# WHAT 01

I have the privilege of being John Tabb's friend and pastor. I can honestly say I have never met a more genuine faith in anyone I have ever pastored. John's love for the Bible and understanding of its pages has been a challenge to our congregation, a witness to our community, and the bridge that has led many to faith in Christ.

In the following pages, you will discover real wisdom for life's everyday questions. I believe you will find yourself growing in confidence in God's word to address all areas of faith and practice. This book will be used as a reference tool throughout one's life and ministry. May you find not only the "wisdom to make you wise unto salvation" (2 Tim. 3:15), but also "everything pertaining to life and Godliness through the true knowledge of Him" (2 Peter 1:3). You are in for a great discovery!

Glad the Tomb is Empty,
Matt Taylor
Pastor, First Baptist Church Lebanon

# TRUTH

# TRUTH

## FOR THOSE SEEKING THE TRUTH

## JOHN TABB

TATE PUBLISHING
AND ENTERPRISES, LLC

Published by Tate Publishing & Enterprises, LLC
127 E. Trade Center Terrace | Mustang, Oklahoma 73064 USA
1.888.361.9473 | www.tatepublishing.com

Tate Publishing is committed to excellence in the publishing industry. The company reflects the philosophy established by the founders, based on Psalm 68:11,
*"The Lord gave the word and great was the company of those who published it."*

Book design copyright © 2014 by Tate Publishing, LLC. All rights reserved.
*Cover design by Rtor Maghuyop*
*Interior design by Jake Muelle*

Published in the United States of America

ISBN: 978-1-63063-067-6
Religion / Christian Theology / General
13.12.03

# DEDICATION

This book is dedicated to God the Father, God the Son, and God the Holy Spirit. I would like to thank my wife, Karen, for her support. I would also like to thank Richard for his challenging questions and Matt for his encouragement.

# TABLE OF CONTENTS

# INTRODUCTION

I wrote this because God told me to do so. I had had a burden for a while for people to know the truth of what God says in the Holy Scriptures so that we will live our lives as God intended and know him better. I have felt burdened for seminary students to not be deceived, or discouraged, by knowing the truth. Then ministers can boldly proclaim the word of God to a hopeless, dying world that desperately needs to hear the truth of God's piercing, convicting, loving, and life-giving word. There have been numerous books written about the evidence that the Bible is true and authentic, primarily using historical evidence, and this book is not attempting to replicate that. The fulfilled prophecies of the first thirty-four verses of Daniel chapter 11, written during the seventy-year captivity of the Jews in Babylon, which was from 605–536 BC, is enough evidence for the validity of the Bible, if one is an honest student of history and the Bible. These prophecies about conflict involving the promised land were fulfilled from about 530 BC until the mid-100s BC. It is important for people to know the truth of what God says in the Holy Bible so they will not be deceived. As I have studied God's word, the more I realized the similarity between the Old Testament and the New Testament. This should not be surprising since God is the same yesterday, today, and forever.

I have done my best to write what the Holy Spirit told me to write: Truth as God has seen fit to show me so far.

This book is not a substitute for the Bible because there is no substitute for studying the Bible. Instead, this book is meant as a study aid to reading and studying the Bible and to help saints find truths from the Bible more quickly than they would otherwise. I thought about titling the book *Truths from the Bible*, but then all truth comes from God (Jn. 14:6), so that would have been a redundant title. In some instances, I wrote obvious truths, but it was necessary to oppose Satan who has convinced people to believe lies. When interpreting scripture, it is important to forgo all previously held beliefs and just believe what the Bible says. Also, when interpreting scripture, it is important to interpret with all scripture in mind. Scripture does not conflict with other scripture because men wrote all scripture as they were inspired by God. The early church leaders gave their lives for God's word and the Lord, so it is reasonable to believe they put into the Holy Bible truths from God. Since God inspired the writings that were put into the Bible, it is reasonable to expect God to have directed the early church leaders to have put exactly what God intended into the Holy Bible. Literal interpretation of scripture is best unless it is obvious allegory or parables. One cannot pick and choose what scripture is right and God inspired to one's liking. This is to determine what is right and wrong, which is to play god. Only God can determine what is right and what is wrong because only he is good and he is the Creator.

I do not mean the references to be exhaustive. Not every book of the Bible has its own chapter. Those books, instead, may be included in writings on other books. I only wrote as I felt the Holy Spirit wanted me to for the benefit of others, so there are many passages without comment. Also, begging forgiveness, modern editing does not allow capitalization of adjective or pronoun references to God.

I am convinced American Christians spend too much time on how to make more money when we should be spending more time reaching lost souls and downtrodden souls around us. I have been guilty of this out of fear of how my wife and I would afford to live out our retirement years. This is because of my childhood filled with uncertainty as to where our next meal would come from or where we would sleep the next night. This is the sin of lack of faith in our loving Heavenly Father. Others spend too much time on seeking money out of the sin of pride or greed.

When our motivation is greater comfort in life, then God is our judge whether it is sin or not, and where one is starting from plays a large role in that. Are we starting as a street urchin or a wealthy person? Also, how much is enough?

> "For I the Lord will speak, and whatever word I speak will be performed. It will no longer be delayed, for in your days, O rebellious house, I will speak the word and perform it," declares the Lord God.
>
> Furthermore the word of the Lord came to me saying, "Son of man, behold, the house of Israel is saying, 'The vision that he sees is for many years from now, and he prophesies of times far off.' Therefore say to them, 'Thus says the Lord God, "None of My words will be delayed any longer. Whatever word I speak will be performed, " declares the Lord God.'" (Ezekiel 4:25–28)

Even so, come, Lord Jesus. (Rev. 22:20b)

# GENESIS

1.　God is the beginning and the end. He always was, is, and will be. He is Father, Son, and Holy Spirit (Gen. 1:1, 2; Jn. 1:1, 2, 10:30; Rev. 21:6).

2.　God created and creates everything. God created the heavens and the earth out of nothing (void). Evolution, and by that I mean macroevolution where one kind of creature becomes another kind of creature, is not true. There is even no fossil evidence of macroevolution. Adaptation, which some people call microevolution, occurs. An example of this is how people's skin tans from sun exposure to help protect the skin from damage from the sun (Gen. 1:1–2, Ps. 100:3, Is. 29:16, Is. 45:12, Jn. 1:3, Col. 1:16–17, Heb. 1:2).

3.　God created everything for its own purpose, even the wicked for the day of evil (Prov. 16:4, Is. 45:7).

4.　There is only one god, and he is the God of Abraham mentioned in the Old Testament of the Holy Bible and in the Pentateuch. He is God the Father, God the Son Jesus, and God the Holy Spirit (Gen. 1:2, 26; Is. 44:6; Jn. 1:1–3). Daniel 11 prophesies that were fulfilled hundreds of years after Daniel wrote them is proof of the God of Abraham as the one true God. There was no god before God and will be no other god after him (Is. 43:10).

5.　The light in Genesis 1:3 that God created on the first day of creation was the light from God and not the sun and moon since they were created on the fourth day. The light he created on the first day was not Jesus since Jesus is without beginning and without end (Rev. 1:8). Jesus was in the beginning with God (Jn. 1:2). The light was life that Jesus, the Son of God, gave to the earth. With life came the creation. Jesus was with God, and they created all things (Jn. 1:1, 3, 4). Darkness, Satan with his forces and people who do not follow God, do not comprehend Jesus and the love, life, and power in him (Jn. 1:5).

6.    God created heaven above the earth (Gen. 1:7–8). God created heaven and earth in about 4004 BC using the Bible's chronology. Although, the earth could be six thousand years older given 2 Peter 3:8, or older if this verse is figurative. However, given the genealogy of the Bible, mankind has only existed since about 4004 BC.

7.    God created huge animals. These are probably what we refer to as dinosaurs (Gen. 1:21).

8.    Man was made in the image of God from dust. Man is like God in his appearance (Gen. 1:26, 27; 9:6). God also made man a living soul that, like God, can last forever (Gen. 2:7, 1 Cor. 15:45). A person then has a physical aspect, the body, and a spiritual aspect, the soul. The soul leaves the body when a person dies (Gen. 35:18) and either goes to heaven, if he or she is a faithful follower of God (Lk. 23:43), or to hell, if he or she is not a follower of God (Lk. 16:19–31). Each person's soul is who he or she really is because the body (flesh) dies and then decays after it dies, but the soul of the faithful follower of God lasts forever, like God (Rev. 20:6). The souls of those who are not faithful followers of God will perish in hell and then the lake of fire (Lk. 12:4, 5; Ac. 3:23; Rev. 20:5, 6, 12–15). As the psalmist said, we are "gods" and children of the Most High in this way (Ps. 82:6, Jn. 10:34). Sometimes people get confused about the difference between the soul and the spirit of persons. In the Bible, spirit is used many different ways such as the nature, or personality, of someone (1 Pet. 3:4); the will of someone (Mt. 26:41); or even interchangeably as the soul (Ac. 7:59). So it is best to

think of the word *spirit* when used regarding people as a word with various meanings and to interpret its meaning in context each time it is used.

9. Man was appointed to rule over the earth. This is an awesome responsibility (Gen. 1:26, 28).

10. God made man and woman. This helps explain where the wives of Cain and Abel came from if one understands this to mean God made more than one man and one woman. He also told them to populate the earth. This also means the sexes are not the same. It also means the gender someone is born as is the gender God intends him or her to be, and it is a sin to try to be the other gender/sex (Gen. 1:27–28). Discussing ambiguous genitalia and mosaicism would require another book. For those interested in a godly approach to those situations, I would recommend the well researched writings of Paul R. McHugh, M. D.

11. Before the fall of man (the first sin by Adam and Eve), God made humans, beasts of the earth, and birds to be vegetarian (Gen. 1:29–30).

12. Satan is described as a snake and separate from Adam in Genesis 3, so Adam and Satan are not the same as some have proposed.

13. Mankind has been able to judge what is good and what is evil since Eve and Adam partook of the tree of knowledge of good and evil. Public nudity is wrong (Gen. 3:5–10, 22).

14. Sin is rebellion against God's will (Gen. 3, 1 John 3:4). Sin is sin for both the saved and lost (those not saved) (Acts 17:30, Col. 2:13).

15. Unconfessed sin before God is sin (Mark 1:15, Acts 17:30, 1 John 1:9). We are also to confess our sins to other believers (James 5:16).

16. Satan and our fleshly desires cause us to sin (Gen. 3).

17. Only two people have not died, Enoch and Elijah. God took them to heaven (Gen. 5:24, 2 Kgs. 2:11).

18. Sons of God had sex with women, who then gave birth to the Nephilim, a mighty and giant race. These sons of men were most likely fallen angels whom God bound in hell during the time of Noah (Gen. 6:1–6; Num. 13:33; 2 Pet. 2:4, 5; Jude 1:6).

19. Mankind's lifespan is limited by God to 120 years due to the corruption of mankind. This should be looked at as the usual case because there are known exceptions in the Bible (Gen. 6:3). The usual lifespan given by God is seventy years, though eighty years if by strength (Ps. 90:10).

20. In about the year 2349 BC, God flooded the whole earth, saving Noah, his family, and creatures to repopulate the earth (Gen. 7–8).

21. God promised to never flood the whole earth again, giving us the rainbow as a sign of that first covenant (Gen. 9:8–17).

22. The earth was all one land mass until it was divided in the days of Peleg in about 2247 BC (Gen. 10:25). This verse explains how the edge of continents seem to fit together millennia before mankind was aware of the continents.

23. The people of the whole earth spoke one language sometime after the flood until God caused them to speak in different languages (Gen. 11:1–9).

24. God promised to give Canaan to the seed of Abraham. That seed is the Messiah, Jesus, who will rule the earth from there during the millennium and the Old and New Testament saints will rule with him there. Jesus's mother could trace her lineage back to Abraham, so Jesus was the seed of Abraham (Gen. 12:7).

25. Shem, one of Noah's sons, was the ancestor of Eber who beget Peleg and other children. Descendants of Eber are known as Hebrews by several theologians (Gen. 11:10–18). Abraham was called a Hebrew for the first time in Gen. 14:13.

26. God told Abraham to go to the land of Canaan, who was a son of Ham, and settle there and that he was giving the territory of Canaan to Abraham and his descendants, which would be a nation there (Gen. 12:1–7).

27. God said those who blessed or cursed Abraham and Israel would likewise be blessed or cursed. And God said in Abraham (Jesus) the families of the earth would be blessed (Gen. 12:3). God will not forget Israel (Is. 44:21).

28. The tithe was started by Abraham as 10 percent of earnings (Gen. 14:20, 28:22). God instructed his people, during the time of Moses, to give this to the Levites since they serve him and have no possessions of land (Num. 18:21). God instructed his people to give another tithe of their produce every third year for the Levites, orphans, and widows for food (Dt. 14:28–29). Jesus instructed us to do justice, love mercy (be kind), love God (be faithful to God) as more important matters but to not neglect to pay the tithe (Mt. 23:23, Lk. 11:42).

29. God promised (covenant) to Abraham that he would have descendants even though his wife Sarai was barren, and God reckoned it as righteousness to Abraham for believing him about this (Gen. 11:30, 15:5–6).

30. God is a shield of protection for Abraham (Gen. 15:1).

31. God promised to Abraham and his descendants the land from the river of Egypt to the Euphrates River. God's covenant is with Isaac and his descendants and not Ishmael (Gen. 15:18, 17:18–19).

32. God knows the future, and he did not give the promised land to the descendants of Abraham for a long time because the iniquity of the Amorites was not complete (Gen. 15:13–16). From Genesis 15:16 and 2 Tim. 3:13, we know that the more sins a society accepts, the more immoral it will become.

33. Circumcision was a sign of the covenant God told Abraham to use for him and his household and their descendants (Gen. 17:9–12).

34. God destroyed Sodom and Gomorrah because of their great sinfulness, including homosexuality (Gen. 19).

35. As demonstrated by the bisexual men of Sodom, sinful people do not like their sins condemned and like to say those condemning their sins are judging them (Gen. 19:9).

36. God promised to make a great nation out of Ishmael (Gen. 21:18).

37. God said all the nations of the earth would be blessed through Abraham because he was obedient to him. This blessing is through Jesus, the messiah (Gen. 22:18). All nations are blessed because salvation, through making Jesus as one's Lord and Savior, is offered to all people.

38. Abraham knew his children should not marry Canaanites (Gen. 24:3).

39. Marrying distant relatives (including cousins) is okay but not close ones (Gen. 24:15, Lev. 18:6–18, Joshua 15:16–17).

40. God gives warning before great calamities that would affect a large number of people (Gen. 41, Jonah).

41. What people do for evil God can make into good (Gen. 50:20, 1 Cor. 2:7–8).

# EXODUS

42. The Jews/Hebrews/descendants of Jacob/Israel were enslaved by the Egyptians but freed by God through signs and miracles, and he used Moses (Exodus).

43. God called Moses from the midst of a burning bush that did not burn up at mount Horeb (Ex. 3:1–5).

44. The place where Moses stood by the burning bush God called holy and told Moses to take off his sandals because of that. Not until Moses was there, near God in the burning bush, did God tell Moses to remove his sandals and call the place holy, so not all ground is holy ground (Ex. 3:1–5).

45. God called himself the God of Moses's father, the God of Abraham, the God of Isaac, and the God of Jacob. God also called himself "I am" (Ex. 3:6, 14).

46. God sees what happens here on earth, and he answers the prayers of his people (Ex. 3:7–9). God punishes his people when they continue to rebel and sin against God without repentance as evidenced by the persecution by Assyria and then by the Babylonian captivity. God will not answer the prayers of his people for help while he is punishing them for their sins (Lam. 3:8, 44).

47. God can affect how people think (Ex. 3:21, 4:21).

48. God almost killed Moses because of his disobedience of not circumcising his son, so total obedience to God is what God requires even to those who have been called by God for something great (Ex. 4: 24–26).

49. God chose the nation of Israel as his people (Ex. 6:7, Dt. 10:15, 1 Chron).

50. God allows some people to have craft to do things that are or appear to be supernatural, but they cannot create anything from inanimate dust. This is to test people's obedience to God (Ex. 7:11–12, 22; 8:7, 18–19; Dt. 13:1–3).

51. God established the Passover (Ex. 12:1–32).

52. God led the nation of Israel by a pillar of cloud by day and a pillar of fire by night from Egypt through the wilderness (Ex. 13:21).

53. God parted the Red Sea so the nation of Israel could escape the Egyptian army, then moved back over the Egyptians, drowning them after Israel crossed over (Ex. 14).

54. The Ten Commandments from God to people: (1) Have no other God (Ex. 20:3, Ex. 22:20, Dt. 6:13–15, Ac. 14:15), (2) make no idol (Ex. 20:4, Dt. 27:15, 1 Jn. 5:21), (3) do not use God's name in vane (Ex. 20:7, Lv. 24:15–16, Jas. 5:12), (4) keep the Sabbath holy (Ex. 20:8, Nu 15:32–36, but Mk. 2:27, Ac. 15, Rom. 14:5, and Col. 2:16 nullifies this), (5) obedience to parents (Ex.20:12, Ex. 21:15–17, Eph. 6:1), (6) do not murder (Ex. 20:13, Ex. 21:12, 1 Jn. 3:15), (7) do not commit adultery (Ex. 20:14, Lv. 20:10, 1 Co. 6:9–10), (8) do not steal (Ex. 20:15, Ex. 21:16, Eph. 4:28), (9) do not bear false witness (Ex. 20:16, Dt. 18:16–21, Col. 3:9–10), (10) do not covet (Ex. 20:17, Pr. 3:29, Eph. 5:3).

55. Property rights are God given, but the land is God's for us to use (Ex. 22:1–14, Lev. 25:23).

56. Sex outside of marriage is a sin for those who voluntarily participate. If a man and previously unmarried woman do have sex before they are married, they are to get married. He is to pay her father a virgin's dowry if her father refuses to allow them to marry (Ex. 22:16–17, Dt. 22:28–29). The

time that the couple is committed to marrying before the marriage is the engagement period (Dt. 20:7).

57. Sorcery is a deadly sin (Ex. 22:18). We are not to participate in fortunetelling or turn to mediums or spiritists (Lev. 19:26, 31). This includes witchcraft, sorcery, trying to contact the dead or interpret omens (Dt. 18:10–11).

58. Sex with an animal is a deadly sin (Ex. 22:19, Lev. 18:23).

59. God cares about the oppressed, widows, and orphans and tells us to help them, even if they are strangers (Ex. 22:21–22; Dt. 10:18–19; Ps. 10:14, 17–18).

60. Do not have partiality for the poor in a dispute (Ex. 23:3).

61. Be kind to your enemies (Ex 23:4–5; Mt. 5:44; Lk. 6:27–29, 35; Rm. 12:20).

62. God required the same amount of money from poor men and rich men when he had them take the first census (Ex. 30:15). This was early in the Jewish nation's history, when people had similar wealth. Since the time of Moses, God said his people (all who love and follow him) are to give to him the tithe, which is 10 percent of what they earned. This equalizes the relative amount that each person gives to God, whether rich or poor (Num. 18:21, Lv. 27:32, Mal. 3:8–10, Lk. 11:42).

63. God gives us talents (Ex. 31:1–6).

64. God will be gracious and compassionate to whom he chooses (Ex. 33:19).

65. No one has seen God's face and lived, including Moses. When the Bible says Moses talked to God face-to-face as a man speaks to his friend, in Exodus 33:11, it is describing the situation that God and Moses spoke to each other directly, rather than through an angel or vision (Ex. 33:20).

66.     Moses went without food or water for forty days and forty nights while he was on Mount Sinai receiving God's word and writing the Ten Commandments (Ex. 34:28, Dt. 9:9). Elijah did likewise (1 Kgs. 19:8). Jesus fasted forty days and forty nights also in the wilderness as he was led by the Holy Spirit. Jesus resisted the devil's three temptations after his fast. So it is possible for people to go without food or water for forty days if they are led by the Holy Spirit to do so. A significant sidenote is that Jesus, God the Son, was led by the Spirit of God (Holy Spirit). How much more should we seek and submit to the leading of the Spirit of God? (Mt. 4:1–11).

67.     Besides the tithe, God wants us to give as our heart directs us (Ex. 35:5).

# LEVITICUS

68. It is okay for men to masturbate (Lev. 15:16), but they should not imagine having an adulterous encounter (Mat. 5:28).

69. Polygamy was allowed by God (Jacob had two wives at the same time; Moses had two wives at the same time) (Num. 12:1–15). God gave instructions for those with more than one wife (Dt. 21:15). People were not to marry close relatives such as aunts, uncles, siblings, one's children or grandchildren because this is incest (Lev. 18:6–18). God established the union of one man and one woman as a married couple as his plan. Gen. 2:24, Mt. 19:5—these two verses use the similar original word meaning singular instead of the number 1 because obviously people could remarry after the death of a spouse and 1 Cor. 7:2. And Jesus clarified that adultery included not just the act but the lust of another person than your spouse, and a person does not naturally marry a person if they do not desire them sexually (Mt. 5:28). If the requirements for bishops and deacons included only having one wife at a time, as opposed to one wife for life (except remarriage when allowed such as death of spouse or divorce for adultery), then polygamy was acceptable to the early church and thus should be today (1 Tim. 3). However this contradicts Mt. 5:28 and 1 Cor. 7:2.

70. Homosexuality is sin. It is an abomination and a deadly sin (Gen. 19:1–29, Lev. 18:22, Lev. 20:13, Rom. 1:27, 1 Tim. 1:10). Dressing or acting like people of the other sex than what one was born as is sin also. Doing so is rebellion against God and how he created that person (Dt. 22:5, 1 Cor. 6:9).

71. We are to love our neighbor as ourselves (Lev. 19:18, Gal. 5:14).

72. Poor people are to go to their countrymen who are not poor and work for them as a hired hand and then after working seven years they will be free to leave with their earnings (Lev. 25:35–46). As an alternative, those who are able are to loan to the poor in their own town generously without demanding repayment (Dt. 15:7–8, Mt. 5:42, Lk. 6:34). Those who have borrowed are to pay their debts when they can (Pr. 3:28). God will bless those who give to the poor without grudge (Dt. 15:10, Ps. 41:1, Pr. 22:9). There will always be poor people (Dt. 15:11, Mat. 26:11, Mk. 14:7, Jn. 12:8). Land was to be returned to original owners or their heirs every fifty years, jubilee year (Lev. 25). Debts of Jews to Jews were to be forgiven every seven years (Dt. 15:1).

# NUMBERS

73. Retirement at age fifty was instructed by God to the Levites. They were to do volunteer work after retirement. So retirement has been around since the Exodus (Num. 8:25).

74. Sons of God had sex with women, who then gave birth to the Nephilim, a mighty and giant race. These sons of men were most likely fallen angels whom God bound in hell during the time of Noah (Gen. 6:1–6; Num. 13:33; 2 Pet. 2:4, 5; Jude 1:6).

75. Unintentional sin is still sin (Num. 15:27).

76. Sheol/hell/hades/nether world is first mentioned in Numbers 16:30 as a destination for the disobedient. In Ecclesiastes it is referenced as a common destination for all the dead of the body. Jesus clarified the concept of sheol/hell/hades in Luke 16:19–31: Sheol was used as the place for all the dead in the Old Testament where all the dead were separated from the living (in the flesh), but for those who will spend eternity with God, their soul will go to heaven, and for those who will not spend eternity with God, their souls will go to hades/hell where they are tormented. Psalm 9:17 also clarifies that the wicked and all people that forget God will be cast into hell. Those who are like Satan try to be equal with God will go to hell. Hell is underground (Isaiah 14:9, 15; Ez. 32:18–21). Those who trust God and die before Jesus's second coming (Hezekiah in this case) will go to the grave sheol as opposed to hell sheol (Is. 38:10). In Revelation 20:11–15, the devil, hades/hell, and all those people not written in the book of life will be cast into the lake of fire where the beast and the false prophet will have already been cast

to be tormented forever (Num. 16:30, Lk. 16:19–31, Rev. 20:11–15).

77.     The Holy Spirit has been around since God, the Alpha and Omega, but only entered people at times for special occasions before Jesus went back to heaven. Since Jesus and the day of Pentecost, the Holy Spirit indwells all believers in Jesus as the Christ (Num. 24:2; Jdg. 3:10, 6:34, 11:29, 13:25; Is. 61:1; Ez. 2:2, 3:24; Jn. 14:26, 20:22; Acts 1:8, 2:1–4).

78.     Balaam prophesied ships from Kittim (Rome) shall afflict Asshur (Assyria, then later northern Syria, northern Iraq, northwest Iran, and southeast Turkey) and Eber (Hebrews) (Num. 24:24). This was fulfilled when Antiochus IV, from Syria, invaded countries south of him, but ships from Kittim (Romans) fought against him and stopped him (Dan. 11:30). Rome later conquered Syria and Israel.

# DEUTERONOMY

79. God helped not only the descendants of Jacob (Israel) and Ishmael but also the descendants of Esau and Lot. God gave the descendants of Esau and Lot lands (Dt. 2:5, 9). God helps people other than the Jews (Joshua 24, 2 Kgs. 5:12). Israel will not be forgotten by God (Is. 44:21). God offers salvation to all the people of the earth (Is. 45:22).

80. Giants existed in the past (Dt. 3:11 and 1 Sa. 17:4).

81. Changing God's word will be punished by God (Dt. 4:2, Prov. 30:6, Rev. 22:18–19).

82. God has chosen the descendants of Israel to be his people out of all the people of the world and they are to be a holy people (Dt. 7:6).

83. Testing of both the wicked and righteous is done by God. God tests us whether by hunger, false prophets or worker of miracles whose prophesies or wonders come true and then try to get us to follow other gods, or other means. The reason is to know what is in our hearts, whether we will obey him or not (Dt. 8:2, 16; Dt. 13:1–3; Jg. 2:22; Ps. 11:5).

84. Man (people) do not live by bread alone but by the Word of God (Dt. 8:3, Mat. 4:4, Luke 4:4).

85. All the Lord God requires of us is to fear him, to serve the Lord our God with all our heart and all our soul and to keep the Lord's commandments and statutes (Dt. 10:12–13).

86. God's commandments and statutes are for our good (Dt. 10:13).

87. We are to teach our children God's word several times a day and display God's written word on our homes (Dt. 11:19–20).

88. God stopped speaking directly to people and instead started using prophets at the Jews' request (Dt. 18:15–18). God also talks to us in dreams and visions (1 Kgs. 3:5) and throughout the Bible.

89. If a prophet is true, his prophecies will come true (Dt. 18:22).

90. People cannot be convicted of a sin on the witness of only one person (Dt. 19:15).

91. Rebellion by children is a deadly sin (Dt. 21:18–21).

92. If someone finds something of value, they are to restore it to the rightful owner. If the owner cannot be found, then it may be kept until the owner is known; then it is to be given to the owner (Dt. 22:1–4).

93. It is an abomination for women to wear men's clothing and men to wear women's clothing (Dt. 22:5).

94. If a woman, who is engaged or married to another man, and a man have sex, both of them commit a deadly sin (Dt. 22:22–24).

95. Rape is a deadly sin; it is like murder (Dt. 22:25–27).

96. Fellow believers are not to charge one another interest on loans (Dt. 23:19–20).

97. Kidnapping is a deadly sin if the kidnapper handles the victim violently or sells them (Dt. 24:7).

98. Parents are not responsible for their children's sins, and children are not responsible for their parents' sins. Each person is responsible for their own wrongdoings (Dt. 24:16).

99. People, while they are living and not after they are dead only, are to leave their excess for the poor (Dt. 24:17–21).

100. God told Moses ahead of time that the Israelis would rebel against him (Dt. 31:16–18).

101. God will destroy this heaven and earth with fire and heat and make a new heaven and a new earth (without any sea) (Dt. 32:22; 2 Pet. 3:10,12–13). This will occur after the millennium and judgment day (Rev. 21:1–7).

# JUDGES

102. God expects us to keep our vows to him even if it is something he doesn't want us to do. Jephthah made the vow to God without God asking him to. Israel had started doing things/traditions that were against God's will. The Jews had become as bad as the people whose land they took over to the point of human sacrifice to false idols. Jephthah planned on something or someone other than his daughter would come out the door when he returned (Jg. 11:30–40, Ecc. 5:4). We need to be prepared for worse case scenarios when we make a vow. Married couples need to remember that they take a vow to God when they get married to stay married till death separates them.

103. We should not worry about what career we pursue but stay obedient to God's word. God will make sure we do what he wants as long as we live a life obedient to Him. Our career is secondary and not to be the focus of our life. But men do need to provide for themselves and their families (Jg. 13:12–14, 1 Tim. 5:8).

104. God can empower people to do amazing feats (Jg. 13:1–16:31, 1 Kgs. 18:46).

# 1 SAMUEL

105. God wants people to want him to be their king/ruler in addition to their god (1 Sam. 8:7).

106. To obey God is better than sacrifice or good works (1 Sam. 15:22). What does the Lord require of us but to do justice, to love kindness and to walk humbly with our God. God delights in obedience more than thousands of sacrifices (Mic. 6:7–8).

107. God initiated anointing His chosen, when He chooses them, by His servants with oil (1 Sam. 16:1, 12).

108. God looks at people's hearts and not their appearance to judge them. People's hearts are what they love and desire and what they reject. People's appearance can be a show, not revealing what is in their hearts, at least for a time (1 Sam. 16:7).

109. The Holy Spirit of God entered David when Samuel anointed him with oil. The Holy Spirit continued in David until he died (1 Sam. 16:13).

110. God took the Holy Spirit from King Saul when David was filled with the Holy Spirit and sent a distressing spirit to trouble him. This distressing spirit was probably a demon that God allowed to trouble Saul regularly (1 Sam. 16:14, 23).

111. God sometimes allows the devil and his demons to influence people directly that do not have the Spirit of God in them (1 Sam. 18:10, 12) or affect their lives in a bad way, usually as a test (Job).

112. Mediums can conjure up the dead to speak to us but it is sin (1 Sam. 28:11–15; Lev. 19: 26, 31).

113. We will be recognizable after we die (1 Sam. 28:11–15, Lk. 16:19–31).

# 2 SAMUEL

114.   God promised to establish and keep David's kingdom forever (2 Sam.7:16). This will be accomplished by Jesus. Jesus' earthly parent's heritage can be traced back to David: Joseph's in Matthew 1:1–17 and Mary's in Luke 3:23–38. This was possible through the work of the Holy Spirit (Lk. 1:26-33).

115.   God plans ways for those that are banished from heaven (do not follow him) to go to heaven just like he provided a means of escape for those banished from society for accidental manslaughter through sanctuary cities. Indeed, even God sent his son to provide a way for all to go to heaven if they just believe in him (2 Sam. 14:14, Jn. 3:16, John 5:25).

# 1 KINGS

116. God wants complete obedience from us. We should not believe others if what they tell us contradicts what God says (1 Kgs. 13).

117. Telling God we are unhappy with how God is dealing with our lives is okay as long we are respectful and not selfish. (1 Kgs. 17:20).

118. Repeating what one prays, even if it is a request of God, in the same prayer is okay as long as it is not vain (thoughtless or without reverence, submitting one's will and desires to God) (1 Kgs. 17:21–22; Ps. 36; Mt. 6:7, 26:44; Rev. 4:8).

# 2 KINGS

119. Elisha did miracles as Jesus would do like raise the dead to life and feed more people than possible with too small a quantity of food (2 Kgs. 4).

120. God has mercy on people other than the Jews (2 Kgs. 5:14).

121. People other than Jews worshiped God when God opened their eyes to the truth (2 Kgs. 5:17).

122. God determines events, including famine. God gives warning for ones that affect many people (2 Kgs. 8:1, Ps. 103:19, Jonah).

123. God determines leaders of nations, both good and bad ones (2 Kgs. 8:13, Rom. 13:1, Ps. 103:19).

124. God will sometimes change the timing of his plans as he did with the timing of Hezekiah's death after Hezekiah prayed to live longer (2 Kgs. 20:1–11).

125. God reversed the earth's rotation, making the shadow created by the sun to reverse course a ways, in answer to Isaiah's prayer request (2 Kgs. 20:10, 11).

126. Age of accountability is generally felt to be twelve, but God knows people's hearts and is righteous and will judge each one of us in righteousness. So some people may be mentally retarded and be held accountable at a different age or however God chooses (2 Kgs. 21:1–2; Lk. 2:42, 49).

127. Women can be prophets (prophetesses) also (2 Kgs. 22:14).

# 1 CHRONICLES

128. All other gods than the God of Israel are idols/false gods (1 Chron. 16:26).

129. The Lord (Jesus) is coming to judge the earth. Isaiah indicates this will be during the millennium (1 Chron. 16:33; Ps. 96:10, 13; Is. 11; Mt. 25:31–46; Rev. 19:15).

130. God is good, and his loving-kindness is everlasting (1 Chron. 16:34, Lk. 18:19).

# 2 CHRONICLES

131. No other king was given as much wisdom, wealth, and honor by God as Solomon (1 Kgs. 3:12–13; 2 Chron. 1:12; 2 Chron. 9:22).

132. The glory of God filled the original temple in Jerusalem that Solomon built (2 Chron. 5:13, 14) and will fill the temple in Jerusalem built for the millennium (Ezk. 43:1–9). There will be no temple after this heaven and earth are destroyed and a new heaven and earth are made by God after Satan is cast into the lake of fire and the final judgment at the great white throne because God the Father and Jesus are the temple in the new Jerusalem (Rev. 21:1, 2, 10, 22).

133. God has chosen Jerusalem that his name would be there (2 Chron. 6:6). God has chosen Zion (Jerusalem) for his dwelling place (Ps. 132:13).

134. If God causes a drought or sends the locusts to devour the land or sends pestilence among his people and the people who are called by his name humble themselves and pray and seek God's face and turn from their wicked ways, then he will hear from heaven, will forgive their sins, and will heal their land (2 Chron. 7:13–14).

135. When the Jews sought God, they found him, but when they forsook God, God forsook them (2 Chron. 15:2).

136. The eyes of the Lord move to and fro throughout the earth that he may strongly support those whose heart is completely his (2 Chron. 16:9).

137. Mechanical weapons of warfare that were used on towers like launchers for great large stones and arrows were

invented under the kingship of Uzziah, king of Judah in about 750 BC (2 Chron. 26:15).

138. The Artaxerses in Ezra 4 is actually Pseudo Smerdis, who the Persians referred to as Berooyeh Doroughi, and not the son of Xerses, the more famous Artaxerses. Pseudo Smerdis falsely claimed to be a son of Cyrus and ruled Persia several months in 521 BC.

# JOB

139. God will accept challenges from Satan and allow Satan to harm people who are faithful to God without cause on the part of the person being persecuted. This harm can be financial or illness or death to family or the individual being persecuted to prove to Satan our faithfulness to God (Job 1–2).

140. The fear of the Lord is wisdom and understanding is to depart from evil said God (Job 28:28).

141. A large creature lived during the days of Job that sounds like Apatosaurus. God made this animal, of course, as he made all things. It lived on land and water (Job 40:15–24).

142. A large sea living creature that breathed fire and had scales, which is where the idea of dragons came from, existed during the time of Job (Job 41).

143. Sincerely praying for and forgiving those who have wronged us can bring about God's blessings, but we dare not presume God will bless us. We should not be mad at God if he does not bless us because God is God, and we are just one of his creations (Job 42:10–17).

# PSALMS

144. Godly people, those who delight in and meditate day and night on the law of the Lord, will be sustained by God. God will make prosper what they do for him. The wicked's ways will not prosper. Though the wicked may be rich monetarily while they are here on earth, they will not stand in the judgment of God to come (Ps. 1, Ps. 10:5,14–18).

145. David, by the Holy Spirit, prophesied that the nations of the world, including Israel, would devise ways of opposing God and the Messiah. The nations feel that God and the Messiah bind them from doing what they want to do. But God will establish the Messiah as king upon mount Zion, and he will reign over the nations of the world with a rod of iron (Ps. 2:1–9). The crucifixion of Jesus fulfilled the first part of David's prophecy in that Pilate, Herod, and the Jewish leaders acted together against Jesus. The Jewish religious leaders also fulfilled it with the early Christian church (Ac. 4:23–30). The Antichrist and his followers will fulfill this prophecy about devising and opposing God and Jesus (Rev. 19:19). Jesus will destroy the Antichrist and his followers and then reign over the earth one thousand years (Rev. 20:1–6). Zion is where the Lord of hosts will reign and the precious cornerstone (Jesus) is placed (Is. 24:23; 28:16; Rom. 9:32, 33; 10:11; Eph. 2:20; 1 Pet. 2:6). Isaiah 42:1 also prophesied about the Messiah ruling over the nations. And finally Satan will inspire the world to oppose God and Jesus as the prophecy says after the millennium, before their destruction (Rev. 20:7–10).

146. The only old testament verse referring to the Son (capitalized) of God is in Ps.2:7. He is also referred to

as begotten of God, and he will rule the earth with a rod of iron (Ps. 2:7–9). The Son, Jesus, was God before all creation, but Jesus is called begotten because he was born in the flesh with his first incarnation. He was not created by God in any way before that. The Son has always existed as has the Father and the Holy Spirit (Gen. 1:26, Mt. 28:19, Rev. 1:8). He was God and man at the same time while he was here on earth (Ps. 2:7; Ac. 13:33; Heb. 1:5; 5:5).

147. The Lord separates the godly from the rest of humanity, and he hears when they call to him (Ps. 4:3).

148. Righteousness is as sacrifice to God (Ps. 4:5). To do righteousness and justice are desired by God even more than sacrifice (Prov. 21:3).

149. Those that know and love God can sleep in peace (Ps. 4:8. Prov. 3:24).

150. No evil dwells with God (Ps. 5:4).

151. God hates people who are wicked (Ps. 5:5, 6; 11:5).

152. God blesses and surrounds with favor and protection as a shield people who are righteous (Ps. 5:11–12). No good thing will he withhold from those who walk uprightly (Ps. 84:11). God is a rewarder of those who diligently seek him (Heb. 11:6). God gives protection to those who trust God and whose life is centered on God (Ps. 91).

153. God made people a little lower than angels (Ps. 8:5).

154. God made people to rule over God's creation (Ps.8:6).

155. God will judge the world in righteousness (Ps. 9:8).

156. God is a stronghold for the oppressed (Ps. 9:9).

157. The wicked people and all the nations who forget God will go to hell. This tells us God judges individuals as well as nations of people (Ps. 9:17). Righteousness exalts a nation, but sin is a disgrace to any people (Prov. 14:34).

158. God hears and helps the humble (Ps. 10:17, Jas. 4:6, 1 Pet. 5:5).

159. No one is good or without sin without help from God (Ps. 14:1–3; 53:1–3; Rom. 3:10–12, 23).

160. God's children tend to reject people who reject God and honor those who follow God. Godly people are honest (Ps. 15:4).

161. David prophesied that Jesus ("Your Holy One") would not decay in the grave, implying a bodily resurrection (Ps. 16:10). This tells today's Jews the Messiah had to die after he arrived here on earth in the flesh. The Messiah does not just come to earth once and be king of Israel forever in the flesh.

162. Darkness is changed into light by God for those who love God. Dread and despair are changed into hope and love. Uncertainty about our future is changed into certainty of a bright future (Ps. 18:28).

163. Protection and provision are given from God to those who take refuge in him and fear God (Ps. 18:30, 23, 28:7–8, 31:3, 33:18–19, 34:7–10). God favors those who fear, love, and wait for God (Ps. 147:11). This does not mean the righteous will not suffer many afflictions (Ps. 34:19).

164. We are trained for battle by God. He does not do all the fighting for us but trains us to win and helps us win (Ps. 18:34, 39).

165. We should pray asking God to make the words of our mouth and the meditation of our heart acceptable to him (Ps. 19:14).

166. Prophetic scriptures dealing with Christ/Jesus: (1) The virgin birth and his name shall be Immanuel (Is.7:14. Mt.1:23). (2) A stone of stumbling and rock of offense (Is. 8:14, 15; Rom. 9:33; 1 Pet. 2:8). (3) He would make disciples (Is. 8:16). (4) He was a light to the people of

Zebulun and Naphtali, Galilee of the gentiles (Is. 9:1, 2; Mt. 4:12–16). (5) The deaf are made to hear and the blind made to see. The poor and afflicted are given joy. The lame are healed (Is. 29:18, 19; 35:3–6; 61:1, 2; Mt.11:5; Lk. 4:18–21). (6) First and second advent preceded by witness of John the Baptist and the two witnesses, respectively (Is. 40:3–5, Mt. 3:3, Mk. 1:3, Lk. 3:4–6, Jn. 1:23, Rev. 11:1–19). (7) Christ brings salvation offer to all people, not just Hebrews (Is. 49:6, 52:7; Rom. 10:15). (8) Jesus beaten and spat upon (Is. 50:6; Mt. 26:67; 27:26, 30; Mk. 14:65; 15:19; Lk. 22:63; Jn. 18:22). (9) He was rejected of men, and his appearance was not attractive (Is. 53:1–4, Jn. 12:38). (10) He was oppressed and afflicted yet was silent (Is. 53:7; Mt. 26:63; 27:12–14; Mk. 14:61; 15:5; Lk. 23:9; Jn. 19:9; 1 Pet. 2:23). (11) Jesus/Christ is the lamb of God who died for all people's sins (Is. 53:7–9, 11, 12; Jn. 1:29; 1 Pet. 1:18, 19; Rev. 5:6). (12) Jesus was sinless (Is. 53:9; 1 Pet. 2:22). (13) The crucifixion: He was betrayed by the one who ate bread with him (Judas) (Ps. 41:9). Words of Jesus on the cross (Ps. 22:1, Mt. 27:46, Mk. 15:34). Scoffers mocking Jesus on the cross (Ps. 22:8, Mt. 27:43). He was pierced and beaten (Is. 53:5). The Messiah was to be rejected as the chief cornerstone (Ps. 118:22–23, Mt. 21:42, Mk. 12:10–11, Lk. 20:17, Ac. 4:8–12, 1 Pet. 2:7). Pierced hands and feet (Ps. 22:16, Is. 53:5, Zec. 12:10, Jn. 20:25). Some cast lots for Jesus's garments (Ps. 22:18, Mt. 27:35, Mk. 15:24, Lk. 23:34, Jn. 19:24). Jesus's bones were not broken even though that was customary for a crucifixion (Ps. 34:20, Jn. 19:33). (14) The Resurrection (Ps. 16:10). (15) The millennial reign of the world by Jesus and worship by all the nations then. He will continue the Davidic lineage (Ps. 2:8–9; 22:27–31; Is. 9:6, 7; 11:1–16; Rev. 20:4–6).

167. The world and all those in it are the Lord's (Ps. 24:1). Satan is the god or prince of this world (Jn. 12:31, 2 Cor. 4:4, Eph. 2:2, 2 Tim. 2:26). But all authority has been given to Jesus in heaven and on earth (Mat. 28:18).

168. Waiting on God will prevent shame (Ps. 25:3). It will also strengthen us and give us courage (Ps. 27:14). Being hasty brings poverty (Prov. 21:5).

169. Humbleness allows God to teach us his ways (Ps. 25:9). It also allows God to teach us things not known to others (Ps. 25:14). Whoever loves discipline loves knowledge, but the one who hates reproof is stupid (Prov. 12:1).

170. Direction from God is given to those who fear God (Ps. 25:12, 31:3, 32:8, 37:23, 48:14).

171. God's loving-kindness is throughout the world (Ps. 33:5).

172. The nation whose god is the Lord is blessed (Ps. 33:12).

173. Desires of the heart will be put in Christians' hearts and fulfilled by God if we delight ourselves in him and commit our way to him (Ps. 37:4–5).

174. Famine will not kill the righteous. God will provide for them and their children (Ps. 33:19, 37:19, 25; Prov. 10:3).

175. God helps those who help others (Ps. 41:1–2).

176. The thoughts of people are known to God (Ps. 44:21; 139:1–2).

177. God reigns over the nations; he sits on his holy throne in heaven (Ps. 47:8).

178. People are born sinners. Sin is in everyone's heart, and no one is good enough to go to heaven (Ps. 51:5, 53:1, 3; Rom. 3:9, 23).

179. Cast your burden upon the Lord, and he will sustain you. He will not suffer the righteous to be moved (Ps. 55:22).

180. Prayers of the unsaved God does not hear except the prayer of seeking Him and of repentance and salvation.

Sin causes a separation between people and God. God does not answer the prayers of the saved with the wrong motives either (Job 27:9; Ps. 66:18; Jn. 9:31; Prov. 1:28–29; 28:9; Is. 1:15, 59:2; Jer. 11:11; Ac. 10:1–4, 34, 35; Jas. 4:3).

181.  A thousand years is as one day to God (Ps. 90:4; 2 Pet. 3:8).

182.  The Lord has established his throne in the heavens (Ps. 103:19). Heaven is God's throne, and the earth is his footstool (Is. 66:1).

183.  Praying to God can result in him changing his mind or stated plans (Ps. 106:45, Am. 7:3, 6, Jon. 3:10). Since he is omniscient, he knew he would change his mind or stated plans, but prayerful request by a child of his is required.

184.  The Messiah was David's Lord (Ps. 110:1). Jesus declared he was David's Lord referred to here (Mt. 22:44–45; Mk. 12:36–37; Lk. 20:42–44).

185.  Wisdom is begun by fear of the Lord (Ps. 111:10).

186.  Those who sow in tears shall reap with joy. Those who have a burden for the lost and witness will have joy, whether here on earth or in heaven, when they see some saved as a result of their witnessing (Ps. 126:5–6; Mt. 10:22; Gal. 6:9).

187.  Unless a house, city, or nation is dedicated to the Lord, it is not assured of continuing. God's plan will be done while man's plans that do not follow God's plans will not last (Ps. 127:1).

188.  No one can do enough good deeds to earn their way to heaven, but forgiveness of sins is offered by God to those who accept the Lord as their God and Savior. People who like to quote, "Judge not lest ye be judged," need to understand that telling people what God says is sin, in the Bible, is not judging the own who sins. God has already

judged what is sin and will judge all who do not repent of their sins and accept Jesus as Lord come judgment day. For those who say they cannot judge any action is a sin, there is no need for a Savior if there is no sin (Ps. 130:3–8; Jn. 3:16; Rom. 3:23–26). People's natural inclination is to do evil, and even righteous people will not be continually good and not sin (Ecc. 7:19, 8:11, 9:3).

189. God will accomplish with his children what he wants to despite our imperfections (Ps. 138:8, Prov. 16:3, 9, Php. 1:6). Praise God.

190. God formed people in their mother's womb. He ordained each of our days before we are born (Ps. 139:13–16). Even before he formed each of us in our mother's womb, he knew us (Jer. 1:5). This tells us how special each of us is in God's eyes. This should also tell us it is wrong to abort babies.

191. The question is not why bad things happen to good people but why any good occurs on earth. The devil is prince of this world, but God intervenes many times (Ps. 139:8).

192. God is slow to anger and good to all, whether they love God or not (Ps.145:8–9; Mt. 5:45; Jn. 3:16; Rm. 5:8).

193. The children of God (followers of him) will have the honor of carrying out God's judgment during the millennium (Ps. 149:9, Rev. 20:4).

# PROVERBS

194. The fear of the Lord is the beginning of knowledge/wisdom. The fear of the Lord is to hate evil (Prov. 1:7, 8:13, 9:10).

195. Debt and being a guarantor for a neighbor is to be avoided like a trap (Prov. 6:1–5, 11:15).

196. Laziness leads to poverty (Prov. 6:6–11; 12:24; 24:33–34; Ecc. 10:18).

197. Rulers and kings of this earth are established and removed by God (Prov. 8:15, Dan. 2:21, Mt. 28:18, Rom. 13:1, Col. 1:16). God also controls the decisions they make (Prov. 21:1).

198. Reprove not a scoffer or wicked person but reprove a wise person when they need it (Prov. 9:7–8).

199. Being wealthy is not sinful unless it is acquired by dishonest means. Wealth is a reward to those who are diligent, but it is not promised to all. But we sin if we focus on wealth, which is useless in the day of wrath (day of judgment by God). We are not to weary ourselves about gaining wealth. Instead we are to focus on righteousness, which is obedience to God. A person who trusts in his riches will fail. The person who mismanages his possessions will come to financial ruin (inherit the wind) (Prov. 10:2–4; 11:4, 28, 29; 23:4; 24:3–4). Attempting to get rich quickly (this includes gambling and lotteries) will lead to poverty and will not go unpunished (Prov. 28:19–20). The love of money is the root of all kinds of evil (1 Tim. 6:10).

200. The wicked and foolish enjoy sinning, but the righteous enjoy the fear of the Lord and doing his will (Prov. 10:23).

201. Life is prolonged for the righteous and shortened for the wicked by God (Prov. 10:27). The wicked can prolong their life though (Ecc. 7:15).

202. Deceit and lying are abominations to God (Prov. 11:1, 12:22).

203. A city that is blessed to be led by the upright is exalted, but a city in which the predominant voice is wicked will be destroyed (Prov. 11:11, 12:26). When the righteous increase, the people rejoice, but when a wicked person rules, the people groan (Prov. 29:2).

204. Wise counsel by many helps make big plans successful, but when counsel is not sought failure typically occurs (Prov. 11:14, 15:22, 20:18, 24:6). Counsel of the wicked is deceitful (Prov. 12:5). A fool is right in his or her own eyes and will not listen to counsel, but the wise listen to counsel (Prov. 12:15).

205. Generosity and mercy to people and giving the tithe and other gifts to God are rewarded by provision from God. The generosity and giving to God must not be grudgingly. The more generous a person is, the more they will be blessed by God. God will provide plenty for the one who is generous to others so they continue to bless others, in God's name, as this is one way God gives to the poor (Prov. 3:9–10, 11:25, 28:27; Mt. 5:7; 2 Cor. 9:6–9).

206. Righteous people have regard for their animal's life (Prov. 12:10).

207. There is a way that seems right to people, not in obedience to God, but in the end, it leads to destruction or eternal separation from God (Prov. 14:12, 16:25, Is. 56:11).

208. God sees everything that happens on earth (Prov. 15:3).

209. The sacrifice of the wicked is an abomination to the Lord, but the prayer of the upright delights the Lord (Prov. 15:8).

210. A joyful heart makes a cheerful face (Prov. 15:13).

211. The Lord weighs the motives of people (Prov. 16:2, 21:2, Jer. 17:10).

212. Everyone who is proud in heart is an abomination to the Lord, and pride comes before destruction (Prov. 16:5, 18).

213. Sweetness of speech increases persuasiveness (Prov. 16:21).

214. He who mocks the poor taunts his Maker, and he who rejoices at calamity will not go unpunished (Prov. 17:5).

215. Do not rejoice when an enemy falls or stumbles or God will be displeased and turn his anger away from them (Prov. 24:17–18).

216. He who justifies the wicked and he who condemns the righteous, both of them alike are an abomination to the Lord (Prov. 17:15, 24:24).

217. Those who rebuke the wicked will be blessed (Prov. 24:25).

218. A joyful heart is good medicine, but a broken spirit dries up the bones (Prov. 17:22).

219. It is a man's glory to overlook a transgression against him (Prov. 19:11). Keeping away from strife is an honor for a man (Prov. 20:3). We are to let God repay evil rather than ourselves (Dt. 32:35, Prov. 20:22, Mt. 5:39, Lk. 6:29, Rom. 12:17–19, Heb. 10:30).

220. Drinking alcohol (including strong drink) is okay unless one drinks enough to be intoxicated/drunk (Dt. 14:26; Prov. 20:1, 23:20–21, 29–35; Eph. 5:18; 1 Cor. 5:11; 1 Tim. 5:23). Alcohol can help one get through miserable times Prov. 31:6–7. Drinking alcohol is forbidden for kings and rulers (Prov. 31:4–5). Wine makes life merry (Ecc. 10:19).

221. Gluttony of food is a sin (Prov. 23:20–21, 25:16; Tit. 1:12).

222. A good name/reputation is more desirable than great wealth (Prov. 22:1).

223. Train up a child to live a Godly life and to study, and meditate on, God's word (the Bible), and when that child is old, they will not depart from it (Prov. 22:6). Children tend to be foolish naturally, but corporal punishment will remove it (Prov. 22:15, 23:13–14). Parents who do not use corporal punishment on their children hate their children (Prov. 13:24). Letting a child get their own way brings shame to a mother, but a corrected child gives a parent comfort (Prov. 29:15, 17). However punishment is not to be too severe and should be less often than kind words to children so they will not be provoked to anger. Parents are to instruct children about God and what God says in the Holy Word/Bible. Fathers are to discipline their children as best they can, emulating God, but fathers will not be perfect as is God (Eph. 6:4, Heb. 12:5–11).

224. The borrower is the lender's slave (Prov. 22:7).

225. Do not be critical in jest (sarcastic) (Prov. 26:18–19, Eph. 5:4).

226. An excellent wife does good things for her husband and not evil. She speaks and acts kindly. She looks well to the ways of her household and is not idle. She fears the Lord (Prov. 31:10–31).

# ECCLESIASTES

227. There is a time for everything under heaven (Ecc. 3:1).

228. God has put into the heart of mankind to consider the concept of eternity (Ecc. 3:11).

229. Knowledge of some things such as details of the beginning and end of this world has been hidden from mankind by God (Ecc. 3:11, 8:17).

230. History repeats itself, and things occur in cycles, and this is done by God (Ecc. 1:9, 3:15).

231. Judgment by God at the great white throne of God will be done to both the children of God and those not his children (Ecc. 3:17, 12:14). The judgment will occur at the end of the millennium (Mt. 10:15; 2 Pet. 2:9, 3:7; Rev. 20:11–15).

232. Two or three people working together is better than an individual laboring alone (Ecc. 4:9–12).

233. He who loves money will not be satisfied with money (Ecc. 5:10).

234. Money helps with life's needs, but wisdom preserves the life of its possessor (Ecc. 7:11–12, 10:19). Divest your investments so one calamity does not ruin all your investments (Ecc. 11:1–2).

235. A wise man's heart directs him toward the right, but the foolish man's heart directs him toward the left (Ecc. 10:2).

236. The meaning of life is to fear God and keep his commandments. For God will bring every act to judgment, everything which is hidden, good or bad (Ecc. 12:13–14).

# ISAIAH

237.   The millennium will begin when the Lord returns. On
that day, people will try to hide from the Lord in places
like caves because the day of the Lord is upon them (Is.
2:21, Rev. 6:16). The Lord Jesus will rule and judge the
earth during the millennium from Jerusalem/Mt. Zion.
There will not be warfare between the nations during
this time. The people of the world will go to Jerusalem,
worship the Lord Jesus, and learn of him (Is. 2, Hos. 3:5,
Mic. 4:1–3, Rev. 20:1–10). During the siege and captivity
by Babylon, the Jews were scattered by God among the
nations (Ez. 20:23, 22:15; Zec. 7:14), but during the
millennium, Israel will be restored the way God intended,
and the Hebrews who love God will be brought from
throughout the world to Israel (Ez. 20:33–44). This is not
the current situation with Israel because not the whole
house of Israel serves the Messiah and because not all
the nations of the earth have acknowledged the Messiah
is holy. Christ is of the lineage of David. Israel will be
free of hostility of other nations during the millennium
(Ez. 34:11–31). Israel is not free of hostilities from other
peoples now, so the current Israel is not the regathering
of Israel by God referred to in the Bible. When a person
becomes saved, their heart of stone becomes a heart of
flesh. The Jews that have been and will be filled with the
Holy Spirit and become Christ followers (Christian) and
will dwell in Israel during the millennium (Ez. 36:25–31).
Those who were obedient to God before the millennium
will be called the priests of the Lord (Is. 61:6). People who
were and will not be followers of God and who are dead
when Christ Jesus returns will not be resurrected until

after the millennium for judgment (Rev. 20:5–6). The Israelites who are restored to the promised land by God after Christ's return will plant vineyards and gardens and fruit trees. They will also rebuild the ruined cities (Am. 9:13–15). God will restore the promised land to the tribes of Israel according to the borders he promised to Jacob (Ob. 1:19, 20). Jerusalem will be the obvious center of the earth spiritually and socially. Gentiles, including whole nations and distant nations, will come and worship Jesus and learn from Jesus. Jesus will judge for them. There will be peace throughout the earth during the millennium (Mic. 4:1–5, Zec. 8:22). God will protect Jerusalem during the millennium (Zec. 2:5). Many nations will join themselves to the Lord and will become his people (Zec. 2:11).

238. Isaiah prophesied the Messiah was to be born of a virgin (Is. 7:14).

239. The king of Assyria and his armies are referred to as the Euphrates River (Is. 8:7). Assyria is called the rod of God's anger (Is. 10:5), which God used to punish the Jews for their disobedience. Isaiah 8:7, 8 tell of the king of Assyria sweeping over the promised land or Holy Land. This prophesied of the Assyrian invasion before the Babylonian empire. It may also prophecy about a future invasion. In Revelation 16:12, it is prophesied God will dry up the Euphrates River so the way for the kings from the east would be prepared for invasion of the Holy Land for Armageddon. This means either the river Euphrates will literally be dried up for the kings of the east to invade the Holy Land or the Assyrians will be destroyed before the armies, including these from the east, gather to Armageddon. These kings from the east are not the same as the country from the east that disturbs the Antichrist,

along with news from the north, because these kings from the east help the Antichrist at the battle of Armageddon.

240. Second Advent. Isaiah 9:1–7 prophecies of the advent of the Messiah following a gloomy period. This speaks of the time being ruled by the Romans (first advent) and the Antichrist (second advent.) The second advent will bring in the millennium. Israel will be made a ruin before the Messiah comes to rule it (Ez. 21:27). Isaiah 10:1–19 prophecies about the evil society that the Jews made and Assyria's conquering of the Holy Land and eventual destruction at the hand of God. This is similar to Ezekiel 38 prophecy of invasion by Gog with the help of Persia, Cush (Ethiopia), Put (Libya), Armenia, and Turkey. The reference to the king of Babylon in Isaiah 14:4 could be the Antichrist. Isaiah 10:17 refers to the destruction of the Assyrian army in one day by fire, which is like Armageddon in Ezekiel 39 (adds hail and brimstone) and Revelation 19:17–21 (the sword of Jesus destroys all nations' armies at Armageddon gathered to battle Jesus). The sun and moon will be darkened, the stars of the sky will fall to earth, and there will be a great earthquake heralding the return of Jesus and the destruction of the beast of the sea and his followers (Is. 13:9–13; Ez. 38:19, 20; Mt. 24:29; Rev. 6:12, 13). The day of wrath or vengeance is the day the Lord returns. The battle of Armageddon occurs on this day (Is. 10:17, 61:2, 63:2–4; Rev. 14:20). The Lord will come in fire and conquer the Antichrist and his armies (Is. 66:15–16). This is followed by return of the remnant of Jews who are loyal to God to Israel, as after the Babylonian captivity, at the beginning of the millennium (Is. 10:20–34, Ez. 39:27). Chapter 18 of Isaiah seems to prophecy about the United States of America unless things change with time. It could be

Ethiopia since it talks about the land beyond the rivers of Cush, but Cush and Ethiopia are felt to be the same.

However Cush can also be the Cush that is in the area of the Garden of Eden where the Euphrates and several rivers are, where they empty into the Persian Gulf. That would be Persia or any country east from there. The land of whirring wings—this could refer to helicopters, and helicopters were invented by the USA. Sending envoys to Israel by papyrus vessels on the surface of the water by the sea. Papyrus is paper, and ships would not be made of paper but planes can be. Sending envoys by plane over the sea would be done by a distant country rather than Ethiopa. A land divided by rivers seems particularly descriptive of Bangladesh or the USA because they are divided by rivers more than other countries. Chapter 18 also says this nation is powerful and oppressive. Bangladesh does not fit that description but the USA does. In Isaiah 18:2, it is mentioned swift messengers, which are most likely angels because prophets, while messengers of God, are not swift. Then in verses 5 and 6, it is mentioned before the harvest there will be a pruning of this country that birds of prey will feast on. When the Bible talks about the battle of Armageddon, it also talks about birds of prey feasting on the corpses after that great battle, so this would indicate a loss of many American lives, most likely in the battle of Armageddon. The harvest is most likely the harvest of saved souls from this earth associated with the Lord's second coming.

When a tree or plant is pruned, it is to remove what is useless or dead. In verse 7, it is mentioned that the people from this country will come to give a gift of homage to the Lord. This would only occur during the millennium. So this country, which is most likely the USA, will have a pruning of people who reject Jesus as Lord by angels sent from God. This could be because these people who reject Jesus join the Antichrist in the battle of Armageddon or they die from punishments sent on the earth by God during the great tribulation.

Because not all of the people of this country are destroyed but pruned of its people who worship the Antichrist, there will be people who will give homage to Jesus after he returns. The saved people of all the world, both dead and alive, will be gathered to the Lord when he returns, so that would mean there will be some, or maybe even many, people in this country (presumed USA) who do not join the Antichrist and yet not be saved prior to Jesus's return. These people will pay homage to Jesus, because it will be obvious that Jesus is God the Son, during the millennium and bear children and repopulate the country.

Isaiah 19 prophesies about Egypt. It will be ruled by a cruel master in verse 4. This was the Assyrian king in the seventh century BC and later Nebuchadnezzar but also prophesies about the Antichrist who will invade Egypt (Dan. 11:42). In addition to the Antichrist conquering Egypt, the Nile canals will be dried up (Is. 11:15, 19:4–7; Ez. 30:12), and poverty (Is. 19:15) will be in Egypt. Egyptians will turn to the Lord, and he will rescue them and be their Savior in verses 19 and 20 bringing in the millennium. Babylon will fall in one day as opposed to its gradual fall when it fell to the Medes and Persians (Is. 21:9, Jer. 51:8, 49, Rev. 14:8, 18:2). Jeremiah 50:2 was fulfilled when Media Persia conquered Babylon. Isaiah 11 prophesies about the rule of the earth by the Messiah/Jesus during the millennium from Jerusalem (Ez. 43, 44, 45, 46, 47, and 48, Rev. 20:1–6).

241. The Spirit of the Lord, the Holy Spirit, will rest on the branch from the root of Jesse, the Messiah (Is. 11:1, 2, Mt. 3:16, Mk. 1:10, Lk. 3:22, Jn. 1:32).

242. Three works/spirits/evidences of the Holy Spirit: wisdom and understanding, counsel and strength, knowledge and fear of the Lord (Is. 11:2).

243. The king of Babylon in Isaiah 14:4 could be referring to the Antichrist or just a king of Babylon of the Babylonian empire period.

244. Satan is sometimes called Lucifer, which means star of the morning as he is called in Isaiah 14:12–14. He was also called son of the dawn in verse 12. Satan was proud and said he would ascend to heaven (he was appointed as cherub in the garden of Eden as referenced in Ezekiel 28:14) and raise his throne above the stars of God. These stars may refer to angels. Job 38:7 indicates morning stars are angels. Lucifer said he would make himself like the Most High God, which led to his fall. Satan is described in Ezekiel 28:11–16. There he is referred to as the king of Tyre, but it is evident these verses refer to Satan because it describes him as being in the garden of Eden, and neither Tyre nor any man other than Adam was around during the garden of Eden days. Also Adam was the only man in Eden. The scripture does not say a garden of your (king of Tyre) god but the garden of Eden of God. Also the king of Tyre, or Satan, is described as a cherub (angel) appointed to cover the garden of Eden in verse 14. Then he is said to have been blameless from the days he was created until unrighteousness was found in him in verse 15.

Even though Satan was evil from the beginning as explained below, his actions were not evil from the beginning. One can be a murderer in their heart and not in action as Jesus said in Matthew 5:22. Then he is said to be cast from the mountain of God in Ezekiel 28:16. No human fits these descriptions. Satan is described as full of wisdom and perfect in beauty, but he was internally filled with violence and sinned in Ezekiel 28:12 and 16. Also in verse 16, it says the king of Tyre was filled with violence by his trade or merchandise (what he was selling). This could fit either the human king of Tyre, if the king was involved in a merchandise, or Satan, if one understands this as what Satan deals in [lies and death (getting as many people he can to go to the second death described in Revelation 20 in particular)]. Jesus said Satan was a murderer from the beginning in John 8:44. This would indicate Satan was like Judas Iscariot, the disciple, in that he appeared the same as those around him who served God, but inside him was evil. God created both Satan and Judas this way to serve his purposes. Jesus is also called the bright morning star in Revelation 22:16, so morning star is most likely a general term for spiritual beings other than the souls of humans.

Ezekiel 28:17–19 could describe the human king of Tyre as well as Satan. Satan, the devil (slanderer), is also called Beelzebul (Lord of the flies—Matt. 12:24), and Belial (lawless—2 Cor. 6:15), the evil one (1 John 5:19), the tempter (1 Thess. 3:5), the prince of this world (John 12:31), the god of this age or world (2 Cor. 4:4), the prince of the power of the air (Eph. 2:2), the accuser of the brethren (Rev. 12:10), disguised as an angel of light (angel of light meaning a "good" angel or in other words an angel serving God, 2 Cor. 11:14), a serpent (Genesis 3, Rev. 12:9), and a dragon (Rev. 12:3). It is felt Satan took a third of the angels with him when he was cast out of heaven from the mount of God (Rev. 12:4). These fallen angels may be demons (Mt. 12:24).

However these fallen angels may not be the same as demons because they are bound in hell for judgment day (Jude 6, 2 Pe. 2:4). Or this may be the abyss where demons, or fallen angels if they are the same, go when they are cast out of someone (Lk. 8:31). Demons are spiritual forces of wickedness (Ep. 6:12). Satan is not a brother of Jesus or another son of God (Jn. 3:16). Satan is a created being, created by God (Ez. 28:15), and as such is subject to eternal torment in the lake of fire (which he will) (Rev. 20:10). Jesus has always existed and will always exist (Rev. 1:8, 21:6, 22:13).

245. Egypt was the first kingdom to rule over the Jews (Is. 10:24, Rev. 17:8–11).

246. Babylon, who will persecute Christians in the last days, will be judged and destroyed by God in one day with plagues, pestilence, famine and fire. This day will be the day of the Lord's return (Is. 13:6, 9,10, 13, Rev. 18). This will lead into the millennium (Is. 14:1–7). These verses would seem to indicate that the Antichrist will be Babylonian or at least Babylonians (today's Iraq) would be in league with the Antichrist in persecuting Christians.

247. In the last days (we know this is in the last days because some of the prophecies in Isaiah chapter 19 have not been fulfilled), there will be civil war in Egypt (Is. 19:2). The current situation in Egypt is the first civil war in Egypt since the prophecy of Isaiah. Then the Egyptians will be demoralized, and God will confound their strategy, so they will turn to idols, ghosts of the dead, mediums and spiritists (v. 3). Then God will deliver Egypt over to the Antichrist, and the waters of Egypt will dry up (Is. 19:4, 5). Then the Egyptians will be grieved and have high unemployment (v. 10, 15).

248. The Lord will deliver Egypt from the Antichrist because they turn to the Lord (Is. 19:18–21).

249.    Isaiah prophesied the fall of Babylon to the Medes and Persians, the fall of Edom to the Assyrians, and the fall of the Arabians in the Kedar region to Babylon (Is. 21).

250.    When a country is beyond repentance to God for its sins and sees it is about to be attacked, the people may just decide to eat, drink, and be merry one last time before they assume they will die. This was done by the Jews in Isaiah 22:1–3, 12, and 13. It was also done by the Babylonians, under Belshazzar, before Babylon was sacked by the Medo-Persians (Dan. 5).

251.    Isaiah prophesied of the fall of Tyre, a previously unconquered city, to Alexander the Great. But its devastation would last only seventy years. As prophesied, Tyre was rebuilt after this relatively short period of devastation (Is. 23).

252.    When the Lord comes to rule the earth, the whole earth will tremble with a great earthquake (Is. 24:1, 18). The sun and moon will give up their light. And the Lord of hosts will reign on mount Zion (Is. 24: 23, Ps. 2:6). There will be a harvest of the bodies of Old Testament saints (otherwise this would not be in the Old Testament) and New Testament Saints (Is. 24:13, 26:19). Unbelievers will be separated from the saints when the Lord returns, with the sound of a trumpet, like a harvest of wheat and tares (Is. 27:12, 13). Saints' souls go to heaven when they die (Lk. 16:19–25, 23:43). We will receive our new imperishable bodies then when Jesus returns (1 Cor. 15:50–57). People from the west will cry out in joy for the Lord during the millennium (Is. 24:14). People of powerful nations will worship the Lord Jesus (Is. 25:3).

253.    God will keep in perfect peace the mind of the person whose mind is stayed on God and who trusts in God (Is. 26:5).

254. Satan, that old serpent who tempted Eve, is destroyed come judgment day after the millennium (Is. 26:21–27:1; Rev. 20:10–15).

255. God's people who turn against God and try to hide their sins saying to themselves even "the Lord does not see" are inviting God's wrath (Is. 29:15, 47:10, Ez. 8:12, Ps. 94:7).

256. The Messiah's advent will be heralded by the appearance of Elijah who will clear the way for the Lord and make smooth the highway of God. The spirit of Elijah was in John the Baptist and will be in one of the two witnesses who appear soon before his coming. Elijah in this way will bring people to repentance before the Lord's second advent as he did in John the Baptist (Is. 40:3–5, 11; Mal. 3:1, 4:5–6; Mt. 11:14; Lk. 1:17; Rev. 11). There will be a period of deep darkness covering the earth prior to Christ's second advent. This follows Christ's first advent by an unstated amount of time (Is. 60:1–3). There will be birth pains (the tribulation period where hurtful things happen to the earth and its inhabitants by God and the believers of God are persecuted by those who do not follow God) prior to God delivering this earth and its inhabitants from the devil with Jesus's second coming (Is. 66:9, Jer. 30:6, 7, Mat. 24:4–31).

God tells us the new Israel (which is the Israel during the millennium) cannot be brought about in one day but must be a long process that involves pain to the current Jews (Is. 66:8). God also tells us Israel brings forth her son before her tribulation (Is. 66:7). This Son is the Lord Jesus (Rev. 12:5), and the Jews have certainly been persecuted since the time of the Romans. God will hide and protect many Jews during the three-and-half-year period in which the Antichrist attempts to kill Jews (Rev. 12:6, 13–16). Satan and Antichrist will be enraged because of God's deliverance of Jews, so they will persecute Christians during this three-and-half-year period (Rev. 12:17). There will be everlasting joy among the obedient to God after the second advent of Jesus (Is. 61:7). Jerusalem and Jesus, the Messiah, will both be called the Lord is our righteousness during the millennium (Jer. 23:6; 33:16).

257.    God is the creator of good and evil. He causes well-being and calamity (Is. 45:7). This contradicts the notion that God does not cause bad things to happen such as natural disasters. He does. He does for the good of people. Salvation with an eternity with God is more important than comfort in this life, and this is sometimes the reason for calamities. Sometimes God punishes a people for great sin as he did with Sodom and Gomorrah. Sometimes he allows the devil to do things to hurt people, as he did with Job, to test their faith.

258.    Chapter 47 of Isaiah is a warning not only to Babylon but to any nation that becomes haughty and thinks they are great on their own and not by God's hand. God will bring destruction to such nations, just as he did with Babylon when they became too proud.

259.    For Jews: God said Israel would bring forth her son before her tribulation (Is. 66:7). The Messiah does not come once to earth and start his eternal rule of Israel, but He will be cut off (killed in the flesh) before he starts his eternal rule of Israel (Dan. 9:26). Jesus fulfills all the prophecies of the Messiah in Isaiah 53. He was not attractive. He was despised. He bore our griefs and sorrows. He was considered smitten of God. He was pierced for our transgressions, crushed for our iniquities. The Lord caused the iniquity of us all to fall on him. He did not speak during his trial. His grave was assigned with wicked men, but he was buried in a rich man's grave. The prophecy of Psalm 2:7 was fulfilled by God (Mt. 3:17).

260. A nation that does not know Israel will run to it because of the Lord God. This could be America since America has developed close ties with Israel (Is. 55:5).

261. God's word will not return to him empty, without accomplishing what he desires and without succeeding in the matter for which he sent it (Is. 55:11, Jer. 1:12).

262. All people who are obedient to God will be with him forever, not just Jews (Is. 49:6, 56:8).

263. Wicked people cannot be quiet. They speak and act in evil ways and will not have peace inside them (Is. 57:20–21).

264. The saints will be called the priests of the Lord. Old Testament saints are followers of God before Jesus Christ's first advent. New Testament saints are followers of God after the first advent of Jesus Christ and believe Jesus is the Messiah. They are called Christians or believers (Is. 61:6, Ac. 11:26).

265. Prayer. We are to remind father God in our prayers of his promises and give him no rest until he establishes his kingdom here on earth (the millennium) (Is. 62:6–7, 64:1–2; Mt. 6:10).

266. The Holy Spirit has been in existence since the beginning with God the Father and God the Son (Is. 63:11). The Holy Spirit moved on people in Old Testament times (Jdg. 14:6). The Holy Spirit first indwelled in John the Baptist, while he was in his mother's womb (Lk. 1:15). His parents were also filled with the Holy Spirit (Lk. 1:41, 67).

267. The new heaven and new earth will be created by God after the millennium and the final battle where Satan is cast into the lake of fire. There will be no weeping or crying or pain in the new heaven and earth. There will be no temple there for God the Father and Jesus the Lamb are its temple. There will be no night and day, sun or moon

because the Lord will illumine them (Is. 65:17–20, Rev. 20:7–22:5). People other than those with a new eternal body (the saints) should live to be one hundred years old (Is. 65:20). These people will also build houses and plant vineyards (Is. 65:21). Former enemies will live at peace with one another such as the wolf and lamb (Is. 65:25).

# JEREMIAH

268. God told Jeremiah of things to come like the conquest of Judah by Babylon and that he must speak to his countrymen about this and their sins, but his countrymen would reject him and fight against him. God said he would not allow Jeremiah's countrymen to overcome him though (Jer. 1:11–19, 4:5–7, 15:19–21).

269. Israel was the first of God's harvest (Jer. 2:3). The final harvest will be when Jesus, the Messiah, returns (Mt. 24:29–31, Rev. 14:14–20).

270. The Jews had gotten to the point of rebellion against God; they worshipped false gods and even idols made of wood and stone. They also believed in evolution if one considers evolution as a theory of the beginning of the earth and all that is in it by means other than God such as spontaneous development or seeding by aliens.(Jer. 2:27, 7:18; Is. 29:16, 65:11). The theory of evolution was imagined even during king David's time (Ps. 100:3). Rebellion got to the point of burning their sons and daughters in fire in worship to false gods (Jer. 7:31). This was the same as the evil people God had the Jews destroy from the promised land (Lv. 18:21, 20:2–5; Dt. 12:31).

271. The Jews had hardened their hearts so much that they said they had not sinned even though they had (Jer. 2:35, 8:6). This after they had killed the prophets God sent to them (Jer. 2:30). God could not find one man who was Godly in Jerusalem, as he could not find ten righteous men in Sodom (Gen. 18:32, 19). The rebellion against God involved all social classes from the poor to the leaders of the country (Jer. 5:4).

272. The Jews denied that God would cause calamity to come on them, and when it did, they denied it was from God until the captivity (Jer. 5:12, 25). The reason for some of them could have been that they thought since they were God's chosen people God would not punish them. This is somewhat similar to people today who say God never punishes anyone for sin because he is a God of love. This is contrary to scripture where God judges the unrepentant throughout the Bible. God is a God of love but also a God of righteousness. Some people seem to go without God's punishment here on earth for their disobedience to God, but unless they are saved, they will be punished in the lake of fire come judgment day. For other Jews, it was because they did not even believe in the existence of God.

273. When the Jews finally acknowledged God was punishing them, they still did not acknowledge it was because of their sin. Instead, they questioned God why he was punishing them (Jer. 5:19, 24).

274. When a people become too ungodly so that their conscience no longer bothered them for sinning, God allowed leaders like false prophets and priests or ministers to tell the people lies they want to hear (Jer. 5:31, 8:12, 10:21; 2 Tim. 4:3).

275. God reserves drought for use by himself and not Satan. He uses it to try to get people to repent and turn to him (Jer. 3:3, 9:12, 13, 12:4). God allows Satan to affect weather, in other ways like storms as what happened with Job.

276. Israel will return to God and not waver; then the other nations will bless themselves in him (Jer. 4:1, 2). This will occur during the millennium.

277. God sometimes tells his people to not pray for someone or some people (Jer. 7:16, 11:14, 14:11).

278. When a people are rebellious and unrepentant to the point of a seared conscious, as was the case with the Jews in Jeremiah, there will be no salvation of souls (Jer. 8:13, 20). Without repentance, there is no remission of sin and salvation (Lk. 13:3).

279. The more people turn from God, the more they lie (Jer. 9:5).

280. God punished the Jews, for their rebellion against him, with drought, pestilence, wormwood, wild beasts, and war (Jer. 4:5–7, 9:12–16, 14:12, 15:3; Am. 4:7–10). This is similar to the last days of this present earth (Rev. 6:3–8, 8:10, 11).

281. Just as God blesses all nations each day, the day will come when he will punish all nations/peoples disobedient to him (Jer. 9:24–26, 10:25).

282. When God is wroth, the earth quakes (Jer. 10:10).

283. God made heaven and earth and controls them (Jer. 10:12, 13, 16).

284. The Jews were God's chosen people (Jer. 10:16). Gentile Christians are too and are able to share in the inheritance of the Jews by becoming spiritually engrafted into the family of Abraham (Rom. 11:13–25, Gal. 3:29). Since Jesus came, Jews have to believe in him as the Messiah to go to heaven just like all people of the earth (Jn. 14:6).

285. God sometimes does not want believers to pray for people who enjoy, or regard in their heart, wickedness (Jer. 7:16, 11:11, 14:11; Ps. 66:18).

286. God is the same yesterday, today, and forever. He uses similar means to deal with people. He used the sword, famine, pestilence, and wild beasts to punish the Jews for their sins (Jer. 14:12, 15:3) and will use these means to punish the world's population for sinning/rebellion in the end times (Rev. 6:8).

287. God determines each person's future, including the way we die. Those who use the sword to defend themselves are doing God's will even though they die by the sword (Jer. 15:2, Lk. 21:24, Rev. 13:10).

288. Blessed is the person who trusts in God and not mankind (Jer. 17:5, 7, 17).

289. The heart of people is wicked. People are wicked without the love of God in their heart to help them do right. Therefore all people are doomed to an eternity in the lake of fire without the love of God in their heart (Jer. 17:9, 10, Rom 3:23). This can only occur through belief in Jesus as Lord (Jn. 14:6).

290. God can change the future calamity for a nation or people from what he spoke if they repent (Jer. 18:7, 8). This tells us prayer changes things, including God's will (Am. 7:6.)

291. If a nation or kingdom that was originated and blessed by God does evil in God's sight by not obeying God's voice, God may bring calamity to that nation or kingdom (Jer. 18:9–11). America needs to pay heed to these verses.

292. People can become so rebellious they will not repent of their sins even when they see their calamities are from God and will continue sinning saying that is the way they are (Jer. 18:12). We see that today with proponents of sin like homosexual activists and those addicted to sinful behavior because of continued rebellion against God. Their conscious initially convicts them, but as they continue in their sin, they eventually give into it and embrace it so their conscious is seared and no longer bothers them.

293. Jeremiah became discouraged because the prophecies he spoke had not happened yet and people were mocking him. So he did not want to prophecy any more. But to speak God's word was like an unquenchable fire in him, so he continued to prophecy (Jer. 20:7–9).

294. Those who know God help the afflicted and needy (Jer. 22:16).

295. The Messiah, the Righteous Branch, will come to reign as king. Judah and Israel will be saved and dwell securely during the millennium. The Messiah will be called the Lord our righteousness (Jer. 23:5, 6). Jerusalem will be called the Lord is our righteousness (Jer. 33:16).

296. The prophecies in Jeremiah 50 and 51 were about the Babylonian and Medo-Persian empires, so they have already been fulfilled.

297. The length of the Jews exile in Babylon was prophesied to be seventy years (Jer. 25:11; 29:10). The exile was seventy years from ca. 605/04 BC to 536/35 BC when Cyrus decreed for the return of the Jews. This allowed the promised land to have the number of years of rest God intended from King Saul through the Babylonian exile that it had not had because of the Jews not honoring the Sabbath law (2 Ch. 36:21).

298. God intended good for the Jews as he does for all people if they would just seek and obey him with all their heart (Jer. 29:11–13).

299. God promised a new covenant to come where his laws would be within his followers and written on their hearts (Jer. 31: 31–33). This occurs when the Holy Spirit indwells believers' hearts upon becoming saved (Jn. 14:15–17, Ac. 1:8, 2:1–4).

300. Medo-Persia is the one who conquered Babylon from the north in Jeremiah 50:3, 51:11, 27, 28. This is because the Babylonians rejoiced at the calamity of the Jews (Jer. 50:11).

# LAMENTATIONS

301. God is good to those who wait for him, to the person who seeks him (Lam. 3:25).

302. Both good and bad things happen as God speaks them into being (Lam. 3:38). This is not to say God tempts people to sin or does evil himself (Jas. 1:13). He allows evil to occur to fulfill his will, but all good things come from God (Jas. 1:17).

303. When God is punishing a country for sin and unfaithfulness to him and the people are at their lowest and repent and cry out to God for forgiveness and relief, then God will turn his wrath away. There is a time during this punishment God will not listen to the requests for help and relief from God, even if Noah, Daniel, and Job were in their midst (Lam. 3; Ez. 14:6, 11–14). God has no pleasure in the death of anyone who dies, even as a result of God's punishment for society's or his or her sins, so he asks us to repent and be obedient (Ez. 18:32, 33:11). We will know we are in the last days when the world's people stop repenting of their sins (2 Tim. 4:3). Then the judgments from God on the world, as written in Revelation, will be justified.

# EZEKIEL

304. Prophets are held responsible by God for the lives of the people God tells them to warn. They are to speak God's word to the people whom God tells them to warn of calamity to come because of sin (Ez. 3:18, 33:1–6).

305. Similarities exist between the Babylonian siege and captivity and the last days. Ezekiel saw in a vision four living creatures that were like the four John saw in Revelation (Ez.1; Ez. 10:15, 17, 20; Rev. 4:6–8). Judgment will be on the whole earth in the last days, like it was on Israel and Judah during the Babylonian captivity, after all the nations have heard and many reject the gospel (Mt. 24:14). Most Jews stopped following God before God's judgment on them occurred with the Babylonian captivity (Ez. 8). There will be many Christians who will stop following God (a great falling away) in the last days before God sends Jesus to Judge the earth (Mt. 24:10, Lk. 8:13–14, Gal. 5:4). These Christians that stopped following God may not have been saved to begin with (1 Jn. 2:19).

Famine, wild beasts, and plague will kill people (Ez. 5:17, Rev. 6:8). God will save a remnant of Jews from persecution and death (Ez. 6:8, Rev. 7:1–8, 12:13–16). The Jewish temple is profaned (Ez. 7:22). This was first fulfilled by Antiochus (Dan. 11:31). This will occur in the last days (Dan. 9:27, Mat. 24:15). Before God judges people on earth with various calamities and death, he will have 144,000 Jews that are followers of him marked on their foreheads so the six angels who punish mankind will not touch them (Rev. 7:3). These six angels that blow the six trumpets that herald these judgments are in

Revelation 8 and 9. They blow their trumpet before the last/seventh trumpet is sounded by an angel that heralds the return of Jesus to earth, and saints, both dead and alive, will be gathered to Jesus (Mt. 24:30–31, 1 Cor. 15:52, 1 Th. 4:15–17, Rev. 11:15). There were six angels sent by God to kill Jews who were not sealed on their foreheads (followers of God) during the Babylonian siege (Ez. 9:1–6). The iniquity by Judah and Israel was great before the judgment, and they said "the Lord does not see" (their sins) (Ez. 9:9–10). Iniquity will be great throughout the earth prior to God's judgment with the six angels with the trumpets (2 Tim. 3:1–7, Rev. 8 and 9). Evil leaders cause nations to sin and bring God's judgment (Ez. 11:1–2, 15, 21, 2 Th. 2:3). Sword (war), famine, pestilence, and wild beast killing people were used by God for judgment on the Jews for their iniquity, and God warned this is for any nation that rebels against him (Ez. 14:12–23). These are God's four severe judgments (Ez. 14:21). God will use these in the end times (Rev. 6:8).

306. God has made Jerusalem the center of the nations of this world (Ez. 5:5). All prophecies center around Jerusalem.

307. When God punishes a country for unfaithfulness to him, his punishment will affect not only the evil people of a country but also the seemingly innocent people, including children (Ez. 9:6, 14:12–23). Only the elect people who bemoan sin in their land will be sealed and saved from the punishment to come from God (Ez. 9:4). This is like the 144,00 Jews who will be saved as a remnant of Israel to serve the Lord after he returns (Rev. 7:1–8). For a nation to become unfaithful to God, it first had to be faithful to him. Only two nations in history have been founded on God's word: Israel and the United States of America. The verses Ezekiel 9:9-10 are a warning the United States of America. The USA is being filled with innocent blood

of aborted babies. These babies are human sacrifice on the alter of Baal. If one says Israel started when Joshua divided the land to the twelve tribes (ca. 1398 BC) and ended when Israel was divided into the northern and southern kingdoms (931 BC), Israel lasted about 467 years. If The USA does not repent of the sin of abortion and its many other sins like acceptance of homosexuality and other sexual sins and get right with God, the USA will receive the four severe judgments from God just as Israel received (Ez. 14:21).

308. The glory of God left the temple in Jerusalem during the Babylonian captivity due to the Jews unfaithfulness to God and stood over the Mount of Olives to the east of Jerusalem (Ez. 11: 23). The glory of God will return from the east and fill the temple built after the destruction of Gog and his allies by God at the battle of Armageddon (Ez. 43:1–9).

309. The Messiah, who is Jesus, is described as the tender branch that God will plant on the high mountain of Israel, and birds of every kind will nest under it. Gentiles from all over the world, as well as people of Jewish heritage, will make their abode with Jesus forever when he returns (Ez. 17:22–24). The Lord will conquer the Antichrist and his armies. The Lord will stand on the Mount of Olives when he returns, and the mount will be split in two so that half will move toward the south and half toward the north. Then the Lord's millennial reign here on earth will begin (Zec. 14:3–9).

310. Jews were saying the way of God was wrong before and during the Babylonian captivity (Ez. 18:25, 29). People do that today. They say the God of the Bible is not just in having the Jews kill people to take the promised land, even though those people God told the Jews to kill were terribly evil to the point they sacrificed their children to

false gods. People today also say God is not just in saying that Jesus is the only way to heaven. They also say some sins like sexual sins are not sin, changing God's word to reflect their viewpoint of saying the Bible is wrong, just words written by men and not God, "if there is a god." So sinners say what is right and wrong, making themselves out to be God.

311. Political and spiritual leaders of the Jews were acting in cahoots together for each other's gain for power and wealth. They called things that were good bad and those things that were bad good (Ez. 22:23–28). During the end times, political and spiritual leaders of the world will do the same. Many leaders of Christian churches are joining the political leaders of today and other sinners in no longer calling homosexuality sin and saying there is more than one way to heaven.

312. Ammonites and Moabites were absorbed into the Arabian peoples as God told Ezekiel would happen in the future (Ez. 25:11).

313. The king of Tyre in Ezekiel 28:11–16 appears to be the devil. See comments about Isaiah 14.

314. People who do not repent and do as God says at the warning of a prophet cannot blame God or the prophet for their calamity; the blame is on the one warned (Ez. 33:4).

315. The prophet must warn people as God tells him to, or he is responsible for the deaths of those God told him to warn of calamity to come (Ez. 33:6).

316. Pastors/priests are held accountable for feeding Christians God's word (Ez. 34:1–10).

317. God will send over his people, both Jew and Gentile, one shepherd, the Messiah, during the millennium (Ez. 34:22, 23).

318. Beasts will not harm saints during the millennium (Ez. 34:25).

319. The resurrection of the dead who were followers of God will occur before Israel is gathered back together and ruled by Christ the King (Ez. 37). Israel will be despondent before this (Ez. 37:11) and call on the Lord for help and recognize Jesus as the Messiah (Mt. 23:39). Since the resurrection of the dead occurs when the Lord returns (1 Th. 4:16-17) and the Lord has not returned yet, we know the gathering together of the Jews that led to the formation of Israel in 1948 is not the gathering together of the Jews referred to here.

320. Gog of the land of Magog, chief prince of Meshech and Tubal, with his allies, will invade Israel under the influence of God (Ez. 38:1–6, Mic. 4:11, 12). The sons of Japheth were Gomer, Magog, Madai, Javan, Tubal, Meshech, and Tiras. Also Togarmah was a son of Gomer according to Genesis 10:2, 3. Magog is a large region to the north and west of the Caspian Sea according to ancient Hebrew maps. There are several historical references to the Scythians as descendants of Magog. The Scythians, as best as other historians can tell, were descendants of Gomer that were tribal nomadic Persians that probably inhabited lands from Assyria, or mostly Syria today, through the Caucasus to much of Asia as far north as Russia. Meshech and Tubal may be Moschoi and Tibarenoi, respectively, mentioned by the ancient historian Herodotus, which were in modern-day Turkey. Or they could be Mushku and Tabal mentioned by the Assyrians.

   First century AD Jewish historian Flavius Josephus thought Meshech was Cappadocian Mosocheni and Tubal was Caucasian Iberia. The Iberians were ancestors of modern-day Georgia and other peoples that may include some in Italy and Spain. According to sixteenth century scholars, Moscow was founded by descendants of Meshech, son of Japheth, son of Noah. So Gog is from Magog and thus could be from Syria, Turkey, or Iraq up through the Caucasus region, into eastern Europe and on into Asia. Meshech and Tubal are in modern-day Turkey or somewhere in the Caucasian region of Asia Minor. Joining Gog in the attack on Israel will be Persia (modern-day Iran), Ethiopia, Put (modern-day Lybia), Gomer (descendants live anywhere from modern day Turkey to eastern Europe, Russia, and China) and Beth-togarmah (region in modern-day Armenia and Turkey) (Ez. 38:1–6). The Antichrist will not be from Persia (modern-day Iran) since Ezekiel says Persia will join Gog in the invasion of the Holy Land. This narrows the area from which the Antichrist will be from since he is referred to as the prince of Meshech and Tubal: modern-day Turkey. This invasion is either the invasion by the Antichrist and his armies spoken of elsewhere in the Bible or the war of Gog and Magog spoken of in Revelation 20:7–10.

This invasion of Israel will occur during a time that Israel is gathered together as a nation and a time of peace with unwalled villages and no bars or gates. The invading army will cover Israel (Ez. 38:7–12). The people from Sheba, in western Arabian Peninsula (in modern-day Saudi Arabia), Dedan, in eastern Arabian Peninsula (possibly modern day Saudi Arabia, United Arab Emirates, and Qatar), and Tarshish (Greek historian Herodotus identified this as a Tartessus, a merchant city in southern Spain) will ask Gog if he means to profit from this invasion (Ez. 38:13). So these countries will not be participants in the invasion. Since Spain is mentioned, it would imply at least some of the western countries will not be in support of Gog. Also, much of the people of the

Arabian Peninsula will not be in support of Gog. More on this later.

Since this is a time of peace for Israel with its people gathered from throughout the world, as Isaiah says, it would either be during the millennium or before the return of Christ when the Antichrist makes a seven-year peace covenant spoken of in Daniel 9:27. The latter seems the only possibility since the battle of Armageddon occurs just before the millennium. The Lord's anger will mount up when Gog enters Jerusalem with his armies, and there will be a great earthquake, and the Battle of Armageddon will ensue (Ez. 38:18–20). This will occur in the valley of Jehoshaphat, Har-Magedon/Armageddon (Joel 3:12, Rev. 16:16). Har-Magedon means Mt. Megiddo, which is sixty miles north of Jerusalem. The size of the army of the Antichrist/Gog will be so large though that it will encompass a large area around Mt. Megiddo. The desolation is near when Jerusalem is surrounded by armies (Lk. 21:20). Then the Jews (the remnant) must flee to the mountains (Lk. 21:21).

Gog, the Antichrist, will capture Jerusalem, and then women will be ravished, houses plundered, and half of the city exiled (Zec. 14:2). The harvest will be ripe, and the dead in Christ will be resurrected, and those who are alive and remain who are Christian will meet the Lord in the air as he returns (Joel 3:13, 1 Th. 4:16, 17, Rev. 14:14–16). God will destroy Gog and his armies with hail, fire and brimstone and they will also kill each other (Ez. 38:21–22). The Lord will conquer the Antichrist and his armies. The Lord will stand on the Mount of Olives when he returns, and the mount will be split in two so that half will move toward the south and half toward the north. Then the Lord's millennial reign here on earth will begin (Zec. 14:3–9). God will shake all the nations with earthquakes before his return and the temple is rebuilt. The Lord is going to shake the heavens and the earth when he returns (Hag. 2:7, 21, 22). It will take seven years to burn what is left of the weapons of the war and seven months to bury the dead bodies (Ez. 39:9–12).

This is followed by the restoration of the Davidic kingdom in Israel ruled by the Lord and the regathering of the house of Israel to Israel for the millennium. God's Holy Spirit will indwell the house of Israel. This can only be after they believe Jesus is the Messiah (Mt. 23:39), which may come about from their desperate situation of losing to the Antichrist and his armies. It will be evident from his awesome return and destruction of the enemies of Israel and God (Ez. 39:25–29). There is a temple made in Jerusalem after the battle with Gog and his armies (Armageddon) that the glory of God fills (Ez. 40–43). Sacrifices will be made on the altar, including by a prince (Ez. 43:18–27, 45:22). This prince is not named, but we know it is not Jesus because he makes sin offering for himself and all the people in the promised land, which would not be necessary for Jesus (Ez. 45:22).

The sacrifices during the millennium include the atonement of the new altar (Ez. 43:18–26), the New Year (Ez. 45:18), the Passover (Lv. 23:5, Ez. 45:19–24), the feast of unleavened bread (Lv. 23:6–8, Ez. 45:24), and the feast of Booths (Lv. 23:33–44, Ez. 45:25). The sin offerings will not be necessary for the saints of God as the sacrifice Jesus made was all that was needed for those who believe Jesus is the Son of God and love him (Heb. 9:28, 10:10, 1 Pet. 3:18). Those who are in heaven before Jesus's return going all the way back to Adam and Eve as well as the Christians alive when Jesus returns will be included in this group. The mystery of the Lord is that Jesus's sacrifice makes all who believe in him and forsake all for him (repent and become saved) become part of the family of God. This means gentile Christians are fellow heirs of the kingdom of God with the Jews who were in heaven at the time of Jesus's death (Eph. 3:2–6, Col. 1:27).

The mystery of the Lord is justification before God offered to all people through faith in Jesus as the Messiah (Rom. 3:21–26). The mystery of the Lord is finished when Jesus returns because all people on earth will see he is God the Son, and faith will no longer be needed to know that (Rev. 10:7). I know this is hard for many Christians to accept because we believe Jesus paid the sacrifice necessary for all who believe he is the Christ. But again faith will no longer be necessary as it will be obvious to all people that Jesus is Lord. Jew and Gentile people born on earth after Jesus's return and people that were already alive when Jesus returns but are not saints will be the ones that will need to offer sacrifices for their sins, through the Levitical priests, to be justified with God. Gentiles will join and attach themselves to the Jews in the promised land (Is. 14:1). We know that eventually many will rebel against God when Satan is released after one thousand years (Rev. 20:7–9). These will not be the saints as saints are sealed (Ep. 1:13) and already have a new eternal body. Saints are those that follow God, the God of Abraham and Father of Jesus, from Adam until Jesus returns. Christians are saints that follow God after Jesus's first advent and, by faith, given to them by God, believe Jesus is the Messiah, God's Son. There is no temple in the new Jerusalem of the new heaven and earth, which replace this heaven and earth after the war of Gog and Magog, which occurs at the end of the millennium (Rev. 20:7–10; 21:22).

Therefore, since Ezekiel prophecies about the temple in Jerusalem after the battle of Gog of Magog mentioned in chapters 38 and 39, this battle in chapters 38 and 39 must be the battle of Armageddon against the Antichrist. There is no sacrifice in the new heaven and new earth since there is no temple or altar and no mention of sacrifice in the new heaven and new earth in scripture. Some have theorized the Antichrist is the Mahdi or twelfth Imam of Islam and that he invades Israel in the last days with a great army, as written in Muslim prophecies. That is possible. The Antichrist could also be the leader of Russia leading a great army invading Israel with the support of its allies in the region, which are Muslim countries devoted to the destruction of Israel. In either case, if it happens with the current religious and government arrangements in that area of the world, Saudi Arabia and possibly its neighbors to the east on the Arabian peninsula will not be in support of the Antichrist as touched on before. There are two main factions in the Muslim religion that frequently oppose and even fight one another: Sunni and Shia. Saudi Arabia is one of the largest countries of Sunni Muslims. The countries with a large percentile or total Shia populations are Iran, Iraq, Pakistan, Lebanon, Turkey, Azerbaijan, Afghanistan, Syria, India, and Yemen. (Bahrain has a high percent of Shia, but it is a small island in the Persian Gulf.)

These top ten Shia countries could be the ten kingdoms that comprise the Antichrist's empire, or the first eight, together with Libya and Ethiopia, could make up the ten kingdoms that comprise his empire. With the traditionally poor relations between India and Pakistan, it is hard, but not impossible, to imagine them uniting. Hinduism is the main religion in India as well so perhaps Bahrain, or another country (things could change dramatically in the future), would replace India in the ten countries of the Antichrist's empire. Armenia may be a country that supports him, but it is uncertain, and currently Armenia is predominantly Christian and not friendly with Turkey. If the Antichrist will be the leader of Russia, the countries between Russia and Israel would have to submit to him if he invades on land from Russia. They may even all support him and be part of his ten-nation empire. Some have said the Antichrist will be Roman, as part of a revived Roman Empire, and will bring a European army invading Israel. If the Antichrist is European, it is hard to imagine Spain not supporting him. The fulfillment of the prophecies about the Antichrist may not occur until many years in the future, and the current world situation may not exist. The Muslim religion may not exist then and so the cause for the nations mentioned in scripture uniting could be different.

We think of the scriptures speaking metaphorically when it mentions horses, spears, shields, and bridles in the battle of Armageddon, but it may occur far enough in the future that armies go back to fighting on horseback. This might occur if fossil fuels are in too short supply or other reasons. Babylon, who will persecute Christians in the last days, will be judged and destroyed by God in one day with plagues, pestilence, famine, and fire. This day will be the day of the Lord's return (Is. 13:6.9,10, 13, Rev. 18). This will lead into the millennium (Is. 14:1–7). These verses would indicate that the Antichrist will be Babylonian (Is. 10:17), referring to the destruction of the Assyrian army in one day by fire, which is like Armageddon in Ezekiel 39 (adds hail and brimstone) and Rev. 19:17–21 (the sword of Jesus destroys all nations' armies at Armageddon gathered to battle Jesus).

The area of Assyria today is eastern Turkey with northern sections of Iraq and Syria. The sun and moon will be darkened, the stars of the sky will fall to earth, and there will be a great earthquake heralding the return of Jesus and the destruction of the beast of the sea and his followers (Is. 13:9–13, Ez. 38:19, 20, Mt. 24:29, Rev. 6:12, 13). The day of wrath or vengeance is the day the Lord returns. The battle of Armageddon occurs on this day (Is. 10:17, 61:2, 63:2–4; Rev. 14:20). The Lord will come in fire and punish the Antichrist and his armies (Is. 66:15–16). This is followed by return of the remnant of Jews who are loyal to God as after the Babylonian captivity and the millennium (Is. 10:20–34, Ez. 39:27). If Revelation 17:8–10 means the Antichrist will be of the kingdoms that ruled over Israel beforehand but not at the time of John (Rev. 17:8), then the Antichrist would not be Roman but would either be Egyptian, Assyrian, Babylonian, Medo-Persian, or Greek. The Antichrist will not be from Persia (modern-day Iran) since Ezekiel says Persia will join Gog in the invasion of the Holy Land (Ez. 38:5). The Antichrist will fight against Egypt, so he won't be from Egypt (Is. 19:4, Dan. 11:40).

As mentioned above, from Isaiah, the Antichrist will either be from the area of Assyria or Babylon. The Messiah will deliver those in the Holy Land from the Assyrian after the Assyrian has trampled under foot the Holy Land. Jesus will destroy Antichrist's weapons. This seems to confirm that the Antichrist will come from the region of ancient Assyria because all of Israel's enemies have never been cut off as they will when the Lord returns. Since ancient Assyria is modern-day Turkey, northern Syria, and northern Iraq, this would imply the Antichrist will be from one of these three countries (Mic. 5:5, 6, 9, 10). The Antichrist will subdue three kings, or leaders (Dan. 7:24). Could it be that these three kings are the leaders of Turkey, Syria, and Iraq? The descendants of Lot are Ammon and Moab and of Esau the Edomites. Ammon is today's Syria. The Moabites and Edomites made today's Jordan. The honorable Ammonites, the Moabites and the Edomites will be rescued from the Antichrist, as he conquers Israel and subsequently conquers Egypt (Dan. 11:41). So the honorable Syrians and the Jordanians will not follow the anti-Christ. Turkey and Iraq then seem the two most likely countries from which the anti-Christ will arise.

321. The promised land will be divided among the tribes of Israel during the millennium according to the promise God gave Abraham and Jacob. The kingdom will be the Lord's (Ez. 48, Ob. 1:17–21).

# DANIEL

322. Daniel (Belteshazzar), Hananiah (Shadrach), Mischael (Meshach), and Azariah (Abed-nego) were given knowledge and intelligence by God. Daniel even understood all kinds of dreams and visions because God revealed them to him (Dan. 1:17).

323. The kingdom of God was to be set up during the days of the kings that ruled over Israel: Babylonian, Medo-Persian, Greek, and Roman (Dan. 2:44). This occurred when Jesus came to earth during the Roman Empire days and started the church age. Some people say this refers to the millennium and thus say the Antichrist will be of one of the above kingdoms.

324. Hananiah, Mischael, and Azariah refused to worship the golden image of King Nebuchadnezzar so they were put into a fiery furnace at the order of King Nebuchadnezzar. They did not know if God would rescue them or not but still refused to worship the golden image because God forbids us to worship anything other than him (the first commandment). God did rescue them from the furnace. There was another in the furnace that king Nebuchadnezzar could see that he said looked like a son of God, so he was either preincarnate Jesus or an angel (Dan. 3).

325. God put Nebuchadnezzar in power and humbled him when he was too proud. God is ruler over the realm of mankind and sets up and brings down rulers (Dan. 5:18–21).

326. Daniel was protected by an angel, sent from God, from the lions in the lions' den because he trusted in God. It was not because the lions were not hungry (Dan. 6:22–24).

327.    There will be a kingdom that will be different than all other kingdoms that ruled Israel in that it will rule the whole earth. Out of this kingdom, ten kings will arise. Then another king will arise and subdue three of the previous kings. This new king is the Antichrist and will speak publicly against the Most High God. The last three and a half years of the Antichrist's presumed seven-year reign he will wage war on, and over power, the saints. He will intend to make alterations in times and laws. God will destroy this boastful king though and start the one-thousand-year reign of Christ here on earth (millennial kingdom) (Dan. 7:21–27, 9:27; Rev. 13:7, 8). The Messiah will deliver those in the Holy Land from the Assyrian after the Assyrian has trampled under foot the Holy Land. Jesus will destroy Antichrist's weapons. This seems to confirm that the Antichrist will come from the region of ancient Assyria because all of Israel's enemies have never been cut off as they will when the Lord returns (Mic. 5:6, 9, 10). Since ancient Assyria is modern-day Turkey, northern Syria, and northern Iraq, this would imply the Antichrist will be from one of these three countries. The Antichrist will subdue three kings, or leaders (Dan. 7:24). Could it be that these three kings are the leaders of today's Turkey, Syria, and Iraq?

328.    God showed Daniel, by Gabriel the angel, that Greece would replace Media and Persia as ruling the promised land. He also showed him that the Grecian king would die, and his kingdom would be divided into four kingdoms. There would follow a king, in the latter years of this divided Grecian kingdom, that would oppose God and magnify himself. History showed this would be Antiochus who profaned the temple in Jerusalem (Dan. 8:21–26).

329.    God told Daniel, through Gabriel the angel, that Israel had to suffer seventy weeks for their rebellion against

God. Each of these weeks are best understood as seven years. Prophecy and vision would be ended at the end of the seventy weeks since the temple of the millennium would be anointed. The Persian king Artaxerxes I decreed in his twentieth year of reigning that Jerusalem be rebuilt. Secular ancient historical records are not exact, and often conflicting with one another, so the years that Artaxerses I reigned, and therefore the exact year that he gave this decree, are debatable. The revealing of Jesus as the Messiah, with his triumphal entry into Jerusalem, occurred the same year of his crucifixion. After the Messiah was to be revealed, he was to be cut off (killed in the flesh) and the people of the prince who is to come will destroy the city and sanctuary. After much investigation and calculations, the Messiah Jesus was crucified AD 30-34. Attempts to be more specific on the year of the revelation and death of the Messiah, even using 360-day years, prove to be uncertain. The Romans destroyed Jerusalem and the temple under general (future emperor) Titus in AD 70.

This prince to come is commonly thought of as the Antichrist. The people then that he is of could range from Roman to Gentile, going from the most to the least specific. Gentile means anyone that is not of the seed of Israel (Jacob or whose bloodlines trace back to the man Israel). Revelation 17:8 seems to tell us that the Antichrist will be of one of the kingdoms that ruled Israel before the Roman Empire but not Roman. So then the Antichrist will not be part of a revived Roman Empire. In the Antichrist's time, there will be war and desolation. His people will destroy Jerusalem and the Jewish temple. The people that have destroyed the Jerusalem and the temple so far since this prophecy are the Romans, but they made no seven-year peace treaty. The ant-Christ will make a covenant of peace with many for one week or seven years.

Why would he do that unless a powerful force threatened him? Could this force be the USA, which might be too weak to force the people of the Antichrist from Jerusalem but able to help broker a seven-year peace treaty? Or is this peace covenant between other nations in conflict over the Holy Land? This is the final or seventieth week to make atonement for iniquity and to make an end of sin. It does not have to follow the sixty-ninth week immediately, and history has shown it has not occurred yet. In the middle of this seven-year covenant, the Antichrist will put a stop to sacrifice in the temple in Jerusalem, implying a temple will be rebuilt in Jerusalem before he stops the sacrifice. The temple could be built in the first three and a half years of the peace covenant. He will commit the abomination of desolation at three and a half years also. This could be him sacrificing swine on the altar as Antiochus IV did or him declaring himself to be a god or the erection of the image of the beast/Antichrist in the temple. We know he will declare himself God, and the false prophet will erect an image of the Antichrist and force people to worship the image (Dan. 9:24–27, 11–36; 2Thes. 2:4; Rev. 13:15).

330. God determines world events. Satan's demons are involved in spiritual warfare with angels to try to change God's plan, but Michael, the archangel, is mightier than any demon or fallen angel (Dan. 10:12–21).

331. The book of Daniel begins in 605 BC when Babylon conquered Jerusalem and exiled Daniel. Daniel lived beyond the time in Daniel 10:1 (536 BC). It seemed reasonable that Daniel wrote, or at least finished, his book not long after 536 BC given his age at the time. Daniel was written in Aramaic, which adds to its authenticity. Daniel prophesied about three kings of Persia after the time of Cyrus and then a fourth great king (Xerxes) who

would attack Greece. Then a mighty king from Greece would rule the area. This was to be Alexander the Great. He tells that Alexander's kingdom would not go to his heirs but would be divided into four realms by the compass, as it was. He goes onto prophesy of the various conflicts over the promised land (Israel) in detail that was fulfilled hundreds of years later to verse 35 in chapter 11. The accuracy of these detailed prophecies proves that the God of Abraham and Israel is the one true God.

Antiochus IV Epiphanes, king of Syria, did the abomination of desolation of the temple in Jerusalem by stopping the daily sacrifice and having sows broth spread on the altar working together with apostate Jews. He also desecrated the temple and erected a statue of the Greek god Zeus in the temple. Verse 35 transitions to the end times leading to Christ's return. Verses 36 to 45 describe the Antichrist who is yet to come because no one has fulfilled all the prophesies of him, and the earth is not ruled by Christ from a rebuilt temple in Jerusalem following a devastating defeat of the Antichrist by God that is obvious to all people of the earth. He will be boastful and speak against God. He will show no regard for the gods of his fathers nor for any god. He will magnify himself above all gods. He will show no regard for the sexual desire of women. The Hebrew text for verse 37 about the desire for women is the same word used in Proverbs 6:25, which describes sexual desire. This could be because he is homosexual or he is too power hungry to care for women in a sexual manner. In verse 38, it tells us he will honor a god of fortresses and a god that his fathers did not know with gold and other treasures.

Verse 39 interpretation is either he will take action against the strongest of fortresses (according to 2 Sam. 22:33 this could be interpreted as God) with the help of a strange god. Today we see alliances between Muslims, some socialists/unions, and some communist countries as their common enemies are Israel and Christianity. Traditionally, the first thing socialists and communists do when they take over a country is to get rid of religion that keeps people happy (the opiate of the masses per Karl Marx). This allows them to make people happier with social programs given to the masses by the government. This also makes people more dependent on government so the government has more power. More recently, they give people benefits first so people are not dependent on God but on the government. In communist countries, God is replaced by government by the government (historically this has consistently been done forcefully by the government), so people rely on the government for their needs and not God. So communism or atheism are their god.

Then verse 39 says he will divide land to people loyal to him. Verse 40 says the king of the south, which earlier in Daniel was repeatedly Egypt, will push against him. The Antichrist will then defeat Egypt with the aid of Ethiopia and Libya. He will overthrow many countries but the choice people of Ammon (Syria), Edom (descendants of Esau who are in present day Jordan), and Moab (descendants of Lot who are in present day Jordan) will escape him. He will set up his royal pavilion in between the Mediterranean Sea, the Dead Sea, and the Mount of Olives. Rumors from the east and the north will disturb him, and he went forth and conquered. This implies he will defeat those from the east and north who are against him, but it does not say he will conquer them per se.

The countries north and east of the nations surrounding Israel, which invade Israel, of significant military power currently are Russia and China. So if Russia and China are the countries that disturb the Antichrist, then Russia and China will not be in agreement with him, at this future point anyway. Could the Lord cause revival in peoples' hearts in Russia and China so that they are more obedient to God than other nations at this point? Since the west, the United States of America being the current foremost power of this area of the world, is not mentioned, one would have to assume the west is either too weak to resist him or in league with him. In 2 Thes. 2:4, it is more specific in that it tells us he will exalt himself above all gods and objects of worship and take his seat in the temple of God, displaying himself as the one true God.

In chapter 12, Daniel continues with at that time the Antichrist does this there will be distress. This is in agreement with other scripture saying the Antichrist will pursue the Jews to kill them, but God will rescue a remnant from him. The Antichrist will then be enraged and will then persecute Christians for three and a half years (Dan. 7:21, 25; Mat. 24:15–22; Rev. 12:17, 13:3, 7). Daniel then says many of the dead will arise. The followers of God that are resurrected will begin their eternal life in a new body. Those that did not follow God will not arise then but right after Satan is put in the lake of fire after the millennium (Rev. 20:5–15). People who have understanding of the Bible will lead many to Christ and shine brightly like the stars. Daniel says, in Daniel 12:12, from the time the daily sacrifice is taken away and the abomination of desolation occurs, which is when the Antichrist is revealed for who he truly is (2 Thes. 2:3), there will be 1,290 days or three and a half years. He then says, in Daniel 12:13, blessed is he who waits and comes to 1,335 days, a little over three and a half years, after the abomination of desolation. I have long wondered what these two verses in Daniel specifically meant and had thought that maybe at 1,290 days those who were dead in Christ arose then and then at 1,335 days was when those saints who are alive meet the Lord in the air when he returns but dismissed it because no one knows when the Lord will return but Father God (Mt. 24:36; Mk. 13:32).

However, after a time of fasting and prayer, at 2:30 a.m. on the morning of January 8, 2013, I felt God tell me that the 1,290 days is the number of days from the abomination of desolation to when the dead in Christ will rise, and the 1,335 days is how long after the abomination of desolation the Lord will return and harvest those who love and believe in him and are alive and remain on the earth, to meet the Lord in the air. This does not contradict the word of our Lord who said no man knows the day of his return except the Father because the people alive on the earth would not know when the resurrection of the dead occurred, unless God revealed it to them, and we do not know the day of the abomination of desolation. The word of God also says the day of the Lord, which is the day the Lord returns and defeats his enemies, will not come except the son of perdition, which is the beast or Antichrist, is revealed (2 Thes. 2:1–4).

I know feelings can be wrong, but how many times have we been a part of or heard people witness of giving to others exact gifts that they felt the Lord lead them to do? The main and first test of what we feel are words or a word from God to us is conformation to scripture. If the word or words do not conform to scripture, then it is either from Satan or from our own imagination and therefore dangerous and to be rejected. The dead in Christ will rise first; then, we who are alive and remain on earth will be caught up with them to meet the Lord in the air, when the Lord descends from heaven with the voice of the archangel and the sound of the last trumpet (1 Cor.

15:51–54, 1 Thes. 4:16–17). What I feel God revealed to me conforms to these scriptures also because "we (those who are alive on earth who are His)…with them (the dead in Christ)" does not necessarily mean at the same moment because otherwise God would not make the distinction.

While testing with scripture what I felt God tell me on the early morning of January 8, 2013, I read 1Thes. 4:14 and 15 which says, "For if we believe that Jesus died and rose again, even so God will bring with Him those who have fallen asleep in Jesus. For this we say to you by the word of the Lord, that we who are alive and remain until the coming of the Lord, will not precede those who have fallen asleep." The key part is the last part of verse 14, which says, "will bring with Him (the Christ Jesus) those who have fallen asleep in Jesus." Those who have fallen asleep in Jesus means Christians, not saints who died before his first incarnation. This means the resurrection of the dead will occur before the Lord returns, the day of the Lord. On the day of the Lord, saints who are alive (in the flesh) and remain on earth will be transformed and receive our eternal bodies and meet the Lord in the air, when he returns to establish his kingdom here on earth. I am still somewhat concerned in that it times the day of the Lord from the abomination of desolation (1,335 days), but what comfort these words from Daniel will be to those children of God going through the last three and a half years of tribulation at the hand of the Antichrist. Those who know the scripture will know that the Antichrist only has three and a half years to persecute them but without this knowledge they might begin to question, "What then?" or "Now what?"

Also, if the Lord does not return exactly three and a half years after the abomination of desolation and the beginning of the tribulation of the saints, will they not then question the truth of the Holy Scriptures, the Bible? So knowing they have to wait until 1,335 days after the abomination of desolation will be a comfort. If I am wrong, then God forgive me. Perhaps the exact day of the abomination of desolation will not be so clear. Regardless, the Lord will return and destroy the Antichrist and start his millennial kingdom here on earth with the saints. Daniel will be a book read by God's children here on earth in the last days for understanding. The book of Daniel will also be inspirational for saints in the last days. There will no doubt be people pressuring saints to receive the mark of the beast, even quoting scripture as Satan did to Jesus in the wilderness. We must obey God rather than our government when the government's law conflicts with God's will as Daniel, Hananiah, Mischael, and Azariah did when the government where they lived made laws that conflicted with God's will and chose to obey God rather than their government with threat of death. They did not know if they would survive the tortuous death penalties they were given, but still they chose to obey God rather than man. Some saints will die under the leadership of the Antichrist, but God will spare some as well.

332. In Daniel 12:14, God is speaking, via the angel, specifically to Daniel about him personally to persevere to the end of his life, then he will enter into rest in heaven, and when the end of this age comes, he will receive his portion, or reward, and eternal life God intends for him.

# HOSEA

333.   God likens our relationship to our spouses to our relationship with him (Hosea). God hates divorce (Mal. 2:16). Our struggle is not against flesh and blood but against the rulers, against the powers, against world forces of this darkness, against the spiritual forces of wickedness in the heavenly places (Eph. 6:12). So if we are having marital problems, we need to battle Satan and the spiritual forces of evil in this present darkness with fasting and prayer so that we may defeat the enemy and restore our marriages. We must be committed to our spouses as we are committed to God and not get divorced. Would we not fear to divorce ourselves from God? Then so we must not divorce our spouses but work through our problems from the starting point of not getting divorced no matter what. This puts both spouses in the position that they have no other choice but stay married together so they have incentive to make the relationship as pleasant as possible.

If a person is in a physically abusive relationship, they should seek counseling and separate themselves from harm while asking fellow saints to talk to their spouse and help the couple make their marriage a safe and happy one. This will also give the abusive spouse some people to fear since he or she has shown they are not fearful enough of God ["For vengeance is Mine, I will repay", says the Lord' (Rom. 12:19) and saints as well as sinners will all be judged by God and held accountable for our sins (Rom. 14:10–12)], if they are ever abusive again to the other spouse. In a verbally abusive relationship, each person has to make their own decision based on their consciousness if they should separate themselves from the relationship and seek counsel so that they can get back together in a healthier relationship. When counseling is necessary, it is best if both spouses receive counseling because counseling is not just identifying where we do wrong and improving our ways but also improving how we handle situations that do not go as they should.

334. The children of Judah and Israel will be gathered together in the future into the promised land and appoint for themselves one leader. This will be the Messiah in the millennium (Hos. 1:11, Am. 9:11–15, Mic. 2:12, 13). The children of Israel and Judah that are gathered are those that God provides a way to escape from the Antichrist (Is. 4:2, 3, Ob. 1:17). Gentiles will join the children of Israel and will follow God and attach themselves to them (Is. 14:1, Zec. 8:20–23). The promised land is divided among the tribes of Israel during the millennium. It will have the boundaries God promised to Abraham and Jacob and as existed in the days of Solomon (Ez. 48).

335. The Lord will be called Ishi (husband) rather than Baali (master) during the millennium (Hos. 2:16). The church (saints) are called the bride of Christ (Rev. 21:9).

336. God will become God to gentiles in the future (Hos. 2:22, 23). This was fulfilled when God called Peter to preach to gentiles in Acts 10.

# JOEL

337. There will be drought sometime in the last days before the day of the Lord (the day the Lord returns to earth to rule the earth) and will involve more countries than the one during Joel's time. The locusts that destroyed the land in Joel's time did not cause as much devastation as the ones in Revelations (Joel 1:14–20; Rev. 6:7, 8, 9:1–12). This may or may not be at the request of the two witnesses (Rev. 11:6).

338. God promised Holy Spirit would come and be in his children, and they will prophecy, dream dreams, and see visions (Joel 2:28, 29). This started on the day of Pentecost (Ac. 2:1–4).

339. There will be wonders in the sky and on the earth, and the sun will be turned into darkness and the moon into blood (look red as blood) on the day the Lord returns. Whoever calls on the name of the Lord on that day will be saved (Joel 2:30–32).

340. God promised to save a remnant of Israel from the Antichrist (Joel 2:32, Rev. 7:1–8).

341. God will draw the surrounding nations around Israel to war against Israel. At this time, many multitudes of people will be indecisive about following God, even though there will have been many fulfillments of his prophecies. The Lord will return, sending the angels to reap the harvest of saints and destroying those who invade Israel (Joel 3:9–17). The blood of the destroyed enemies of God at the battle of Armageddon will be so massive it will be like wine from the wine press, up to the horses' bridles for a distance of two hundred miles (Rev. 14:20).

# AMOS

342. God chose Israel among all the nations of the earth as his (Am. 3:2). But God cares about all people, including enemies of Israel and Judah as evidenced by his bringing other peoples from harsh environments (Am. 9:7). Also, God so loved the whole world that he gave his only begotten Son that whosoever believes in him shall not perish but have eternal life (Jn. 3:16). All people sin and fall short of the glory of God (Rom. 3:23). The wages of sin is the second death of an eternity in the lake of fire, but the free gift of God to those who believe in Jesus as Lord is eternal life in Christ Jesus our Lord (Rom. 6:23). If anyone does not believe in Jesus as Lord and thus does not have the Spirit of God in them, they do not belong to the Lord (Rom. 8:9). If anyone believes in their heart that God raised Jesus from the dead and confesses with their mouth that Jesus is Lord, they will be saved (Rom. 10:9).

343. Before God punishes a people, he gives warning through prophets (Am. 3:6, 7).

344. Before the Assyrian invasion of Samaria, God tried to get the Jews to repent of their sins by holding the rain three months before the harvest on various cities rather than be harsher and cause drought throughout the nation. He also used scorching wind, mildew, and caterpillars. So God first tried to get the Jews to repent of their rebellion against God with drought, limited to about three months and to limited cities, and then scorching wind, mildew, and caterpillars. But they would not repent, so God sent plague. The reasons they did not repent are the same as with people today: they did not believe God was doing all this and/or they desired to continue in their sin more than

obey God. They knew God was a forgiving god and had forgiven them for many years so they thought he would continue do to so. Finally, he sent conquerors with the sword (Am. 4:7–10). God can do likewise today to any nation he wants to repent of their sins. If a nation that once used God's word as it's guide becomes sinful and God does not do this, it is not sinful enough in God's eyes. If a nation never tried to abide by God's word, it is probably reserved by God to be an adversary to God's people. That is not to say there can be those that follow God in those nations. God cares about even nations that never claimed to follow him and holds them responsible for their sins as evidenced from the book of Jonah where God was going to punish Nineveh for it's sins.

God also destroyed Sodom and Gomorrah for its immorality, specifically pointed out in scripture its sin of homosexuality (Gen. 19). Sometimes those peoples can be warned by God and repent as was the case with Nineveh. Even the leaders of Nineveh fasted and repented to God (Jonah 3:5–10). God is gracious, compassionate, slow to anger, and abundant in loving kindness to all people. He relents concerning his calamities he intends for people if they will just repent (Jon. 4:2). Over one hundred years later, Nineveh was conquered by Babylon because of its sins it reverted back to, which included prostitution, both carnally and spiritually, and sorcery (Nah. 3:4).

345.   When evil reaches a certain level of predominance in a nation, prudence requires even good people to not speak out against the sins for their own safety. People reach a point of sin where they rationalize and think they justify their sins and deny they sin (Am. 5:13, Ecc. 3:7, Hos. 4:4). But saints (followers of God) should still do good and hate evil. This may cause God to not be so harsh with a nation (Am. 5:15).

346. God brings about pestilence, plagues, and other punishments on people when he desires without involving the devil (Am. 7:1, 9:3).

347. Praying to God can result in him changing his mind (Am. 7:3, 6, Jon. 3:10). Since he is omniscient, he knew he would change his mind, or stated plans, but prayerful request by a child of his is required.

348. God sometimes will not give a word to a nation when they are too sinful, such as what happened with Israel and Judah, even though they petitioned God for a word (Am. 8:11, 12).

349. Hell is below us, and heaven is above us (Amos 9:2). Hell is a hot place of torment where people who are not saints go. Heaven is where saints go. There is a great chasm between hell and heaven. Therefore, those who want to go from heaven to aid those that are in hell and those that want to go to heaven to escape hell cannot (Lk. 16:19–31). This parable of the rich man and Lazarus by Jesus also tells us that at least some of those in heaven and hell can see each other.

# JONAH

350. God loves all people and is merciful to all people who repent of their sins (Jonah).

351. God cares about animals. People are more valuable to God than the rest of creation though (Jon. 4:11, Mt. 10:29–31).

# MICAH

352. The Lord Jesus will judge and rule the earth during the peaceful millennium (Mic. 4:1–4).

353. God admits he makes the lame and outcasts and otherwise afflicted people of earth, but he has reserved a special place for them with him in Jerusalem during the millennium. He will make a strong nation of the outcasts of society (Mic. 4:6, 7). He will turn their shame into praise and renown (Zep. 3:19).

354. The Messiah was to be born in Bethlehem. The Messiah has existed since eternity. He will rule Israel (Mic. 5:2).

355. God will give the children of Israel up to other peoples until the time of their travail is ended and the remnant are delivered from her (to escape the Antichrist). Later the remnant will return to Israel after the return of Christ (Mic. 5:3). This verse then goes on to say the remnant of the children of Israel will return to the children of Israel. The remnant of Israel that God rescues from the Antichrist will return to Israel where Jesus and the Old and New Testament saints will go as he returns. The saints will be gathered to Jesus as he returns to the promised land.

356. Assyria, which as we saw from the fulfillment of prophecies about Antiochus from Numbers 24:24 and Daniel 11:30 is mostly southeast Turkey, northern Syria, and northern Iraq today, will invade Israel and trample it underfoot in the last days. This sounds like the Antichrist. Then the Jews will raise against the leader of Assyria (Turkey, Syria, and/or perhaps Iraq) seven shepherds and eight leaders of men (Mic. 5:5). I have read many thoughts as to what these shepherds and leaders of men in this prophecy are.

Shepherds are religious leaders. I do not think we know who these shepherds and leaders of men will be till this end-time prophecy is fulfilled.

357.   The Messiah will deliver those in the Holy Land from the Assyrian after the Assyrian has trampled under foot the Holy Land. Jesus will destroy Antichrist's weapons. This seems to confirm that the Antichrist will come from the region of ancient Assyria because all of Israel's enemies have never been cut off as they will when the Lord returns (Mic. 5:6, 9, 10). Since ancient Assyria is modern-day Turkey, northern Syria, and northern Iraq, this would imply the Antichrist will be from one of these three countries. The Antichrist will subdue three kings or leaders (Dan. 7:24). Could it be that these three kings are the leaders of Turkey, Syria, and Iraq?

358.   The remnant of the Jews will not only be in the Holy Land, but they will be throughout the world during the millennium. The people of the world that are not saints then will fear the remnant, and nations will fear the Lord and serve him (Mic. 5:7–9, 7:17; Zep. 2:10, 11, 3:8–10). The nations of the world will bring their wealth to the rebuilt temple of the millennium, which will be more glorious than the temple Solomon built (Hag. 2:7–9).

359.   Jesus will tear down the Antichrist's fortifications. Jesus will rid the world of false gods and sorcery. Jesus will execute vengeance and wrath on any who do not obey him (Mic. 5:11–15, Zep. 3:11). God will not retain his anger but will forgive and love because of the sacrifice of Jesus (Mic. 7:18, 19).

360.   What does the Lord require of people? To do justice, to love kindness, and to walk humbly with your God (not just any god but God) (Mic. 6:8, Mt. 23:23, Lk. 11:42). Saints will do these things because the love of God is in them.

# NAHUM

361. The Lord is slow to anger (Nah. 1:3). God is patient with mankind, giving us time to come to him.

362. The Lord is good, a stronghold in the day of trouble. And he knows those who trust in him (Nah. 1:7).

# HABAKKUK

363.　Habakkuk 2:1–8 seems to prophecy about Babylon but also the United States of America (USA/America). It could be about any nation that is proud, goes into debt, and is the center of the world in some fashion-like economics. Verse 3 tells us the prophecy will be in the distant future from Habakkuk's time. There will be contrasting people in this country: those that are proud and those that are righteous (v. 4). The proud and haughty people of the nation are never satisfied. America has grown economically because of greed to a large extent (v. 5a). America has gathered all nations to itself at the United Nations. America has also done this by being the center of the world economically. It has the world's largest economy. Trade is done in dollars; the language of business in the world is English (v. 5b). Nations will taunt this nation because of its great debt (v. 6). The USA has the largest debt of any nation in the world. The prophecy says the creditors of this debtor nation will rise up suddenly and plunder this debtor nation. The USA is the strongest nation militarily currently, so this is hard to envision as a military invasion.

However, the USA is vulnerable economically several ways since it has the largest debt of any nation and the United States's debt is greater than its gross domestic product. Creditor nations would just have to lose faith in the credit of the United States and thus no longer accept dollars for the United States to be brought to its knees economically. This would force the United States to give up tangible assets it did not want to lose in order to pay creditors (be looted) (vv. 7, 8). Other western nations, like Great Britain, could be seen as fulfilling these prophecies through the centuries since Christ was here on earth, but no nation has had the United Nations in it like the United States.

# ZEPHANIAH

364. The people that believe in, and follow, God in a country that is in rebellion against God should seek righteousness and humble themselves before God so that perhaps God will spare them of at least some of the punishment God will inflict on the rebellious nation (Zeph. 2:3).

365. Millennium (Zeph. 3:8–20).

# HAGGAI

366. If we withhold giving to God as we should such as the tithe, we invite the withholding of God's blessings and even provisions we take for granted such as rain. If our focus becomes worldly things, we will not be satisfied, always desiring more (Hag. 1:2–11).

367. The nations of the world will bring their wealth to the rebuilt temple of the millennium, which will be more glorious than the temple Solomon built (Hag. 2:7–9).

# ZECHARIAH

368. Zechariah describes a vision of four horns and four craftsmen. The four horns are four kingdoms that have ruled over the Jews and scattered them up to that point in time. Those kingdoms would have been Egypt, Assyria, Babylon, and Medo-Persia. The four craftsmen terrified the four kingdoms that ruled the Jews and caused these four to fall. The craftsmen may be the subsequent kingdom, or leader of the kingdom, that overthrew the previous kingdom. For example Nebuchadnezzar overthrew the Assyrians (Zec. 1:18–21).

369. The Lord will choose Jerusalem from which to rule the earth during the millennium (Zech. 2:12).

370. The day the Lord returns he will remove the iniquity of the remnant of the Jews who have not become saints before then and did not side with the Antichrist (Zec. 3:9, 12:10–14; Rom. 11:25–29).

371. Zechariah is given a vision of the golden lampstand with seven lamps and two olive trees. The two olive trees probably represent the kingly and priestly offices of Israel, the two anointed ones who stand by the Lord of the whole earth. At the time of the vision, the king was Zerubbabel and the priest was Joshua (Zec. 4:1–14). The lampstand with the seven lamps is the word of the Lord saying, "Not by might nor by power, but by My Spirit says the Lord" (Zec. 4:6). For we wrestle not against flesh and blood but against principalities, against powers, against the rulers of the darkness of this world, against spiritual forces of wickedness in heavenly places (Ep. 6:12). The two witnesses in Revelation are called the two olive trees and two lampstands before the Lord as well (Rev.

11:4). Jesus fulfills both kingly and priestly roles in the millennium (Zec. 6:12, 13). There are seven Spirits before God in heaven, which are the seven lamps of fire burning. This is a description of the Holy Spirit in heaven. These seven lamps are the eyes of the Lord, which range to and fro throughout the earth (the Holy Spirit searches the earth for God) (Zec. 4:2, 6, 10; Rev. 1:4, 4:5).

372.    Wickedness will be exalted in the last days. People will build a temple in the land of Shinar, Babylon, in the last days. An image, most likely a statue, of wickedness will be made and put on a pedestal in the temple (Zec. 5:8–11). This is not the temple that the Antichrist will profane (Dan. 9:27). That temple will be in Jerusalem.

373.    The four spirits of heaven will go forth between two bronze mountains in the last days (Zec. 6:1–10). Most likely these two mountains are Mount Zion and the Mount of Olives, between which is the Valley of Jehoshaphat, or Kidron Valley. Bronze was used in the serpent, and altar used by the Jews where sin was dealt with. Thus this is where God's judgment of the earth will begin. These four spirits of heaven are sent by God for his judgment of an evil earth. These four spirits of heaven are described as red, black, and white and dapple horses with chariots, like the four horses in Revelation 6. The black horse(s) go(es) first to the north country. The black horse in Revelation is described as scarcity of food or famine (Rev. 6:5, 6). In the Old Testament, the north country repeatedly refers to Syria or Assyria (present-day northern Iraq, northern Syria, and southeastern Turkey mostly). Following the black horse(s) to the north country are the white horse(s). Revelation describes the white horse with a rider going forth conquering (Rev. 6:2). This is usually thought of as God allowing the Antichrist to conquer many nations. The dappled (ashen) horse(s) go

into the south country. The south country in the Old Testament repeatedly means Egypt. In Revelation 6, the ashen horse is described as death. As described earlier in the Bible, Egypt is conquered by the Antichrist. The red horse(s) go throughout the earth. In Revelation, the red horse is described as peace taken from earth and conflict between people on earth with people slaying one another (Rev. 6:3, 4).

374.    The Jews would be brought back from the west and the east to the promised land it was prophesied in Zechariah 8:7. This was not possible until the Romans scattered some Jews west to Rome.

375.    The Messiah would arrive in Jerusalem humble and mounted on a donkey, even a colt (Zec. 9:9, Mt. 21:1–5).

376.    Chapter 9 of Zechariah prophesies of the conquest of lands by Alexander the Great. In verse 8, it tells of God's divine protection of Jerusalem from destruction from Alexander the Great as he passed by it twice as he entered into and returned from Egypt. This was fulfilled as God told Zechariah. The Jews would have some success in battle against the Greeks (Seleucids) (Zec. 9:13–15). The Maccabean revolt fulfilled this in about 166 BC.

377.    Jesus, the Cornerstone, will come from the tribe of Judah. Jesus has been around since eternity with God, but his human form, in the first advent, was as a descendent of the tribe of Judah (Zec. 10:3b-4, Is. 28:16, Mt. 1:2–16).

378.    Two of the reasons the Jews were punished by God by the Assyrians and Babylonians were slavery of even their own people and greed. This caused God to remove his hedge of protection from them (this is what he means by breaking his covenant) as he said he would before these times. God did not break his word but fulfilled it (Zec. 11:4–11).

379. Prophecy given to Zechariah by the Lord Jesus of thirty shekels of silver to be the price at which he was to be valued by those who opposed him. The Lord himself spoke to Zechariah about this (Zec. 11:12, 13; Mt. 26:15, 27:3–10). This was the price of a slave in Mosaic law (Ex. 21:32).

380. God brought about shepherds (spiritual leaders/priests) who did not care for the Jews spiritual life but cared for themselves. The sword was upon these shepherds right eye and arm, meaning they were blinded to the truth, and their strength (by Babylon) was taken away by God. These verses in Zechariah do not appear to be talking about the Antichrist because nowhere else in scripture does it talk about the Antichrist having a withered arm (Zec. 11:16, 17, Ez. 34:2–4, Jer. 23:1).

381. All the nations of the earth will be gathered against Jerusalem in the last days. Accounting for Ezekiel and Daniel, Spain, the choicest people of Syria, Saudi Arabia, Jordan, and Egypt will not be partakers of the attack on Jerusalem in the last days. God will destroy the armies of those nations that attack Jerusalem (Zec. 12:3–9).

382. The Jews in Jerusalem and those of the house of David will have their eyes opened to see that Jesus, the one they pierced, is the Christ. They will weep bitterly and repent and follow Jesus as Lord (Zec. 12:10–14). Then the Lord can return as he said (Mt. 23:39).

383. Zechariah 13:7 prophesies of the Good Shepherd, Jesus, being struck (crucified) and his flock scattered as a result. The persecution of the church, after Jesus's crucifixion, allowed the gospel to be spread further as Christians fled from persecution.

384. Zechariah 13:8 and 9 prophesy of two-thirds of Jews killed in the last days. The remnant will include the 144,000 in

Revelation 7:4 that are sealed. The remnant will worship Jesus as Lord.

385.    Zechariah 14 prophesies of the battle of Armageddon. It says Jerusalem will be captured by the invading army and half of the city exiled, houses plundered, and women ravished. Then the Lord will fight for his people and destroy the invaders. The Lord will return on that day, and his feet will stand on the Mount of Olives, on the east side of Jerusalem. The Mount of Olives will thus split in two so that half the mountain will move toward the north and half move toward the south. Jesus will return in like manner that he left (Ac. 1:11, 12). The invaders flesh, eyes, and tongues will rot in them. They will fight each other. Judah will fight also and gather riches from the battle. The Lord will be king of the earth, and all the inhabitants will worship him. If any do not come to the Feast of Booths, God will cause drought in their land (Zec. 14).

# MALACHI

386.    To call what we give to God a valuable offering and it is not very valuable to us is sin. To give to God our second best is wrong. We should honor and respect God. Mal. 1:6–14.

387.    Tithing is expected of us by God. To not give one's tithe is to rob God. God will bless those that tithe above their tithe. Mal. 3:8–12.

388.    The Lord told Malachi he was going to send forth his messenger to clear the way before him. This was John the Baptist for his first advent. Mal. 3:1; Mt. 11:10. This was by the spirit of Elijah in John the Baptist, as the Lord said. Mt. 11:14. The two witnesses will clear the way for his second advent. Rev. 11. John the Baptist and the two witnesses are necessary to prepare people's heart for the coming of God the Son. Repentance is paramount as people prepare to meet God the Son, who will judge all people. Jn. 9:39. Rev. 20:11. The spirit of Elijah will be in one of the two witnesses in the last days. He will restore the hearts of the fathers to their children and the hearts of the children to their fathers, so that Jesus will not come and smite the land with a curse. This means if there was not a repentant remnant God would destroy the whole earth. Mal. 4:5, 6.

389.    God will condemn those that don't follow him to the lake of fire and give blessings to those that do love and serve him. Mal. 3:16–4:3; Rev. 19:20; 20:11–15.

# THE GOSPELS

390. John the Baptist was fulfillment of the prophecy from Malachi 3 of one preparing people's hearts for the coming Son of God. John was filled with the Holy Spirit in his mother's womb. When a person becomes saved is when the Holy Spirit fills the person, so John was saved by God while in his mother's womb (Lk. 1:15–17). This is similar to Jeremiah (Jer.1:5) where Jeremiah was called by God to be a prophet before he was born. This shows the sovereignty of God over salvation. John went in the spirit and power of Elijah to turn the disobedient to an attitude of righteousness (Lk. 1:17). Both Jeremiah and John were called by God to be prophets before they were born (Jer. 1:5, Lk. 1:76). The Holy Spirit filled Elizabeth, John the Baptist's mother, at least for a time (Lk. 1:41). Zechariah, John the Baptist's father, was filled with the Holy Spirit at least for a time and prophesied (Lk. 1:67).

391. The birth of John was a miracle because his parents, Zachariah and Elizabeth, were advanced in years just as the birth of Isaac to Abraham and Sarah was a miracle because of their old age (Lk. 1:18; Gen. 18:11, 21:2).

392. The genealogy of Jesus the Messiah to his earthly father, Joseph, who raised him but did not father him (Mt. 1:1–17). The genealogy of Jesus through his mother Mary (Lk. 3:23–38). Joseph is named the son of Eli (v. 23), but this is through marriage since Eli had no sons of his own. Both lineages reach commonality in King David.

393. Jesus was born of the Virgin Mary fulfilling Isaiah 7:14 prophecy. The Holy Spirit caused Mary to be pregnant with Jesus. Both Joseph and Mary were of the lineage of Judah and David, fulfilling the prophecy from Zechariah

10:3b–4 and Micah 5:2 that the Messiah would be from the tribe of Judah (Mt. 1, Lk. 3:23–38). The timing of Jesus' birth has been subject to much study with proposed years ranging from 8 BC to AD 1. John the Baptist was born about six months prior to the Lord's first incarnation (Lk. 1:36). John the Baptist began his ministry in the fifteenth year of the reign of Tiberius Caesar (Lk. 3:1), which was August AD 27 to August AD 29, depending on if Luke was using the Syrian or Roman calendar. Jesus was about thirty years old when he began his ministry (Lk. 3:23), which was probably shortly after John's ministry began, given the writing of Luke chapter 3. St. Clement of Alexandria (150-215 AD) dated Jesus birth as 3 BC. King Herod's death was proposed to have been 4 BC by Johannes Kepler because of Josephus writing in Antiquities of the Jews (17.6.4) that there was a lunar eclipse when Herod died. However, NASA's web site shows that eclipse did not affect Jerusalem. Lunar eclipses that affected Jerusalem that period of time occurred in the years 1, 2, and 3 BC. It is known Jesus was born before Herod the Great's death because of the Slaughter of the Innocents. Given all of this information, the year of Jesus' birth can be narrowed to between 5 and 1 BC.

394.  Jesus was born in Bethlehem as Micah prophesied in Micah 5:2 (Mt. 2:4–6).

395.  Angels were sent by God to announce the birth of Jesus to shepherds so they were the first to see Jesus. Lk. 2:8–20. Shepherds were dirty from their work, so it was very difficult for them to participate in religious activities in the temple. By giving the good news of salvation through repentance and forgiveness of sins (Lk. 1:77) first to the shepherds, God demonstrated his love for all people and that salvation is offered freely to all people (Lk. 2:32).

396.  Jesus fulfilled the prophecy given to Simeon (Lk. 2:25–35).

397. A star guided the wise men to where Jesus was (Mt. 2:9).

398. God spoke to the wise men from the east in a dream and sent an angel to speak to Joseph in a dream (Mt. 2:12, 13, 19, and 22). This tells us God can speak to people in dreams.

399. Joseph moved his family to Egypt for a while to escape Herod's attempts to kill Jesus. This fulfilled the prophecy from Hosea 11:1, "…out of Egypt I called My Son." (Mt. 2:15).

400. Herod's killing of children to try to kill the young King of the Jews fulfilled the prophecy from Jeremiah 31:15 (Mt. 2:16–18).

401. John the Baptist fulfilled the prophecy of Isaiah 40:3 telling of one crying in the wilderness, making ready the way of the Lord and making smooth his highway (Mt. 3:1–3, Mk. 1:2–4, Lk. 3:3–6, Jn. 1:23).

402. John the Baptist baptized people in the Jordan River as they repented, but Jesus would baptize with the Holy Spirit those that repent and with fire for those that do not repent. John was clothed with camel's hair and a leather belt. He ate locusts and wild honey. Jesus baptizes with the Holy Spirit and fire (Mt. 3:1–12, Mk. 1:1–8, Lk. 3:3–16, Jn. 1:19–34).

403. The Holy Spirit descended on Jesus like a dove when Jesus arose from being baptized (Mt. 3:16, Mk. 1:10, Lk. 3:21, 22, Jn. 1:32).

404. God spoke where people could hear immediately after Jesus was baptized, saying, "This is My beloved Son, in whom I am well pleased." (Mt. 3:17, Mk. 1:11, Lk. 3:22). This fulfilled prophecy from David (Ps. 2:7).

405. Jesus fasted forty days and forty nights in the wilderness after his baptism, at the leading of the Holy Spirit, to be tempted by the devil. Moses on Mount Sinai (Dt. 9:9) and

Elijah on Mount Horeb (1Kg. 19:8) also fasted forty days and forty nights. Moses went without food and water, and Elijah went without food, and perhaps water. Jesus went without food and, perhaps, water also. It is not clear from scripture if Jesus went without water, but it would be in character of God for Jesus to do as much as did Moses. He was with the wild beasts and angels ministered to him. Angels assist those who are God's. Jesus was then hungry. The devil tempted Jesus three times. First with a request that Jesus make bread out of stones for his own belly. Second he tempted him to miraculously rescue himself from a deadly fall purposely. The devil quoted scripture out of context in this temptation. He changed the meaning of the scripture from trusting God to testing God. Thirdly, he tempted Jesus with great wealth and power if only Jesus would worship him. Jesus quoted scripture in each of his refusals to give into temptations from the devil (Mt. 4:1–11, Mk. 1:12, 13, Lk. 4:1–13). Likewise, quoting scripture, silently or out loud, helps us to not sin when tempted.

406. Jesus began his ministry in the region of Zebulun and Naphtali, fulfilling prophecy from Isaiah 9:1, 2 (Mt. 4:12–16). This was in Galilee (Lk. 4:14, 15).

407. Jesus preached to people to repent and believe in the gospel for the kingdom of heaven is at hand (Mt. 4:17, Mk. 1:14, 15). Since this was Jesus's message, it should be ours.

408. The disciples left their jobs and families when Jesus called them to follow him and to do his work (Mt. 4:18–22, Mk. 1:16–20).

409. Jesus healed people of all kinds of diseases and delivered people of demons. Demons can possess only sinners (people who are not saved) (Mt. 4:23, 24).

410. Jesus had a large following of people (Mt. 4:25).

411. Jesus sat when he gave the Beatitudes. Blessed are the poor in spirit, for theirs is the kingdom of heaven. Blessed are they that mourn, for they shall be comforted. Blessed are the meek, for they shall inherit the earth. Blessed are they who hunger and thirst after righteousness, for they shall be filled. Blessed are the merciful, for they shall obtain mercy. Blessed are the pure in heart, for they shall see God. Blessed are the peacemakers, for they shall be called the children of God. Blessed are they who are persecuted for righteousness's sake, for theirs is the kingdom of heaven. Blessed are those who are reviled, persecuted ,and lied about for Jesus's sake. These are to rejoice and be glad, for great is their reward in heaven: for so were the Old Testament prophets persecuted. All Christians should fit any of these descriptions except some Christians are not persecuted, for a variety of reasons. Christians vary in how intense they fit into each of these categories of the blessed from day-to-day, but they will all receive these promised blessings because the Holy Spirit in Christians conforms them to these Beatitudes (Mt. 5:1–12, Lk. 6:2–26).

412. Jesus said believers in him are the salt of the earth. Salt is used to bring out the full flavor in food and as a preservative and wound healing medicinal. So Christians, when they do as they should, make life here on earth more like God intended (bringing out the near full flavor). Also Christians help preserve this world and its inhabitants from decay brought about by the devil. If Christians were not here, this world would be so decadent God would have to destroy it. Christians preserve other people from decay when they lead them to the Lord, so those people are no longer doomed to the lake of fire for eternity but will inherit eternal life with God. Salt was used in Biblical times and, for many years after, to help wounds heal without

infection. The salt hurt when it was put in a wound, but it brought about good. So when Christians use the Word of God that is in them to effect the world around them, it is hurtful to the unbeliever. But if the unbeliever receives the salt (Word of God) and allows it to cleans their dirty wounds, it will bring about healing. There may be scars left if the wounds (sins) are deep (severe), but they will be made clean and healed (Mt. 5:13, Mk. 9:49, 50).

413.   Jesus goes on to say that if the salt has lost its savor it is no longer good for anything but is thrown out and trampled under foot of men. Mt. 5:13. This may mean that if Christians are not different than the world in their heart they do no good for God and are thus good for nothing. They must repent and make their heart right with God so they can then affect the world for good as directed by God. It could also mean that if the believer no longer has the Word of God in them because they rejected God after once being saved they are no longer good for anything and can no longer be saved so they are cast out (Heb. 6:4–6; 2 Pet. 2:20–22; 2 Th. 2:3; 1 Tim. 4:1; Jas. 5:19, 20; Col 1:23; Rev. 2:5, 3:5).

414.   Christians are the light of the world, a city set on a hill. This means we are to show the world the light that is in us, Jesus, by our good words and works so they will be lead to Christ and glorify God. We are not to hide what is in us from the world safe and secure, avoiding injury by the world, but let our light shine. We are to set a good example for others to follow in all things (Mt. 5:14–16).

415.   Jesus did not abolish the Old Testament laws but fulfills them. We are not to follow traditions made up by men but God's word (Mt. 5:17–20). God's teachings written in the Old Testament are valid today except God did tell Peter what food was prohibited to eat in the Old Testament is acceptable to eat after Jesus was sacrificed. This showed

God is able to make all people clean through belief in His Son Jesus as Lord and people are no longer held under the curse of eternity in the lake of fire because of sin. Circumcision of a man's foreskin and sacrifices to atone for one's sins are no longer required to go to heaven since Jesus's sacrifice on the cross. His sacrifice fulfilled these Old Testament requirements. So Jesus said the Old Testament teachings from God are still valid today and not to be forsaken. Indeed, Jesus said all of the Old Testament law will be accomplished. He went on to anyone who annuls even the least of God's laws and teaches others to do the same shall be called the least in the kingdom of God (Mt. 5:18, 19). The Pharisees came up with hundreds of traditions over the years after the Mosaic law was given. God did not give these traditions. Jesus taught us in verse 20 that we can not justify ourselves before God in doing good works as some like the Pharisees do but that we are to live our lives based on the two great commandments Jesus told us to abide by: to love the Lord our God with all our heart, soul, mind, and body and to love others as we love ourselves (Mk. 12:30, 31).

416.    Imagining committing sins is as bad as actually committing the sins Jesus taught. We are all guilty of this (Mt. 5:21–28).

417.    If we remember a fellow believer has something against us, we are to go to that fellow believer and be reconciled with them before we can ask God for forgiveness or other petitions (Mt. 5:23, 24).

418.    If part of a person makes he or she sin, then he or she should get rid of it so that he or she does not go to hell (Mt. 5:29, 30, 18:8, 9; Mk. 9:43–48). This does not apply to believers because we cannot sin too much to go to heaven (Mt. 18:22) but to unbelievers in whom this aspect of themselves keeps them sinning and from repenting.

419. Divorcing someone, except for unchastity, causes him or her to commit adultery. Jesus said whoever marries a divorcee commits adultery. Jesus said this to everyone and did not specify believers or unbelievers, so this pertains to all of us. Jesus said whoever divorces his wife, except for adultery on her part, and marries another, commits adultery. God wants each married couple to stay married (Mt. 5:31, 32, 19:8, 9). A Christian is also free to divorce an unbelieving (not a Christian) spouse if that unbelieving spouse leaves them (1 Cor. 7:15). This does not mean a separation for a short period but abandonment. This implies that a Christian who becomes divorced from an unsaved spouse, due to abandonment, then is free to marry again. This also implies that in the case of two Christians married to each other, if one abandons the other, they are not free to divorce. Unsaved people begin a new life when they become saved, so divorced unsaved people may very well be free to remarry after they become saved, with 1 Cor. 7:15 in mind.

420. Swearing, or making an oath, by anything, including God, is not to be done, Jesus taught (Mt. 5:33–37). In the Mosaic law from Lv. 19:12, God said to not break an oath to God. Jesus made clear that God intends for us not to bind ourselves by oaths because he holds us to them. The exception to this is the oath of marriage, which spouses make to each other, as God forbids sex outside of marriage. This makes evident that God upholds the institution of marriage. And if just living together was right in God's eyes, then there would be no need for marriage because there would not be a difference in relationships between men and women who are joined together whether they were married or not.

421. Be doubly generous to those who harm you or request assistance from you, Jesus taught (Mt. 5:38–42). He also

taught that the Mosaic law of "an eye for an eye and a tooth for a tooth" was not meant to give people license to retaliate for harm done to them but was the God-given law for society as a whole of the legal principal of the punishment being the same as the crime. This prevented society from making punishments too harsh, which is unjust to the criminal, or too lenient, which is unjust to the victim.

422. Love your neighbor and hate your enemy was the principle the Jews had lived by for a long time. This was from the Mosaic law of love your neighbor (Lv. 19:18) but twisted by the Pharisees to add hate your neighbor. God never advised people to hate their enemies. Jesus taught us that God's law of loving our neighbor applied to our enemies and those who persecute us also (Mt. 5:43–48). Jesus went on to explain that God is good to good and bad people by giving both rain and sun, and we need to be like him by being good to both good and bad people.

423. Doing good works to be noticed by people instead of in secret will cause us to not receive a reward from God when we get to heaven since we receive our reward from people here on earth (Mt. 6:1–4).

424. It is better to pray in secret rather than to pray to receive praise of people who see you pray (Mt. 6:5, 6). This does not mean you should pray only in secret because Jesus prayed privately (Lk. 5:16, 6:12), with fellow believers (Lk. 9:18, 28), and publicly (Mk. 10:16; Lk. 3:21, 23:34; Jn. 11:41, 42). Jesus was not saying that a person has to pray in secret but that one must beware they do not pray to be seen of people so they will receive praise from people for praying. In other words, the motive for prayer should not be for one's self-glorification, which would be to give in to the sin of pride (1 Jn. 2:16).

425.    The Lord's Prayer is an example of how saints should pray (Mt. 6:9–13, Lk. 11:1–4). It does not pertain to the unsaved since God only listens to the prayer of repentance and salvation of unbelievers. It teaches saints to start prayer with an attitude of awe and reverence of God and to voice the same. We are to pray for God's millennial kingdom come so that his will will be done on earth as it is in heaven without being effected by Satan's interference, as it is now. This is the first request of God in the Lord's Prayer showing Christians that this should be the foremost desire, and thus prayer request, of Christians.

We desire the return of the Lord and the millennium because we love the Lord and want to be with him. And as Jesus taught that the two great commandments of God are to love God with all that we are and the second is like unto it, that being to love others as yourself; therefore I would add along with this desire and prayer request a Christian should desire, and pray for, to be used by God to lead others to salvation and a full knowledge of God's word. Satan challenges God to test the faithfulness of saints, as he did Job's faithfulness. When we pray, God's will will be done, and pray for God to lead us not into temptation and to deliver us from evil we are praying for God to not listen to Satan's accusations about us and Satan's requests of God to allow him to do us harm. He is prince of this earth, so he tempts all to sin, and he will be bound during the millennium so he will not be able to do that or challenge saint's faithfulness to God.

Until the millennium comes, we are to submit our will to his so that at least in our lives his will will be done through us (Mt. 6:33). We are to ask God to provide what food we need each day and not worry about tomorrow. We are to ask for God to forgive us of our sins as we forgive others who have sinned against us. (Jesus goes on to explain in verses 14 and 15 if we do not forgive others, then God will not forgive us of our sins. This does not mean saints who do not forgive others will not go to heaven since we have the promise of Jn. 3:16, but we will have to answer for our sins to God if we do not forgive others. If saints forgive others of sins, we will not have to answer to God for our sins since God will forgive them. We are to ask God to lead us not into temptation but deliver us from evil. God does not tempt people to sin. But God tests his saints' faith as he did Job. We are to acknowledge God is King and he has all power and glory.

426.  Forgiving and confessing sins (Mt. 6:12, 14, 15, Mk. 11:25, 26). Jesus told us that if we do not forgive others, neither will God forgive us of our sins. This does not mean all sins a Christian ever committed, even those before salvation, are not forgiven if they do not forgive someone (Col. 2:13). Christians are to forgive all other people (sinners and saints) without limitation on the number of sins or the types of sins. Christians need to remember God forgave them for their many sins, without limit, so they are to forgive others without limit (Mt. 18:21–35, Lk. 11:4). This does not mean Christians who do not forgive others will not go to heaven (Rom. 7:25–8:1), but they will have to answer to God for not forgiving others, unless they do forgive all others. Not forgiving others leads to bitterness, strife, and poor mental and physical health (Eph. 4:31, 32). It gives place to Satan to do evil (Heb. 12:15). 1 Jn. 1:9 says, "If we confess our sins, He is faithful and just to forgive us our sins and to cleanse us from all unrighteousness."

The confession of sins in this verse is to God. This forgiveness, as well as redemption, is possible because of the sacrifice Jesus made of himself for all, through his blood (Eph. 1:7, Col. 1:13, 14). In 1 John 1:9, John is writing as a Christian to other Christians because he uses the word we here as well as in verse 7. There are three different viewpoints on the meaning of this verse regarding Christians: (1) repentance (asking God for forgiveness with the intent to sin no more) is necessary for sins committed after salvation to be forgiven, (2) all sins (past, present, and future) are forgiven at the time of salvation and that this verse only pertains to the repentance of a sinner when they become saved so that future repentance of sins is no longer needed for forgiveness of sins, and (3) the same as the first except continual confession and repentance of sins is not necessary for forgiveness of sins, but God will not forgive unforgiveness of other people or blaspheme against the Holy Spirit. Support for the first viewpoint: The scripture says *if* we (Christians) confess our sins, we (Christians) are forgiven. So unrepentant sins done by Christians are not forgiven. But unforgiven sin does not keep the Christian from entering heaven and being partaker of the kingdom of God (Eph. 1:13, 14).

Christians with unrepentant, and thus unforgiven, sins will have to answer to the Lord for these sins (1 Cor. 3:15, 2 Cor. 5:10, 1 Thes. 4:6). A sinner who claims to be a Christian but is not a Christian, like a sinner who does not say they are Christian, will be unrepentant of their sin(s) and will try to justify them so they can continue committing the sin(s). They may say their sins are not sins, even though the Bible clearly says they are sins, or they may say God forgives them of their sins, and that is just the way they are, so they are going to continue doing whatever they desire. Sometimes Christians will also try to justify their sins, including not forgiving others, and be unrepentant for a time, or until their death. Until they repent of these sins and forgive all others of their sins, they will have to answer to God for these sins. So the confessed sins a Christian commits are forgiven by God, and God will not bring them up when they stand before God. Hebrews 8:12, which says the Lord will remember saints' sins no more, seems to go against this viewpoint since there are many Christians today with several unconfessed sins.

Support for the second viewpoint: All a sinner's sins are forgiven when they become saved (Col. 2:13). Another supporting verse for the second viewpoint is Hebrews 8:12. If these verses pertain to sins after salvation, then why did Jesus say God would not forgive Christians if they do not forgive others, and if anyone blasphemes the Holy Spirit, it is unforgivable? From the second viewpoint, all sins a Christian commits will be forgiven, and the verses 1 Cor. 3:15 and 2 Cor. 5:10 mean Christians will just receive less reward in heaven, the worse they behave here on earth, and 1 Thes. 4:6 refers to sinners defrauding Christians and will be held accountable. Usually those who hold this viewpoint feel forgiveness of all sins is necessary to enter heaven and that Christians will never blaspheme the Holy Spirit and that Jesus was not really meaning God would not forgive Christians if they do not forgive others but that they would be less clean.

It is dangerous though to say Jesus did not really mean what he said. The parable of the unforgiving servant that Jesus told makes it clear he meant what he said. The third viewpoint seems to hold up to scriptural scrutiny the best. To be clear, all three viewpoints hold that Christians will go to heaven. There are some people who have the opinion that Christians who do not confess their sins will not be forgiven and thus will not go to heaven, but this does not stand to scriptural scrutiny. Christians are to confess their sins to one another and pray for one another (Jas. 5:16). This means Christians are to confess their sins to other

Christians and then ask God for forgiveness. Jesus said, "Therefore if you are presenting your offering at the altar, and there remember your brother has something against you, leave your offering there before the altar and go; first be reconciled to your brother, and then come and present your offering." (Mt. 5:23, 24).

These verses in Mathew and James tell Christians are to confess their sins to other Christians, but it would also be a good witness for Christians to confess their sins to sinners. Perhaps the reason God does not answer prayers of Christians then is because of unconfessed sins by the offender (leading to the offender's unanswered prayers) to the victim and/or because of unforgiveness by the victim (leading to the victim's unanswered prayers). God sometimes also leads Christians to confess their sins before the church. To disobey God is sin.

427.    Mt. 6:16–18. Fasting is to be a regular part of a Christian's prayer life. Jesus said whenever we fast, indicating that Christians will fast. Fasting is to be done in secret so that others will not know we are fasting. We are not to make it obvious we are fasting so that others will think well of us as the hypocrites do. God looks at the heart, so if someone becomes aware we are fasting despite our trying to not let it be known, then God will honor the fast. Fasting, as well as prayer, is not to be done for our own selfish desires or lusts but for others or God. It can be part of a prayer of repentance, prayer for others, prayer of worship of God, prayer of beseeching God's protection and guidance. Is. 58:3–6; Ac. 13:2, 3; 14:23.

428.    Wealth. Greed or coveting (Mt. 6:19–34, Lk. 12:13–15). Jesus said we are not to store up treasures here on earth, which can be lost anyway. Instead, he said, we are to store up treasures in heaven. Jesus, in Luke 16:9, describes these treasures as souls we lead to the Lord and in Matthew

19:21 as giving to the poor. We cannot serve two masters. We either serve God or money. Whatever our mind is preoccupied with, whether wealth and things of this world or God and how we might serve him, shows which we serve. This does not mean Christians are to all become beggars because Jesus and his disciples were not beggars. They did not have homes to live in though so they could be free to do God's work instantly. Homes require wealth to purchase and time for upkeep so they can distract us from doing God's work. This is similar to what Paul said about being married in 1 Corinthians 7:32–35, but it is not wrong to be married or own a home.

While the Lord did ask the rich, young ruler to sell all that he had and give to the poor, and follow him, the Lord did not ask all to sell all that they had and give to the poor. Some Christians of the early church worked and used money they earned to support those who were involved in full-time ministry (1 Cor. 9:1–14). As more believers did give all they owned to support other believers in need and were involved in full-time ministry, the higher the number of salvations (Ac. 2:43–47). As shown in Acts 5:4, God recognizes the right of property ownership and does not ask all people to give up all they have to further the gospel. We must all be willing to help fellow believers in need though (Rom. 12:13). Those who do give up all they have for Christ's sake will be blessed many times more (Mt. 19:29, 30). Because we need food, shelter, and nourishment to survive, it is natural to worry about the adequate, continual supply of those needs for the duration of our life. In Matthew 6:25–34, Jesus tells us to not worry about these needs though because God promises to meet those needs for us. Since Jesus told us not to worry about these needs to do so is sin. Jesus told us in Matthew 6:33 to seek first God's kingdom and his righteousness, and all these things (our needs) will be added to us. We can depend on this promise.

429. Mt. 7:1–5. Judging. Jesus told believers to not judge or they would be judged. He then said in the way we judge, we will be judged. He told us to take the sin out of our own life so we can see more clearly to judge a fellow believer. In Matthew 7:15–20, Jesus told us we can discern, judge, who is truly a believer in Christ and who is not by their fruits. In John 7:24, Jesus told believers to judge not according to appearance but with righteous judgment. Determining what a person does is a sin based on what the Bible says is not judging that person in that this does not condemn them to hell. Taken together, these verses tell believers they will be held accountable by God for their judgments of others, so they need to be careful but determining right from wrong actions is necessary. Believers need to judge and hold one another accountable for sins but not sinners (Mt. 18:15, 1 Cor. 5:12, 13).

On judgment day, which occurs at the end of the millennium, God will judge all people (Rom. 2:16, Ac. 17:31, 1 Cor. 4:5, Rev. 20:11). When believers feel someone is wrong about something, they need to first look at themselves to see if there is sin in themselves they need to take care of before passing judgment. They may find that selfishness in themselves is causing them to think ill of someone else. We do not know all the life circumstances of others and what others are thinking or planning so we may form the wrong opinion of others. There may be exceptional circumstances where the Holy Spirit gives a Christian knowledge of a secret thing or thought of a person to fulfill God's will though (Ac. 5:1, 2).

Telling others what God says about things written in the Bible is not judging but imparting knowledge of what God says to others. God expects us to do this, but if the listener rejects it, they are as described by Jesus as dogs or swine hating the Word of God. If they are this way, we are not to continue to share with them what the Word of God says (Mt. 7:6). This is not judging them, but they are revealing who they are by their fruits. So it is wrong to say that Jesus taught believers to not say anything anybody does is good or bad because "Jesus said judge not lest ye be judged."

430.    Prayer requests (Mt. 7:7–11, Lk. 11:9–13). Jesus said everyone who asks receives, and he who seeks finds, and to him who knocks it well be opened. We must have no doubt in our mind when we ask God for something or he will not answer it (Jas. 1:6–8). Persistence in prayer requests of God will cause God to answer those requests (Lk. 11:5–8). This does not mean whatever we ask of God he will give it to us if we just have enough faith. If we have wrong motives such as for our own pleasure, it will not be answered (Jas. 4:3). Also God may not give us the response to our petition to him we ask for. He may give us a different response, such as no, as he did with Paul in 2 Corinthians 12:7–10. So Jesus was saying believers will receive from God answers from God for their prayers, but it will not necessarily be what we ask for. It will be a better answer many times, spiritually, but not one we would like physically or emotionally sometimes. The answer will always be best for God, and thus humanity in the long run, because God loves his creation.

431.    Golden Rule: Do unto others as you would have them do unto you, for this is the law and the prophets (Mt. 7:12). Jesus taught here that we are to treat others well as we would want to be treated. This is the way we put into action obedience to God's laws. Being kind and caring for others not only includes caring for their physical

needs but attempting to rescue them from Satan's hold by witnessing to them of sin and the gospel.

432. Wide is the gate and broad is the way that leads to destruction, and there are many who enter through it. Small is the gate and narrow is the way that leads to life, and there are few who find it. Most people will go to hell and the lake of fire. There are many ways and religions that lead that way. Few will go to heaven because few will believe that Jesus is the only way to heaven and make him Lord of their lives (Mt. 7:13, 14).

433. False teachers or prophets have and will exist. They have evil motives. The way to tell them is by their fruits, which are their teachings, disciples, and acts. If they do not agree with the Word of God, then these teachers or prophets are false. If good fruit (which is teaching, disciples, and acts in agreement with the Word of God) are seen, then that teacher or prophet is true (Mt. 7:15–20).

434. Many people will say they are followers of the Lord but not do the will of God the Father. They may even appear to have done many good any miraculous things and think by doing these acts they will earn their way into heaven, but they will go to hell because their heart was never surrendered by them to God (Mt. 7:21–23).

435. Those who do as God and Jesus have said they should do, and not just read or listen to God's word, will be able to withstand adversity with a dependable faith. They are like the man who built his house on a solid foundation. Those who listen to God's word but do not act accordingly are like the foolish man who built his house on the ground without foundation, and when adversity comes, they will fall (Mt. 7:24–27, Lk. 6:46–49). Those who merely listen to God's word and do not do what God's word says delude themselves in thinking they are saved and going to

heaven (Jas. 1:22). Because James wrote this about people deluding themselves indicates there are people who think they are saved but are not. They would think themselves saved only if they had said they believe in Jesus as Lord. To clarify the term saved, being saved means saved from Satan's family or kingdom (Jn. 8:44, Mt. 10:25, 1 Jn. 3:10) and instead being a member of God's family or kingdom (Jn. 1:12, 13) and saved from the punishment all people deserve for their sins, which is the lake of fire after hell. (Rom. 3:23, 6:23; Rev. 20).

To become saved, a person must repent of their sins (Mk. 1:15, Ac 3:19), confess with their mouth Jesus as Lord, and believe in their heart that God raised Jesus from the dead (Rom. 10:9, 10). Acts 16:31 tells us believing in Jesus is all it takes because belief will lead to repentance and confession. There are other people who think they are going to heaven through ways other than Jesus, but this verse does not pertain to them because they are not even listeners to the word of God. They are obviously not saved and so not going to heaven. Doing God's word shows obedience in a person's heart to God. This is in agreement with Jesus's teaching a few words earlier (Mt. 7:15–20) where he said by a person's fruit you will know them. A person's actions, good or bad, show whether he or she is saved (a repentant child of God) or not saved (not a child of God), respectively. Christians are not to be the same as unbelievers, indulging the desires of the flesh and mind, but doing good works, which God has prepared in advance for his people to do (Eph. 2:1–10). Christians still sin even after being saved, but their desire is to not sin (Rom. 7:14–8:19).

436.  Jesus taught with authority and not as the scribes (Mt. 7:28, 29, Mk. 1:22). He used writings from what Christians call

the Old Testament as well as his own words to teach (Mk. 7:6–13, Lk. 4:16–21).

437. Gentiles will share in the inheritance of Jews who are followers of God (Mt. 8:11).

438. Those who go into full-time ministry can be married, as shown by Peter being married. It is not right to say one should be single or divorced to go into full time ministry (Mt. 8:14). Paul did make the point that it is easier to do full-time ministry if one is single, and so a Christian might consider not marrying so he or she could devote themselves to full-time ministry without being distracted by caring for his or her spouse and family. However, if a Christian's desire for sex is too strong to avoid fornication, they should marry (1 Cor. 7:25–40). Also, to be fully effective for ministry, one must be willing to give up family and worldly possessions for God (Mt. 8:22, 19:29).

439. Many illnesses are not caused by demons or the devil (Mt. 8:5–14, 9:27–31).

440. A storm was rebuked by Jesus, and it stopped (Mt. 8:26, Mk. 4:35–41, Lk. 8:22–25). This indicates the storm was started by the devil. Weather can be affected by Satan if allowed to by God as shown in the scripture of Job and here. Both of these instances involve storms, and there is no scripture where Satan causes drought or earthquakes. Only God directly causes drought and earthquakes in scripture. When God grants Satan storms, it is to test the faith of God's children (to clarify, God's children are followers of him and not all people).

441. Demons can possess people and animals and cause them to have amazing strength and do bad things. Demons can be cast out of people by Jesus and saints who do it in his name (Mt. 8:16, 28–34, 10:1; Mk. 5:1–20; Lk. 8:26–39).

Sometimes it requires fasting along with prayer (Mk. 9:29; Ac. 16:18, 19:11).

442. Demons confessed, and still confess, that Jesus is the Son of the Most High God (Mt. 8:29; Mk. 3:11, 5:7; Lk. 4:41, 8:28).

443. Demons confessed that there is coming a day of judgment for them (Mt. 8:29).

444. Jesus healed the sick and lame. So can Christians, in his name. The purpose is usually to bring people to salvation (Mt. 4:24, 8:1–16, 10:1, 15:30, 31, 21:14; Ac. 3:7-8, 9:32–35.

445. The Lord desires mercy and not sacrifice (Hos. 6:6, Mt. 9:13). Obedience is greater than sacrifice (1 Sam. 15:22).

446. Religious ceremonies based on tradition are not to be done by Christians. Our ceremonies, such as baptism and communion, are to be based on Biblical teaching. God created a new covenant of salvation through faith in Jesus as his Son and not a few new laws to add to Jewish traditions to lead one to heaven (Mt. 9:16, 17, Mk. 2:21, 22).

447. Jesus raised the dead to life. So can Christians, in Jesus name (Mt. 9:18, 25, 10:8; Lk. 7:11–17; Ac. 9:36–43).

448. When Jesus said he felt power proceeding from him as the woman who had a hemorrhage for twelve years, he was not saying he was weakened. He just felt the power proceed from himself to someone, which is what happened when she touched his garment and was healed instantly. Jesus told her that her faith in him made her well (Mt. 9:20–22, Mk. 5:25–34, Lk. 8:43–48).

449. The blind received their sight by Jesus (Mt. 9:27–30, 20:29–34, 21:14).

450. Jesus wants Christians to do his work like he did (bearing good fruit) while He was here on earth. He said the workers are few, so all Christians need to pray for God to send laborers (Christians) to go out in the world and do as he did and be willing to go themselves (Mt. 9:35–38, 10:8–10; Lk. 10:2). He also said the fields are white unto harvest, meaning the world is ready for witnesses. Jn. 4:35. He also said some sow and others reap, meaning we may not see someone become saved when we witness to them, but someone else may lead them to the Lord (Jn. 4:36–38). So Christians need to go and tell others the gospel and not be discouraged if they don't directly see someone become saved.

451. The gospel (good news of salvation through Jesus) was first preached to Jews and then to Samaritans and Gentiles, as Jesus directed (Mt. 10:5, 6).

452. Christians are to freely use the power and gifts He freely imparts to them (Mt. 10:8).

453. Those in full-time ministry are to be supported by saints who are not in full-time ministry (Mt. 10:10). This implies Jesus knew not all Christians would be involved in full-time ministry, but this allows support for those who are by those who are not. So not all Christians are called to full-time ministry. Jesus also tells those who go into full-time ministry to not accumulate money, food, or more clothes than what they are wearing. He was speaking to the disciples who had left their homes and wives and families, for those who were married, so this tells us this does not pertain to those who do not forsake all for ministry. Those who do will be blessed in heaven for forsaking all for Jesus (Mk. 6:8, 9). Another time (before his trial) Jesus told the disciples to take with them money, extra clothes in a bag, and a sword for protection (Lk. 22:35–38). So sometimes God wants Christians to go with no provision than faith

alone, and other times, he wants them to take what is necessary for their fleshly needs.

454. When a missionary or minister visit a town or city they are to inquire who in it is worthy (obedient servant of Christ) with which to stay and stay there until they leave. If the household is worthy, they are to give the household a blessing of peace. If it becomes evident, the household is not one that wants to follow God they are to take back the blessing of peace. If a household or town does not receive the worker of God or word of God, the worker of God is to not take anything of that household or town, even to the point of dust on their shoes, with them. It will be more tolerable for Sodom and Gomorrah than for that town on the day of judgment (Mt. 10:9–15, Mk. 6:10, 11).

455. Christians are to be obedient to God and the laws of the land wherever they are, as long as the laws do not contradict what the word of God tells us how we are to be (Mt. 10:16; Rom. 13:1–7; Dan. 3:28, chapter 6).

456. Persecution of believers will happen, Jesus said, so believers need to be shrewd and careful how they speak (Mt. 10:24, Jn. 15:20). The Holy Spirit will speak through Christians when they are persecuted and imprisoned for the gospel's sake. Close relatives will even betray Christians, and Christians should expect this because Jesus was persecuted. Believers should not fear people even though they can harm and kill them because they have no power over the souls of believers. Rather believers are to fear God who has power over everything, including people's souls. People accused Jesus wrongly of being of the house of the devil, so Christians should expect to be accused of worse things. Those who deny Jesus before others, Jesus will deny them before God the Father. This does not mean those who are persecuted for their faith and deny Jesus due to a temporary wavering of their faith

with their mouth but not their heart, as in the case with Peter during the trial of Jesus (Lk, 22:56–62) will not go to heaven. Those who deny Jesus and no longer put their faith in him will not go to heaven even though they once professed a faith in Jesus as Lord. Whether these people never truly believed in Jesus (as Southern Baptists believe) or once believed and later rejected Jesus with heart, soul, and mind is debatable. The end result is the same (Mt. 10:16–36).

457. The gospel will be preached in all the cities of Israel before Jesus returns (Mt. 10:23). This had not happened by AD 70, so the notion that the millennium began when the Romans destroyed the temple in AD 70 is false.

458. Saints can expect to be misaccused by sinners (Mt. 10:25).

459. Fear God who determines where each person spends eternity, and not people, though they may harm or kill us (Mt. 10:28–31, Lk. 12:4–7).

460. Those who deny Jesus before other people will be denied by Jesus the right to enter the kingdom of God (Mt. 10:32, 33; Mk. 8:38; Lk. 9:26, 12: 8, 9; 2 Tim. 2:12). Peter was chosen by Jesus to do his work after the resurrection (Jn. 21:15–19). The example we have of Peter's denial of Jesus during his trial, and yet he was later chosen by Jesus to spread the gospel shows us that the denial Jesus speaks of in these verses is a denial in the heart as well as the mouth. A denial of Jesus by mouth only and not the heart, during persecution, will not doom a believer to the lake of fire. But those who do not deny Jesus during persecution will be rewarded in heaven with the crown of life (Jas. 1:12, Rev. 2:10) and a greater resurrection (Heb. 11:35).

461. God requires us to love him more than any person, including ourselves (Mt. 10:37–39).

462. God will reward those who assist prophets and other workers for God (Mt. 10:40–42).

463. Jesus fulfilled prophesies of the Messiah from Isaiah 53 and 61:1 in that the blind received sight, the lame walked, the deaf heard, the lepers were cleansed, the dead were raised up, and the poor had the gospel preached to them (Mt. 11:5).

464. John the Baptist fulfilled the prophesy from Malachi 3:1 in that he was the messenger clearing the way for the Lord (Mt. 11:10, Mk. 9:11–13, Lk. 7:27). The spirit of Elijah was in John the Baptist (Mt. 11:14, 17:10–13). This does not mean that John was a reincarnation of Elijah. John denied that himself (Jn. 1:21). The spirit of Elijah will also be in one of the two witnesses who prepare the way for the second return of Jesus (Mal. 4:5, 6). God will perform miracles the two witnesses ask of him similar to those he did for Elijah (Jas. 5:17, Rev. 11:5, 6).

465. Even the least of the saints in heaven are greater than the greatest of those alive in the flesh on earth (Mt. 11:11). This is because once we get to heaven, we are without sin.

466. People have and will violently oppose the kingdom of God (Mt. 10:16–36, 11:12). They have done and will do this under the influence of Satan (Rev. 12:13–17).

467. Many people reject the gospel no matter how it is presented or what miracles are done (Mt. 11:16–19, Lk. 7:31–35).

468. God typically does not choose intelligent people but those who believe God's word with childlike faith, without skepticism (Mt. 11:25, 18:3).

469. Jesus invites all who are weary and heavy-laden, and he will give them rest. He went on to say those who become a Christian and learn of him will find rest for their souls, for he is gentle and humble in heart. What he asks of

his followers is easy and not burdensome (Mt. 11:28–30). Believe Jesus will help you with life's burdens.

470. The Sabbath (Mt. 12:1–21, Mk. 2:23–38, Lk. 6:1–11). Jesus is Lord of the Sabbath (Mt. 12:8, Lk. 6:5). God did not want people working on the Sabbath to profit themselves (Ex. 20:8, 11). God did not prohibit all physical effort on the Sabbath so that harvesting enough food to eat (Mt. 12:3,4), service to God (Mt. 12:5, 6), and acts of mercy (Mt. 12:7, 8, 11–13) were not prohibited by God. In verse 7, the Lord Jesus said he desires compassion and not sacrifice anyway. The idea of the Sabbath was to rest from labor that profits oneself. The person who thinks that by avoiding any physical exertion on the Sabbath he or she is being more holy than someone who does physical exertion, without intent of profit, or someone who helps others or does work for the church/God is wrong (Rom. 14:5, Col. 2:16). We need to not neglect God every day though. God has given us laws for our own good because he cares for us, his creation. Resting the mind and body weekly rejuvenates us for our weekly tasks.

471. If a person is not for Jesus, that person is against Jesus. People who do not help gather people into the kingdom of God scatter them from God (Mt. 12:30, Mk. 9:40, Lk. 11:23).

472. Blaspheme against the Holy Spirit is an unforgivable sin both in this age and in the age to come (Mt. 12:31, 32, Mk. 3:29, 30). Based on whom Jesus was speaking to here, this verse pertains to all people. What does Jesus mean by blaspheme against the Holy Spirit? It could mean speaking against the Holy Spirit. It could mean denying the work of the Holy Spirit when one is aware of it. In Mark 3:30, the Bible explains that denying the work of the Holy Spirit is the work of God, or at least claiming the work of the Holy Spirit is the work of Satan, is blaspheme against the

Holy Spirit. I believe someone who God has predestined to go to heaven will not do this. When a person who was saved and then consciously turns against the Lord (not just having doubts or backsliding), it is impossible for them to be saved again because they have committed the unforgiveable sin of blaspheme against the Holy Spirit having done a work in themselves and crucified Christ again to themselves (Heb. 6:4–6).

473.    Lukewarm. If a person is saved, they will bear good fruit. Good fruit is things like Jesus did: heal the sick, cast out demons, teach the truths from scripture, lead people to God for salvation, and disciple people. God does not want Christians to be lukewarm. He wants people to be hot or cold, good or bad, meaning fully committed to God in word and deed or not (Mt. 12:33–35, Rev. 3:15, 16).

474.    All people will be accountable for what they say. Our words could justify us or condemn us before God (Mt. 12:36, 37). This does not mean a Christian will go to the lake of fire if they say *too many* bad things. Jesus said people will have to give an accounting for every careless word they say. Christians will be justified by their repentance and acceptance of Jesus as Lord, but they should minimize their careless words to minimize how much they have to give an accounting.

475.    Jesus was three days and three nights in the heart of earth after his death. Mt. 12:40. This would not be possible if Jesus was buried on Friday and raised from the dead on Sunday, two days later. One could say it was three days, but three nights cannot be fit into that time frame. The answer is that there were two Sabbaths, or holy days. Mark 16:1 and 2 say Mary Magdalene and Mary, the mother of James, and Salome bought spices with which to anoint Jesus after the Sabbath, on the first day of the week (Sunday). Passover begins on 15 Nisan each spring

and lasts one week. No work is permitted on the first day of Passover (Lev. 23:5–7), like weekly Sabbaths, so it is referred to as a Sabbath by some. Luke 23:56 says these women prepared these spices and perfumes before the Sabbath, after Jesus's death. This would have been the weekly Sabbath. Jn. 19:31 says Jesus was buried before not just a Sabbath but a high Sabbath or holy day. If this was Friday, the first day of Passover, that would help explain Mt. 12:40. According to Mark 14, the Lord's last supper with his disciples was the first day of Passover, which begins at sunset on Nisan 14. Jesus was crucified the next day, which would have been the first day of Passover, Nisan 15. The Sabbath in Luke 23:56 would have to be a weekly Sabbath. So to fit Jesus's words about himself from Mt. 12:40, he was crucified on a Thursday and resurrected on Sunday (Mk. 16:9). This fits all the scripture about his crucifixion and resurrection.

476. If a person is not saved after a demon leaves them, it is likely that person will be possessed by more than one demon at some point (Mt. 12:43–45). Per verse 44, a person who is occupied by the Holy Spirit, someone who is saved, cannot be demon possessed.

477. Jesus said whoever does the will of his father who is in heaven is his brother, sister, and mother (Mt. 12:50, Mk. 3:35, Lk. 8:21).

478. Jesus spoke in parables, fulfilling prophecy from Psalm 78:2. (Mt. 13:34, 35).

479. Parable of the Sower (Mt. 13:3–23, Mk. 4:2–20, Lk. 8:4–15). When anyone hears the word of God (seed) but does not accept it or understand it, the evil one (Satan) comes and snatches away what has been sown in their heart. People who accept God's word they hear but have no firm root to their faith give up their faith when persecution or

affliction come. Some people receive the word of God, but the worries of this world and the deceitfulness of wealth choke out the word, and they become unfruitful. They are still believers though. Some people receive God's word and are fruitful to varying degrees.

480. Parable of the Wheat and Tares (Mt. 13:24–30, 36–43). The devil has enticed people to be unrepentant sinners, tares. Jesus called these people sons of the evil one (Satan). These people corrupt the world, but God wants the wheat, worldwide Christian church, to mature before he gathers the wheat to himself and burns the tares in the lake of fire. The harvest is the end of the age, and the harvesters are angels (Mt. 13:39).

481. Parable of the Mustard Seed (Mt. 13:31, 32, Mk. 4:30–32, Lk. 13:18, 19). The kingdom of heaven is like a grain of mustard seed, which even though it is smaller than all other seeds grows to be larger than other garden plants and even becomes a tree that even God's other creatures (e.g. birds) may find rest in them. God makes great things out of what appears to have little potential.

482. Parable of the Leaven (Mt. 13:33, Lk. 13:20, 21). The kingdom of heaven is like leaven, which even though very small in comparison to its surroundings grows and affects all its surroundings.

483. Parables of the Hidden Treasure and Pearl of Great Price (Mt. 13:44–46). When a person becomes aware of the kingdom of heaven they realize it is more valuable than anything else.

484. Parable of the Dragnet (Mt. 13:47–50). At the end of the age, angels will separate the saints from those who are not saints and throw those who are not saints into the furnace of fire.

485. Parable of the Householder (Mt. 13:51, 52). Those saints who write will bring to light treasures or truth from God's word both before and after Jesus's first incarnation. Jesus explained and showed God's word because he was the Word of God. The Holy Spirit helps saints today understand God's word, which is the Holy Bible.

486. A prophet is not without honor except in his hometown and in his own household (Mt. 13:53–57, Mk. 6:1–6).

487. The Lord limits the miracles he does because of unbelief both in him as Lord and his capability of doing miracles (Mt. 13:58, Mk. 6:1–5).

488. Jesus miraculously fed five thousand men and an untold number of women and children with five loaves of bread and two fishes at Bethsaida by the Sea of Galilee. After all had eaten, there were twelve baskets full of fragments remaining (Mt. 14:13–21, Mk. 6:31–44, Lk. 9:11–1, Jn. 6:1–13). In a separate incident, Jesus fed four thousand men, besides women and children, with seven loaves of bread and a few small fishes. There were seven large baskets full of leftovers after everyone was satisfied with enough to eat (Mt. 15:32–38, Mk. 8:1–10). The larger amount of people fed and larger amount of leftovers, with fewer loaves of bread and fishes, contradicts logic, so God is glorified all the more.

489. John the Baptist was beheaded by King Herod (Mt. 14:1–12, Mk. 6:14–29, Lk. 9:7–9).

490. Jesus often went off to himself to pray. He often went by himself to the wilderness to pray (Mt. 14:13, 23, 15:29; Lk. 5:16).

491. Jesus walked on water. Peter did also for a while because Jesus willed it so. When Peter doubted his ability to walk on water, he began to sink, but Jesus pulled him back up and kept him up till they got into the boat. This shows

God can do miraculous things that defy natural laws. He can also help us to do miraculous things if it is for his glory. If we doubt or look at our surroundings too much, we cannot expect God to do miraculous things, but God is always there to increase and sustain our faith so we can do miraculous things to glorify him (Mt. 14:25–33, Mk. 6:45–52, Jn. 6:15–21, Jas. 1:6, 7).

492. The Jewish religion, in the time Jesus, was here on earth in the flesh, had become a religion of traditions, following traditions of men rather than of heartfelt true worship of God, obeying God's word (Mt. 15:8, 9). This was the case before the Babylonian captivity as well (Is. 29:13).

493. Eating certain kinds of food or drink or eating with unwashed hands do not defile a person. What a person says from their evil heart defiles she or he (Mt. 15:11, 15–20).

494. A heartfelt, prayerful request, in humbleness and faith, of the Lord that helps his creation and glorifies him he will answer even if he was not intending to do so before the request (Mt. 15:21–28).

495. Evil people seek signs rather than God himself. They believe what they see rather than have faith in him. Jesus said the only sign the unbelieving Jews would see was the sign of Jonah. This sign was that as Jonah was in the belly of the fish three days and three nights so was Jesus three day and three nights in the earth (Mt. 12:40, 16:1–4; Mk. 8:11, 12).

496. Believers are to beware of and avoid false doctrine. False doctrine is like leaven in that it can start out small and seemingly unremarkable but grow and change all who do not reject it for the worse (Mt. 16:5–12, Mk. 8:14–21).

497. Jesus said he is the Christ, the Son of the living God (Mt. 16:16, 17).

498. Jesus is the rock his church is built on and not Peter as even Peter said. Simon was called Peter, which means stone, by Jesus, but Peter was not the cornerstone of the church (Mt. 16:18, 19; 1 Pet. 2:6, 7). Some say that Jesus was referring to Peter as the rock on which the church is built and that the Catholic church is the Christian church Christ was referring to because church tradition is that Peter died in Rome. However, Peter's main ministry was to the church around the Middle East, with Jerusalem being the headquarters of the first century church (Ac. 15:4–22). The church is built on the foundation of all of the apostles and prophets with Jesus Christ being the cornerstone (Eph. 2:20).

499. All authority in heaven and earth is given to Jesus, and he has given it to his followers. The gates of Hades (hell) shall not prevail against the church (body of believers here on earth) (Mt. 16:18, 19, 18:18–20, 28:18; 1 Pet. 2:4, 5). This is particularly true when two or three believers gather together and agree in prayer in regard to something. Miracles have and will be done through believers by God. Though the church has been, and will be, persecuted by the devil the church has and will prevail. This does not mean Christians can get anything they ask of God (Jas. 4:3). In the verse John 20:23, Jesus gave authority to the disciples, and by extension all saints, to retain or forgive the sins of people. This does not mean Christians have the power to forgive sins because only the Lord God has that authority. But it may mean that Christians who have sin not forgiven by other Christians will have to answer to God for their unforgiven sins (all people who are not saved will be judged by God at the great white throne). What this may also mean is Christians have the word of God to guide them in determining whether a person is forgiven by God or not.

A forgiven person is repentant of their sins. An unrepentant person is not forgiven of their sins and will perish in the lake of fire (Lk. 13:3). This person is not saved so will not go to heaven unless they repent and become saved. A Christian who does not forgive other people is not forgiven by God for their sins after that (Mt. 6:15, Mk. 11:26). This does not mean this unforgiving Christian will not go to heaven when they die. When we become saved we are justified by Christ's sacrifice to go to heaven (Jn. 5:24, Rom. 8:1, Eph. 1:7). So the lack of forgiveness referred to in Mt. 6:15 and Mk. 11:26 means God will not let the unforgiving Christian go unpunished while here on earth. He will chasten the unforgiving Christian to help them come to repentance for their unforgiving heart and forgive those who wronged them (Heb. 12:5–7). It may also mean Christians who have not forgiven others will have to answer to God when they get to heaven about their unforgiveness.

500. Even solid Christians can speak words that are not of God that need to be rebuked (Mt. 16:21–23, Mk. 8:32, 33). We all need to be prayerful before speaking our minds, being careful not to seek our own benefit. Fear can also make us speak things we should not speak.

501. Everyone should be willing to give up everything for God (Mt. 16:24–26, Mk. 8:34–38, Lk. 9:23–26).

502. All people will be repaid according to his or her deeds by Jesus when he returns (Mt. 16:27).

503. In Mt. 16:28, Mk. 9:1, and Lk. 9:27, Jesus prophesied to a crowd that included his disciples (Mk. 8:34) there that some of those present would not taste death until they saw the Son of Man (Jesus) come with the kingdom of God. Some have hypothesized Jesus was referring to the disciples Peter, James, and John who saw the transfiguration

of Jesus six days later. They say the transfiguration was a glimpse of what the kingdom of God will be like. These three disciples did not die until some time after they saw the transfiguration, so Jesus was talking about the transfiguration in Mt. 16:28, Mk. 9:1 and Lk. 9:27. However, Jesus clearly was speaking of his second coming immediately prior to speaking in Mk. 9:1 and Lk. 9:27 as evidenced from Mk. 8:38 and Lk. 9:26. Jesus also said whoever saves his life will lose it and whoever loses his life for his sake will find it (Mk. 8:35 and Lk. 9:24) immediately prior to his prophesy. This means whoever does not surrender their lives spiritually to the Lord will die spiritually. This spiritual death is called the second death and described in Revelation 20:6, 10, 14, and 15. It is reserved for the devil, the beast, the false prophet, death, hell and all who do not surrender their lives to the Lord.

The spiritual death I speak of, or second death, is of the soul and is not the end of the soul as one might think of it, given the term death, but eternal torment in the lake of fire (Rev. 20:10). The first death is death of the physical body, which is the vessel for a person's soul, comes before the second death. The soul lasts for eternity and so should be thought of as the true self. To clarify, the Lord Jesus existed from the beginning as God the Son and those who followed God prior to his first coming in the form of a man (Old Testament saints) will not taste of spiritual death ever, just as New Testament saints (Christians) will never taste of spiritual death. Jesus said there were some in his audience who would not taste of death until after his second coming. These people are those who never surrendered their lives to him and died without being saved. They will be thrown into the lake of fire with the rest of unrepentant sinners thus suffering the second death from the great white throne of judgment.

This judgment occurs at the end of the millennium (Rev. 20:7–15), which is ushered in by the second coming of Jesus (Rev. 19:11–20:6). Jesus looks at things from an eternal perspective, and the first death is almost nothing in comparison to the second death.

504.   During the transfiguration, Jesus became bright as the sun. Moses and Elijah appeared with him. During the transfiguration God said about Jesus, "This is My beloved Son, with whom I am well-pleased; listen to Him." (Mt. 17:1–8, Mk. 9:2–13, Lk. 9:28–36.

505.   John the Baptist had the spirit of Elijah in him (Mt. 17:12, 13).

506.   There was a demon the disciples could not drive out of a boy. Jesus rebuked him, and the demon came out. Jesus told the disciples it was because of the littleness of their faith that they were not able to drive the demon out (Mt. 17:14–21, Mk. 9:14–29, Lk. 9:37–42). Jesus also said this kind of demon does not go out except by prayer and fasting [Mk. 9:29 and perhaps Mt. 17:21 (some manuscripts do not have verse 21 in Mathew 17)]. Regardless, to drive all demons from people requires faith in God to do it and not faith in oneself. Perhaps there is a kind of demon that requires fasting as well as prayer to drive out of someone.

507.   Faith the size of a mustard seed (Mt. 17:20, Mk. 11:23, 24). If a Christian has even a small amount of faith (mustard seed is one of the smallest seeds) in Jesus, he or she can pray and ask anything according to God's will (1 Jn. 5:14) and it will be done, even to the point of moving mountains. Life experiences tell us that what we pray for and what God does are not always the same. God has the best plan for all of us so we need to trust him and submit our will to him. Healing of an illness may or may

not take place, depending on God's will, but we are to pray regardless.

God's spoken plan, through the prophet, for king Hezekiah to die was changed by the king's prayer to ask God to let him live longer. This is an example from the Bible where prayer changed what God said he was planning on doing: prayer changed things. Since God is omnipotent though, one would have to say God knew Hezekiah would pray to live longer, and he would change his spoken plan to what he would do all along from the beginning. Still, Hezekiah's prayer was part of it all so prayer is important. Jesus prayed that he would not have to endure the trial and crucifixion, but he said God's will be done and not his. This sets the example for us to submit our will to God's will no matter how hard life circumstances may be, even to the point of losing our lives.

Jesus tells us God can do great miracles such as moving mountains, so we need to have faith that if God will answer whatever we ask of him if he wills it. God knows our needs and says we should not worry about them (Mt. 6:25–34). We should not pray for our own selfish desires. We should not pray for things that would increase our pride. If God does not answer our prayer the way we want him to we need to thank him anyway and ask him to help us understand him and what he is doing in our life better.

508.  Jesus foretold his death and resurrection three days later (Mt. 17:22, 23, Mk. 9:30–32, Lk. 9:43–45).

509.  There was an annual tax for the upkeep of the temple in Jerusalem called the two-drachma tax. Peter impetuously told the tax collectors for this tax that Jesus paid this tax. Jesus made it clear that he as God's son was exempt from the tax but to avoid offense to the collectors Jesus told Peter to collect the money from a fish and give that as the tax (Mt. 17:24–27). In Matthew 22:15–22, Pharisees and

Herodians tried to trap Jesus about paying tax. Jesus let it be known that things of this world, like money, are for the world, like country leaders. He also let it be known that the things of God, like souls, are God's.

510.    Jesus said unless we are converted and become as children, we would not enter the kingdom of heaven (Mt. 18:3). This means unless we have obedience to, love for, dependence on, and heartfelt faith in God, we will not enter into the kingdom of heaven. He is not endorsing temper tantrums and selfish behavior as children can exhibit.

511.    Whoever humbles themselves as a child will be the greatest in the kingdom of heaven (Mt. 18:4). A child does not think of himself or herself as more important than an adult. Likewise, Christians are not to consider themselves as more important than other people.

512.    Whoever receives a child in Jesus's name Jesus said is like someone receiving Jesus (Mt. 18:5). This tells us how important children are to Jesus.

513.    Whoever causes a child who believes in Jesus to stumble in their belief in him will be punished severally. Their punishment will be worse than drowning with a heavy millstone around their neck. This punishment may take place while they are alive in the flesh or it may take place after he or she dies (Mt. 18:6, Mk. 9:42).

514.    Do not despise children for their angels continually see the face of Father God who is in heaven (Mt. 18:10). These are angels are referred to as guardian angels commonly.

515.    Stumbling blocks cause people to sin and Jesus said it is inevitable that they come. He warned those persons through whom stumbling blocks come will be punished for causing people to sin (Mt. 18:7).

516.    Parable of the stray sheep (Mt. 18:12–14, Lk. 15:4–7). Jesus likened the backslidden Christian as a stray sheep.

Some have called this lost sheep but Jesus said a stray sheep that was a member of his fold, so it would be incorrect to call this a lost sheep, given the tendency to describe people that are not saved as lost. Jesus said Father God does not will that any should perish so he will pursue the stray sheep, or backslidden Christian, to bring she or he back into a right relationship with him.

517. Christians are to hold each other accountable, with a loving attitude of restoration. If we know a person who claims to be a fellow believer sins we are to go to that person and show him or her their fault in private. Again, it is to be done with a heart and attitude of restoration and love and not mean spirited. If he or she listens and does what is right, then all is well. If they do not listen, then the Christian is to take one or two witnesses with them to discuss the sin with the one who sinned. If that person refuses to listen even then, the sin is to be told to the church (local body of believers meeting together regularly). If the unrepentant member of the church refuses to listen even to the church, then he or she is to be treated as an unrepentant sinner. That means they are to be removed from church membership, but they are to be prayed for and witnessed to so that they will repent and turn to the Lord (Mt. 18:15–17).

518. Jesus said there is no limit to how many times Christians should forgive another person, just as there is no limit to how often forgives saints of their sins. God will not forgive our unforgiveness of others until we forgive others (Mt. 6:15, 18:21–35; Lk. 17:4).

519. Marriage. When a man and woman become married, they are to leave their father and mother and become one in the flesh (Mt. 19:4–6, Mk. 10:6–9). First of all, Jesus made no provision for same sex marriage or for changing one's sexual identity. These are contrary to the way God created

us, so they are sin. The married couple obviously does not literally become one body, but they are to act together in unison. They are to not let their parents make decisions for them anymore, but they are to make their own decisions. Their loyalty to each other is to be more than their loyalty for their parents. This is not to say they should neglect their parents. Their parents are still to be honored and cared for by them as needed, including financial assistance (Mt. 15:3–7, Mk. 7:10–13).

520. It is harder for a rich person to enter the kingdom of God than one who is not rich because they have more of this world to distract them from God. Also a rich person has more to give up than a poor person if they give up all to follow the Lord so they are naturally less inclined to do so. The natural man (mortal self) lives in this world and cares about the things of this world, whose lord is Satan. The spirit of a saint strives with their natural inclinations because the kingdom of God is not of this world (Mt. 3:22, 19:16–26; Mk. 10:17–27; Lk. 18:18–27). Zaccheus was an example of a rich man who humbled himself before the Lord and gave half of his wealth to the poor and said he would pay back four fold to any he defrauded. Salvation came to Zaccheus's house after this. Jesus did not ask Zaccheus to give up all his belongings and follow him, but I believe Zaccheus would have if Jesus had asked this of him. Lk. 19:1–10. God wants people, both rich and poor, to be willing to give up all they have for him and obey him, giving him first priority in their lives. He has not asked many people to give up all they have, but he expects us to be willing to do so.

521. The twelve apostles will judge the twelve tribes of Israel during the millennium. Matthias took Judas's position (Mt. 19:28, Ac. 1:15–26).

522. Christians who have worked for a shorter period for God than those older in their faith will likewise receive eternal life with God (Mt. 20:1–16).

523. God recognizes the right of people to do as they will with what is theirs (Mt. 20:15).

524. Jesus foretold of his trial and death and his resurrection to follow three days later (Mt. 20:17–19, Mk. 10:32–34, Lk. 18:31–34).

525. God wants us to put other people above ourselves as opposed to selfish ambition. As we do so, we will be rewarded in heaven (Mt. 20:20–28, 23:11, 12; Mk. 10:35–45).

526. Jesus fulfilled the prophecies about the Messiah coming mounted on a donkey from Zechariah 9:9 and declaration of blessed is he who comes in the name of the Lord from Psalm 118:26 (Mt. 21:1–9, Mk. 11:1–10, Lk. 19:29–38, Jn. 12:12–15).

527. Jesus drove out the money changers and merchants from the temple in Jerusalem saying the temple was to be a house of prayer for all the nations and not a den of thieves (Mt. 21:12, 13, Mk. 11:15–17, Lk. 19:45, 46). There is no mention of a scourge of cords in these accounts and these accounts are written later in Jesus's ministry in the first three gospels, so this may have been a second cleansing of the temple by Jesus. The account in the gospel of John is written as if it was earlier in his ministry, and he used a scourge of cords (Jn. 2:13–18). It would not be surprising Jesus would have to do this more than once since the Jewish religious leaders did not recognize him as a man of God, let alone the Son of God. It is better to confront evil in a house of God than be silent before it, even if it makes people mad and changes the way things are.

528. Out of the mouth of babes and infants, God prepared praise for himself (Ps. 8:2, Mt. 21:15, 16).

529. God will do miracles even if it appears to harm the environment (Mt. 21:18–22).

530. Psalm 118:22 prophesied the Jews would reject the Messiah, Jesus. Isaiah 8:14 and 15 prophesied this stone, the Messiah, would be a stumbling block to the Jews (Mt. 21:42–45, 1 Pet. 2:7, 8).

531. The kingdom of God was taken from being exclusively available to the Jews to all people (Mt. 21:43). The Jews who believe(d) in Jesus as Lord are part of the kingdom of God. The kingdom of God is God the Father, God the Son, God the Holy Spirit, heaven and all beings therein, and all those who serve God in heaven and earth (saints and angels). Righteousness, peace, and joy of the Holy Spirit are thus part of the kingdom of God (Rom. 14:17). This world and the cares of this world are not part of the kingdom of God at this time.

532. Jesus said the Jews would reject him, and so God would invite gentiles to the wedding of the Lamb and be with him forever (Mt. 22:1–10, 25:1–13; Rev. 21:2, 9, 22:17).

533. Many people are called, but few are chosen for salvation. Called means summoned. Many will hear the gospel. Few however will accept the Lord as the Savior. Those who become saved choose to accept the Lord as their Savior but even this faith is God-given. There are people who call themselves children of God but are not (Mt. 22:11–14, Eph. 2:8, 9).

534. Relationship of this world to the kingdom of God and since we are of both how we are to respect both (Mt. 22:15–22, Mk. 12:13–17, Lk. 20:20–26). This world is run under the influence of Satan, the ruler of this world (Jn. 12:31, 14:30, 16:11). The way this world works, like

its financial systems, are under the rule of Satan. The kingdom of God is not of this world (Jn. 18:36), so we are not to try to master or rule in this world. Jesus tells us to pay taxes due because we live in this world. The world asks us to pay taxes with money, which is of this world (Caesar's). The kingdom of God consists of God, Jesus, the Holy Spirit, heaven and all that are there, angels, and the souls of all saints now. Later it will include the future millennium kingdom of Jesus on earth, and when this heaven and earth pass, it will be the Holy Trinity, the heavenly host, and all saints in the new heaven and earth.

535. When Christians die, they become like angels in heaven and cannot die anymore. They are also not married nor given in marriage as they might have been on earth (Mt. 22:23–33, Mk. 12:18–27, Lk. 20:27–40).

536. Resurrection (Mt. 22:31, 32; Mk. 12:26, 27; Lk. 20:37, 38, 23:40–43). When a saint dies, their soul lives on forever with God, currently in heaven. When Jesus returns, their bodies are raised and instantly changed into new imperishable bodies. Those saints that are alive in the flesh when Jesus returns meet the Lord in the air in a new imperishable body, given to them the instant he returns (1 Cor. 15:42–52). Unbelievers' souls go to hell when they die, where they are tormented with fire until judgment day after the millennium, and then they are cast into the lake of fire where they are tormented forever. There is no travel between heaven and hell by souls. There is no purgatory where souls await final disposition by God to either heaven or hell (Lk. 16:19–31).

537. Love the Lord your God with all your heart, all your soul, and all your mind is the greatest commandment. The second greatest commandment is to love your neighbor as yourself. On these two commandments hang all the law and prophets (Mt. 22:34–40, Mk. 12:28–34).

538. Jesus let it be known he might be called the Son of David because of his lineage through his mother, but he is David's Lord (Mt. 22:41–45, Mk. 12:35–37, Lk. 20:41–44).

539. Jesus condemned pride (Mt. 23:1–14, Mk. 12:38–40, Lk. 20:45–47).

540. Jesus told Christians to only call God Father and not to call another Christian father, like some religious leaders are called. This is in reference to a spiritual father, not the father who fathers a child. In the Bible where people like Paul are said to be as a father to others, it does not say those people called them father but that they were as a father to them. Jesus also told Christians to not call another teacher, Rabbi, or leader but brother or sister because he is our teacher, rabbi, and leader (Mt. 23:8–10). So we are not to use the term "father" as a reverent term for anyone but God. Also, we are not to use the terms "Rabbi" (teacher) or "leader" for any person with the mindset that they know all and can teach us all truth.

541. We are obliged to keep our word by whatever we swear (Mt. 23:20).

542. Justice and mercy to other people and faithfulness to God (obedience to God) are as important to God as giving our tithe to him (Mic. 6:8, Mt. 23:23, 24, Lk.11:42).

543. Having the appearance of godliness without actually being so is like the Pharisees. When a person becomes godly inside, their outward appearance changes to reflect that (Mt. 23:25–28).

544. Jesus prophesied the Jewish leaders would persecute Christians and future prophets he would send (Mt. 23:34–37). The Jews persecuted Christians for many years, just as they did the Old Testament prophets. This also tells us there will be prophets after Jesus's death and resurrection.

545. The Jews will one day recognize Jesus as the Messiah, saying, "Blessed is He who comes in the name of the Lord," and then Jesus will return (Mt. 23:39, Ps. 118:26, Rom. 11:24–27, Is. 59:19, 20).

546. Regarding the end of the age, the first caution Jesus gives the disciples, and by extension Christians in general, is to make sure not to be deceived by those falsely claiming to be Christ. He said many would come claiming to be Christ and will mislead many. He also said there would be false prophets and that these false prophets and false Christs will show great signs and wonders that if it were possible they would mislead even the elect. So they will not be able to mislead the elect (Mt. 24:4, 5, 23–28, Mk. 13:5, 6, 21–23, Lk. 21:7–9). Always abound in the word of God rather than follow the crowd. There will be no doubt when Christ returns. All people of the earth will know it when it happens, when he appears in a cloud in the sky after the sun and moon are darkened and stars fall from the sky. The roaring of the sea and waves will perplex men (Mt. 24:29–31, 26:64; Mk. 13:24–27; Lk. 21:25–28; 1 Th. 4:16, 17; Rev. 19:11–16).

547. The first signs of the end of the age are wars and rumors of wars and, in various places, famines and earthquakes (Mt. 24:6–8, Mk. 13:7–8, Lk. 21:9–11). Before (Luke) and after (Matthew) these sign come about, sinners will deliver Christians to trials and tribulations and will kill many Christians. The Holy Spirit will tell Christians what to say to our persecutors so we are not to worry about or plan on what to say. It will be opportunity for us to give our testimony. Christians will be hated of *all* nations because of Jesus Christ's name. Many will fall away from the faith and betray one another and hate one another, including family members (Mt. 24:9, 10, Mk. 13:9–13, Lk. 21:12–19). One could say the persecution of Christians that was

to take place before the period of wars and famines Jesus referred to was that which occurred to the early Church at the hands of the Jews and Romans. Then the persecution Jesus referred to in Matthew in which Christians will be hated by all nations after the wars and famines begin is in reference to the end times. The great falling away of Christians, I will address later. Because lawlessness will increase the love of many will grow cold (Mt. 24:12). God will put the fear of him in those that are his to keep them from turning away from him. Jer. 32:40.

548. When Jerusalem is surrounded by armies, the abomination of desolation, spoken of by Daniel, is near (Lk. 21:20, Dan. 9:27). The gentile armies will capture Jerusalem and persecute those that are there so when it is surrounded those in Jerusalem must flee to the mountains without hesitation. Rome already occupied Jerusalem when Jesus said this, so he was not speaking of the ancient Roman Empire. Christians are to pray that the time of this flight not be in the winter or on the Sabbath. This abomination of desolation occurs in the middle of a seven-year treaty the beast, Antichrist, makes with the Jews. It is thought this abomination of desolation will be the Antichrist declaring himself to be God and demanding worship by all while he is in the holy place. It may also be erection of the image of the beast in the holy place (Mt. 24:15, Mk. 13:14). Involved in the abomination mentioned in Daniel (Dan. 9:27) is the Antichrist putting a stop to grain offering and sacrifice.

This implies the Jews will reestablish the Jewish temple and have grain offering and sacrifices occurring before the abomination of desolation by the Antichrist. However, Psalm 51:16 says the sacrifices of God are a broken spirit, one that submits their will to God, and Hebrews 13:15 says praising God is sacrifice to him, and thanking God is the fruit of our lips, which is like a grain offering. Matthew 24:15 then says let the reader understand. Since Jesus did not say the listener but said the reader understand, we have to take this to mean the ones who read and study the Bible will understand more about the abomination of desolation such as its location. Since Jesus came to earth, the temple of God is the worldwide church, the body of believers, or all saints in the world. This temple is built on the foundation of the apostles and prophets, Jesus Christ being the chief cornerstone. Eph. 2:19–22. Jesus said the abomination of desolation would occur in the holy place. It could be argued that the center of the Christian church is historically the Vatican, the holy place from the perspective of the largest Christian denomination. If the Vatican is where the abomination of desolation occurs, then perhaps the last Pope would be the Antichrist or the Antichrist would take over the Vatican. Mark 13:14 says those in Judah should flee to the mountains when they see the abomination of desolation occur so this would make one think the abomination will occur in Jerusalem. The holy place in Jerusalem today is the Wailing Wall, and so Bible prophecy could be fulfilled if Jewish sacrifices are instituted there. In that case, the abomination could occur at the Wailing Wall. With these two possibilities in mind, end times Bible prophecy could occur without a rebuilding of the Jewish temple as it was before the Romans destroyed it.

549.  In the end times, many Jews will be killed and led captive to the nations. False Christs and false prophets will arise and deceive many during this time but not the elect (Mt. 24:15–28, Mk. 13:14–23, Lk. 21:20–24, Rev. 13:10). God will rescue a remnant of Jews (Rev. 12:13–16). This remnant may be the 144,000 in Revelation 7. Then the Antichrist under the influence of Satan will make war

with Christians and have power to persecute them for three and a half years (Rev. 12:17, 13:5–7).

550. After this three-and-half-year period of tribulation for Christians, the Lord will return in the clouds. Even then we will not know the day of his return, most likely because the beginning of the three-and-half-year tribulation period will be unclear. The Lord will return in clouds with great power and glory. People will faint, and their hearts will fail them because the powers of the heavens will be shaken and expectation of things to come. Those that are not saved will try to hide from Jesus when he returns even calling on the mountains and rocks to fall on them and hide them from the Lord and the wrath of the Lamb (Lk. 23:30, Rev. 6:16). At that time, he will send the angels to gather the souls of all the saints, from dead and alive bodies, Old and New Testament saints (Mt. 24:24–31, Mk. 13:24–27, Lk. 21:25–28). Matthew 24:28 refers to the battle of Armageddon.

551. Christians are to live their lives as if the end times could start during their lifetime. This means putting priority on witnessing to (keeping our lamps lit), baptizing and discipling people [the great commission (Mt. 28:19, 20)] (Lk. 12:35–40). Jesus warned people to not think he would not return during their lifetime. When the beginning of the signs of the end of the age comes, then be ready for the Lord's return (Mt. 24:32–51, Mk. 13:28–37, Lk. 21:29–48). When Jesus said this generation will not pass until all these things come to pass in Mt. 24:34, he could be referring to the generation of the time of the beginning of the end times. The word Jesus used for generation was also used for age, so he could have been referring to this present age or this heaven and earth as this generation.

552. Parable of the Virgins. There are, and will be, people who are not prepared to meet their Creator. They put

off becoming saved for a variety of reason, including the enjoyment of sin, until it is too late. They die before they plan on becoming saved. There will also be a day the Lord will return before people are ready (Mt. 25:1–13).

553. Parable of the Talents. Christ entrusts each professing believer with various ministries here on earth. People that do not do any of what Jesus entrusts them to do show that they never fully believed in Jesus as Lord and will not go to heaven but suffer eternity in the lake of fire (Mt. 25:14–30). Jesus told the disciples, and by extension all Christians, to witness to people that are not saved so they will have opportunity to become saved. All Christians are to teach the newly saved what Christ taught (Mt. 28:19, 20).

554. Jesus will judge all nations sometime after his return (Mt. 25:31–46). Jesus will judge the live and the dead when he returns in that the saints who are dead will rise first and then the saints who are alive will meet him in the air (1 Th. 4:16, 17). The sinners who are alive will be judged in that he will destroy many who are against him and with the Antichrist. He will spare some of the people who are alive on earth, and they will worship him. In these verses, Jesus tells his sheep (his followers) to come and inherit the kingdom prepared for them from the foundation of the world. Then he tells the goats (those who rejected him because they rejected, and cared not for, his followers) to depart into the lake of fire. However, when Jesus returns, he will destroy those who oppose him, sparing some who will worship him during the millennium (Zec. 14:16). There may be others in the world who do not join the Antichrist in the battle of Armageddon. These will also worship Jesus for they will see him for who he is, Lord of lord's and King of kings. Any who do not worship him and celebrate the Feast of Booths will not receive rain on their

lands (Zec. 14:17–19). The people who are dead and did not follow God prior to Jesus's return will not be raised for judgment until after the millennium (Rev. 20:5). So the people whom the devil deceives after the millennium are some of the people born during the millennium. Jesus will sit in the great white throne and judge all people who will have ever existed after the millennium, and after Satan, death and hell are thrown into the lake of fire. There is a day appointed for this, so when it says, in Matthew, the goats are to depart to the eternal fire of the lake of fire, it is most likely talking about the day all of us stand before the great white throne of judgment. Hell will deliver all who are dead in it before it is thrown into the eternal fire (Jn. 5:22–29, Ac. 17:31, Rev. 20:10–15).

555.     Predestination. God chose who would be saved before he made the world (Mt. 25:34; Eph. 1:4, 5, 11, 2:10; 2 Thes. 2:13). We do not know whom God has chosen to be saved, so we are to witness to all people we can, knowing that God will convert those whom he will from sinner to saint. Faith comes by hearing the word of God (Rom. 10:17). So those people whom God has chosen for salvation will not become saved until they have heard the word of God, whether by a person or vision from God. People receive salvation by God's grace, a gift we do not deserve (Rom. 5:1, 2, Tit. 3:5–7). The Holy Spirit accomplishes this in those God predestined to be saved and washes them, making them reborn from their old self, sanctified, and making them justified to be with God (1 Cor. 6:11, Tit. 3:5–7). Ephesians 2:8 tells us that even a person's faith to believe and become saved is from God. Arminianism, a theology that includes the philosophy that all people can become saved if only they will have the faith to believe in the gospel and that God has not predestined (and thus does not foreknow) those who will go to heaven

contradicts these verses. Calvinism, the theology that God predestined those who would and would not go to heaven at the foundation of the world does conform to these verses. However, if one takes an extreme, unbiblical view of Calvinism in which one thinks there is no need to witness to others because God has predestined who will and will not go to heaven, then they contradict Romans 10:17 and 2 Timothy 2:10.

556.   The chief priests and elders of the Jews plotted to kill Jesus (Mt. 26:3, 4).

557.   Mary, the sister of Lazarus whom Jesus raised from the dead, anointed Jesus's head and feet with a pound of very costly perfume of pure nard six days before the Passover. Jesus said she was anointing him for burial. This took place in Bethany. Judas Iscariot and some other disciples were indignant about this, saying it would have been better for the perfume to be sold and the money given to the poor. Jesus responded by saying the poor will always exist, but he would not be with them forever. He meant he would not be in the flesh with the believers of the time much longer. In saying this, Jesus also let it be known there will always be poor people. He was also saying he was more important than people. This should not be surprising because he is God. Jesus said what Mary did would be spoken of wherever the gospel is preached in the world in memory of her (Mt. 26:6–13, Mk. 14:3–9, Jn. 12:2–8).

558.   Judas betrayed Jesus for thirty pieces of silver, which was the price of a slave (Ex. 21:32) (Mt. 26:14–16, 27:3–10; Ac. 1:18, 19; Mk. 14:10, 11; Lk. 22:3–6). This fulfilled prophecy from Zechariah 11:12 and 13. Hebrew canon was divided into three sections of books: law, writings and prophets. The reason Matthew 27:9 references Jeremiah rather than Zechariah is probably because they are both

part of the Book of Prophets and Jeremiah came first in that book.

559.   Jesus identified Judas as the one who was betraying him (Mt. 26:25). I suppose the reason the other disciples did not understand this was that they did not hear or understand the words Judas and Jesus spoke to one another.

560.   Communion or the Lord's Supper was instituted by Jesus for Christians to commemorate the sacrifice Jesus made. It took place during the Passover week (Mt. 26:26–29, Mk. 14:22–25, Lk. 22:19, 20, 1 Cor. 11:23–26). The unleavened bread represents his body, which was given for all. The wine represents the blood of the new covenant, whereby people are saved through belief in and confession of Jesus as Lord. Only Christians are to participate in communion. Before Christians partake in communion they need to examine themselves and forgive anyone they have not forgiven, then ask God's forgiveness for their sins (1 Cor. 11:27–32).

561.   The disciples fell away from the Lord after he was arrested as Jesus said they would and in fulfillment of Zechariah 13:7. (Mt. 26:30–35, 69–75; Mk. 14:26–31, 66–72; Lk. 22:34, 39, 55–62; Jn. 13:37, 39, 18:15–18, 25–27).

562.   Jesus did not want to suffer because of the pain he knew he would have to endure and the time of separation from God on the cross when he took on the sins of all, but he submitted his will to God the Father, praying, "Father, if You are willing, remove this cup from Me, yet not My will be done but Your will be done." (Mt. 26:42, Mk. 14:34–36, Lk. 22:42). Jesus herein sets the example for prayer requests of God by believers. It is fine for Christians to ask God to spare them of pain and suffering, but they are to submit their will to God and ask God's will be done. To

help in this, a believer can ask God to help them accept his will.

563. Jesus was in such agony as he prayed in the garden of Gethsemane; his sweat became drops of blood (Lk. 22:44).

564. Angels ministered to and strengthened Jesus when his faithfulness to God was tested with the forty-day fast and in the garden of Gethsemane (Mt. 4:11, Mk. 1:13, Lk. 22:43).

565. When Peter cut off the ear of Malchus, the high priest's servant, while Jesus was being arrested, Jesus healed the ear back. Jesus also said he who kills by the sword must die by the sword, which is God's law (Gen. 9:6, Mt. 26:51, 52, Jn. 18:10). The Lord told us in Revelation 13:10 that during the tribulation period for Christians at the hand of the Antichrist those who kill by the sword will die by the sword. He also said there that those predestined to go into captivity will be led into captivity.

566. When Jesus asked those who came to arrest him whom they sought and they said Jesus of Nazareth, he said, "I Am." When he said this, they fell backward, demonstrating the power of the word of God (Jn. 18:6). God first called himself "I Am" when Moses asked what was God's name (Ex. 3:14).

567. Jesus made those who arrested him to leave his disciples alone to fulfill his word (Jn. 17:12, 18:8, 9).

568. Peter denied he was associated with Jesus three times before the rooster crowed, just as Jesus said would happen. Then Peter went out and wept bitterly for his sin of denying Jesus (Mt. 26:69–75; Mk. 14:30, 66–72; Lk. 22:55–62; Jn. 13:38, 18:15–27). Peter was repentant, showing that in his heart he did not deny Jesus even though he denied Jesus with his mouth. Therefore Jesus did not deny Peter before the Father, so he did go to heaven.

569. Jesus did not speak to defend himself during his trials as the sacrificial Lamb (Is. 53:7; Mt. 26:63, 27:12–14; Mk. 14:61, 15:5; Lk. 23:9; Jn. 19:9; Ac. 8:32, 33; Rev. 5:6).

570. The Jews took responsibility for Jesus's death from the Romans (Mt. 27:25). But Jesus went willingly to the cross to pay the price for all mankind's sins (Is. 53:5, Mt. 26:53, 54, Jn. 10:17, 18).

571. Jesus was mocked and beaten by the Roman soldiers. A crown of thorns was placed on his head. He was so weakened by his torture, the Roman soldiers made a Cyrene man named Simon help Jesus carry the cross to Golgotha where he was crucified (Mt. 26:67, 68, 27:27–34; Mk. 14:65, 15:18–22; Lk. 22:63–65, 23:26–33; Jn. 19:17).

572. They tried to get Jesus to drink wine mixed with myrrh, but he would not drink it when he tasted it because the myrrh in it would dull his senses, and he had said at the Last Supper he would not drink wine again until he drank it in the kingdom of God. He did drink sour wine or vinegar just before he died when he was thirsty. These fulfill prophecy from Psalm 69:21 (Mt. 27:34, Mk. 15:23, 36, Jn. 19:28–30). The vinegar, or sour wine, he drank on the cross was not from grapes but some other fruit because he said he would no longer drink of the fruit of the vine until that day he would drink it new in the kingdom of God (Mt. 26:29, Mk. 14:25, Lk. 22:18). This will be in the millennium.

573. While he was crucified, his garments were divided up between the soldiers by casting lots fulfilling prophecy from Psalm 22:18 (Mt. 27:35, Mk. 15:24, Lk. 23:34, Jn. 19:23, 24).

574. The Romans put a sign above Jesus's head on the cross, saying, "This is Jesus the King of the Jews." (Mt. 27:37,

Mk. 15:26, Lk. 23:38, Jn. 19:19). This proclaimed the truth. This also indicates Jesus was crucified on a cross with part of the vertical section of the cross above the transom rather than a T-shaped cross that was also used during that time.

575. Jesus was crucified with thieves/transgressors fulfilling Isaiah 53:12 (Mt. 27:38, Mk. 15:27, 28, Lk. 23:32, 33).

576. One thief that was crucified with Jesus was saved on the cross. Jesus said he would be with him the day they were crucified in Paradise (heaven) (Lk. 23:40–43). This tells us Christians' souls go to heaven when they die.

577. The crucifixion lasted from 9:00 a.m. until 3:00 p.m (Mt. 27:45, Mk. 15:25, 34, Lk. 23:44–46).

578. Darkness fell upon all the land from noon until 3:00 p.m. while Jesus was on the cross because the sun was obscured (Mt. 27:45, Mk. 15:33, Lk. 23:44).

579. At that moment, Jesus said, "My God, My God, why have you forsaken Me?" He was experiencing separation from God because he had taken on himself the sins of all mankind (Ps. 22:1, Is. 53:12, Mt. 27:46, Mk. 15:34, 2 Cor. 5:21).

580. When Jesus voluntarily yielded up his spirit and died in the flesh, the veil of the temple was torn in two from top to bottom, there was an earthquake, and rocks were split. When the centurion, who was standing in front of Jesus, saw these things, he said, "Truly this was the Son of God." He also praised God (Mt. 27:50, 51, 54, Mk. 15:37–39, Lk. 23:44–47, Jn. 19:30). Jesus took away the separation of God from believers spiritually when he died, so God took away the separation physically by tearing the veil in the temple in two. This veil was to separate the holy of holies of the temple, where God was, from all else in this world.

Only the high priest could go there, and he could only go there at certain times.

581. When Jesus died in the flesh, the bodies of many saints who had died before him were raised from the dead and appeared to many in Jerusalem (Mt. 27:52, 53). Since the scripture says they appeared and does not say they continued here on earth, I would say these saints were given their glorified, eternal, spiritual bodies and went to heaven after they appeared to people in Jerusalem. They went to heaven after Jesus arose from the dead and went to heaven (1 Cor. 15:20).

582. The Roman soldiers broke the legs of the two thieves who were crucified with Jesus to hasten their death. Since Jesus was already dead, they did not break his bones, but one of the soldiers pierced his side with a spear anyway (Jn. 19:31–37). This fulfilled scripture for the sacrificial lamb from Ex. 12:46 and Nu. 9:12 and prophecy from Psalm 34:20 and Zechariah 12:10.

583. Though Jesus was crucified with thieves and would have been buried like them, he was buried in the tomb of a rich and righteous man named Joseph of Arimathea, fulfilling prophecy from Isaiah 53:9. The Jews convinced Pilate to place guards over the grave to make sure no one took Jesus's body out of the grave and claim he was resurrected as he claimed he would be three days after his death (Mt. 16:21, 27:57–66; Mk. 8:31, 15:42–47; Lk. 9:22, 23:50–55; Jn. 19:38–42).

584. Jesus was three days and three nights in the heart of earth after his death (Mt. 12:40). This would not be possible if Jesus was buried on Friday and raised from the dead on Sunday, two days later. One could say it was three days, but three nights cannot be fit into that time frame. The answer is that there were two Sabbaths, or Holy days.

Mark 16:1 and 2 say Mary Magdalene and Mary the mother of James and Salome bought spices with which to anoint Jesus after the Sabbath, on the first day of the week (Sunday). Passover begins on 15 Nisan each spring and lasts one week. No work is permitted on the first day of Passover (Lev. 23:5–7), like weekly Sabbaths, so it is referred to as a Sabbath by some. Luke 23:56 says these women prepared these spices and perfumes before the Sabbath, after Jesus's death. This would have been the weekly Sabbath. Jn. 19:31 says Jesus was buried before not just a Sabbath but a high Sabbath or Holy Day. If this was Friday, the first day of Passover, that would help explain Mt. 12:40. According to Mark 14, the Lord's last supper with his disciples was the first day of Passover, which begins at sunset on Nisan 14. Jesus was crucified the next day, which would have been the first day of Passover, Nisan 15. The Sabbath in Luke 23:56 would have to be a weekly Sabbath. So to fit Jesus's words about himself from Mt. 12:40, he was crucified on a Thursday and resurrected on Sunday (Mk. 16:9). This fits all the scripture about his crucifixion and resurrection.

585. The first day of the week (Sunday), there was a severe earthquake, and Jesus was resurrected. The angel of the Lord appeared to Mary Magdalene, Mary the mother of both James the Less and Joseph, Joanna, and other women who were the first to arrive to the tomb when the sun had just risen. The Roman guards shook for fear of the angel and became as dead men (probably feinted). The angel told the women that Jesus was risen and that they were to quickly go and tell the disciples that he was risen. The angel also told the women that Jesus was going ahead of them to Galilee where they would see him. Jesus did greet them as the angel said and they worshiped him. While Mary Magdalene was worshipping him, she

touched him, and he told her to not touch him because he had not ascended to heaven yet. Perhaps he told this to Mary because she was clinging to him wanting him to stay. Or perhaps he was not to have anything of earth on him, such as her skin oil, before he went to be with God the Father. This would mean he went to heaven to be with God before his appearances to the disciples and other Christians and then his ascension forty days later, because he offered Thomas to touch him (Mt. 28:1–10, Mk. 16:1–11, Lk. 24:1–11, Jn. 20:1, 2, 11–18).

586. Upon hearing what the women said, Peter and John ran back to the tomb and saw that the stone was rolled away. They saw that Jesus was not there, but only the linen wrappings and face cloth for his burial were there. Then they went back to where they were staying (Lk. 24:12, Jn. 20:3–10).

587. The Jewish chief priests and elders conspired with a lie that the disciples stole the body of Jesus from the grave while the soldiers were sleeping. This lie is continued to today (Mt. 28:11–15). This is preposterous as the Roman soldiers were professional soldiers, and there is no record in history of a whole Roman detail falling asleep on duty. They passed out when the angel appeared.

588. Jesus appeared to two men, who followed the Lord, as they were walking on the road to Emmaus (tradition has it that Emmaus is today's Kubeibeh, seven miles northwest of Jerusalem). One of these men was named was Cleopas. During this time, the men tell us their hearts burned within them while Jesus was explaining the Scriptures to them. This tells us our hearts burn within us when truth is revealed to us from the Scriptures (Mk. 16:12, 13, Lk. 24:13–35).

589.     While these two men were telling the ten apostles (Judas was dead and Thomas was not there), on a Sunday evening, Jesus appeared to them. He told them they could touch him to help them believe because a spirit does not have a body that can be felt. He showed them his pierced hands, body, and feet. He also ate while he was with them, showing he was alive in spirit and body. He told them some of the signs of those who are believers: in his name they will cast out demons, they will speak in new tongues; they will pick up serpents, and if they drink any deadly poison, it will not harm them; and they will lay hands on the sick, and they will recover. He breathed on them and said to them, "Receive the Holy Spirit. If you forgive the sins of any, their sins have been forgiven them; if you retain the sins of any, they have been retained." Since the disciples did not receive the Holy Spirit until the day of Pentecost about forty days later (Ac. 1:8, 2:1–3), Jesus is here saying the word to make it happen at that future date. He is not saying we have the power to forgive others' sins and determine whether they are then allowed into heaven. Only God has that authority. Perhaps he is saying we can choose whether or not to forgive others of their sins and to pray to God that he will forgive their sins. Jesus himself prayed to God the Father to forgive those responsible for crucifying him (Lk. 23:34). A person is forgiven when they are saved, so when we pray to God to forgive those that are not saved, we are asking God to save them. God will honor this prayer, as he did with Paul, who was consenting to the stoning death of Stephen, who prayed to God to forgive those responsible for his death (Mk. 16:14–18, Lk. 24:36–43, Jn. 20:19–25, Ac. 7:58-8:1).

590.     Eight days later, he appeared to the apostles, including Thomas, because Thomas did not believe the other disciples that they had seen Jesus. He told Thomas to do

as he said was necessary for him to believe that it was Jesus the other disciples had seen: put his finger into the piercings of Jesus's hands and his hand into the pierced side of Jesus. Thomas then believed. Jesus said blessed are those who believe without seeing him with their natural eyes (Jn. 20:24–29).

591.    Jesus appeared to five hundred brethren at one time before his ascension (1 Cor. 15:6).

592.    All authority has been given to Jesus in heaven and earth (Mt. 28:18). Jesus told us that so we would use his authority in heaven and earth to do his work despite opposition and without fear. He told the disciples to wait until they were filled with power from the Holy Spirit before they went forth to witness to the world. Lk. 24:49. The Holy Spirit came into all Christians on the day of Pentecost. Since then the Holy Spirit indwells every newborn Christian (Ac. 1:1–8, 2:1–13).

593.    Jesus opened the minds of the disciples to understand the Scriptures. The Holy Spirit will do this for the believer who asks God to help them understand the Scriptures. God will open the believer's mind to understand however much he chooses at a time. Sometimes a believer is not ready to understand some Scripture at a point in their life, but later they might be ready, and it is then God allows them to understand (Lk. 24:45).

594.    The Great Commission to all Christians. In Galilee, Jesus commissioned (gave orders to, with authority) the eleven disciples, and by extension all Christians, to go and make disciples of all nations, baptizing them in the name of the Father and the Son and the Holy Spirit, teaching them to observe all that Jesus said. Jesus went on to promise he is with the disciples, and by extension all Christians, to the end of the age (this present heaven and earth) (Mt. 28:19,

20). So witnessing to the lost and teaching new believers God's word is the duty of all Christians. We are to do this throughout the world, but those who are not able to travel to other nations are to witness to the lost and teach God's word to new believers where they are. Christians are to preach repentance for forgiveness of sins in Jesus name (Lk. 24:47).

595. When Jesus cast out demons, sometimes he allowed the demons to speak, but usually he just told them to be quiet and come out. Jesus sent demons to the abyss and in one instance into swine (Mk. 1:25, 34, 5:9–13; Lk. 8:26–33). When dealing with demons a Christian should be sensitive to the direction of the Holy Spirit. God may not have Christians deal with each demon the same way.

596. A servant of God may be told by God to leave an area that is responsive to the gospel and wants the servant to stay (Mk. 1:37, 38).

597. Because Jesus was in a fleshly body during his first advent, he was limited where he could work (Mk. 1:45).

598. The twelve disciples of Jesus were Simon (whom he called Peter); Andrew, Simon Peter's brother; John and James the sons of Zebedee (whom he called Boanerges, Sons of Thunder); Philip; Bartholomew; Matthew; Thomas; James, the son of Alphaeus; Thaddeus (Luke 6:14–16 and Acts 1:13 refer to him as Judas the son of James while John 14:22 refers to him as Judas, not Iscariot); Simon the Zealot; and Judas Iscariot, the one who betrayed Jesus (Mk. 3:13–19).

599. Jesus explained Isaiah 6:9 and 10: sinners who do not want to turn away from their sin but love the approval of men more than the approval of God will not be allowed to understand God's word, so they will not become saved

(Mt. 13:14, 15, Mk. 4:12, Lk. 8:10, Jn. 12:37–43, Rom. 11:8).

600. Parable of the Lamp. What Christians learn and experience of God they are to share with other people. Those who do this will receive more knowledge from God to share with others. Those who do not, even what they have will be taken from them (Mk. 4:21–25, Lk. 8:16–18).

601. Jesus taught people to be careful what we listen to in Mark 4:24. This seems to coincide with Matthew 7:2, which would indicate a caution from Jesus to not believe gossip at face value. Taken with 1 Timothy 4:6, Jesus is telling Christians to not listen to words that would hurt our faithfully following him. This would mean to not entertain false doctrine as possibly true. It also means Christians are not to listen to music that would decrease our faithfulness to Jesus. Obviously this would include songs that encourage immoral behavior, have cursing in them, and speak badly of Christianity.

602. Parable of the Growing Seed (Mk. 4:26–29). The Word of God spoken to someone who believes it with all their heart will grow in them resulting in that person having a good root system from studying the word of God. They will be solid in their faith. Though the wind (trials of life and attacks of Satan) may bend them, testing their faith, they will always return to the straight and narrow looking to the Son, the supplier of all their needs. They make seed of their own that they spread around them. The seed is the word of God. It is natural to the believer to share the word of God with others because they want others to share in the joy of salvation and to experience the love of God. The farmer waits until his crop is mature, and he will get the maximum amount of harvest to harvest the crop. So too God will wait until he knows the number of mature Christians is at the maximum, and there are

mature Christians wherever he has planted on earth before he will harvest the earth.

603. Jesus told the disciples, and by extension all Christians, to rest even from God's work from time to time (Mk. 6:30–32, Lk. 9:10).

604. Jesus said to honor one's father and mother. He said money and other assistance given to one's parents could not be counted as an offering to God (Mk. 7:9–13).

605. Jesus declared all food is fit to eat (Mk. 7:15–19). A Christian can even eat food offered to idols if they do not do it in worship to the idol. If a weaker Christian would be offended by eating food offered to an idol, then one should not eat that food so that the weaker Christian does not stumble in their faith (1 Corinthians 8).

606. What immoral things a person says defiles him or her. Lies, filthy language with curse words, and abusive speech are sin and proceed from evil in the heart of a person (Mk. 7:15–23; Eph. 4:29, 5:4; Col. 3:8). From the heart of men proceed evil thoughts, fornications, thefts, murders, adulteries, deeds of coveting, deceit, sensuality, envy, slander, pride, and foolishness.

607. A blind man was healed by Jesus with Jesus spitting on his eyes and laying his hands on him. The man could see partially so then Jesus laid His hands on his eyes and the man could see well (Mk. 8:22–26). Jesus could have healed the man's eyes without even being with the man, but Jesus did it this way for the benefit of the man. The blind man probably had been blind a long time and a sudden ability to see normally without the touch of Jesus may have scared him.

608. Jesus preached that hell existed and those that are not his (evil) will go there (Mt. 5:22, Mk. 9:42–50).

609. The widow's mites (Mk. 12:41–44, Lk. 21:1–4). Jesus taught that God counts an offering greater if it is a higher percent of a person's wealth than an offering of greater monetary value.

610. The great tribulation will occur during the last three and half years of the Antichrist's reign. Christians will go through it as well as sinners (Mk. 13:14–20).

611. Eternity with God was no longer possible through being of Jewish heritage, and sacrifices in the Jewish tradition after John the Baptist started his ministry of repentance and baptism. Salvation through repentance and forgiveness by God was now the way for eternity with God. Evidence of a person being saved was their good fruit (Lk. 3:8, 9, 16:16). Good fruit is works of righteousness out of love for God. This love for God causes Christians to love other people as we should.

612. A sinful woman, most likely a prostitute, anointed Jesus's feet with perfume while he was in Galilee. This is a different episode than when Mary, the sister of Martha and Lazarus, anointed Jesus's feet. That took place in Bethany. Also Mary was not described as a sinner. There is no reason to say this woman was Mary Magdalene. Jesus told this sinful woman her faith had saved her. Jesus told the Pharisee and those dining with him that those who are forgiven little love little. She was forgiven even though she had sinned much. This teaches us the magnitude of our sins does not keep us from being saved by God. We cannot sin too much to be saved (Lk. 7:36–50).

613. Christians have the light of life, God, in them. No one who has this in them hides it but displays it for all too see (puts the lamp on the lampstand) so they can see the light and come to it (God) (Lk. 8:16). Christians are to bear witness to the world, wherever we are, about the Lord.

614. Jesus came to save people's lives (Lk. 9:56).

615. Parable of the Good Samaritan (Lk. 10:30–37). It is sin to ignore the needs of others with whom we come into contact. We are to help others that we know of are in need and that need is not being met. By doing this we obey God's command to love others as ourselves. However, enabling people to live corrupt lives by assisting them is not the right way to help them. For instance, we should not give money to a destitute alcoholic on the street because they will most likely just use the money to buy alcohol rather than use it for a greater need. In such an instance, it would be better to provide the person with food or clothing, if they need it.

616. It is better to spend time with God than to spend time in the cares of this life. Mary chose to spend time with Jesus while he was visiting rather than doing as Martha did, preparing a meal. God will provide for our needs, so we are not to worry about them. However it is evident one cannot spend all of their time in meditating without taking care of oneself or one's family. But when the cares of this life take up our whole day so that we do not spend time with God, every day we miss out on the best God has for us (Lk. 10:38–42).

617. Looking in a person's eyes gives one an idea of whether that person is obedient to God or not (Lk. 11:33–36).

618. Planning for the future without consulting God is wrong. We cannot determine how long we will live, so it is arrogant to assume we can determine our future (Lk. 12:16–21).

619. The Lord Jesus will return with fire to deal out retribution on people who choose not to know God and do not obey the gospel of Jesus Christ (Lk. 12: 49; Is. 66:15; Joel 2:30; Am. 1:7, 10–14, 2: 2, 5; Mal. 3:2; 1 Cor. 3:13; 2 Th. 1: 7, 8).

620. Evil done to people by other people is not necessarily the judgment of God for some sin they have done. God did send the Jews to destroy the evil people in Canaan before they established their nation there. But the Romans killing the Galileans while they were offering their sacrifices to God was not judgment from God (Lk. 13:1, 2).

621. Repentance is necessary to enter the kingdom of God (Lk. 13:3). Repentance leads to salvation.

622. People from all over the world, including gentiles, will enter the kingdom of God (Lk. 13:29).

623. He who exalts himself will be humbled, and he who humbles himself will be exalted (Lk. 14:11).

624. Parable of the Prodigal Son (Lk. 15:11–32). The son who squandered his inheritance is like unto people who live their life their own way. Then when they reach a point in their life they become desperate, they come to the Heavenly Father and repent of their sins. The father in this story is like our Heavenly Father who forgives all who come to him and ask for forgiveness, making them his children with the right of inheritance of the kingdom of God. The obedient older brother who stayed at home with the father but was jealous of all the father did for the younger brother is like the Jews who were jealous the gentiles would become part of the kingdom of God. Jesus explained they should rejoice together for the entry of the repentant sinner into the kingdom of God. Jesus makes it clear that riotous living leads to ruin but that there is hope for those who have done this. This can also be a lesson for the backslidden Christian that there is hope for restoration with repentance and returning to obedience to God.

625. Jesus told a story showing that the unsaved (both master and servant) are shrewd with financial matters, thinking

of the future. Christians should use their finances to influence the unsaved to become saved. Many of the unsaved prepare for coming disaster (the servant), so when they become aware of what awaits those that are not saved, they may repent and become saved to avoid judgment (Lk. 16:1–9).

626.   He who is faithful in a very little thing is faithful in much, and he who is unrighteous in a very little thing is unrighteous in much. If a Christian is unrighteous in matters of money or possessions, then God will not entrust spiritual matters to him or her. We cannot serve two masters. Either we are devoted to God or wealth. We cannot serve God and wealth (Lk. 16:10–13).

627.   Christians should not be proud in doing what is right and obeying God since this is what God expects of us (Lk. 17:10).

628.   The kingdom of God is not only those in heaven but also those here on earth who serve God (Lk. 17:20, 21).

629.   Parable of the Woman and the Judge (Lk. 18:1–8). Here He taught Christians ought to pray at all times and not to lose heart. He reassured persecuted believers that God will bring about justice for believers quickly. Quickly in God's eyes is different than in our eyes since we have a short lifespan, relative to eternity. He follows this statement with asking when the Son of Man returns will he find faith on earth? This tells us that the justice he was speaking of comes when he returns. This question also lets us know that persecution and temptation will be so strong here on earth before his return that there will be few Christians, the very elect, on earth who will be faithful to Him during the last days of this age. Jesus taught Christians to pray that they might have strength to

escape all the persecution and tribulation of the end times and to stand before him, the Son of Man (Lk. 21:36).

630. Parable of the Pharisee and Tax Collector (Lk. 18:9–14). This parable reinforces the word of God that says God resists the proud but gives grace to the humble (Ps. 138:6, Pr. 3:34, Jas. 4:6, 1 Pet. 5:5). It is better to repent and humble oneself to God than to do what is right and be proud about it, thinking that by doing good acts one can earn their way into heaven and that these good acts make oneself better than sinners.

631. Jesus prophesied the Jews would reject the Son of God, him, so that God would give the inheritance of the kingdom of God to gentiles. The Jews said, "May it never be." But Jesus quoted to them the prophesy from Psalm 118:22, "The stone which the builders rejected is become the chief corner stone." (Lk. 20:9–18).

632. God predetermined Judas Iscariot to betray Jesus. He was also destined to go to hell because he would not be a believer but deceive others into thinking he was a believer in Jesus as the Messiah (Lk. 22:22).

633. Pontius Pilate, Roman prefect of Judah, and Herod Antipas, tetrarch of Galilee and Perea, both tried Jesus at the request of the Jewish religious leaders (Lk. 23:1–25). Herod Antipas was the son of Herod the Great, who tried to kill Jesus when Jesus was a child. Herod Antipas was the one who had John the Baptist beheaded.

634. After Jesus blessed the believers, he ascended up in a cloud to heaven and sat at the right hand of God. Two angels told the believers that Jesus would return just as he was taken up into heaven (Lk. 24:50–52, Mk. 16:19, Ac. 1:9–11).

635. Jesus is the Word of God. Jesus was in the beginning with God (Jn. 1:1, 2). The light was life that Jesus, the Son of

God, gave to the earth. With life came the creation. Jesus was with God, and they created all things (Jn. 1:1, 3, 4). Darkness, Satan with his forces, and people who do not follow God do not comprehend Jesus and the love, life, and power in him. Jn. 1:5.

636.    In John 1:5–9, Jesus is referred to as the Light. This is not the same light that God created on the first day of creation because Jesus was not created, but he has always been as is God (Jn. 1:2). John the Baptist was a witness that testified of the coming Messiah to the world so that all might believe in him and be saved.

637.    Jesus's own people, the majority of the Jews, rejected him but as many as believed in him received the right to become children of God. All believers are born again in the spirit, not in the flesh (Jn. 1:10–13).

638.    Jesus, the Word of God, became flesh and dwelt among us, full of grace and truth. The law was given through Moses; grace and truth were realized through Jesus (Jn. 1:14–17).

639.    No one has seen God but Jesus who explained God to people. Since he is God, God revealed himself to us through him (Jn. 1:18, 6:46; 1 Tim. 6:16; 1 Jn. 4:12).

640.    John the Baptist denied being Elijah, but the angel who appeared to his father told him he would be a forerunner to the Messiah in the spirit and power of Elijah (Lk. 1:17, Jn. 1:21). Malachi 4:5 promises that Elijah will return before Messiah establishes his earthly kingdom. John the Baptist knew he was not Elijah in the flesh, so it is reasonable that he denied being Elijah. God placed the spirit of Elijah in him though so he would witness as he did. One of the two witnesses will be Elijah in spirit and maybe in the flesh since Elijah was taken up to heaven without dying (2 Kg. 2:11).

641. John did not initially recognize Jesus as the Messiah, but God said to him, "He upon whom you see the Spirit descending and remaining upon Him, this is the One who baptizes in the Holy Spirit." (Jn. 1:32). So God told John he would show John who was the Messiah this way. We don't know how God spoke to John, but since God stopped speaking directly to people and instead started using prophets at the Jews' request (Dt. 18:15–18), he probably spoke to John via the Holy Spirit, as he does with Christians today. This is not an audible voice but a quickening of the soul, a knowing that this knowledge is from God. God also talks to us in dreams and visions (1Kgs. 3:5), by angels, and through his words in the Bible. There is no mention of John having been visited by an angel, but it is possible God spoke to John in a dream or vision.

642. Jesus changed Simon's name to Cephas, or Peter (Jn. 1:42).

643. The first miracle recorded that Jesus did was turn water into wine at a wedding feast. This despite his will was to not start his ministry yet. Because his mother asked and believed he did it (Jn. 2:1–12).

644. Jesus drove the moneychangers and those who sold animals for sacrifice out of the temple of God in Jerusalem, early in his ministry, out of zeal for God's house (Jn. 2:13–25). The temple was meant for worship of God and a place of repentance, but most of the Jews had made it a place of religious tradition without heartfelt repentance and worship of God. Also, the moneychangers and those that sold animals for sacrifice were in the outer courts of the temple making business transactions when it was to be used only for sacrifice and worship of God.

645.    Jesus said unless one is born again, born of water and the Spirit, they cannot enter the kingdom of God. Born of water is a person's birth in the flesh from their mother. When a person is born again, they are born of the Spirit, a new creation, a child of God and not just of their fleshly parents. All people are creations of God, but only those who love and follow the Lord are children of God (Jn. 1:12, 3:4–7). Once a person is born of the flesh, they are destined to the kingdom of God or the lake of fire. Only when a person becomes a child of God are they destined for the kingdom of God.

646.    Jesus said the Holy Spirit is like the wind. We do not know where the wind comes from and where it is going, but evidence of it, such as the sound of it, is undeniable. Likewise, we don't fully understand or know all there is to know of the Holy Spirit, but it is undeniable. The effects of it are evident such as the changes in people's hearts to repent and believe in Jesus as the Son of God and that God raised him up after his sacrifice and confess this with their mouth. Then the Holy Spirit enters the newborn Christian and compels him or her to obey God and do good instead of bad (Jn. 3:8).

647.    For God so loved the world that whoever believes in him should not perish but have everlasting life (Jn. 3:16). Salvation, and eternity with God, is offered to all people. God did not send his Son to judge the world but that the world might be saved through him (Jn. 3:17). Judgment of the world will come when Jesus returns, but God gave his Son as the one and only sacrifice for all people's sins so that they may become children of God and enter the kingdom of God. God desires that all people would be saved (2 Tim. 2:4, 2 Pet. 3:9). However, most people do not choose to follow God so they will go to the lake of fire. Few follow God and enter the kingdom of God (Mt.

7:13, 14). God gives people free will to choose whether to follow God or not. People are without excuse now since Jesus came into the world. Jn. 3:19. Most people choose darkness rather than the Light. Everyone who does evil hates the Light, Jesus, and does not come to the Light for fear their deeds will be exposed (Jn. 3:20). The Son, Jesus, was God before all creation, but Jesus is called begotten because he was born in the flesh with his first incarnation. He was not created by God in any way before that. The Son has always existed as has the Father and the Holy Spirit (Gen. 1:26, Mt. 28:19, Rev. 1:8). He was God and man at the same time while he was here on earth.

648. Jesus had his disciples baptize new believers with water (Jn. 3:22, 4:1, 2).

649. A man cannot have an effective (effective for God) ministry unless it is given to him by God (Jn. 3:27).

650. God does not give the Holy Spirit by measure to persons that become saved. It is all or nothing (Jn. 3:34).

651. Since Jesus was in the flesh, he felt the feelings we feel, such as fatigue (Jn. 4:6), hunger (Mt. 4:2), and anger, at the hardness of heart of the Pharisees against healing on the Sabbath (Mk. 3:4, 5). He also experienced temptation (Heb. 4:15), yet without sin.

652. Encounter with the Samaritan woman at the well (Jn. 4:3–42). Jesus chose to travel directly, through Samaria, from Judea to Galilee. This was contrary to Jewish tradition of traveling around Samaria to avoid interacting with Samaritans, whom the Jews considered impure. It is believed by Bible scholars that the Samaritans were the progeny of the ten northern tribes of Israel who married the people groups the Assyrians brought into the territory of the northern kingdom after the Assyrians had conquered it. Jesus met a Samaritan woman at a well

there and asked her to give him water to drink. She was surprised he interacted with her since he was a Jew. He told her that if she asked he would give her living water and would never thirst again.

He meant spiritually she would never lack of being sustained by God. He told her things about her a stranger would not know such as her many marriages and her current situation of living in sin, living with a man with whom she was not married (This tells us living with someone without being officially married in God's eyes is sin). She thought He was a prophet after hearing this so she asked Him whether the Samaritans or the Jews worshiped God correctly. Sometimes people want to win arguments over differences of opinion. He told her the Jews were correct in worshiping God as God revealed to Moses and the prophets but not the Samaritans in worshiping God at Mount Gerizim, in the tradition of Abraham. So he told her the truth but did not argue with her.

He also told her in essence the argument between the Samaritans and Jews was irrelevant because now was the time that worship of God was to no longer be confined to Jerusalem or Mount Gerizim. He then said true worshipers of God must worship God in spirit and truth, because God seeks such people to worship him and he is spirit. She then perceived Jesus was the Messiah. In unique fashion, he plainly told her that he was I Am. This is the same name God used for himself with Moses. She went and told her village of him so they came to see him. Many people became saved after listening to Jesus.

653. Living together is not the same as marriage. Jesus told the Samaritan woman things about her a stranger would not know such as her many marriages and her current situation of living in sin, living with a man with whom she was

not married (This tells us living with someone without being officially married, sometimes called common law marriage, is sin) (Jn. 4:16–18).

654. Salvation for the world is from the Jews, through Jesus (Jn. 4:22).

655. Jesus told his disciples his food was to do the will of God the Father who sent him (Jn. 4:34). Doing God's will nourishes our soul.

656. God the Father has given judgment of all people to the Son, Jesus, so that all will honor the Son as even they honor the Father. He who does not honor the Son does not honor God the Father (Jn. 5:22–24).

657. Just as God the Father has life in himself, even so he has given to the Son to have life in himself. Jn. 5:26. This is how Jesus raised himself up on the third day after his crucifixion. Jn. 10:18. Jesus will raise up the dead when he returns; those who did good deeds because they are saved to a resurrection of life those who did evil deeds because they are not saved to a resurrection of judgment (Jn. 5:29). The resurrection of the wicked will occur after the millennium, as opposed to the resurrection of the children of God when the millennium begins with Jesus's return (Rev. chapter 20).

658. The works that Jesus did testify that God sent him. Jn. 5:36. The scriptures testify of Jesus as the Messiah (Jn. 5:39).

659. Jesus prophesied that the Jews, in general, would follow a false messiah (Jn. 5:43). This happened before AD 70 when the Roman army destroyed the rebellions that these false messiahs instigated. This may also mean that the majority of Jews will believe that the beast, the Antichrist, is the Messiah.

660. The disciples asked what should they do so that they do the work of God. Jesus answered them, saying, "This is the work of God, that you believe in Him whom He has sent." (Jn. 6:28, 29). This is faith. With good works (bearing fruit), faith is perfected (Jas. 2:22). From the love God places in a believer's heart, they will do good works, in the name of the Lord, for other people and God. From the love for God, a Christian desires to please God, which leads to many goods works. Rather than listing various works for Christians to do, Jesus said what must be done to incite a person to do those things that please God, with the right motives.

661. The bread of God is life from heaven. This life is Jesus, and he will give eternal life to all who believe in him as Lord. He is the bread of life come down from heaven (Jn. 6:33–35, 50, 51).

662. "Once saved always saved" versus "giving up salvation." All people who God gives to Jesus (saves), Jesus will not cast out (Jn. 6:37). Other verses that support the doctrine of once saved always saved: Jn. 10:28, 29, 14:16, 15:16, 17:2; Rom. 8:38, 39; and 1 Pet. 1:5. Matthew 18:22 teaches that God does not have a limit on how much a person sins, and so God takes away their salvation or determines that person will not be saved because they have sinned too much. So a Christian cannot sin too much, or backslide, and as a direct result lose their salvation. However there is scripture, in context, that support the doctrine of a Christian rejecting their salvation: Col. 1:23; Heb. 6:4–6; 1 Tim. 4:1 (2 Thes. 2:3); Jas. 5:19, 20; 2 Pet. 2:20–22; Rev. 2:5, 3:5. All scripture is true and from God, so how do we reconcile these seemingly contradictory verses? An explanation could be that a Christian doesn't lose their salvation at the hand of another such as Satan or other principality or power or by God rejecting them but that

the Christian consciously and deliberately rejects the Lord Jesus and no longer follows him as Lord. They commit the unpardonable sin of blaspheme against the Holy Spirit (Mk. 3:29, 30). So that the cause of a Christian "losing salvation" is really not losing it because Jesus said no one will be able to snatch them out of his hand but them giving it up by deliberately rejecting Christ after having once believed in, and followed, Christ Jesus.

It is also clear from Hebrews 6:4–6 that once a person rejects Jesus after having been saved it is impossible for that person to be saved again. Those who believe in once saved always saved interpret Hebrews 6:4–6 to be a presalvation experience of people where they are convicted of their sins but still reject the Lord and never come to salvation. However, scripture is clear no one can be made a partaker of the Holy Spirit, have the Holy Spirit in her or him, unless they have been saved (Jn. 7:39, 14:17, 20:22; Ac. 1:8, 2:1–4, 38; 1 Cor. 12:3). Partaker means one who takes part in something. Partake means to possess or share a certain nature. However, John 14:16 says Jesus intends for the Holy Spirit to be in believers forever. Does everything that God intends happen? He wants all people to be saved (2 Tim. 2:4, 2 Pet. 3:9), but most people reject him and are not saved. God knew before he created the world who would be saved and have the Holy Spirit in them forever though. This is a difficult topic and one which some Christians get riled up about if other Christians do not agree with them.

There is only one truth, so only one interpretation is right. Whether the truth is once saved always saved or a Christian can throw away their salvation deliberately, not by backsliding or sinning too much and "lose their salvation" at the hand of God, it seems knowledgeable Christians may never agree. To call the other's opinion blasphemy is wrong and gives place to Satan to cause division in the church of God. So we should respect the other's opinion, even if we don't agree, on the matter and work together on saving the lost, while there is yet time.

663. God wills that of all who are saved Jesus will lose none but raise them up on the last day of this age (Jn. 6:39, 40). God also wills that all people would be saved and to come to the knowledge of truth (1 Tim. 2:4). However, not all people are saved, and God is omnipotent, so not all people are saved so that prophecies will be fulfilled. The Lord has not returned yet because God is patient, not willing that anybody would perish in the lake of fire but for all to come to repentance (2 Pet. 3:9). This tells us that either Peter was talking about all people, or all people that God has predetermined to be saved, are saved. If it is the first, even though God wills all people to be saved, it does not happen because he gives people free will. This is the Arminian philosophy. In the Calvinist philosophy, the "all" in 2 Pet. 3:9 refers to all people God has predetermined to be saved. Jesus told us most people choose the way of perishing (Mt. 7:13, 14).

664. God chooses who is saved. He gives faith to believe in Jesus as Lord to whomever He chooses (Jn. 6:64, 65, 15:16, 17:2, 6; Rom. 9:18, 12:3; Eph. 2:8). Since God wills that all be saved, then why does he not save all? Prophecies about the end times and the words of Jesus would not be fulfilled if God saved everyone, and God said his word will be fulfilled, so it is necessary that most people not be saved but reject Christ. Even prayer cannot change this, but the Scripture tell us prayer changes God's mind (that are not contrary to Scripture). Examples are: God allowed Hezekiah to live longer than he said he would (2 Kgs. 20:1–11, Is. 38:4, 5), God relented of punishing Job's friends in response to Job's prayer request (Job 42:8,

9), Jesus turned the water into wine at the request of his mother even though He had not intended to do it (Jn. 2: 4–9), Jesus delivered the gentile woman's child of a demon even though it was not his plan to touch the lives of gentiles yet (Mk. 7:24–30). God is merciful and has more love for all people than anybody can imagine, and he listens to the prayers of his saints.

The effectual fervent prayer of a righteous man accomplishes much (Jas. 5:16). One might then ask, "Why didn't God determine all people to be saved before he spoke to people and Scripture was written since he does not want any to perish?" In other words, "Why did God create Satan and allow sin to enter this world?" If God had made people to not have free will and Satan to not exist then worship by people would be less meaningful than if people had a choice to worship God or not. In a perfect world without Satan, there is little or nothing to draw people's hearts from God, even with the will of the self. This is evident as we read how the world will worship him during the millennium and then turn against him when he lets Satan free in Revelations. How much more meaningful to God is the worship of people who have a choice of whether or not to worship him, especially with the enticements from Satan to the contrary.

665. Jesus did not lie to his brothers about going to the feast of Booths in Judea but wished to go privately, as opposed to publicly (Jn. 7:1,10).

666. If anyone is willing to do God's will, he will be taught of the teachings of God by God and Jesus (Jn. 7:17). The one who seeks God's will seeks for God to receive the glory and not him or herself to receive glory. God reveals to the one who seeks him and desires to do God's will truths from his word in the Holy Scriptures, the Holy Bible.

667. Jesus taught believers to not judge according to appearance but judge with righteous judgment (Jn. 7:24). First of all, Jesus is telling Christians to judge. Christians must tell those of the world that sins are sins, because unsaved people are going to hell when they die unless they repent of their sins and accept Jesus as their Lord. Without sin, there is no need for a savior. To say one cannot judge the actions of another are sin contradicts Jn. 7:24. This means when a believer is tempted to judge someone for appearing to disobey God, the believer must take into account all factors and motivations, as well as other teachings of God.

668. Some of the Jews had believed in tradition that no one would know where the Messiah would come from. This is not scriptural (Jn. 7:27). However, scripture said the Messiah would come from Bethlehem (Mic. 5:2). Some Jews remembered this scripture, so they were confused when they were told Jesus was from Galilee (Jn. 7:41, 42). Had they been earnestly seeking the truth, they would have discovered Jesus was from Bethlehem. Knowledge of the scripture is important to avoid being fooled, but one must also seek truth and desire to love God and others as oneself.

669. The Pharisees were wrong to claim no prophet arises out of Galilee (Jn. 7:52) because Jonah was from Galilee.

670. The woman caught in adultery (Jn. 8:1–11). The Pharisees and scribes caught a woman in the act of adultery and tested Jesus to see if he would follow Mosaic law of stoning those caught in adultery (Lv. 20:10). The law taught that both the man and woman caught in adultery should be stoned and these Pharisees and scribes did not bring the man to Jesus to be stoned. This showed that their intent was not about being obedient to God. Mosaic law was from God, so one would imagine that Jesus would have said they would be right in stoning her, but he tells

them he who is without sin cast the first stone. This puts everything in proper perspective. All these men had sinned at least in their hearts, probably the sin of adultery, so they knew they were guilty in God's eyes also, so they had no right to stone her.

To catch this woman in adultery and test Jesus probably involved planning all of it so they were not about restoring her to God but trying to make Jesus out to be a false prophet or teacher of God. Jesus brings to light here the new covenant of God to mankind that forgiveness and salvation is offered to all sinners who repent of their sins and believe in Jesus as Lord and reject Satan, sin, and self for Christ. Some people like to use this passage to say that Jesus is teaching that all people sin so no one can judge someone else for sinning. Jesus is the judge of all people (2 Tim. 4:1). In John 7:24, Jesus told believers to judge not according to appearance but with righteous judgment. Determining what a person does is a sin based on what the Bible says is not judging that person in that this does not condemn them to hell. Believers will be held accountable by God for their judgments of others so they need to be careful but determining right from wrong actions is necessary. Believers need to hold each other accountable for sins (Mt.18:15).

When believers feel someone is wrong about something they need to first look at themselves to see if there is sin in themselves that they need to take care of before passing judgment. They may find that selfishness in themselves is causing them to think ill of someone else. We do not know all the life circumstances of others and what others are thinking or planning so we may form the wrong opinion of others. There may be exceptional circumstances where the Holy Spirit gives a Christian knowledge of a secret thing or thought of a person to fulfill God's will though (Ac. 5:1, 2). Telling others what God says about things written in the Bible is not judging but imparting knowledge of what God says to others. God expects us to do this, but if the listener rejects it, they are as described by Jesus as dogs or swine hating the Word of God. If they are this way, we are not to continue to share with them what the Word of God says (Mt. 7:6). This is not judging them, but they are revealing who they are by their fruits. Also, this passage of the woman caught in adultery tells us that no one is sinless, therefore righteous enough, to carry out the death penalty for sins that God said deserve the death penalty to Moses.

The Mosaic laws are still valid except for the specific ones addressed in the New Testament like circumcision. God tells us here in John 8:1–11 that the penalties that men can carry out are changed with the new covenant. Also, with the new covenant, the Lord offers forgiveness to those who believe in him as Lord and Savior. All sins though condemn mankind to death so we all die in the flesh, and are worthy of death, spiritually. Those that are not saved when they die will suffer the second death after they are judged at the great white throne of judgment (Rev. 20:11–15).

671. People who do not believe that Jesus is Lord will die in their sins and will go to hell and then the lake of fire (Jn. 8:24).

672. Jesus taught what God the Father taught him (Jn. 8:28, 14:24).

673. True believers in Jesus continue in his word. True believers are obedient to God. If they backslide, they repent and return to God (Jn. 8:31).

674. Believers, not unbelievers, who continue in the Lord's word will know the truth, and the truth will make them

free from the bondage of sin and Satan's hold (Jn. 8:31, 32–36).

675.  Satan is described as a murderer from the beginning (Jn. 8:44). This is most likely in reference to him taking eternal life in the flesh from Adam and Eve. In this verse, Jesus also describes the devil as a liar and the father of lies. This means the devil is never to be trusted. Common lies he tells people are they are not worthy of salvation or to live, to get them to not accept Jesus as Lord, or to kill themselves. He also tells people lies of the validity of the Bible so they will continue in rebellion against God. Also, in this verse, unbelievers in Jesus, sinners, are called children of the devil because they want to do the desires of the devil.

676.  Christians hear the word of God believe it and understand it (Jn. 8:47). This is because God allows believers to hear his word and understand it. Believers do not usually understand everything the Bible says when they first hear or read it, but God opens their minds to understand as much of his word as he knows they are ready to understand. A Christian may not understand a passage of scripture until they have read another passage of scripture later, for instance.

677.  Faithful saints will never die in that they will receive eternal bodies when Jesus returns (Jn. 8:51). Though their fleshly body they are born into dies their soul, lives on forever, and will receive their new imperishable bodies when Jesus returns.

678.  Jesus said, "Truly, truly, I say to you, before Abraham was born, I Am." This is so powerful I can't think of anything else to say regarding it (Jn. 8:58).

679.  An illness, even blindness, is not necessarily because of sin in a person's life or their parents' lives. Sometimes it is so

God's healing works may be displayed so God will receive more glory (Jn. 9:1–3). Also, this chapter shows us that God will sometimes heal sinners who are not saved.

680.    Because of opposition from Satan and the world, resulting in a lack of faith, no one (except the two witnesses in chapter 11 of Revelation) will be able to do the works of God such as miracles and public witnessing for a period during the end times of this age. So Christians must do the work of God while we are free to do so (Jn. 9:4). This verse does not mean miracles and other works of God ceased when Jesus ascended to heaven after his crucifixion. Evidence of that are the miracles mentioned in the New Testament after the gospels.

681.    God does not hear the prayers of sinners except the prayer of seeking him and of repentance and salvation. God hears the prayers of those that are his (Ps. 66:18, 145:19; Jn. 9:31; Ac. 10:1–4).

682.    Jesus does not drive but leads his followers (Jn. 10:3). A Christian can know they are in the will of God when they do not feel conflicted. When a believer seeks to determine whether God is leading he or she regarding something, it is important to remember that love, not guilt, leads a believer to do God's will other than repentance. Guilt only leads a person to repentance, which is the typical first step in a person's salvation, but even after being saved, we sin and need to repent of those sins, but love can likewise lead to repentance. Otherwise, guilt is not from God. The devil drives, but God leads. The Lord's leading is typically peaceful and full of grace and love. That is not to say there can be times when, out of zeal for God, a Christian will not speak boldly to condemn sin and lies. An example of this is when Jesus drove out the moneychangers and those that sold animals for sacrifice from the temple.

683. The devil seeks to steal and kill and destroy (Jn. 10:10). The devil wants to steal faith, love and peace from saints. He also wants to steal people from God and steal people of an eternal life full of grace, love, peace, joy, and mercy from God. The devil seeks to get as many people to die and go to hell and then suffer the second death in the lake of fire as he can. The devil seeks to destroy God's creations (people's lives, marriage, families, the church), causing such things as discord, divorce, mental illness caused by unforgiveness of others, and murder.

684. Jesus brings life, an abundant life. All who believe and follow him will inherit eternal life in the kingdom of God. Saints will also have abundant life here on earth and, after they die, in heaven and then the new heaven and earth. This abundant life is not life full of riches of this world like money and worldly possessions. The Lord's kingdom is not of this world (Jn. 18:36). This abundant life Jesus spoke of is of God's riches of forgiveness, peace, love, and other things we have no idea of yet.

685. The good shepherd lays down his life for the sheep. Jesus is this good shepherd (Jn. 10:11–15, 26, 27). False shepherds flee when danger comes. The sheep (believers) hear and know who the good shepherd (Jesus) is.

686. Jesus said he was going to bring gentiles into the fold of saints that was full of Jews before his first incarnation (Jn. 10:16).

687. Jesus had the power to lay down his life willingly as a sacrifice for all people and to take it up again as he did on the third day after his crucifixion (Jn. 10:17, 18). There is no reason to be angry at the Romans or the Jews for crucifying Jesus because he did it willingly because we all needed him to for our sakes.

688. All Scripture, Old and New Testament, is true and relevant. Jesus fulfilled the Mosaic law and did, and will, fulfill prophecies from the Old Testament. The Mosaic law was to help people live happy, healthy lives and to keep people in a right relationship with God and each other. Jesus fulfilled this. He provides forgiveness of sins, assistance in our relationship with God and others by the work of the Holy Spirit, and eternity with God, to those who believe in him as Lord and Savior, fulfilling the law (Mt. 5:17–19, Jn. 10:35).

689. Jesus had empathy and emotion that caused him to cry. God has feelings (Dt. 6:15, Jn. 11:33–35).

690. Jesus raised Lazarus from the dead when he had been dead four days (Jn. 11:38–44).

691. The Jewish chief priests and Pharisees refused to believe in Jesus as the Messiah even though they knew he had raised Lazarus from the dead. They were afraid many people would believe in Jesus as the Messiah, and it would cause the Romans to fear an uprising and so take away what freedoms they had and their nation. So they conspired the more to kill Jesus (Jn. 11:45–48, 53).

692. Caiaphas, who was high priest the year Jesus was crucified, prophesied Jesus would die for the nation of Israel (all twelve tribes). He died not just for Jews but all people (Jn. 11:49–52).

693. Judas Iscariot stole money from the moneybag that Jesus and his disciples used to buy things, as they needed to (Jn. 12:6). Nowhere in scripture does it say Jesus or the other disciples took Judas to task for this and asked for the money back that he stole. This is an example Christians need to follow in that we are not to demand what is rightly ours. God will judge those who steal from us.

694. God spoke to Jesus where people could hear (Jn. 12:28).

695.　Jesus prophesied that the ruler of this world, Satan, would be cast out of it (Jn. 12:31). This occurs when the devil is bound by an angel of God for a thousand years during the millennium (Rev. 20:1–3).

696.　The refusal of the majority of the Jews to believe in Jesus as the Messiah was prophesied by Isaiah (Is. 6:9, 10, 53:1; Jn. 12:37–41). If the Jews had believed in the gospel, they would not have crucified Jesus, and then the world would be without hope (1 Cor. 2:7, 8).

697.　People who do not accept Jesus's words will be judged by Jesus's words, which were given to him by Father God (Jn. 12:47–50).

698.　God the Father gave Jesus free choice to do God the Father's will of sacrificing himself for the world (Jn. 13:3). Jesus was in the flesh, so he had human traits and desires: he was tempted like as we are, he felt hunger, he had free will to obey God or not (Mt. 4:1–11, Heb. 4:15). In the garden of Gethsemane, Jesus prayed not his will be done but God the Father's will be done. (Lk. 22:42). So Jesus submitted his will to God's will to the point of the most horrendous death known to mankind at the time. This is the example of how submissive we are to be to God's will.

699.　Jesus washed his twelve disciples' feet. He said this was an example to them that they should also wash each other's feet (Jn. 13:1–17). He is Lord and did this. How much more should Christians humble themselves before one another and care for one another?

700.　When Jesus is glorified, God is glorified (Jn. 13:31, 32).

701.　A new commandment Jesus gave to believers: love one another, even as he loved us, that we also love one another. By this all men will know that Christians are his disciples, if they have love for one another (Jn. 13:34, 15:12, 17). Three times Jesus said his commandment to believers was to love one another. This should tell us how important it is to Jesus that Christians love one another. It is like three exclamation points after Jesus's commandment that Christians love one another!!! Jesus said greater love has no one than this that one lay down his or her life for his or her friends (Jn. 15:13). This is an incredible goal of how much Jesus wants Christians to love one another.

Jesus calls Christians who obey him and love other believers as he commands, his friends (Jn. 15:14). As evidence that Christians are friends of Christ rather than slaves, Jesus made known to us all that the Father told him, which is written in the Bible (Jn. 15:15). Love is greater than spiritual gifts God gives believers (1 Cor. 13:1–13). Faith, hope, having knowledge of scripture or what is spoken in other tongues, speaking in other tongues, and prophesying are not as great as love. So disagreeing over finer points of doctrine that may be controversial such as eschatology to the point of classifying those that do not interpret scripture the same way as someone to be shunned is wrong.

That is a misinterpretation of Galatians 1:9. Paul was speaking to the Galatians about adding to or taking away from the gospel of salvation simply through repentance of sin and belief in, and confession of, Jesus as the Son of God who died for all people's sins and arose from the dead in spirit and body and making him Lord of one's life. Christians can have perfect love because they recognize the love God has for them and accepted it (actually I believe a person embraces it when they become saved). Love for others then comes from the love God has put in a Christian's heart (1 Jn. 4:19), so Christians cannot even brag about their love.

702.    There are many dwelling places in God's house. Jesus has been preparing a place for each saint since he ascended

to heaven. Jesus said he will come again and receive us to himself. He did not say he will collect us to himself without coming again (Jn. 14:2, 3). When Jesus returns, he will descend from heaven with the sound of the last trumpet of God. The dead saints will rise first, and then those saints who are alive and remain on earth will meet the Lord in the air (1 Th. 4:16, 17). This does not say there will be a rapture of the Christians from the earth without the Lord returning. The place that Jesus prepares for each Christian will be greater than imaginable.

703. Jesus said to him, "I am the way, the truth, and the life; no one comes to the Father but by Me" (Jn. 14:6). Herein, Jesus claims to be the only way to salvation and heaven. There is no other way to heaven and God than to become a Christian since Jesus's first incarnation. He also claimed to be the only truth—no other religion is totally truthful and is therefore false, a deceit by Satan. Jesus does not lie. All that Jesus said is truth. He also claimed he is the only way to live forever and that life will be with God. Saints will live forever because of Jesus. Jews were called first to follow Jesus, the Messiah, and then the rest of the world. There is no other way to heaven and God than through belief in Jesus as the Messiah, which is Christianity. All others will perish in hell and then the lake of fire.

704. Jesus said he who has seen him has seen the Father (Jn. 14:9). In that Jesus is God this is possible. People of the time of his first incarnation did not see the Spirit of God the Father, but they saw Jesus, and Jesus and Father God are one. People who never have seen Jesus when he was in the flesh here on earth and yet believe in him know him and hear his voice. We may not know exactly how he, or God the Father, look, but we will know them when we see them.

705.    Saints will do greater works than what Jesus did before
        he returns, Jesus said (Jn. 14:12). Obviously there will be
        more numerous works, including miracles, done by saints
        before the Lord returns because of the time laps since
        he was here on earth and the number of saints doing his
        work. Jesus may have also meant the magnitude of the
        works, or miracles, done by saints will be greater. Time
        will tell. I am looking forward to a saint praying for a
        mountain to move, for the glory of God, and God moving
        the mountain for the whole world to see.

706.    Jesus said, "Whatever you ask in My name, that will I
        do, so that the Father may be glorified in the Son. If you
        ask anything in My name, I will do it" (Jn. 14:13, 14).
        Experience has taught people that this does not mean
        God will answer a Christian's prayer the way the Christian
        wants it to be answered always. Jesus is not a genie at
        the beckon call of Christians. Jesus is talking about a
        prayer request that honors God without self-serving
        intent. Even then the way God answers the prayer may be
        different than the way the Christian asks of God. In the
        Lord's Prayer example to the disciples (Mt. 6: 9, 10), Jesus
        showed believers that when they pray, they should ask for
        God's will be done and not the believer's will be done. For
        instance, when a Christian prays for someone who is ill to
        recover and live, God may not heal the person physically
        but will allow the person to die. Also, the prayer by a saint
        for a sinner to be saved may not result in that person
        becoming saved. In the first instance, God is ultimately
        in control, and we just have to trust him regardless of the
        short-term outcome. In the latter instance, the sinner has
        free will and must decide whether or not to accept Jesus as
        Lord, and even with this, God is in control.

        Also, God sometimes answers a Christian's prayer
        request later than the Christian desires. This teaches the

Christian patience. God may answer the prayer in a way differently than asked for. When a Christian prays to God they need to be careful not to ask God to answer their prayer in such a specific manner that the person praying is not submitting their will to God and is in essence taking God's role of working all the details of how the prayer is to be answered. Again, pray for God's will be done, as Jesus did in the garden of Gethsemane, about whatever is the petition of God. Since God is omnipotent and omniscient, then one could ask why pray since God's will will be done anyway? It helps the believer's heart submit to God's will. Then the believer is compelled to pray to God to help them do as God wills. Prayer also is fellowship time between a believer and God.

A loving father wants his children to talk to him and let their desires be known to him. He will respond to these requests in the best interest of the child. He knows giving his children what they want is not always the best response. A loving father also desires time with his children where the children do not ask him for things but tell him they love him, speak well of him, and just enjoy each other's company. So should believers do this with God. A child who willingly and wholeheartedly does as his loving father desires please his father and shows respect and love for the father. Believers should live their lives this way also, and they will live their lives this way if they love the Lord (Jn. 14:15, 21). This makes a believer's life more meaningful, sweeter and less stressful.

Believers do not always do this because of the struggles we have with our flesh, which cause us to sin. Other people who hear a believer pray for God's will to be done learn how they should pray also. Praying for God's will to be done also asks God to intervene against Satan and his forces, so that rather than Satan's will be done in a matter God's will is done. If, while praying for God's will to be done, the Holy Spirit leads a believer to pray to rebuke the devil and his demons or cast a demon out of someone, then the believer should pray as the Holy Spirit guides them and God will do this. The Holy Spirit does as God wills and guides believers if believers are submissive to God's will enough to hear the Holy Spirit guide them.

707.    The Holy Spirit testifies to believers all the truth. Unbelievers do not receive the Holy Spirit, so they cannot fully understand scripture. The Holy Spirit convicts sinner (the world) of their sins, Jesus' righteousness, and judgment to come so a sinner sees they are in need of the savior Jesus. Verse 26 of John 14 does not say the Holy Spirit would come in the place of Jesus and become the way of salvation, as some say. The Holy Spirit came in the name of Jesus, bearing witness and confirming that he is the Messiah and Lord. The Holy Spirit will never leave believers (v. 16) (Jn. 14:16, 17, 26, 15:26, 27, 16:8–11). If the sinner accepts this conviction by the Holy Spirit, they repent of their sins and ask Jesus to come into their heart and save them. The Holy Spirit then infills the person as they do this, not sometime later and only manifested by speaking in other tongues. The Holy Spirit helps believers understand what the Bible, and therefore God, says. Jesus also said the Holy Spirit will disclose to believers what is to come in the future (Jn. 16:12–15). This was done to John, and that is how he wrote Revelations. Jesus promised he would send the Holy Spirit after he died (Jn. 14:16, 17, 15:26, 16:7; Ac. 1:5, 8). The Holy Spirit has always existed (Gen. 1:2), which makes sense since it is part of God.

708.    People who do not obey God do not love him (Jn. 14:24). This does not mean if a saint sins they do not love God except at the time the sin they show they do not love God

enough to keep them from sinning. The person who sins regularly shows they regularly do not love God. This is evidence of not being saved. If that person claims to be saved, then they should respond to the word of God and repent and change their ways. If they claim to be saved and rebel against the word of God shared by another believer, then they may not be saved; God knows.

709.    Perfect peace is given by Jesus to saints. Not peace as the world knows it but a peace that reassures and quiets the soul (Jn. 14:27). The saint knows they are destined for eternity with the beloved Lord no matter what happens to him or her here on earth.

710.    While Jesus said he and the Father are one, He said, "The Father is greater than I" (Jn. 14:28). Some people take this to mean that Jesus said God is forever greater than him. Jesus said he was here to do the will of the Father (Jn. 4:34). He said he spoke and did as God instructed him (Jn. 12:49, 14:31, 17:8). Jesus prayed not his will be done but God the Father's will be done (Lk. 22:42). Other people take John 14:28 to mean that he was not glorified as much as the Father in his present incarnate state and that he would be in the same glorious state as God when he ascended back to heaven. So they say Jesus meant he was not as great as God only while he was here on earth, but he would go back to his coequal greatness as God state when he returned to heaven. Jesus said, "I and the Father are one" (Jn. 10:30). Jesus came from the Father and was going back to him (Jn. 13:3). After death and hell are cast into the lake of fire, Jesus will be subjected to God the Father so that God may be all in all. This means Jesus will no longer be needed as the Mediator between man and God after the great white throne of judgment so that the Son may resume his former state as before his first incarnation (1 Cor. 15:21–28, 50–57, Rev. 20:14). God

will still be triune as Jesus is the same today, yesterday and forever (Heb. 13:8).

711.   Unfruitful branches in the vine (Jn. 15:1–11). Jesus said he is the true vine and his Father is the vinedresser. He said God takes away from the vine every branch that does not bear fruit, and God prunes every branch that bears fruit. God prunes it so that it will bear more fruit. Jesus appointed Christians to bear fruit (Jn. 15:16). Jesus said to his disciples, and by extension all believers, that they are the branches and that they cannot bear fruit unless they abide in him. If anyone does not abide in Jesus, he or she is taken away from the vine, thrown away, dried up, and then thrown into the fire where they are burned. If a Christian keeps Jesus's commandments, they abide in Jesus's love.

One can make a case that Jesus is talking about Christians that are unfruitful show they no longer believe in the Lord as Lord so they are removed from the vine. To be in the vine to begin with, they had to be saved. Others can make the case that these branches are unfruitful because they are not fully in the vine so they were not saved to begin with. In both cases, a person who claims to be a Christian but does not bear fruit has no part in the kingdom of God and will go to hell. This should motivate Christians to do the work of God, such as witnessing so people will be saved and discipling new believers so they will know the word of God (the Bible).

Remember Jesus's kingdom is not of the world but of the kingdom of God so cares of this life are not near as important as the souls of individuals. This passage also tells us that God prunes Christians who bear fruit so they will bear more fruit. Pruning involves removing parts of a branch that are not desirable by the vinedresser. God is constantly working on fruitful Christians to improve their ability to bear fruit and be the branch that God desires. Sometimes this is painful to the fruitful Christian because there are some things about us we don't want to lose or change but it is for the best. As a Christian is pruned and becomes more Christ-like and as they participate in winning and discipling souls for Christ, they will be full of the joy of Jesus.

712. The world (the people who are not saved) hates Christians. This should not be surprising because the world first hated Jesus (and thus God the Father), and the slave is not above his master (Jn. 15:18–25).

713. Since Jesus came and started his ministry here on earth, during his first incarnation, people have been without excuse for their sins (Jn. 15:22). Before this, the Jews were the only people going to heaven unless God was gracious enough to reveal himself to other people, as he did with Rahab the harlot and Ruth. Creation itself has always declared that God existed and anyone who wanted to follow God could by searching for him. Before the Jewish religion was started by Mosaic law people of the world had creation to witness to them about God, and there are many examples of other people following God in obedience such as Adam and Eve, Job, Noah, Abraham, Isaac, and Jacob. Even after Jesus's first incarnation, creation has declared that God exists, and he has revealed himself to those he has chosen to be with him in his kingdom. However there are no other religions that will get anyone to heaven (Jn. 14:6). If God revealed himself to anyone through dream, vision, or the Holy Spirit, without them hearing about Jesus from another person, God would not reveal another way to heaven than by Jesus (Ac. 4:12).

714. Jesus foretold persecution of believers would occur by people thinking they were doing it in service to God (Jn. 16:2, Ac. 26:9–11, Rev. 6:9). Jews fulfilled this prophecy

when they persecuted members of the early church, many thinking they were doing it in service to God. In the end times, persecution of Christians, including imprisonment and execution, will occur by the Antichrist (beast of the sea/man of lawlessness) and his followers. This occurs after he tries to kill all the Jews, but God rescues 144,000 Jews as a remnant (Jer. 15:2; Lk. 21:24; Jn. 16:20; Rev. 7:1–8, 12:13–17, 13:7–10, 14:1–5). These verses about the end times persecution of believers do not say the persecutors think they will do it in service to God, but perhaps that will be the case. Muslims persecute non-Muslims, thinking they do it in service to God.

715.    The Holy Spirit is the Spirit of truth and speaks to Christians what he hears, even what is to come (Jn. 16:13). This is knowledge for prophecy. The gift of prophecy did not cease with the resurrection of Jesus. If a Christian feels the Holy Spirit has told them something to come that they are to share with others, then they need to first make sure it does not contradict the Bible. If it does conflict with scripture, they are to pray to God to protect them from Satan trying to influence them. If it does not, then they should share it as God directs them. Those who hear it are to test the prophecy to make sure it does not contradict the Bible also. If it does, then they should admonish the one who spoke it. If it does not, then they should obey whatever God compels them to do.

716.    When Jesus returns, saints will not question him about anything (Jn. 16:22, 23). Saints will not need to ask about things we didn't understand while in the flesh because the Lord will reveal things fully when he returns (1 Cor. 13:12).

717.    When we pray requests to God in Jesus's name, it is not like Jesus in turn makes those requests of God. God hears

them directly and answers them because he loves us (Jn. 16:26, 27).

718.   Even though Christians have trials and tribulations here on earth, Jesus told us to take courage because he has overcome the world (Jn. 16:33). Christians need to look at their lives with the perspective of eternity with confidence in the Lord. Whatever tribulations we endure here on earth will be short compared to an eternity with the Lord.

719.   Jesus's prayer for the eleven disciples before his crucifixion (Jn. 17:1–19). I say eleven because Judas was predestined to be a false disciple and betrayer of Jesus (Ps.41:9, 109:8; Zec. 11:12, 13). Jesus said his word, which came from God, gave the disciples joy. He prayed that the disciples not be taken from the world even though the world hated them because of God's word, but he prayed they would be kept from the evil one (Satan). History showed the disciples suffered, and many were martyred for their faith, so when Jesus prayed to keep them from Satan, he wasn't praying that Satan would never harm them. The eleven disciples were kept safe from death long enough to spread the Lord's word as God intended, and they were kept from turning away from their faith.

This is evident when Jesus follows, in his prayer, saying they are not of the world even as I am not of the world. Jesus asked God to sanctify them in the truth, saying God's word is truth. This tells us sanctification of believers comes from God's word (the Bible). Sanctification means to set apart or become holy. As a saint submits their will to God, studies the Bible, and applies it to themselves and their lives, and prays to God they become more and more apart from the world and more like Jesus, who was the only perfect man on earth. Saints will never be perfect until they die in the flesh and their soul goes to be with the Lord, because they are not Jesus. A saint will have more struggles with sin the less time they spend in God's word and conforming to his word. Jesus said he sent the disciples into the world even as he came into the world. So believers are to go into the world and witness and make disciples of people whenever and wherever they can.

720.  Jesus's prayer for all believers (Jn. 17:20–26). Believers are to be as one even as the Son and the Father are one. This tells us the Lord wants believers to be in agreement on doctrine and what we say is truth. This also tells us we are to love one another as Jesus and God love each other. This way the world will be more likely to believe in Jesus as Lord, sent by God. He goes on to say believers are to be perfected in unity. The way this can be done is through study of God's word, submitting our thoughts, pride, and desires to God, willing to be wrong to be made right. This tells us God does not want the divisions and various denominations that are among his church (all believers) in the world. Stubbornness, pride, and jealousy are some of the causes of these divisions in the church. Jesus prayed that all believers would be with him where he was. So believers will be with him always: When we die, our soul goes to be with him in heaven; when he returns, our souls will be placed in an eternal body, and we will be with Jesus here on earth during the millennium; and when this earth and heaven are replaced with the new heaven and new earth, we will be with Jesus there forever. Jesus makes the point he existed and was loved by God before creation. Jesus makes God known to believers so that the love God has for his one and only Son may be in believers and Jesus himself in them. Sacrificial love for others is a sign of a true believer. It is self-evident that Jesus is in believers spiritually, not physically.

721. When Jesus said, "I Am" (original scripture does not have "he" in Jesus's response) in the garden of Gethsemane to those who were seeking to capture him, they fell backward. This is his same response when Moses asked the Lord who he should say sent him when the Jews asked him when he goes to bring them out of Egypt. The power of the word of God is evident in that his captors fell backward when he said, "I Am" (Jn. 18:6).

722. Jesus secured the safety of his disciples, telling his captors to let his disciples go their way, in fulfillment of his word, "Of those whom You have given Me I lost none" (Jn. 18:8, 9, 17:12).

723. Jesus said his kingdom was not of this world (Jn. 18:36). Jesus's kingdom is the kingdom of God. When Jesus returns, this world will become part of his kingdom (Rev. 11:15). He will reign over this world for a thousand years during the millennium. Jesus did not fight over this world while he was here on earth, so neither should we. Christians' concerns and efforts need to be for the kingdom of God.

724. When a Christian is suffering persecution, they need to know that the persecutor does not have power over them except what God allows (Jn. 19:11). This is not to say we should not try to defend ourselves, as Paul defended himself before leaders.

725. Not all sin the same, perhaps. Even though all sin destines those who are not saved to hell and then the lake of fire, not all sin is the same in God's eyes. There are degrees of evil or sin and thus degrees of punishment by God for sinners. Knowledge of the truth before the sin seems to play a role in this (Mt. 12:31, 32, Jn. 19:11, Heb. 10:26–29, 1 Jn. 5:16, 17). The various degrees of punishments God told the Jews to use for various sins showed that God

views sins in degrees of severity. These were for civil law but also show the heart of God. The worst sins then were sins worthy of death of the physical body of the sinner: murder, adultery, homosexuality, bestiality, various forms of incest, rape of a woman who is engaged, witchcraft (witch, spiritist, or medium), cursing or striking one's parents, kidnapping and violently treating or selling the victim, idolatry or worshipping any other god than God, blasphemy against God, false witness in a capital case, breaking the Sabbath, and being a false prophet.

Proverbs 6:16–19 says there are seven things which are an abomination to God: pride, lying, killing of an innocent person, a heart that devises wicked plans, desire to do evil, false testimony, and spreading strife among fellow believers of God. All people sin and fall short of the glory of God (Rom. 3:23), and the wages of sin is death (Rom. 6:23), an eternity in the lake of fire. So all unrepentant (unsaved) people will go to hell. The degree of sin an unrepentant person does not determine if he or she is going to hell and then the lake of fire, but it determines the degree of punishment from God. The Bible does not say how God will vary his punishment but that all sinners will be tormented forever in the lake of fire. James 2:10, 11 tells us that if we are guilty of transgressing one law of God we are guilty of transgressing all laws. This then seems to equalize sinners, so all are unworthy of going to heaven except through salvation by belief in Jesus as Lord.

726.   Jesus breathed on the disciples after his resurrection and said to them, "Receive the Holy Spirit" (Jn. 20:22). The Holy Spirit was in men in rare instances before the day of Pentecost. Examples were king Saul; King David; Samson; Elizabeth and Zecharias, the parents of John the Baptist; and John the Baptist. Here Jesus is either promising the coming of the Holy Spirit after he ascends to heaven or

he is giving them the Holy Spirit so they can have the power of the Holy Spirit to start God's work without interruption. The former seems the most likely because Acts 2:3 says the disciples received the Holy Spirit on the day of Pentecost.

727. Jesus said blessed are those who have not seen him and yet believe in him as Lord (Jn. 20:29).

728. The disciple John said Jesus performed many more miracles than what is recorded in his gospel and that he recorded the ones he did to help people know that Jesus is Lord (Jn. 20:30, 31).

729. The third time Jesus appeared, after his resurrection, to the disciples was while the disciples were fishing. He miraculously helped them catch many fish. Here he also told Simon Peter to feed and tend to his sheep three times (Jn. 21:1–19). The disciples were called to full-time ministry rather than typical work for a living.

# ACTS

730. Luke was most likely the author of Acts (Lk. 1:3, Ac. 1:1). Luke traveled with Paul (Col. 4:14).

731. Jesus appeared to believers over a period of forty days, after his resurrection until his ascension (Ac. 1:3).

732. Jesus promised Christians they would be baptized with the Holy Spirit not many days from the time between his resurrection and ascension (Ac. 1:5). So the Holy Spirit had not come yet into saints as a routine. The Holy Spirit had filled some believers over the course of history such as Samson, King David, King Saul, and Zacharias, but the only person the Holy Spirit stayed in, as in Christians after Pentecost, was King David (1Sam 16:13) and probably John the Baptist. John the Baptist is the only person in the Bible said to have received the Holy Spirit in his mother's womb (Lk. 1:15).

733. The Father determines future events and when the Lord will return (Ac. 1:7).

734. Jesus said the apostles, and by extension all Christians, would receive power after that the Holy Spirit would come upon them and that they shall be witnesses all over the earth, starting at Jerusalem (Ac. 1:8). This tells us the Holy Spirit is to give Christians power to witness.

735. Jesus ascended up into heaven in a cloud. Two angels told those that saw him ascend that Jesus would return in like manner (Ac. 1:9–11).

736. The apostles fulfilled prophecy (Ps. 109:8) in choosing Matthias to replace Judas Iscariot's place among them (Ac. 1:15–26).

737. Day of Pentecost—Feast of Weeks (Ex. 34:22, 23) or Harvest (Lv. 23:16)—where the offering of first fruits was given and celebrated fifty days after the Passover (Acts 2). This is fulfillment of Jesus's promise of sending the Comforter, which is the Holy Spirit, to believers (Jn. 14: 16, 17, 15:26, 16:7; Ac. 1:5, 8). On the day of Pentecost, the Holy Spirit came from heaven with a noise like a violent rushing wind and there appeared to about 120 disciples (Ac. 1:15), including the 12 apostles, tongues as of fire distributing themselves and resting on each of the disciples. And the disciples were filled with the Holy Spirit and began speaking in other tongues, as the Spirit gave them utterance. They were speaking in several different languages of people in the area where those people could hear them, speaking of the mighty deeds of God. Some thought the disciples were drunk, while others were amazed since the apostles had no way of knowing all these languages.

Peter told the listeners that they were not drunk but that this was fulfillment of the prophecy of Joel: "And it shall be in the last days God says, that I will pour forth of My Spirit on all mankind; and your sons and your daughters shall prophesy, and your young men shall see visions, and your old men shall dream dreams; even My bondslaves, both men and women, I will in those days pour forth My Spirit and they shall prophesy. And I will grant wonders in the sky above and signs on the earth below, blood and fire and vapor of smoke. The sun will be turned into darkness and the moon into blood, before the great and glorious day of the Lord shall come. And it shall be that everyone who calls on the name of the Lord will be saved." Here Joel's prophecy ends with the requirement to be saved is to call on the Jesus, which would require belief he is Lord. God made it possible for the disciples to witness to many people from several countries of various languages to hear the gospel of Jesus on the day of Pentecost. They believed and were saved so then they took the gospel of Jesus to their nations and people, who then heard the gospel, and so the gospel spread across these nations and people. This is a marvelous thing. Speaking in tongues is not for proof that someone is saved but for someone to miraculously spread the gospel to those whose language they do not speak and for edification of the one speaking in tongues (1 Cor. 14:4). The Holy Spirit has always existed (Gen.1:2), which makes sense since it is part of God.

738. Jesus descended to hell between his death on the cross and his ascension to heaven (Ac. 2:27–31, Eph. 4:9, 10). While there, he made proclamation to the fallen angels that did evil during Noah's time (1 Pet. 3:19–20). The eight souls delivered in 1 Peter is referring to Noah, his wife, and Noah's three sons and their wives, not to eight souls saved by Jesus's visit to hell. So then Jesus conquered both death and hell and has the keys to them (Rev. 1:18).

739. King David prophesied that the Messiah would be buried but not suffer decay (Ps. 16:10). Jesus fulfilled this prophecy in that he arose three days after his death in body and spirit (Ac. 2:29–36).

740. When asked by those convicted by the Holy Spirit what they must do to be saved Peter told them they needed to repent and be baptized in the name of the Lord Jesus Christ for the forgiveness of sins; and they would receive the gift of the Holy Spirit (Ac. 2:37–38). This tells us to be saved one must repent of their sins seeking forgiveness, in the name of Jesus. This implies that the one repenting believes the gospel that Jesus is Lord and that he died for the sins of the world but is raised in body and spirit. With this in mind, the one repenting would readily confess

what they believe. Then the one seeking salvation is to be baptized in the name of Jesus Christ.

The examples given in the New Testament are full emersion in water after the person repents of their sins, and believes and confesses the truth of the gospel of Jesus. Peter finishes with saying, "And you will receive the gift of the Holy Spirit" after having repented and gotten baptized. This implies the Holy Spirit enters a new believer after they have become saved and then are baptized in water. However scripture says the Holy Spirit is in those who obey God and become saved (Acts 5:32; John 3:5; Romans 8:9; 1 Cor. 6:19; 12:13; Col. 1:21–23). So Peter said baptism because that is the first act of obedience of a new believer, not because a person has to be baptized to receive the Holy Spirit.

Peter did not say that this baptism was of the Holy Spirit. "The gift of the Holy Spirit" means the Holy Spirit is a gift from God to all who become saved as a consequence of becoming saved not as a step in becoming saved. "The gift of the Holy Spirit" is not speaking in other tongues though speaking in other tongues is one manifestation of being filled with the Holy Spirit (1 Cor. 12:7–11). Those people who believed in Jesus as Lord and did not receive the Holy Spirit, because it had not come yet into all those who believed, before they died were saved and went to heaven as exemplified by the thief who became saved while he was dying on a cross by Jesus. This example also shows us that baptism is not necessary to be saved and to go to heaven.

741. Whoever Jesus calls to himself will be saved (Ac. 2:39). People who become saved are called by Jesus. Even though people are given free choice the faith to believe in Jesus as Lord comes from God (Eph. 2:8, 9).

742.    The early church showed believers today how the church today needs to take care of its own believers who are in need of necessities and those preaching and teaching full-time. They sold their possessions to help fellow believers in need. They supported those doing full-time ministry work, such as witnessing, so that those doing full-time ministry work could spend all their time doing God's work rather than spending time working to earn a living for themselves and their families. Those who work harder at preaching and teaching should receive more honor, which may mean more money, but not to the point where they have too much or those who work less lack their necessities (Ac. 2:44, 45, 4:32–35, 6:1–7; 1 Cor. 9:3–14; 2 Cor. 8:12–15; 1 Tim. 5:17, 18). They did this voluntarily (Ac. 5:4-"After it was sold was it not in your control?").

It was not communism, where the government takes everyone's possessions, with or without permission of the possessor, and distributes as the government sees fit (usually those who have insider connections receive the most). However scripture also tells us that people who are not willing to work for their necessities are not to even eat (2 Thes. 3:10). Because human nature is to get all a person can with as little effort as possible people will be inclined to take advantage of charity. If a person knows they will not eat unless they work for it, then they will work because of a natural sense of preservation. If a person is totally disabled then their necessities would be greater and the early church example would be to meet their greater necessities.

743.    The early church members were of one mind (Ac. 2:46). There were not doctrinal differences. Selfish desires like pride, lust for power, money, or sex, and envy cause divisions and various denomination in the church (Jas.

4:1, 2). Differences of doctrine, and thus denominations, are not of God but of the flesh and Satan (1 Cor. 14:33).

744. The early church met together daily praising God and even eating together. This unity and sincerity made sinners look favorably on the church's religion and as a result people were being saved daily (Ac. 2:46).

745. God used Peter to heal a lame man (Ac. 3:1–10).

746. The God of Abraham, Isaac, and Jacob in the Old Testament is the same as the God of the New Testament (Father of the Lord Jesus) (Ac. 3:13).

747. Jesus fulfilled the promise God gave to Abraham to bless all nations through his seed because Jesus came from the lineage of Abraham and offers salvation to all nations (Ac. 3:25, Gen 22:18).

748. Peter, filled by the Holy Spirit, spoke boldly and in his native language to his and John's persecutors (Ac. 4:8–12). The persecutors here were Jewish leaders. Peter did not speak in other tongues as the Holy Spirit moved him to speak, but he spoke in understandable language to all that were there so they would be told the truth plainly. God wants all people to hear the gospel of Jesus in understandable language. On the day of Pentecost several foreigners heard the gospel of Jesus miraculously and were saved so that the gospel was sent throughout the world in various languages. So speaking in other tongues is not the only manifestation of being filled with the Holy Spirit.

749. There is salvation in no one else than Jesus. There is no other way to heaven than by Jesus. There is no other name whereby we must be saved. This scripture does not say we are saved by the name of the Holy Spirit, or Holy Ghost as some people like to call the Holy Spirit; it says we are saved by the name of Jesus. Jesus paid the price for everyone's sins. A person must become a Christian,

believer, and follower of Jesus as the Messiah and Lord to go to heaven. The Holy Spirit convicts people to repent and become saved and, when they become saved, it infills them (Ac. 4:12; Mt. 1:21; Jn. 3:16, 10:7–9, 14:6).

750. When mankind's laws conflict with instructions from God such as witnessing or believing in Jesus as Lord and Messiah, it is better to obey God rather than mankind (Ac. 4:18–20, 5:29; Mt. 28:19–20). Though God does not tell us, we have to speak publicly where we would be killed or harmed for witnessing publicly.

751. Persecution of the church fulfilled and still fulfills prophecy (Ps. 2:1–3, Ac. 4:23–30).

752. After Peter and John were released, they went to fellow believers to tell them what had happened and they all rejoiced, remembered God's word, and spoke it as they prayed to God. As soon as they had finished praying the place where they had gathered was shaken and they were all filled with the Holy Spirit and began to speak the word of God with boldness (Ac. 4:31). The Holy Spirit had already been given as a gift to all believers starting on the day of Pentecost, so they had the Holy Spirit in them already, so when the verse says they were filled with the Holy Spirit, it means they were overwhelmingly moved by the Holy Spirit. The Holy Spirit took control of them so much that their flesh was overpowered so they would be completely obedient to God. When this happened, they spoke the word of God with boldness. They did not fear what man could do to them because the Holy Spirit in them overpowered the flesh. Of note, they did not speak with other tongues as some suggest a person has to do when they are saved and filled with the Holy Spirit.

753. Ananias, with his wife Sapphira, tried to receive more honor than they deserved from church members by

saying they sold their property for less than they did and claiming the amount they were giving to the church was all they received for the sale of their property, while pocketing the difference. Peter said they were lying to God by doing this, and God took away their lives that day as Peter confronted them about their deception (Ac. 5:1–11). I imagine similar deception is done today, and I have not heard of people dying because of it suddenly, but these verses teach believers about the seriousness with which God takes dishonesty.

754. Many signs and wonders, including healing of illnesses and delivery from demon possession, were done at the hands of the apostles. This not only benefited the receivers of these miracles but led to many people believing and becoming saved (Ac. 5:12–16).

755. Though the Jewish religious leaders imprisoned and persecuted the apostles, the apostles continued to preach and teach the word of God. God even delivered them from prison (Ac. 5:17–21, 40–42).

756. The Holy Spirit is given by God (gift) to all who obey him (Ac. 5:32). Those who obey God are saints, believers, and followers of Jesus as Lord and Messiah. When a person does this, they become saved. The verse says all who do this receive the Holy Spirit from God. Therefore, when a person becomes saved, in obedience to God's word, they receive the Holy Spirit. Receiving the Holy Spirit is not a required step in becoming saved but a gift from God to those who become saved.

757. A preacher is not to be burdened with taking care of the physical needs, like feeding, of others (Ac. 6:1–4). A preacher is to spend his time praying, studying God's word, and preaching. This does not mean a preacher should not help with the physical needs of others. They

need to be compassionate and do as God directs them. Godly men were chosen to care for the physical needs of others, specifically widows, by the church. Today we call these men deacons. The apostles laid their hands on them after praying (Ac. 6:5, 6).

758.    Stephen was martyred by stoning by the Jews who refused to believe in Jesus as the Messiah. Yet Stephen asked God to forgive those who stoned him (Ac. 7:54–60). This is a great example for us today to forgive those who unjustly persecute us. Saul, whom the Lord later called to be his disciple, was there at Stephens stoning, consenting to it (Ac. 7:58–8:1).

759.    Persecution of the early church made the believers scatter away from their persecutors. This caused the gospel to be preached and many new believers were added to the church in more regions than before the persecution (Ac. 8:1–4). So God made good out of what evil people meant for bad.

760.    Holy Spirit in new believers (Ac. 8:14–40). Because verses 16 and 17 say the Holy Spirit had not yet fallen upon any of the new Samaritan believers that Philip had lead to the Lord, and that these new believers received the Holy Spirit after the apostles laid their hands on them, there are some people who say the Holy Spirit is not in all new believers but comes later. They say a person can be a believer and follower of Jesus as Lord and not have the Holy Spirit in them. They also say if a new believer does not speak in other tongues automatically, then the new believer needs to prayed over with the laying on of hands of someone Spirit filled to receive the gift of the Holy Spirit. They also say the manifestation of being filled with, or baptized by, the Holy Spirit is speaking in other tongues because people spoke in other tongues on the day of Pentecost and apparently here in Acts 8. These same people say that

when Jesus said the Holy Spirit would come in his name (Jn. 14:26) that Jesus meant that the Holy Spirit would take Jesus's place in salvation and that salvation is not in the gospels but through the Holy Spirit.

This is another gospel and is a lie from Satan, and those who continue to preach this after being enlightened to the truth are in danger of judgment by God (Gal. 1:6–9). These ones typically say that when the Bible talks about baptism starting in Acts, it is talking about baptism in the Holy Spirit as evidenced by speaking in tongues. However, scripture says the Holy Spirit is in those who obey God and become saved (Acts 5:32; John 3:5; Romans 8:9; 1 Cor. 6:19, 12:13). Scripture also says that not all Christians speak in other tongues (1 Cor. 12:30). Paul even said he wished all would speak in tongues but even more that they would prophesy (1 Cor. 14:5). This tells us the early church recognized that not all people who are saved and going to heaven speak in other tongues. So why does Acts 8:16 and 17 say what they do? These new Samaritan believers had not spoken in other tongues as had been happening in other places, so the apostles Peter and John wanted confirmation that these Samaritans were truly believers. So they prayed over them, with the laying on of their hands, and God was gracious enough to give the gift of speaking in other tongues to the new converts in Samaria. This edified the new believers as well as reassured the apostles that the new believers were saved.

The last passage where Philip, immediately after this experience in Samaria, lead an Ethiopian to salvation clarifies this. After Philip witnessed to the Ethiopian, the Ethiopian asked, "What prevents me from being baptized!" And Philip said, "If you believe with all your heart, you may." After the Ethiopian said, "I believe that Jesus is the Son of God." Philip baptized him in water.

Philip did not baptize him in the Holy Spirit. Another explanation for verses 16 and 17 is that this is a transition time for how believers received the Holy Spirit. On the day of Pentecost, those who were saved beforehand received the Holy Spirit a variable number of days after they were saved, on the day of Pentecost. The newly saved Christians in Samaria received the Holy Spirit later, as was the case with those on the day of Pentecost, when the disciples prayed over them. Then God changed to where all newborn Christians received the Holy Spirit when they were saved and the Ethiopian eunuch was the first newborn Christian this happened in.

Philip did not make sure he spoke in other tongues nor ask God to baptize or fill the Ethiopian with the Holy Spirit because he knew God gives the Holy Spirit as a free gift to all who believe with all their heart and confess that Jesus is Lord. Philip was definitely obedient to the direction of the Holy Spirit because he witnessed to the Ethiopian due to the Lord and the Spirit telling him to in the first place, and Philip was miraculously taken away immediately after the Ethiopian was baptized with water and taken literally to Azotus. As a side note on baptism, Philip did not sprinkle the Ethiopian with some water but fully immersed the Ethiopian in his baptism.

761. Jesus spoke and appeared to Saul (Paul), who was a devout persecutor of Christians because he thought he was serving God doing this, on the road to Damascus in the form of a light. Paul was the only one in his group that was blinded and heard what Jesus said. Paul fasted from all food and drink for three days subsequent to this (Ac. 9:1–9).

762. Jesus spoke to Ananias in a vision and told him to go to Saul. Jesus told Ananias where he would find Saul. Jesus told Ananias that Saul was a chosen instrument of his

to bear his name before the gentiles and kings and the sons of Israel and that Saul would suffer for his name's sake. Ananias did as Jesus told him despite fearing Saul the persecutor. When Ananias found Saul, he laid his hands on Saul and said the Lord Jesus sent him so that he may regain his sight and be filled with the Holy Spirit. Immediately there fell from Saul's eyes something like scales, and he regained his sight and was baptized. Then Saul ate (Ac. 9:10–19).

763.  Saul spent several days with the disciples. Thus he learned more about Jesus. Saul immediately proclaimed in the synagogues and proved by scripture, that Jesus was the Christ (Ac. 9:19–22). This shows that one is able to prove that Jesus is the Messiah using prophecies from the Old Testament and scripture from the New Testament.

764.  The Jews then planned to kill Saul, so he was let out of the city in a basket over the city wall (Ac. 9:23–25).

765.  When Saul came to Jerusalem, he boldly proclaimed the gospel publicly, despite opposition. The Jews in Jerusalem then planned to kill him, so he went to Caesarea and then Tarsus (Ac. 9:26–30).

766.  Despite threats of death for speaking about Jesus, the church grew because the believers chose to fear God rather than man and spoke the gospel despite the threat of death. Comfort from the Holy Spirit enabled the believers to do this (Ac. 9:31).

767.  God used Peter to heal a paralyzed man named Aeneas in Lydda. Then God used Peter to bring to life a saint named Tabitha (Dorcas, in Greek) who had recently died in Joppa. This led to many new people believing in the gospel (Ac. 9:32–43).

768. God listens to the prayer of a sinner seeking him, as was with the case of Cornelius, a centurion. God gives grace to the humble (Ac. 10:1–4, 25, 34, 35, Ps. 138:6, Jas. 4:6).

769. An angel of God miraculously told Cornelius whom to send for and where he was (Ac. 10:5, 6).

770. In a vision, God showed Peter that what he has declared no longer unclean is to not be avoided. God used as an example creatures that were considered unholy to eat by Mosaic law (Lv. 11). God told Peter to eat these kinds of animals. This showed Peter that God can make what was considered unclean by him to be clean (Ac. 10:9–16).

771. The Holy Spirit told Peter to go with the men Cornelius sent for him. Peter went with them and into the house of Cornelius despite Jewish tradition (this was not Mosaic law) of not associating with gentiles (Ac. 10:19–29).

772. God saves everyone who truly seeks him. The Holy Spirit fell upon Cornelius and the other gentiles with him who Peter was speaking the gospel to when they believed the gospel. Then Peter and the Jewish believers there with him baptized, with water, the new gentile believers (Ac. 10:34–48).

773. Barnabas brought Saul from Tarsus to Antioch, where the disciples were first called Christians. Here Barnabas and Saul met with the church and taught large numbers of people (Ac. 11:25, 26).

774. A Jewish prophet named Agabus, moved by the Holy Spirit, prophesied in Antioch that there would be a great famine all over the world. It is estimated the prophecy was given about AD 40. Though there were famines in diverse places during Claudius's reign, the famine most likely referred to in the prophecy took place in the Middle East, including Israel, about AD 45–46 per the historian

Josephus. Christians from other countries gave aid to fellow believers in need during this time (Ac. 11:27–30).

775. King Herod Agrippa I, grandson of Herod the Great, killed the disciple James, the brother of John, with the sword. He saw this pleased the Jews, so he imprisoned Peter. While saints were praying for him, an angel of the Lord made the shackles fall from him and led him out of the prison and city, opening doors for him, without the guards knowing what was happening in their presence (Ac. 12:1–11).

776. While King Herod Agrippa was giving a speech, the people said, "The voice of a god and not of a man." Because Herod did not give God the glory, an angel of the Lord immediately struck him, and he was eaten of worms and died (Ac. 12:20–24). According to the historian Josephus, Herod endured terrible pain for five days before he died of worms. This tells us God cares when sinners claim to be a god and will strike them with illness and death unless they repent immediately.

777. Before the disciples did anything new, they fasted and prayed until they heard from God, via the Holy Spirit (Ac. 13:1–3). Here the Holy Spirit told them to separate Saul and Barnabas for the work to which the Lord had called them. They fasted and prayed again after hearing from God in this way before they went where God lead them (Ac.13:3, 4).

778. While witnessing on the island of Cypress, Saul, who was also called Paul, and Barnabas were opposed by a Jewish magician and false prophet named Bar-Jesus. While Barnabas and Paul were witnessing to the proconsul, Sergius Paulus, Bar-Jesus opposed them to turn Sergius Paulus from becoming saved. Paul, full of the Holy Spirit, overwhelmingly moved by the Holy Spirit, fixed his eyes

on Bar-Jesus, and said, "You who are full of deceit and fraud, you son of the devil, you enemy of all righteousness, will you not cease to make crooked the straight ways of the Lord? Now behold, the hand of the Lord is upon you and you will be blind and not see the sun for a time." Immediately, he was blinded and the proconsul believed and was saved, seeing what had happened (Ac. 13:4–12).

So the Lord struck this man who tried to keep the truth from being believed by others. This tells us God will strike those who oppose his disciples at times, even though he loves everyone. He knows those who oppose him and actively serve Satan and may let them work their evil for a time, but there will be a day of judgment for them, the second death being the worse judgment to come. This episode in history, as well as others such as the death of King Herod, proves that the message from some people that God does not harm anyone is wrong. He does harm them when he decides it is best for his kingdom.

779.   Barnabas and Paul preached the gospel of Jesus in the synagogue of Perga in Pamphylia to the Jews and others who feared God. Paul used the prophecy of David that God would not allow his Holy One to undergo decay (Ps. 16:10). This prophecy obviously dealt with the Messiah, and since Jesus did not decay but rose from the dead, as witnessed by hundreds of believers, Jesus fulfilled the prophecy, proving that he is the Messiah. The Jews, moved with jealousy, incited the leaders of the city to throw Barnabas and Paul out of the city. However, many gentiles believed the gospel of Jesus and were saved, fulfilling prophecy of the Messiah from Isaiah 42:1, 6 and 49:6 (Ac. 13:13–52).

780.   The Son, Jesus, was God before all creation, but Jesus is called begotten because he was born in the flesh with his first incarnation. He was not created by God in any way

before that. The Son has always existed as has the Father and the Holy Spirit (Gen. 1:26, Mt. 28:19, Rev. 1:8). He was God and man at the same time while he was here on earth (Ps. 2:7; Ac. 13:33; Heb. 1:5, 5:5).

781. Barnabas and Paul preached the gospel of Jesus at Iconium, Jesus allowing signs and wonders at their hands to further the belief of Jesus as the Messiah. Many believed and were saved, but Jews and gentiles who opposed the truth intended to stone the apostles. When the apostles learned of this plot, they fled to Lycaonia, Lystra, and Derbe (Ac. 14:1–7).

782. At Lystra, a man who was lame since birth was made whole at the word of Paul. This made the people there want to offer sacrifice to Paul and Barnabas, thinking they were Hermes and Zeus, respectively. The apostles were barely able to convince the people that they were mere men and that they preached the one true God, the Creator (Ac. 14:8–18). Jews from Antioch and Iconium came there and incited the people against the apostles so much that they stoned Paul. Supposing Paul to be dead they dragged his body out of the city. While the disciples were around Paul on the ground, Paul stood up and went into the city. This showed boldness to opposition by Paul. He and Barnabas then witnessed in Derbe, and many were saved there. They then returned to Lystra, Iconium, and Antioch strengthening the faith of the believers there, saying, "Through many tribulations we must enter the kingdom of God." They appointed elders (pastors) in every church, having prayed with fasting, they commended them to the Lord (Ac. 14:8–23).

783. Some Christians from Judea thought it was necessary to be circumcised to be saved. The apostles met and decided that circumcision was not necessary to be saved. The apostles said four laws of the Mosaic law that the gentiles, and

thus all believers, should abstain from: things sacrificed to idols, eating or drinking blood, eating anything strangled, and fornication, which is any sex other than sex between a man and a woman who are married to each other (without having been divorced, other than for infidelity) (Ac. 15:1–29). This does not mean these are the only Mosaic laws Christians have to obey. For example, God still expects all believers to obey the Ten Commandments, except keeping the Sabbath is now perfected in worshipping God constantly in spirit and in truth (Jn. 4:24, 1 Thes. 5:17). Jesus is Lord of the Sabbath (Mt.12:8, Lk. 6:5). God did not want people working on the Sabbath to profit themselves (Ex. 20:8, 11). God did not prohibit all physical effort on the Sabbath so that harvesting enough food to eat (Mt. 12:3,4), service to God (Mt. 12:5, 6), and acts of mercy (Mt. 12:7, 8, 11–13) were not prohibited by God. In verse 7, the Lord Jesus said he desires compassion and not sacrifice anyway. The idea of the Sabbath was to rest from labor that profits oneself.

784. Paul and Barnabas disagreed sharply about whether to take John Mark with them on a mission trip to churches they had started. So Barnabas took John Mark and Paul took Silas to different locations, strengthening the churches (Ac. 15:36–41). Though Satan meant this for evil God turned it into good in that they involved Silas more in their ministry, and they were able to do what they intended in a shorter amount of time by dividing the labor. Paul and Barnabas eventually forgave each other and resolved their differences (1 Cor. 9:16).

785. Paul circumcised Timothy so Timothy could witness in Jewish synagogues, not because it was necessary to please God. They even preached that circumcision was not necessary but that believers should abstain from the

four things the apostles had said in Acts chapter 15 (Ac. 16:10–14).

786. The Holy Spirit forbade Paul, Silas, and Timothy to preach in Asia Minor (they were intending to go to northern Asia Minor) but instead lead them to Macedonia by a vision (Ac. 16:6–10). While Christians may have good intentions with their plans, they need to be willing to change what they do if God directs them otherwise. While God loves everyone and wills all people to be saved, he has determined world events to fulfill prophecies and that means some people will not be saved to bring evil to it's fullest before Jesus returns. This is similar to the early days of the children of Jacob/Israel (Gen 15:16). God sent the children of Israel into slavery while the evil of the people they were to later conquer increased to it's fullest so that God could then send the children of Israel to destroy the evil people of Canaan.

787. Paul, Silas, and Timothy did not have specific directions from the Holy Spirit as to what they were to do in Macedonia other than preach to gospel (Ac. 16:10). It was a gentile nation so there were not synagogues to preach in as they had done where there were in synagogues, so they went to a place they supposed was a place of prayer after spending several days there (Ac. 16:11–13). A sincere seeker and worshiper of God, Lydia, believed the gospel of Jesus and was saved and baptized (Ac. 16:14, 15). Even though she had not heard the gospel of Jesus she worshiped the one true God. God sent to her Paul and Timothy so she could be saved, as he sent Peter to Cornelius and his friends and family. God said, "I love those who love me; and those who diligently seek me will find me" (Prov. 8:17). Amen. Thank you, God.

788. A demon possessed slave-girl practiced fortune-telling by satanic forces. For several days, she taunted Paul and Silas

by repeatedly telling the truth about them publicly. Paul finally became annoyed and cast the demon out of her. This took her ability to fortune-tell away so her owners had Paul and Silas beaten and imprisoned (Ac. 16:16–24).

789. In prison at about midnight, Paul and Silas were praying and singing hymns loud enough for the other prisoners to hear. Suddenly, God caused a great earthquake that shook the foundations of the prison so that the doors of the prison were opened, but no one was harmed. This was miraculous that the earthquake was great and did such a specific thing. The chains of all the prisoners were unfastened. The jailor sought to kill himself because of what had happened, but Paul told him to not kill himself and let him know no one had escaped. The jailor asked what he must do to be saved and Paul told him, "Believe in the Lord Jesus, and you will be saved, you and your household." He took Paul and Silas to his house where Paul and Silas witnessed to him and his household and all were saved and baptized that night (Ac. 16:25–34). New believers are immediately baptized consistently in scripture. This promise of the jailors household being saved does not necessarily apply to all believers. The jailor could not release them though until he received orders to do so. The leaders of the city asked Paul and Silas to leave their city and they did but only after they had ministered to the believers some more (Ac. 16:35–40).

790. Paul reasoned with those whoever would listen in market places, synagogues and other religious places about the gospel of Jesus (Ac. 17:17). He preached in a way that each of his audiences could understand or relate to (Ac. 17:23).

791. Having overlooked the times of ignorance, God has declared to all people everywhere that they must repent, since the ministry of John the Baptist, and believe in Jesus

as Lord since Jesus's ministry (Ac. 17:30). For people who had and will have not had a chance to be witnessed to by a Christian God will provide a way for them to be saved (Prov. 8:17). This may occur through visions such as is happening now in Muslim countries where it is illegal to witness to others the gospel of Jesus.

792.    Paul worked as a tent maker for a time (Ac. 18:3, 5). This was probably necessary because there was not enough financial support from others to sustain him as well as other disciples in full-time ministry.

793.    The Lord spoke to Paul in the night in a vision to continue speaking the truth of God's word because he had enough believers in Corinth to prevent Paul from being harmed. Paul then taught there one and a half years (Ac. 18:9–11).

794.    Submission of one's thoughts and beliefs to the word of God furthers the kingdom of God greatly (Ac. 18:24–28).

795.    In Ephesus, Paul met about twelve men who had repented and been baptized unto John's baptism of repentance. They had not heard that the Promised One, the Messiah, that John the Baptist had spoken of had come and that his name was Jesus. Paul enlightened them of this and they believed, so Paul immediately baptized them in the name of the Lord Jesus. Paul then laid his hands on them and the Holy Spirit came on them, and they spoke in other tongues and prophesied. This helped these new believers understand that they were now part of the family of God. This also gave them evidence that they were filled with the Holy Spirit since they believed and confessed that Jesus was Lord (Ac. 19:1–7). This does not mean that being filled with the Holy Spirit only comes by laying on of hands on a new believer in Jesus as Lord by a Spirit filled Christian nor does it mean that one can be a believer and

follower of Jesus as Lord but yet not filled by the Holy Spirit and thus not saved (Ac. 8:26–40).

796.   There is a point where opposition to speaking God's word is too great to stay at that location (Ac. 19:9).

797.   God performed great miracles at the hand of Paul, such as healings and exorcisms. Even cloths from him that came in contact with the sick were used by God to heal the sick. Some who tried to cast out demons without believing in Jesus as Lord but still using his name were overpowered by a demon-possessed man after the demon said he knew Jesus and Paul (Ac. 19:1–17).

798.   When a sinner becomes saved, they must get rid of anything of their former life that was evil such as books, television shows, movies, music, etcetera. Doing so will increase their faith and lead to more salvations and miracles of God (Ac. 19:18–20).

799.   Christianity was called the Way in the early church days (Ac. 19:23).

800.   Those who profited from worship of the false god Diana (Artemis) started a riot to do away with the believers who were proselytizing in Ephesus. The town clerk stopped the riot (Ac. 19:21–41).

801.   God brought to life, at the hand of Paul, Eutychus who died from a fall three stories high (Ac. 20:7–12).

802.   The Holy Spirit told Paul he would suffer bonds and afflictions, and yet he continued his ministry out of love for the Jesus and people (Ac. 20:23–26, 21:13). As he said in Ac. 20:26, all Christians need to witness to others to avoid the blood of the lost people we know being on our hands.

803.   Elders are the same as pastors today (Ac. 20:17, 28).

804.    Since the early church age, there have been people wanting to draw people away from the truth (Ac. 20:28–30).

805.    Jesus said, "It is more blessed to give than to receive" (Ac. 20:35). This is the only recording of Jesus saying this. Paul quoted Jesus here while saying that by working hard you must help the weak. The weak here are those who physically cannot provide for themselves. One must provide for oneself if one is physically able (2 Th. 3:8, 9).

806.    After calling out the high priest for doing wrong, Paul was told it was the high priest that he spoke to. Paul then said he did not know it was the high priest he spoke to and quoted Exodus 22:28, which says a person is not to speak evil of God or a ruler of one's people (Ac. 23:5). Here and several times by Jesus, as well as other places in the New Testament, the Old Testament is quoted as applicable to today. So those who say we no longer live under the Old Testament are right in that we are under a new covenant of atonement for sin by the sacrifice of Jesus if we believe he is Lord and Savior, but God's laws are still applicable, except for circumcision and sacrifices because Jesus paid the full price for our sins so that nothing else is needed to be acceptable in God's eyes.

807.    We should try to do right in order to do our best to maintain a good conscience before God and people (Ac. 24:16). But love, not guilt, leads a believer to do God's will other than repentance. Guilt only leads a person to repentance but love can likewise lead to repentance. The devil drives but God leads. The Lord's leading is typically peaceful and full of grace and love. That is not to say there can be times when, out of zeal for God, a Christian will speak boldly to condemn sin and lies. An example of this is when Jesus drove out the moneychangers and those that sold animals for sacrifice from the temple. God chastens those whom he loves (Heb. 12:6).

808. God will do exactly as he tells us, whether by the Bible or by angel or vision (as long as it does not conflict with scripture) (Ac. 27:23–26).

809. All on board the ship that was taking Paul, as prisoner, to Rome went without eating for fourteen days while they were in a storm. God spared all on board even though they were shipwrecked on the island of Malta (Ac. 27:33–44).

810. A poisonous viper bit Paul as he threw sticks on a fire, however he shook it off into the fire. This shows us that even God's creatures can harm those who serve Him if this is God's will. It also shows us that it is appropriate to kill an animal that does this. God allowed no harm to come to Paul from this viper bite and seeing this the natives of Malta thought Paul was a god. From Paul's previous behavior (Ac. 14:11–15) we know that Paul did not allow them to continue to think this. However this opened doors for Paul to minister to them and God healed people by Paul. This allowed the gospel to be preached in Malta (Ac. 28:1–10). God causes all things to work together for good to those who love God, to those who are called according to his purpose (Rom. 8:28).

811. Paul preached, first to the Jews and then to gentiles who came to hear him, the gospel of Jesus and persuaded some concerning Jesus from both the Law of Moses and the prophets. Some believed and some did not. He did this two years from his own rented quarters while under guard and chain (Ac. 28:16–31).

# ROMANS

812. The gospel of Jesus is the power of God for salvation to everyone who believes. First this was available to Jews and then gentiles at the hand of God (Rom. 1:16). This is the mystery of Christ (Eph. 3:2–6).

813. God gives eternal life to those who faithfully believe in Jesus as Lord. The believer becomes righteous in God's eyes because Jesus paid the price for our sins on the cross (Rom. 1:17).

814. God has always made himself evident to all people so that all people are without excuse to not believe in, and follow, him (Rom. 1:19, 20).

815. The wrath of God is against all who resist the truth that he is, prophesying to be wise but are fools (Rom. 1:18, 21–23).

816. God gives hearts of those who resist the truth over to evil so that they even degrade their bodies. God even gives them over to their degrading passions: having passion for and sex with those of the same sex as they. God allows male and female homosexuals to receive the due penalty for their sin of homosexuality, AIDS being an example. God also allows those who are disobedient to him in regards to heterosexual acts to receive their due penalty as well, such as sexually transmitted illnesses (Rom. 1:26, 27).

817. Besides homosexuality, the disobedient to God are allowed by God to give in fully to their evil desires so that they do not want to do those things that are proper but are full of unrighteousness, wickedness, greed, evil; full of envy, murder, strife, deceit, malice; gossips, slanderers, haters

of God, inventors of evil, disobedient to parents, without understanding, untrustworthy, unloving, unmerciful; and though they know what God wants them to do and not do they not only do these sins, but give hearty approval to those who practice these sins (Rom. 1:28–32).

818. Romans chapter two is addressed to self-righteous, unsaved people (Rom. 2:1). Saints are not condemned. These self-righteous unsaved are stubborn and unrepentant, storing up wrath from God to be delivered on judgment day (Rom. 2:5).

819. The unsaved have no right to judge others and will be judged by God (Rom. 2:3).

820. The kindness of God leads people to repentance (Rom. 2:4). Witnesses and preachers need to remember this in order that they will be kind in their efforts to lead others to salvation through Christ Jesus.

821. Tribulation and distress will come to those who do evil, to the Jews (genetically) first and then to gentiles (Rom. 2:9). In the early part of the end of this age the Jews, who have rejected Christ Jesus, will suffer at the hand of the Antichrist and his followers, but God will save a remnant of Jews and pour out his judgments on the Antichrist and his followers in the latter part of the last days. After the remnant of Jews are rescued from Satan, he will inspire the Antichrist to persecute Christians for three and a half years (Mt. 24:15–28; Dan. 7:21; Rev. 12:16, 17, 13:5–7).

822. The Jews (genetically) will be judged first on judgment day and then gentiles; those who will have loved and obeyed God will receive glory, honor, and peace (Rom. 2:10).

823. Not having studied and learned God's word, the Bible, is no excuse for sinning and escaping God's judgment. God places in everyone a conscious, which convicts him or her

when he or she sins and give him or her an instinct to do what God's law says, such as to not kill or steal (Rom. 2:12–16).

824.  Jews (genetically) who claim to Abraham's seed and abide by God's law and therefore are justified before God do not do as they claim. They break God's law at least in their heart and are therefore condemned by God. This hypocrisy makes the gentiles reject God (Rom. 2:17–24).

825.  Circumcision is useless if a person does not love and obey God (Rom. 2:25).

826.  A true Jew is a Jew spiritually and is therefore a child of Abraham (Rom. 11:17) and therefore not one who is genetically a Jew but a person who loves and obeys the God of Abraham, who sent His son Jesus to make the ways of God more clear to us and to pay the price for our sins, so that those who believe that God raised him from the dead and confess with their mouth that Jesus is Lord will be saved and spend a blessed eternity with God (Rom. 2:28, 29, 9:6, 10:9). For ease of understanding though, I will refer to Jews who are Jews genetically.

827.  God chose the Jews to be the oracles of Him (Rom. 3:2). This was done through prophets of the Old Testament. God also spoke sometimes through kings Saul, David, and Solomon.

828.  We should not sin to make grace abound more (Rom. 3:8, 5:20, 6:1).

829.  All people are not consistently good and seek God consistently. All people sin and thus are too impure, without believing in and following Jesus as Lord and Savior, to be in the presence of God who is perfect (Rom. 3:9–23).

830.  Justification is being made worthy to be in the presence of God. Justification is by faith in Jesus as Lord and Savior

(Rom. 3:22, 5:1, 10:9, 10). This faith is not in people on their own part but is given to people by our graceful God (Tit. 3:7), of his choosing (Mt. 25:34; Eph. 1:4, 2:10; 2Thes. 2:13), so saints have no reason to boast (Eph. 2:8, 9). So it is by faith and not works people are justified (Eph. 2:8, 9, Tit. 3:5–7). Justification through faith is made possible because of Jesus's sacrifice of himself, shedding his blood, for the sins of the world and his resurrection (Rom. 4:25, 5:9). People receive salvation and justification by God's grace, a gift we do not deserve (Rom. 5:1, 2, Tit. 3:5–7). The Holy Spirit accomplishes this in those God predestined to be saved and washes them, making them reborn from their old self, sanctified, and making them justified to be with God (1 Cor. 6:11, Tit. 3:5–7).

831. Those who believe in, and follow, Jesus as Lord and Savior are justified before God so that they can be with him in heaven because Jesus paid the price of people's sins through his sacrifice on the cross. Thus God passes over the sins saints commit (Rom. 3:24–26).

832. The law of God is fulfilled in faith in his Son Jesus as Lord and Savior. So saints are justified through faith (Rom. 3:27–31).

833. Abraham was justified before God by his faith in God and what God told him in a vision, that he would father a son despite being childless in his old age and that his descendants would be as numerous as the stars. His faith was credited to him as righteousness (Gen. 15:1–6, Rom. 4:3). This occurred before he was told by God to circumcise himself, his household, and that his descendants were to be circumcised as a sign of the covenant that God promised to make many nations from Abraham (Gen. 17:1–14, Rom. 4:10). So circumcision does not make one righteous. Abraham's righteousness, through faith in God's promise, came before the law also.

834.  Faith in God and Jesus as Lord and savior justifies the ungodly, making them as righteous as a person without sin (Rom. 4:5–8).

835.  Those who are Jews by blood will not go to heaven if they do not have faith in God and Jesus as Lord and Savior because the Mosaic law does not justify someone. The Mosaic law gave man knowledge of how we are to live our lives and the seriousness of sin. The law did not bring about God's promise to Abraham but his faith in God (Rom. 4:13–25).

836.  Saints glory in tribulation, as well as justification by the grace of God, knowing that tribulation increases our patience. God made people such that their characteristics increase by their resisted use, such as muscle strength and knowledge. Without a testing of person's patience by tribulation, then one goes the natural inclination of self-centeredness and selfishness. Tribulation and patience gives people experience of God's grace and mercy and less dependence on one's self. With this comes hope, hope in God, who is loving, omniscient, and omnipotent. With this hope, saints are made not ashamed, assured of the certainty of God, the Lord Jesus, and our salvation. Experiencing God's love in our lives through tribulation and blessings and feeling God's love through the Holy Spirit saints share God's love to other people, desiring the unsaved to experience God's love. The Holy Spirit gives saints love for other people that is beyond their natural ability (Rom. 5:3–5).

837.  God loves people so much he sent his Son Jesus Christ to die for all people while we were ungodly sinners. This is remarkable when one considers how hard it is for us do be willing to die for a good friend, let alone a stranger or enemy. Yet this is how much God loves people (Rom. 5:6–8).

838. Salvation means being saved from the wrath of God, which all people deserve, for our sins. This wrath will be poured out on all people who will have not been believers and followers of God and his Son Jesus as Lord since Jesus came to the earth to show that he is the way to heaven (Rom. 5:9; 1Thes. 1:10; Rev. 6:16, 17, 20:11–15).

839. Sin entered into the world by Adam, and by sin, death of people entered the world. God had created people to live forever, but sin made this impossible, so people have had limited lifespans since Adam. The Mosaic law was given so that people would know how God intended us to live our lives. Those who do not seek and obey God are destined for eternal punishment in the lake of fire. God provided a way for those who do seek and obey him to love forever with a new eternal body. This way is his Son Jesus (Rom. 5:12–21, 6:23).

840. We are not to intentionally sin to make grace abound more (Rom. 6:1, 2).

841. Saints are given a new life through Jesus, so we are to live new lives, not serving sin but God. This is not to say saints will not sin, but we should not willingly sin (Rom. 6:4–22).

842. We struggle with sin, the flesh, and our willingness to obey God warring in our members to either sin or do right. Sometimes we do not do what we know we should do and do what we know we should not do (Rom. 7:15–25).

843. There is no condemnation to those who are believe and follow Jesus as Lord and Savior. That is what it takes to not go to hell when one dies and then an eternity in the lake of fire (Rom. 8:1, 2).

844. Saints walk not after the flesh but after the Spirit, and our mind is preoccupied with things of the God and the Holy

Spirit and not of things of the flesh, or this world (Rom. 8:4, 5).

845. If someone does not have the Holy Spirit in them, they are not saved and vice versa; those that are saved have the Holy Spirit in them (Rom. 8:9).

846. Saints are not in bondage to sin but are children of God, joint-heirs with Jesus, by the grace of God, and empowered by the Holy Spirit (Rom. 8:15–17).

847. Saints and all of creation groans because of sin in the world and waiting, with great anticipation, for the coming of the Lord and the day we will receive our eternal bodies and no longer sin (Rom. 8:22, 23).

848. The Holy Spirit makes intercessory prayer for the saints it indwells with groanings that cannot be spoken. Even though saints do not know what we should pray for the Holy Spirit knows and intercedes for us (Rom. 8:26). Jesus also intercedes for saints according to the will of God (Rom. 8:27, 34).

849. All things work together for good to them that love God, to them who are called according to his purpose. Rom. 8:28. What is good is what is truly good, good according to God and not necessarily according to our natural thinking. As an example, illness usually is not thought of as good according to our natural thinking but it can be good according to God to serve His purpose.

850. Predestination. God chose who would be saved before he made the world. Mt. 25:34; Rom. 8:29, 30; 9:15–18; Eph. 1:4, 5, 11; 2:10; 2 Thes. 2:13. We do not know whom God has chosen to be saved so we are to witness to all people we can and trust that God will convert those whom he will from sinner to saint. We are not to find fault in God's predestination and condemnation of those he predestines

to not be saved because he is God the Creator. Rom. 9:19–24.

851. If God is for us who can be against us. Rom. 8:31. Nothing, neither the devil, his evil forces, nor other people can keep God from performing in saints what he wills. Even our faith will be made as God desires. Heb. 12:2. So saints are more than conquerors. Rom. 8:37.

852. Nothing can separate saints from the love of Jesus and God; including tribulation, distress, persecution, famine, nakedness, peril, sword, principalities, death, life, angels, powers, things present, things to come, height, depth, and any creature. Rom. 8:35, 38, 39.

853. Paul was so sorrowful about the lost state of his countrymen that he could have wished to have taken their place amongst the lost if that would have meant they would have been saved. Rom. 9:2, 3. Paul was speaking rhetorically here in that only Jesus was able to be the substitute sacrifice for the many. But it tells us that it is normal to have great heaviness of heart and continual sorrow for the lost. Even though God wants us to enjoy his blessings and his creation we should be sorrowful about the lost, which then compels us to strive to be used by God to win souls. Paul said his heart's desire and prayer to God for Israel was that they might be saved. Rom. 10:1.

854. God has given salvation to gentiles as well as Jews, through Jesus Christ. Rom. 9:24–30; 10:12, 18–21. Gentiles are not to boast against unsaved Jews that they are saved. Rom. 11:18. Instead gentile believers should fear lest they no longer believe, and then God would cut them out of their inheritance and go to hell. Rom. 11:20–22.

855. The majority of Jews were destined by God to reject Jesus as the Messiah just as they rejected God before the Babylonian captivity. Rom. 9:32, 33; 11:8–10. Is. 8:14;

29:10. But God always makes sure there is a remnant of Jews who believe in him and follow him. Rom. 11:1–4. Rev. 7:4–8. The Jews are blinded by God from the truth of Jesus as Lord by God until the fullness of the gentiles is come, which is when the last of the gentiles is saved, by the mystery of faith in Jesus as Lord, when the Lord returns. Rom. 11:25. When Jesus returns he will deliver Israel from the Antichrist and their blindness to the truth of him as Lord, thus he will turn away ungodliness from Jacob. Rom. 11:25, 26; Lk. 21:24. God will purge away the Jews' sins when the Lord Jesus returns. Rom. 11:27; Is. 27:9. Jews are enemies in regards to the gospel of Jesus but they are chosen and beloved of God. Rom. 11:28.

856.  The Jews had a zeal for God but not according to knowledge of the truth. Desiring to justify themselves they did not humble themselves to God. Rom. 10:2, 3.

857.  What does a person have to do to become saved? They must confess with their mouth that Jesus is Lord and believe in their heart that God has raised him from the dead, for with the heart a person believes unto righteousness and with the mouth confession is made unto salvation. Rom 10:9, 10. Whoever calls on the name of the Lord in whom he or she believes will be saved. Rom. 10:13, 14.

858.  Whoever believes on Jesus as Lord is not ashamed of him. Rom. 10:11.

859.  People will not believe in the Lord Jesus unless they hear the word of God. So it is necessary for saints to preach and teach the gospel of Jesus to sinners. Rom. 10:14, 15, 17.

860.  Not all who hear the word of God will obey God. Rom. 10:16.

861.  The Jews cut out of the olive tree are those Jews who never believed in Jesus as Lord and so were never saved.

Therefore they can become saved and engrafted back into the olive tree. Rom. 11:16–24.

862. As God did not spare the natural branches (Jews by blood) for their rebellion against him, so he will not spare gentiles for rebellion against him (the gospel of Jesus). Rom. 11:21. This does not mean a backsliding Christian (one who has moments of doubt about his or her faith or one that chooses to sin but later repents) will be sent to hell. Jews and gentiles who never believe in and follow God will go to hell because they are in rebellion against God. It probably also means those who were once believers and followers of God and then consciously and deliberately turn against God and never repent and believe in Him again will go to hell (Heb. 6:4–6). This also is a warning to unfaithful nations, which currently only applies to Israel and the United States of America because they are the only nations founded on the word of God and so can be unfaithful (Ez. 14:13). However God will fulfill his promises to Israel and make it a great nation during the millennium.

863. The gifts and calling of God are irrevocable. Rom. 11:29. These ministerial gifts God gives each saint, by the Holy Spirit, will stay with that saint and God could give more in the future. The gifts include prophecy (speaking God's word of truth to any people, whether or not it predicts the future, usually to bring people to a right relationship with God and less commonly could be a word of encouragement), service to others, teaching, exhortation (evangelists generally have this gift), giving (more than the tithe, these people may be made wealthy by God so saints need to not envy other saints who are wealthy because it may be someone with this gift), leading (a pastor should have this gift as well as the gift of teaching), and mercy (Rom. 12:6–8).

They also include the word of wisdom (giving wise advise to others), the word of knowledge (understanding of God's word and speaking it), faith (some saints have more faith than others and can encourage other believers with this), gifts of healing (used by God to heal others), effecting of miracles by God (miracles other than healing can occur today when and where God chooses), discernment of spirits (ability to discern if something or someone is of God or Satan, which is important to avoid deception), speaking in other tongues, interpretation of other tongues (1 Cor. 12:4–10). The calling of each saint by God will be accomplished, meaning we can be assured God will perform his purpose in each of us, despite our failings along the way.

864.    No one knows as much as God or can give counsel to God (Rom. 11:34).

865.    God gives back fully what saints give to him, more so the tithe (Rom. 11:35, Mal. 3:10, 11, Lk. 6:38).

866.    Of God, through him and to him are all things, to whom be glory for ever (Rom. 11:36). These are to be expected of the one true God.

867.    It is reasonable to expect saints to not commit sexual sin (Rom. 12:1, 1 Cor. 6:18).

868.    A saint is not to be conformed to this world but be transformed by the renewing of his or her mind so that he or she may prove, or show, what is that good, acceptable, and perfect will of God (Mt. 6:24; Rom. 12:2; 1 Cor. 10:21; 2 Cor. 6:3, 14–18; Eph. 5:11; 1 Thes. 5:22; Tit. 2:11–14; Jas. 1:27, 4:4, 8; 1 Pet. 2:9; 1 Jn. 2:15–17; Rev. 18:4).

869.    Each saint is to not think more highly of themselves than they ought to think but to think soberly, according as God has dealt to everyone the measure of faith he desires (Rom. 12:3). We are to use the faith God has given to

each of us. God gives more faith to some than others, so the ones with more faith are not to be proud as if they had their faith on their own accord.

870. Saints are to love all people without hypocrisy, which means without self-centeredness, ulterior motives, and guile, but pure and sincere (Rom. 12:9).

871. Saints are to abhor what is evil but cling to what is good (Rom. 12:9). We should hate evil, which is Satan and his demons, and the acts of evil done by others. Saints should not hate people that do not accept the word of God (Mt. 5:44), but saints should not keep company with them either (Mt. 7:15, 10:14; Rom. 16:17; 2 Th. 3:6, 14; Tit. 3:10; 2 Jn. 1:10). Saints should love and adore what is good (what is from God). This comes without effort to a saint.

872. Saints are to be devoted to one another in brotherly love, honoring and giving preference to one another above themselves (Rom. 12:10). How more effective the church would be if the saints would consistently do this. There would not be divisions among saints or various denominations as there are today, even among those who strive to please God.

873. Saints are to not be lazy but diligent in doing what God has called them to do (Rom. 12:11).

874. Saints rejoice in the hope of our future with the Lord, making us able to persevere tribulation (Rom. 12:12).

875. Saints pray regularly (Rom. 12:12).

876. Saints are hospitable with one another and contribute to the needs of other saints (Rom. 12:13). Saints are to bear the weaknesses and burdens of other saints and not just please themselves. For even Christ did not please himself but gave himself as a sacrifice for mankind. This edifies the brother who is weaker and or in need (Rom. 15:1–3).

877. Saints are to not curse, but bless, those who persecute them (Rom. 12:14). We are not to repay evil to anyone for evil done to us (Rom. 12:17).

878. Saints are to rejoice with those who rejoice and weep with those who weep (Rom. 12:15). Saints are to be sensitive and compassionate toward others. We are not to be isolationists or hermits. God made us to be salt to the earth, meaning we are to have contact with others.

879. Saints are to think and feel about other saints the same, regardless of social status. We are not to be proud but associate with the lowly of society. We are not to be conceited, thinking we are wise in and of ourselves (Rom. 12:16).

880. Saints are to respect what is right in the sight of all men (Rom. 12:17). This tells us God has given to people the knowledge of good and evil, since Adam and Eve sinned. This does not mean what people describe what is right is right if they are in a depraved mind, which occurs after continued rebellion against God, for then they will call what is evil good and what is good evil (Is. 5:20; Rom. 1:24, 28; Eph. 2:3, 4:19).

881. If possible, saints are to be at peace with all people (Rom. 12:18). We are to strive for peace and not conflict. There are times when conflict will come to us though, which we are to handle prayerfully and soberly.

882. Saints should never take their own revenge on other people but leave room for God to judge and punish those who wrong us. For it is written, "Vengeance is Mine, I will repay, says the Lord (Rom. 12:19, Dt. 32:35, Ps. 94:1, Prov. 20:22). If our enemy (people who do us wrong) is hungry we are to feed him, and if he is thirsty, we are to give him drink. For in so doing the saint heaps burning coals on his head (Rom. 12:20). This refers to the ancient

Egyptian tradition of those who had done wrong would carry pans with hot coals on their head, which obviously caused pain and was humiliating in that it was public, as a sign of contrition for the wrong they had done. So when saints lovingly help their enemies, it should bring about shame to the their enemies. This is a witness for Jesus to the unbelievers, which should be our motive, and not to cause shame on our enemies just to shame them, because then we are repaying evil for evil in a deceptive way.

883.    Do not be overcome by evil, but overcome evil with good (Rom. 12:21). Speaking and acting good, according to God's word, overcomes evil. This also helps saints overcome evil that creeps into our lives through temptation and the desires of the flesh.

884.    People are to obey their governing authority, which is established by God, except when obedience to the governing authority would require disobedience to God (Rom. 13:1–7; Ex. 1:17; Dan. 3:16–18, 6:7, 10). We know the will of God from the Bible, the word of God.

885.    People should not borrow or they will be slave to the lender (Rom. 13:8). It is not a sin to borrow money. This is wise advice from God to us. However God knows people will borrow so He set rules (Ex. 22:25; Lv. 19:11, 25:35–37; Dt. 15:7–9; Mt. 5:42; Lk. 6:34). So if one does borrow, they need to abide by their agreement with the lender and the lender is to not charge interest to poor fellow saints. Also if the poor fellow saint is not able to pay back the loan by seven years, then the lender is to forgive the debt. If the poor fellow believer asks a saint for something they need the saint being asked to lend is to give what the poor saint needs without asking for it back. The poor saint is to pay back to those they borrow from when and if they can. It is just as sinful to borrow or ask as free gifts things and not work to pay them back, if one is able, as it is to not

lend or freely give to a fellow saint when asked. Here, as in general in life, we are to apply the golden rule of doing unto others as we would have them do unto us (Mt. 7:12, Lk. 6:31).

886.   Saints are to love their neighbors, which means everyone. In this, we fulfill the second law that is like unto the first law of loving God. This will keep us from committing such specific sins as adultery, murder, theft, and coveting (Rom. 13:8–10).

887.   God wants people to believe in his Son Jesus as Lord and Savior and behave properly, not doing anything of which they would be ashamed, imagining themselves standing before God with their sins exposed. We are not to be participants of wild parties, brawls, or riots. We are not to have sex outside of a marital relationship with one spouse of the opposite sex. We are not to get drunk. We are not to look, listen, read, watch, or in any other way participate in things that promote immorality (Rom. 13:11–14).

888.   People are not forbidden to eat various foods or drink various drinks, unless it was in worship to an idol, since Jesus came. However it is sinful to voluntarily intake drugs, which alter one's thinking such that their inhibitions from sinning are gone or to get drunk with alcohol because it causes the same effect. Those who do not think it is right to eat or drink certain things are not to judge those who think it is fine and those who feel there is no restriction of types of foods or drinks or not to judge those who restrict what they eat or drink (Rom. 14:1–4, 20, 22, 1 Cor. 10:28).

889.   To observe the Sabbath or not is up to how each person feels they should do, and we should not judge those who differ from us (Rom. 14:5, 6).

890.   Every knee shall bow to Jesus and every tongue confess that Jesus is Lord. Saints as well as sinners will stand

before the judgment seat of God and give account for their lives and sins. So then, should we not fear God, who holds our eternity in his hands (Mt. 10:28)? Saints will still be able to be with God and not cast into the lake of fire, despite our sins, but we will be judged and held accountable in some fashion by God (Rom. 14:10–12, Is. 45:23, Eph. 2:10, 11).

891. If a saint feels they should not eat or drink certain things, then if they were to eat or drink those things it would be sin. So others should not tempt or in other ways try to get them to eat or drink those things (Rom. 14:13–15, 20, 21, 23).

892. Pursue peace with one another rather than try to convince someone that you are right when either way is fine in God's eyes (Rom. 14:16–19).

893. The Bible, the holy Scriptures, was written for our instruction and can help us persevere tribulation and encourage us so that we have hope. Scripture helps saints be of one mind so that with one accord we may with one voice glorify the God and Father of or Lord Jesus Christ (Rom. 15:4–6).

894. Saints are to accept one another despite our weaknesses just as Jesus accepted us despite our faults (Rom. 15:7).

895. Jesus fulfilled God's promises to the Jews and the gentiles, bringing glory to God for his mercy. To God be the glory for rescuing saints from the devil (Rom. 15:8–12).

896. Knowledge of God's word allows saints to admonish one another (Rom. 15:14).

897. Paul aspired to preach the gospel of Jesus where it had named been preached before. Isaiah prophesied that they who had no news of him shall see, and they who have not heard shall understand (Is. 52:15, Rom. 15:20, 21). The gospel will be preached by the saints God calls for this

purpose to these places before the Lord Jesus returns (Mt. 24:14).

898. Saints are to be on the alert for people who cause dissensions and hindrances contrary to scripture and to avoid them because they do not serve God's will but their own will, deceiving the unsuspecting (Rom. 16:17, 18).

899. Saints are to be wise in what is good and innocent in what is evil (Rom. 16:19). Saints (saints alive today are Christians) are to learn what the Bible says, and so be wise as to the way of God. Also, saints are to be innocent in what is evil and innocent means inexperienced, so saints are to not partake of sinful things like watching movies that are sensual or in other ways evil, even under the guise of trying to relate to sinners so they can witness to them better.

900. God will crush Satan under the feet of saints and bring eternal peace at the battle of Gog and Magog at the end of the millennium (Rom. 16:20, Rev. 20:7–10). However since the verse says soon it also probably means saints will harm Satan through the power of God. God gave Satan power to hurt people in Genesis 3:15, but he gave people to power to hurt Satan more (the head is more vital than the heel), if they are servants of God. We are either servants of God or servants of Satan and servants of Satan do not battle Satan, so only servants of God will harm Satan. This verse also can be applicable to Jesus' crucifixion being akin to a bruise on the heel and his resurrection as a bruise to Satan's head because Jesus paid the price for people's sins once and for all, for those who believe and follow him.

# 1 CORINTHIANS

901. God gives to each Christian the ministerial gifts he wants each to have so that no Christian is lacking a ministerial gift God wants them to have (1 Cor. 1:7).

902. Christians will be blameless, or uncondemned, on the day of the Lord's return because Jesus paid the price for our sins and we accepted that gift of salvation from him. Then we will receive our eternal bodies and no longer sin as well (1 Cor. 1:8).

903. Denominations, divisions, and quarrels among Christians are not God's will. Christians are to humble themselves before God and to each other and settle their differences to the authority of God's word (1 Cor. 1:10–13; 2 Cor. 13:11).

904. An evangelist or preacher does not have to baptize people he leads to the Lord if there are other Christians who can baptize the new believers (1 Cor. 1:17).

905. Saints do not lead other people to salvation by human wisdom or clever speech but as simple mouthpieces for the word of God, the gospel of Jesus. The sacrificial death, burial, and resurrection of Jesus is foolishness to gentiles and a stumbling block to Jews, unless the Holy Spirit helps them understand the truth and convicts them. The simple things of God are far greater than the greatest wisdom and knowledge of mankind, and the weakness of God (the death of God the Son) is stronger than all mankind. The death of Jesus on the cross conquered all sin (1 Cor. 1:17–25). If we convince someone to become a Christian by clever speech or earthly wisdom rather than by the work of the Holy Spirit that person's faith is based

upon the wisdom of men rather than the power of God and thus not lasting (1 Cor. 2:2–5). This is comforting and encouraging to saints to witness to people, knowing that they do not have to worry about messing up or doing something wrong when witnessing, as long as they stay true to the Bible.

906. God chooses more people who are simple, poor, weak, and despised than those that are wealthy, famous, influential in worldly matters, strong and wise (1 Cor. 1:26–28). People need to humble themselves before God. The wisdom or this world is foolishness before God (1 Cor. 3:18, 19).

907. Faith, and thus salvation, comes from God. None of us can boast that it is by our own doing that we are saved. Likewise, wisdom, and thus sanctification, comes from God so that none of us can boast it is by our own doing that we no longer want to sin as much as we did before we were saved and thus behave in a more Christlike manner (1 Cor. 1:29, 30, Eph. 2:8, 9).

908. The Holy Spirit reveals to believers the thoughts and ways of God (1 Cor. 2:10–13). The natural man does not accept the things of the Holy Spirit because they are spiritually discerned and the natural man does not have the Holy Spirit in them. These things are foolishness to the natural man (1 Cor. 2:14–16).

909. Believers (saints) who still exhibit strife and jealousy are acting fleshly like sinners. Saints who are like this cannot understand weightier spiritual matters (1 Cor. 3:1–4).

910. The process of leading a person to salvation is typically done by more than one person over time, with some planting the seed of the word of God in the person, God making that seed grow in the sinners heart and mind, and another person leading the sinner through the sinners prayer and acceptance of Jesus as their Lord and Savior

(1 Cor. 3:5–9). So none involved in this should boast, or feel ineffective for the cause of Christ, but be glad for all involved in leading a person to salvation.

911.    There is no foundation for our faith than Jesus crucified and raised from the dead. Anything else will fail. Trials of this life will test a person's faith. If a person's faith was based on Jesus by the power of God, then they will withstand the trials of life (1 Cor. 3:10–15).

912.    Our bodies are the temple of God so we should treat our bodies with that in mind (1 Cor. 3:16, 17). This means it is sinful to have sex with anyone other than one's spouse of the opposite sex; murder; commit suicide; or harm our, or other people's, bodies intentionally. Ways we harm bodies not only involve physical harm with weapons or blows but include eating so much we become obese, entertaining our minds or bodies with lewdness, drunkenness or use of drugs that cause us to not control our behavior. Sexual sin by saints is particularly abhorrent because saints are one body with Jesus and when a person has sex with someone they are as one flesh. So to have sex with someone other than one's spouse of the opposite sex is to mix sin with what is holy in spirit and flesh (1 Cor. 6:12–20).

913.    Saints are to live their lives realizing they are accountable to the Lord and not man so that we should aim to please the Lord and not man with our actions. Saints are already accepted (justified) by the Lord when they become saved but sins are not acceptable to God (1 Cor. 4:4, Jn. 12:43). Saints are to live lives that would be good examples for others to follow (1 Cor. 4:16).

914.    The apostles lived hard lives. They were hungry, thirsty, homeless, poorly clothed, roughly treated, rejected, lied about, persecuted, and treated as the scum of the earth (1 Cor. 4:11–13).

915. Saints serve the almighty God and not just an empty religion conceived by men (1 Cor. 4:20).

916. Churches are to remove from church membership those so called Christians who openly sin and are not repentant (1 Cor. 5:2, Mt. 18:15–17). This prevents the unrepentant person from being an evil influence on the church (1 Cor. 5:6). When the church openly accepts compromise on sins, then others will perceive that God has no problem with those sins. Christians are then to not associate with so called Christians who are not repentant of their known sins except efforts to bring them to repentance. Regardless of what this person who openly sinned did they are to be forgiven by the saints but still removed from church membership (1 Cor. 5:9–11, 13, 2 Cor. 2:5–11).

917. Christians are not to pray for deliverance from the consequences God gives to those who sin so that the consequences will hopefully bring the unrepentant one to repentance (1 Cor. 5:5). It is better to suffer here on earth for our sins and repent than to continue in sin without repentance, which will lead us to reject Christ (1 Cor. 5:6, 7) and thus to hell (Mt. 5:29, 30). We should not be glad to see others suffer for the wrongs they have done, and if we do, God may punish us (Prov. 17:5, 24:17). Instead, we should help those who suffer, especially fellow Christians, whether they deserve it or not. We should feed them when they are hungry, give them drink when they are thirsty, clothe them when they need clothes, provide them shelter when they need it, and visit them when they are sick or imprisoned (Mt. 25:34–40). If we do not have the desire to help these people, then we need to repent and ask God to change our heart of stone into a heart of flesh, a heart of compassion (Ez. 36:26).

918. Saints are to judge each other, admonish, and love each other to a right relationship to each other and God. Saints

do not judge sinners, but God judges sinners (1 Cor. 5:12, 13). Communicating God's word to sinners is not judging them. If God's word says something a sinner is doing is sin, then it is not the saint communicating God's word to the sinner that judges them but God's word.

919.   Christians (a.k.a. saints) are to not sue each other but resolve their differences among their own Christian community (1 Cor. 6:1). It is better to suffer financial loss at the hands of a fellow saint wrongfully than to sue him or her (1 Cor. 6:7).

920.   Saints will judge the world, and even angels, during the millennium (1 Cor. 6:2, 3, Rev. 3:21).

921.   Sinners will not go to heaven but will go to hell and then the lake of fire. 1 Cor. 6:9; Rev. 20:15.

922.   Saints do sin, but they do not continue in sin as sinners do. Such sins include: fornication; homosexuality; acting like a person of the opposite sex God made them when they were born (genetic sex); adultery; spending thought time and effort on anything more than God, which is idolatry; theft; drunkenness; coveting, or desiring what another person has; troublemaking; and lying. When a saint does such sins, they repent and do their best not to do such sins again, and they do not neglect in admitting that sin is sin (1 Cor. 6:9–11).

923.   Married couples are not to deprive one another of sex except for a mutually agreed upon period so that they may devote themselves to prayer. Each spouse has authority over the other sexually so that if the husband desires to have sex, the wife is to have sex with him when he desires or asks for it, and likewise, if the wife desires to have sex, the husband is to have sex with her when she desires or asks for it. This prevents Satan from creeping in and causing one of the spouses to sin, such as getting sexual

gratification from someone else if their spouse will not have sex with them when they need it (1 Cor. 7:1–5). God gave people the sexual desire and to deny it is to deny what God has made to be part of a marital relationship (it is clear in the Bible that sex outside of marriage of one man and one woman is sin).

924.  Polygamy versus monogamy. We are to have only one spouse at a time (1 Cor. 7:2).

925.  God does not command, but Paul felt, it is better for the unmarried, widowers, and widows to not marry so that they can devote themselves to the work of God, but if they cannot control their sexual urges, then they are to marry. When one is married, one is concerned about the things of this world how he or she may please his or her spouse, so that one's interests are divided from the Lord. It is no sin for a widow or widower to remarry (1 Cor. 7:6–9, 25–40). Here each person may do as he or she sees fit.

926.  Divorce. God commands people to not divorce their spouse, but if one does divorce their spouse, they cannot remarry anyone but their spouse they divorced (1 Cor. 7:10, 11). God does allow divorce for adultery (Mt. 5:31, 32; 19:8, 9), but he would rather the husband and wife stay together. If a saint is married to a sinner, then Paul recommends they do not divorce their spouse. This apparently was in response to some saints of Paul's time thinking they had to divorce spouses that were not saved because they were unequally yoked. The hope is that the saint will lead the unbelieving spouse to salvation. However if the unbelieving spouse divorces the believing spouse, then the believing spouse is under no obligation to stay married. The debatable question then is can the saint who is divorced from a sinner later marry a saint and not sin in doing so.

In Matthew 5, Jesus is addressing a large crowd and not just believers. There he says to marry someone who was divorced, other than for adultery, is committing adultery. With that in mind, it would be sinful even for a saint to marry again once divorced from a sinner, except for the cause of adultery. However, Jesus said to even look at another person and imagine having sex with them was the same as committing adultery (Mt. 5:28). I am not aware of anyone who has gotten a divorce who has not lusted after another person. So practically speaking, the sinner who divorced the saint must have committed adultery, at least in his or her heart.

The saint may have lusted after someone as well. If this is true, once the saint is divorced, they would be free to marry another saint. A person who is dissatisfied with their marriage might be tempted then to encourage adultery to justify their getting a divorce. People must be reluctant to divorce though because God's plan was for people to not divorce one another. Repeated divorces by someone make a mockery of God's plan and fornication is sin. Selfishness, pride, and deceit are not hidden from God. As God said to Cain, "Sin is crouching at the door, and its desire is for you, but you must master it."

927.   It does not matter if a man is circumcised since the Lord brought us salvation by him. What matters is the keeping of the commandments of God. So there is no need to become circumcised if one was uncircumcised when one was saved (1 Cor. 7:17–20).

928.   We are to try to become free from slavery if we are able to legally. This does not mean God endorses slavery. God is against slavery, as it is known today, because it is unjust. He does however want us to be happy in him no matter what state of society we are in. We are not to be mad at God because we are not as well off financially as others.

We are free from the slavery of sin when we become saved, having the power of the Holy Spirit in us to overcome our inclinations to sin (1 Cor. 7:21–24).

929.    There is but one God, the Father, from whom are all things, and we exist for him, and one Lord, Jesus Christ, by whom are all things and we exist through him (1 Cor. 8:6).

930.    We can eat food that was for sacrifice to idols if we do not do so in sacrifice to an idol. If however a fellow believer feels they cannot eat such food in good conscience, then the believer whose conscious is not bothered by eating such food should not eat the food so that the weaker believer is not tempted to do something against their conscious (1 Cor. 8:7–13).

931.    A man who is a minister has a right to marry and take his wife with him wherever he ministers (1 Cor. 9:5).

932.    Believers are to support ministers of God so they can proclaim the gospel as God has directed them and not be hindered by lack of funds or distracted from the work God has for them with another job to make a living. This also allows the minister to proclaim the gospel elsewhere than their home and not ask for money from those who listen. New churches are to support their ministers as well, as best they can (1 Cor. 9:6–18).

933.    Ministers are to have priority on preaching and teaching the word of God so that people will be saved and discipled. If this means they join sinners where they are to be able to do this, then that is fine as long as the minister does not partake in sin. An example would be a minister could witness to a sinner in a bar if the minister did not get drunk and as long as there was nothing lewd happening there such as people dancing in a provocative fashion or people not dressed in a moral fashion (e.g. naked or

dressed as the opposite sex). We should not watch movies or shows that would be displeasing to the Lord or listen to music that is sinful (e.g. cursing) in order to witness to others because then it would be impossible to not partake in what sinful event was occurring.

If a saint finds they are in an environment that is displeasing to the Lord, such as around music that is sinful, then they should ask the sinner if they could speak elsewhere or at another time, if the sinner is not willing at that time to change the environment to one that would not displease the Lord (1 Cor. 9:19–23). Christians are to be as infants when it comes to evil and grow in the knowledge of God (1 Cor. 14:20). That means we are to not have knowledge of evil things, which means we are to avoid situations where we know God would not be pleased with us being there and learning things God would not be pleased with. Breaking God's instruction for this while saying we are doing it to reach lost souls is, at best, deceitful to oneself and at least deceitful to others.

934. Christians are to work for God as if they were in a race to win. We are not to work aimlessly but with a goal in mind. This may be discipling all people the Lord brings you into contact with, who are not saved already, or just one person a month. But Christians are to reach the whole world with the gospel and to set a low goal or no goal is not aiming to win the race. We are to discipline our bodies, while working to win souls and disciple new converts, so that we will not be ashamed. Do not commit sexual sin or be a glutton or be lewd or in other ways act sinfully so that we could be accused of being hypocrites (1 Cor. 9:24–27).

935. The children of Israel during the Exodus were the children of God, as Christians are today, yet most of them sinned, even after knowing who God is. God punished them for their idolatry and open rebellion against him. This is an

example to saints today to not sin in the same way lest God be displeased and punish us. We should not believe God will forgive us of our sins so we can sin all we want and not have a care in the world that God would punish us, because we are under a new covenant. We should not believe freedom under the new covenant means we are free of worries about punishment from God. We should not worry about being punished by God for sins, because he loves us, but we should not tempt God's patience with a care-free attitude about sin either. The Christian who thinks because he stands on the rock of Jesus he does not have to worry about sinning because God forgives all his sins, or forgave all his sins he would ever commit when he or she became saved, needs to be careful lest he or she falls into a sinful lifestyle. A saint who falls into a sinful lifestyle can do immense harm to the cause of the kingdom of God, causing people to doubt the validity of Christianity or turn them completely away from God (1 Cor. 10:1–12).

936. No temptation to sin has overtaken a person but such as is common to man. There is no cause of sin that is new under the sun. Jesus knows our temptations because he was in the flesh while here on earth as a man and tempted as we are, yet without sin. So he knows our temptations and is able to relate to us. God does not allow our temptations to be too much to escape or resist and always provides a way out of our temptations (1 Cor. 10:13, Heb. 4:15).

937. Idolatry, worship of, or sacrificing to any god other than God is sin. False gods are demons. Idolatry provokes God to jealousy and will cause God to punish those who do that, even if they are so-called Christians (1 Cor. 10:14–22).

938. Christians should not live their lives trying to live like sinners as much as they can without sinning with a mindset of doing as many things as they can that are not

specifically forbidden by God. Instead Christians are to live their lives with a mindset of being used by God to further the cause of the kingdom of God. Do all things to the glory of God, not thinking about our own profit, but the profit of others so that God will use us to save and disciple as many people as possible (1 Cor. 10:23, 24, 31–33).

939.  Even though Satan is prince of this world, the world is the Lord's and all it contains (1 Cor. 10:26). So Satan only has the limited power and authority God allows for a limited time. God is in control of all things.

940.  Be imitators of godly men (except their sins) and Jesus. This includes traditions given by both, as written in the Old and New Testament Bible, out of reverence to God: men should not have their head covered while praying or prophesying, women should have their head covered with long hair or a covering of some sort if their hair is short, men should not have long hair like a woman, and women should not have their hair cut short like a man or shave their head, but if they do they should cover their head (1 Cor. 11:1–14).

941.  God is the head of Jesus Christ, who is head of each man, who is head of each woman (1 Cor. 11:3). This is the order of headship God has set up and to not comply with it as well as the traditions in 1 Cor. 11 is to be contentious (1 Cor. 11:16). Jesus said he did all that the Father commanded him to do and followed God's example (Jn. 5:19, 30–32). In this way God the Father and God the Son honor one another and so should men do likewise with Jesus and women with men (Jn. 5: 22, 23). So in the end, all of us do as God the Father does. It should be noted here that God does not force his way on Jesus or people but those who love him are obedient to him. So men who are tempted to use this scripture to force

women to do everything they want are not following God's example and thus not obedient to God. Men have a responsibility to act in a way as Jesus would act. Likewise, women who do not submit to the authority of men who are doing as they see God directing them are in rebellion to God. Obviously these verses do not mean God wants women to sin at the bequest of men. Also it is all right for women to question men as it is all right to question God and Jesus why life is at it is, but if we will study the Bible, we will see our answers to those questions of God. So that if more people studied the Bible, with a submissive heart, they would not even ask God or Jesus why. Men and women need to live their lives to the glory of God and not for their own desires. God may or may not give us our desires, but the purpose in our lives is not to fulfill our desires but the will of God. The great commission Jesus gave *all* Christians was to witness to people about the gospel of Jesus and disciple them in the word of God (the Bible). Love for another will cause obedience with a willing heart.

942.   Church is not for coming together to eat but to study God's word and worship him (1 Cor. 11:20–22). To occasionally eat at the building where we have church is alright if it is not in place of church service and no one goes hungry.

943.   Communion/Lord's Supper. Christians are to have communion, reenact the Lord's Supper, regularly at church in remembrance of the Lord's death, until the Lord returns (1 Cor. 11:23–26). A person is not to partake of communion unless they are saved and examine themselves. To do otherwise is disrespectful of Jesus and is to be guilty of crucifying Jesus at the moment they partake of communion, which invites judgment from God. This means the Christian must look introspectively

at themselves and repent of any ungodly ways before partaking in communion.

944.    No one says, "Jesus is accursed," by the Spirit of God, and no one says, "Jesus is Lord," in reverence, except by the Holy Spirit (1 Cor. 12:3).

945.    Each Christian has an important role to play in the kingdom of God, even those who seem less important. We are all baptized by one Spirit into one body. God gives more abundant honor to those who lack, so that there will be no division, but that the members would have the same care for one another. We Christians are all in this together. When one member suffers, we all suffer, and when one member rejoices, we all rejoice. Perhaps the quote of *The Three Musketeers* is appropriate here, "All for one and one for all!" However the king we serve is God Almighty, who gives us the strength to conquer evil. Though we may suffer and die in the flesh at the hands of those who serve Satan, we know that the One whom we serve wins in the end (1 Cor. 12:13).

946.    All gifts and acts are nothing compared to love and mean nothing without love (1 Cor. 13:1–3). This perfect love is as gifts and comes from God and indwells believers (Jas. 1:17, 1 Jn. 4:7). Perfect, sacrificial love can only have its way in us, and work through us, when we surrender all that we are and our own will and desires to God. Love is perfect, kind, hopeful, faithful, and forgiving. Love is not boastful or arrogant, is not jealous, does not joke at the expense of others, endures all things, does not seek its own, is not easily provoked to anger, does not rejoice in unrighteousness, but rejoices in truth (Prov. 26:18, 19, 1 Cor. 13:4–7).

947.    When that which is perfect comes, when Jesus returns and we receive our eternal bodies, prophecies, gifts of

tongues, and knowledge will cease, but love will never fail (1 Cor. 13:8–10).

948. Believers need to grow spiritually and not stay immature in their faith. This comes by prayer and listening to God speak to us, sometimes convicting us of our sins. To grow spiritually, we also must study and meditate on God's word and apply it to ourselves. We may not understand all of God's scripture and his ways, but we will after Jesus returns (1 Cor. 13:11, 12, 14:20).

949. Saints will not know or understand all there is to know about God until we get to heaven (1 Cor. 13:12).

950. Faith, hope, and love abide in this world because of God, but the greatest of these is unselfish love (1 Cor. 13:13).

951. Christians must first pursue love, but they are to desire ministerial gifts, especially the gift of prophecy. Prophecy is the gift of speaking words from God that people need to immediately apply to themselves for edification, exhortation, and consolation (1 Cor. 14:1, 3).

952. When a person speaks in another tongue, they are not speaking to people, unless God gives an interpretation, but to God. One is speaking the mysteries of God when one speaks in tongues (1 Cor. 14:2). The gift of prophecy is more useful for people because it edifies the church, while speaking in tongues edifies only the speaker, unless there is an interpretation (1 Cor. 14:4, 5). If someone speaks in tongues, they need to pray that God would give them the gift of interpretation so they may edify people around them (1 Cor. 14:13). Saints are not to forbid speaking in tongues (1 Cor. 14:39).

953. Order in church. Saints are to not speak in other tongues out loud in church unless they do it one at a time and with interpretation. Speaking to oneself in tongues silently in church is fine (1 Cor. 14:26–28). Those who speak

prophecy are to do it one at a time. Those who hear the prophecy are to judge if the prophecy is truly from God (1 Cor. 14:29–32). These measures will prevent confusion for God is not a God of confusion but of peace (1 Cor. 14:33).

954.     Women in church. Women are to keep silent in church, and if they have something to say, they are to wait until they get home and talk to their husband there (1 Cor. 14:34, 35). This is in context of what the congregation as a whole would hear so a woman are not to speak to where the whole church would hear what she says. This is hard for modern society to accept, but this is the word of God and our church suffers or at least does not prosper as well as it should because of incomplete obedience to the word of God. Also when we pick and choose what we want to abide by from the Bible we are disobedient in what we do not obey. This is dangerous because one compromise leads to another, and there is no end to compromise. We must submit ourselves to God's word, the Bible. Obviously, these verses mean a woman is not to preach to or teach a congregation. The verse does not say women may not sing or play instruments in church. It is acceptable for a woman to teach a Sunday school that does not have men in it also (1 Tim. 2:12). If anyone does not accept these verses about church, which God commands, they are not to be recognized as a believer (1 Cor. 14:37, 38).

955.     Jesus appeared to some five hundred brethren at once between his resurrection and his ascension (1 Cor. 15:6).

956.     Jesus was the first being who was in human form to be resurrected (1 Cor. 15:20).

957.     Death of the flesh, and after that the second death (eternity torment in the lake of fire), has been the destiny of people since Adam and Even sinned. However in Jesus

Christ all who are his will be given eternal life in a new imperishable, spiritual body. Jesus will rule the earth with the saints during the millennium; he conquered death in himself when he raised himself from the dead and will have the power over death to resurrect the physically dead who are his when he returns. Included in God's power over death will be new, imperishable, spiritual bodies saints will receive when Jesus returns. The final victory over death will occur after the millennium after all people are judged at the great white throne of judgment. Death and hell will then be cast into the lake of fire. God put all things in subjection to Jesus's feet, and it is understood that God is excepted in all things because God put all things but the triune God under Jesus's feet. In verse 28, it says Jesus, the Son, will be subjected to God the Father so that God may be all in all. This means Jesus will no longer be needed as the Mediator between man and God after the great white throne of judgment so that the Son may resume his former state as before his first incarnation (1 Cor. 15:21–28, 50–57, Rev. 20:14). God will still be triune as Jesus is the same today, yesterday, and forever (Heb. 13:8).

958.    The resurrection of the dead in Christ will occur when Jesus returns (1 Cor. 15:23). This precludes the idea of a "rapture" of believers as a separate event from His return. The resurrection of the dead in Christ will occur quickly ("in the twinkling of an eye") at the sound of the last trumpet (1 Cor. 15:51, 52). Jesus will return when the last trumpet sounds (1 Th. 4:16, Rev. 11:15). There is a distinction made between the resurrection of the dead and then those saints who are alive being caught up to meet the Lord in the air (1 Th. 4:16, 17) but it is not certain if this is minutes or forty-five days as perhaps Daniel says (Dan. 12:11, 12). The notion of "the rapture"

occurring any second now, sparing Christians from the tribulation, started in the nineteenth century because Christians of that time were discouraged that the Lord had not come yet and many were scared of going through the tribulation. It is not biblically based. The traditional view of the Christian church since the time of John, who wrote Revelation, was that the Lord would return at the end of the seven year tribulation, resurrecting the dead in Christ and Christians who were alive at the Second Coming would then be caught up in the air, in their new spiritual bodies, to meet the Lord in the air. More discussion of this will be made in Revelation.

959. Bad company corrupts good morals (1 Cor. 15:33). We should therefore not keep company with those people who usually behave badly so that we do not start acting and thinking like them. Saints should witness to sinners, but this scripture plainly says sinners who usually behave badly will corrupt our thinking and behavior, rather than us being a positive influence on them by keeping company ("hanging out") with them.

960. Saints should be serious about their walk with God and do their best to not sin rather than neglecting to make efforts to not sin (1 Cor. 15:34).

961. God, who has the power to create large varieties of plant life from simple seeds and who created the universe, is able to change saints' physical bodies to imperishable, spiritual bodies (1 Cor. 15:35–49). These verses do not mean animals will go to heaven because only humans have souls.

962. Saints must not be discouraged or stop working for God because their work is not in vain, even if it seems so while they are alive in the flesh (1 Cor. 15:58). Seeds planted (words of God shared with others) may grow and cause

salvations, or have other positive influences, after the sower dies.

963. When an evangelist, or visiting speaker, visits a church, the members of the church need to know in advance and set aside what they determine to give the evangelist when he visits, rather than collect money while the evangelist is there. This prevents money collection, while the visiting speaker is visiting a church, from distracting from the work of the Holy Spirit in people's hearts (1 Cor. 16:1, 2).

964. Saints are to be on the alert for the work of Satan, be strong and bold in their faith, and work for God. Whatever we do, we must do in love (1 Cor. 16:13, 14).

965. If anyone does not love the Lord and rejects the gospel of Jesus, he or she is to be left alone by saints (1 Cor. 16:22). This does not apply to people who say they don't know or are confused or need more time to consider the word of God. This refers to people who defiantly trample on the word of God, saying the Bible is definitely false and Jesus is not the only way to heaven or may even deny that God exists. Saints need to apply their efforts for making disciples among people who have not already rejected the Lord.

# 2 CORINTHIANS

966.  God comforts saints in their distresses and saints in turn can comfort each other by prayer and helping saints in need practically. Our sufferings can be to the point of death, but when our sufferings are too much for us to bear, we can depend on God to comfort us. Sometimes our sufferings are to bring us to the point that we realize our hope is not in ourselves, but in God and God alone (2 Cor. 1:3–11).

967.  Paul was not a domineering, hateful person but a loving, selfless disciple of the Lord who wanted people be like Christ (1 Cor. 11:1; 2 Cor. 1:24–2:4, 11:11, 23–29).

968.  We must restore to church membership those saints who desire it and who repent (2 Cor. 2:5–11). Repentance involves asking for forgiveness and discontinuation of committing the sin. That is not to say we will never commit the sin again, but we must do our best to not do it again. Theft, idolatry, and sexual sin involving another person, incest in this case, is easier to not commit again since it is not done in an instant with a sudden rush of emotions such as the sin of cursing when one smashes one's finger.

969.  Thanks be to God who always causes saints to triumph in Christ (2 Cor. 2:14a). This doesn't mean saints will get what they want, but saints will always triumph in the cause of the kingdom of God even with apparent failures along the way. All things work together for good to those who love God and are called according to his purpose (Rom. 8:28). The good God means here is not our fleshly good, but God's good for his purposes. Saints' adequacy for God's tasks comes from God and not from us. The

Holy Spirit, not the letter of the law, gives us the ability (2 Cor. 3:4–6). We do not have to have all of God's word, the Bible, memorized to be adequate for God's tasks. It is more important to know the love and ways of God from meditation on the scriptures than to have much scripture memorized because the work is done by the Holy Spirit and not our own abilities.

970. God manifests through saints the sweet aroma of the knowledge of Christ Jesus in every place we testify of him (2 Cor. 2:14b). People can sense the truth of Jesus when they hear God's word from the Bible. To those whom God has predetermined to be saved, it is the aroma of life, which leads them to salvation and thus eternal life. To those God has predetermined would not be saved (God is the creator and omniscient), it is the aroma of death, condemning them of their unrepentant sins, which leads them to hell and then the second death of eternal punishment in the lake of fire (2 Cor. 2:15, 16). It must be said here that we do not know to whom or when salvation comes, so we need to continue to pray for and witness to, as God give opportunity, those sinners with whom God brings us into contact.

971. New believers are a testimony for saints who helped them come to salvation (2 Cor. 3:1–3).

972. God is not fully, and many times not at all, revealed to those who try to go to heaven by following the traditions and laws of the Jewish religion or any other religion than Christianity. Whenever a person turns to the Lord, the veil is removed, and that person then understands God more fully and sees him for whom he really is. The Spirit of the Lord is in saints and where the Spirit of the Lord is, there is liberty—liberty from sin and from trying to go to heaven by works and other futile religious efforts. We become more and more like the Lord as we are more

and more obedient to him, as the Holy Spirit and the scriptures lead us (2 Cor. 3:7–18).

973.  Saints must not change or compromise the word of God, regardless of the motive or intent (2 Cor. 4:2). The uncompromising word of God is the only way to lead others to salvation and disciple them. Otherwise, there is no salvation and, worse, confusion.

974.  The god of this world, Satan, has blinded the minds of unbelieving so that they would not see and understand the truth of the gospel of Jesus, who is the image of God (2 Cor. 4:3, 4). Jesus is the Light in the darkness of this world, and he shines in the hearts of believers (2 Cor. 4:6).

975.  Saints are bond-servants of the Lord (2 Cor. 4:5). Saints gladly serve the Lord for eternity rather than be slaves to sin. Believers, who are faithful to the Lord, are bound to him forever and will serve God even in the new heaven and the new earth.

976.  Through the power of God, Paul, and by extension all believers, can endure persecution and death without being despondent (2 Cor. 4:7–12).

977.  Though the outer man is decaying, the inner man is being renewed day by day (2 Cor. 4:16). Though our bodies age or we fail in sin, God renews our spiritual, inner self, which is our soul. We are forgiven, rejuvenated, and strengthened for the tasks ahead of us. If anyone is in Christ, he or she is a new creature; the old things and ways have passed away. Behold new things and ways have come. These new things and ways come from God (2 Cor. 5:17, 18). The Lord strengthens saints' inner beings, our souls, with his power through the Holy Spirit (Eph. 3:16, 20).

978.  Saints' afflictions for the sake of God here on earth produce rewards that await us in heaven. Our life after this body dies is eternal with God. With these facts in mind, we

are able to suffer persecutions, which are temporal (2 Cor. 4:17, 18).

979. We know that we will receive an eternal, spiritual body, made by God, when the Lord returns. Saints' souls long for this to come (2 Cor. 5:1, 2, 8).

980. Saints walk by faith and not by sight (2 Cor. 5:7). If we physically saw Jesus as Lord, as will be the case during the millennium for the whole world, then faith that he is Lord would not be necessary. Faith without sight in Jesus as Lord God is the fundamental factor of the new covenant of the gospel of Jesus.

981. All people who will have ever lived, saints and sinners, will be judged by the Lord Jesus before his judgment seat. We all will be recompensed for our deeds we did while we were alive in the flesh, whether good or bad (2 Cor. 5:10). This should make saints and sinners alike tremble and want to live their lives in obedience to God.

982. Christ died for all, so then we should no longer live for ourselves but for the Lord who died and rose again for our behalf (2 Cor. 5:15).

983. Trinity. God was in Jesus Christ, reconciling the world to himself (2 Cor. 5:19). This helps us understand the Holy Trinity. The Son is part of the triune God, and God is in the Son. They are one in the same yet able to be separate, as was the case on the cross. The Trinity is a hard concept for people to understand, but I like that God is not so easily fully understood. Saints will not know or understand all there is to know about God until we get to heaven (1 Cor. 13:12).

984. Saints are ambassadors for Christ, as though God were making appeal through us, so we should be reconciled with God and live as righteous a life as we can. So that no matter what our circumstances, we may live lives full

of faith and the love of God (2 Cor. 5:20, 21, 6:1–10). We know we will not be perfect but should be sober to the fact that we represent Christ to the world. The grace of God that brings salvation has appeared to all people, teaching us that denying ungodliness and worldly lusts, we should live soberly, righteously, and godly in this present world, looking for the return of Christ, who gave himself for us that he might redeem us from all iniquity and purify unto himself a peculiar people, zealous of good works (Tit. 2:11–14).

985. Saints are the temple of the living God so that saints should not entangle themselves with sinners. We should not spend large amounts of our time with sinners as friends, and we should not enter into contracts or partnerships with sinners. It is obvious saints should not be involved in sinful activity with sinners (Is. 52:11, 2 Cor. 6:11–18).

986. Since each saint is a temple of the living God, each of us should cleanse ourselves from all defilement of flesh and spirit, perfecting holiness in the fear of God (2 Cor. 7:1).

987. God offers saints overflowing joy even while we are afflicted (2 Cor. 7:4).

988. Paul and other disciples of Jesus were so afflicted and fearful they became depressed for a time. Therefore, God sent to them Titus who comforted them so that they were no longer depressed. Titus's news from other believers made the disciples such as Paul rejoice and were no longer depressed (2 Cor. 7:5–7). This tells us depression can occur when circumstances seem hopeless. It also tells us we need to say words of encouragement to each other and pray for one another. We should be encouraged that God knows our feelings and thoughts and comes to our aid.

989. Repentant people do not think they should not pay for the sins they committed. They try to right the wrongs they

did, if they can (2 Cor. 7:11). So a person who repents for stealing, for instance, will try to repay the one they stole from. Saints cannot do works to make up for their sins in God's eyes, but they do not have to because Jesus paid the price for their sins. However, a saint who has God's love in them would want to help those he or she wronged as much as possible.

990. Saints need to follow through on their commitments to support ministries as much as is possible (2 Cor. 8:11, 12).

991. Donations by saints are to be according to their abundance so that none prosper while others lack (2 Cor. 8:13–15). This is regarding the donations above the tithe, which is 10 percent of one's income or harvest. (Lv. 27:32, Mal. 3:8–10, Lk. 11:42). He who sows sparingly will also reap sparingly, and he who sows bountifully will also reap bountifully. God gives back to those who give to him, through donations to ministries, proportionately to what percent of their wealth they give to him. Each person must give as he or she desires because God loves a cheerful giver. Better to give a little without grudge than to give more grudgingly. God is able to provide for all of our needs, so giving to him will not result in lack of our necessities. God is God, and so he is able to provide for all of our needs, often through other people. However much we give, we cannot give more than he has given: his Son for our salvation, his indescribable gift (2 Cor. 9:6–15).

992. Though people are in the flesh our war is not with the flesh or of the flesh. For the weapons of our warfare are not carnal, but spiritual and mighty through God to the pulling down of strong holds, casting down every imaginable thing that opposes God and every high thing that exalts itself against the knowledge of God, bringing into captivity every thought to the obedience of Christ, and we are ready to punish all disobedience, whenever a

body of believers' obedience is complete (2 Cor. 10:3–6). Our battle is spiritual against the devil and his demons, who are influencing people to do evil. Prayer and fasting bring about God's power to oppose these evil forces. Saints also have the Holy Spirit in them to win the battle against their flesh, which influences them to sin, and God gives a way to escape temptation so that saints will not sin. When a body of believers, a local church, is obedient to God as a whole, then they are able to root out those who have evil intentions and separate them from the church, if they are not repentant.

993.   When God does great things through a person, that person needs to give credit to God and not take credit for it himself or herself (2 Cor. 10:17).

994.   There is no different revelation from God that would espouse a different Jesus, a different Spirit, or a different gospel than what is in the Bible (2 Cor. 11:4). This warned people to not accept what people of various religions believe and profess, under the influence of Satan, a different Jesus than what is in the Holy Scriptures (Holy Bible). These false beliefs and teachings include: Jesus was created by God, Jesus and Satan are brothers, and Jesus was just a prophet and not God in the flesh. It also warned people of false spiritism that worships angels or other spirits. Angels are not to be worshiped. A message that there is another way to heaven and God than by God the Son, Jesus, or things a person needs to do in addition to believing and confession the Lord Jesus is a false gospel. Another example of a false gospel is the practice of leaders of a church acting as mediators between their parishioners and God, which is in violation of 1 Tim. 2:5. Christians in all churches need to study the Bible and do as the Bible says. This may mean they have to leave their church because of the false teachings of their church.

There are many people in all Christian denominations who call themselves Christian but are not. Christians are genuine believers in Jesus as Lord, who then follow God as they should. Some people have begun to use the word Christian to include people who call themselves Christian and yet do not follow and obey God, some even denying that Jesus is the only way to heaven. These people are not Christians but so-called Christians, hypocrites, destined for hell unless they repent and get right with God.

995. Just as Satan disguised himself as an angel of light, so too do those people who do his work, deceivers trying to influence people away from the truth of the Bible (2 Cor. 11:13–15). They may say outright lies, misquote the Bible slightly, get people to compromise on obedience to God, or try to get people to doubt the validity of the Bible.

996. Three different heavens: The first is the earth's atmosphere (Gen. 1:8, 8:2; Dt. 11:11; 1Kgs. 8:35), the second is the sky we see at night or space (the universe from our perspective, Gen. 1:14–17, 15:5; Ps. 8:3; Is. 13:10), and the third is God's dwelling place, where God's throne is and saints are with God (1 Kgs. 8:30; 2 Ch. 30:27; Ps. 123:1; 2 Cor. 12:2–4; Rev. 2:7, 22:14).

997. The thorn in the flesh. Paul was given a thorn in the flesh, a messenger of Satan to torment him—to keep him from exalting himself. Three times he asked God to deliver him from this evil, but God said his grace was sufficient for him and his power is perfected in weakness. This made Paul content, knowing the power of Christ dwelled in him, for when we are weak, then we are strong (2 Cor. 12:7–10). There has been speculation as to what this thorn in the flesh was, but given it was a messenger (Gr., angellos, or angel) of Satan, one has to wonder if it was a demon that regularly attacked Paul. These attacks kept Paul from being perfect and thus prideful. It could have

been poor vision, as some speculate, because Paul had others do a good amount of his writing. It could have been a recurring sin he committed and repented of, keeping him humble. It could have been depression (2 Cor. 7:6). It could have been the demon making other people oppose Paul's ministry. We do not know for certain, but we do know any of these possibilities are ways God could use to keep us humble, and if God does not free us of any of these after we have asked him to, we have Paul's example from which we can take comfort. As was the case with Paul, we know for where we are weak, then we are strong because the power of Christ dwells in us. So we are kept from being prideful by our thorn in the flesh, knowing that we owe all that we are to the grace and mercy of God.

998. Young children are not responsible to save up for their parents, but parents for their children, while they are children. 2 Cor. 12:14. This does not mean adult children are not responsible for caring for their parents' needs. Quite the contrary, adult children are responsible for their parents' needs. 1 Tim. 5:4. However the parents are to do the best they can to not be in need of assistance from anyone (1 Tim. 5:8).

999. Every fact is to be confirmed by the testimony of two or three witnesses (Dt. 19:15, 2 Cor. 13:1).

1000. Greeting one another with a holy kiss does not mean kissing other people is holy (2 Cor. 13:12). Paul is advising the Corinthians to kiss each other with a holy kiss when they greet one another. Kissing on the cheek was a traditional way to greet one another at the time. Paul is advising to make this kiss a holy one, one without fleshly motives.

# GALATIANS

1001. There is only one gospel, and that is the gospel of Jesus as told in the Holy Bible (Gal. 1:6–9). There is salvation by none other than Jesus, no matter what other people say or even if an angel were to say otherwise.

1002. Saints cannot seek to please other people, as a whole, and serve God at the same time, because mankind is in rebellion against God (Gal. 1:10). The spirit of rebellion in people strives against God.

1003. When God calls a saint to ministry, the saint does not need to consult with other saints. When God calls we should simply obey (Gal. 1:16, 17).

1004. Peter's ministry was primarily to the Jews while Paul was called by Jesus to minister to Gentiles (Gal. 1:16, 2:7, 8).

1005. No one is justified by obeying religious laws. Only through faith in Jesus Christ can anyone be justified before God (Gal. 2:16).

1006. People that are saved are no longer sinners but saints (Gal. 2:17). Believers are part of the body of Christ, and Christ is not a sinner. Christ lives in believers, and believers live by faith in Jesus, the Son of God (Gal. 2:20). Since Christ lives in saints we have the power to not sin (Lk. 10:19; 1 Cor. 10:13, 15:57; Gal. 5:16, 17; Eph. 4:22–27, 6:10–17; Heb. 2:18; Jas. 4:7, 8; 1 Pet. 5:8–10; 1 Jn. 4:4; 5:3–5; Rev. 3:21, 12:11).

1007. Just as Abraham was justified, reckoned as righteous, before God by his faith in God, so too all saints are justified by their faith and are become children of Abraham (Gal. 3:6–9, 29). If someone could live a sinless life, obeying all the Mosaic law in mind, speech, and action, then they would be able to go to heaven, but Jesus was the only perfect person (and he was God the Son). So then the only way to go to heaven is through faith in Jesus as Lord, who took on himself the sins of the world while on the cross. Blessed be the name of the Lord forever.

1008. The Holy Spirit was promised to come and came at Pentecost into believers (Is. 32:15; Joel 2:28, 29; Jn. 7:37–39, 14:16, 26; Ac. 2:1–21; Gal. 3:14). The Holy Spirit has been part of God always and was manifest rarely before Pentecost, such as with David, Samson, and Zacharias, but since Pentecost, the Holy Spirit dwells in all saints.

1009. God promised to give Canaan to the seed of Abraham. That seed is the Messiah, Jesus, who will rule the earth from there during the millennium and the Old and New Testament saints will rule with him there. Jesus's mother could trace her lineage back to Abraham so Jesus was the seed of Abraham (Gen 12:7). The Mosaic law did not nullify the covenant God made with Abraham. From the time the covenant was first given to the Mosaic law was 645 years (Gen. 12:4, 7, 21:5, 25:26, 47:9). God repeated the covenant to Isaac (Gen. 26:24 and then Jacob ca. 1928 BC, Gen. 28:15). The last time we read God repeating the covenant was about 1875 BC (Gen. 46:2–4), 430 years before the Mosaic law was given (Gal. 3:15–18).

1010. The purpose of the Mosaic law was to tutor people leading them to Christ. It gave people knowledge of the desires of God for the way he wants us to live our lives. It also showed that we could not be good enough to go to heaven because no one, except Jesus, can live a perfect life. Now through faith in Christ, saints become sons of God (Gal. 3:23–26).

1011. Saints have a common bond in Jesus. So we are to think of ourselves as belonging to Christ, descendants of Abraham, and not as Jew or Greek, male or female, slave or free (Gal. 3:27–29).

1012. Saints are adopted by God as sons, and he has put the Spirit of his Son into our hearts so that our heart cry, "Abba! Father!" "Abba" being a term of endearment meaning "daddy." Our souls long to be with God. We love him. We honor and respect him. We obey him gladly. We know the joy that we experience now is just a taste of the joy we will have when we are in God's presence (Gal. 4:4–7).

1013. Hagar bore a son to Abraham through the flesh. Hagar was from Egypt and a slave, as were the Jews when the left Egypt under Moses's leadership. The Jews received the law at Mount Sinai and lived under the law. God promised he would make a great nation of Hagar's son Ishmael, and he is the father of the Arabic people. Islam came from the Arabic people and its followers are slave to the laws of Islam. Sarah was a free woman and bore a son to Abraham through promise from God. This son, Isaac, had two sons, but only Jacob received the blessing. So the children of Jacob, the Jews, receive the promise God gave Abraham. However, since Jesus came the promise is available to all, and only to those, who believe in Jesus as Lord. These believers are heirs of the promise of God to Abraham and free children of God (Gal. 4:21–31). He who was born according to the flesh, Ishmael, persecuted him who was born of the Spirit (Sarah was only able to bare Isaac through the work of the Holy Spirit), Isaac, and so it is today. In general the descendants of Ishmael, the Arabs who are not saved, persecute Jews and Christians, who are born of the Spirit. It is then not surprising that Islam, the religion born from Arabs, calls for persecution of Jews and Christians.

1014. Uncircumcised men who convert to Judaism, and thus get circumcised, live under the law of Judaism. Christ was sent to free us from the bondage of the law. Circumcision does not help a person get to heaven (Gal. 5:1–6).

1015. A little leaven leavens the whole lump of dough (Gal. 5:9). We are not to compromise on our walk with God or his truth, the Bible, or we will become wholly affected by this compromise. We will live and teach a life of bondage to this sin.

1016. Saints should not sin since they are free from the law. They should do as the heart of the law intends: love the Lord your God with all your heart, soul, strength, and mind, and love other people as yourself (Gal. 5:13, 14).

1017. The Holy Spirit in saints opposes the flesh in them so that there is a struggle for saints to do good or bad. If saints walk by the Spirit, live their lives devoted to God and giving more thought time for him than anything or anybody else, then they will not carry out the desires of the flesh. The deeds of the flesh include immorality, impurity, sensuality, idolatry, sorcery, enmities (bearing a grudge), strife, jealousy, outbursts of anger, disputes, dissensions, factions, envying, drunkenness, and carousing, and those who practice such things will not inherit the kingdom of God. This does not mean that a saint may in a weak moment do a sin such as some of these, but a saint does not regularly do these things or take pleasure in doing them or seeing them done by others (Gal. 5:16–21).

1018. The fruit of the Spirit is love, joy, peace, patience, kindness, goodness, faithfulness, gentleness, and self-control; against such things, there is no law. Those who belong to Christ, Jesus have crucified the flesh with its passions and desires. Since saints will live forever with God because of the Spirit, we should also walk by the spirit, live our lives devoted to God, and give more thought time for him than anything or anybody else. Then we will not be boastful, proud, envious, selfish, or sensual so that the Holy Spirit helps us exhibit the fruits of the Spirit (Gal. 5:22–26).

1019.   If saints find out another saint sins, they should approach the saint who sinned with gentleness and try to bring him or her to no longer desire to sin and repentance. Those who communicate with the one who sinned must first examine themselves and repent of their sins (Gal. 6:1–5).

1020.   Saints are to share good news with one another such as understanding of scripture or where God has worked in their life. We are to express thanks to the one who teaches us from God's word, and if it blesses us particularly, we need to let the one who taught us know that (Gal. 6:6). This encourages the teacher.

1021.   God is not mocked; what a person sows that they will also reap. If we spend our time and efforts on things of God and witness for him, we will receive blessing from God such as insight in his word and greater ability to overcome sin, and we will be used by God to save sinners and disciple new believers. If we spend our time and effort on things of this world, we will receive things of this world, which will corrupt us. We should do good to others, especially fellow saints. God will then definitely reward us; though our reward may not be imminent (Gal. 6:7–10).

1022.   Paul blessed Israel. This is something American Christians have tended to do also and have been blessed by God in response, according to God's word in Gen. 12:3 (Gal. 6:16).

# EPHESIANS

1023. Believers and followers of God are saints, not sinners. That is not to say saints do not sin. Sinners are not saved and choose sin and self over God. Eph. 1:1.

1024. Father God chose each saint before the foundation of the world. Eph. 1:4, 5. Saints are predestined according to God's purpose who works all things after the counsel of his will (Eph. 1:11). So does God predestine who will be saved, but God makes sure saints do what he purposed them to do. This is reassuring so that saints do not have to be concerned about failing to do God's will. This is possible because saints have a willing heart to do God's will. People who do not want to do God's will are not saved. That is not to say saints are perfect and always stay in God's will. Saints sin also. But they repent and make stronger efforts to obey God.

1025. Saints are holy and blameless before God through Jesus Christ according to God's kind will. So that saints are adopted children of God. When a person becomes saved, they are redeemed through Jesus's blood and forgiven of all trespasses by his grace (Eph. 1:4, 5, 7).

1026. Saints feel the Lord in them and are aware of the mystery of the gospel, which is salvation and oneness with God through faith and confession in Jesus as Lord without seeing him (Eph. 1:9).

1027. God will give an inheritance to each saint, according to his will (Eph. 1:11). I do not know if this is anything more than a dwelling place (Jn. 14:2). But it appears there are greater things in store for saints in the age to come, new heaven and new earth (Eph. 2:7).

1028. Believers are sealed in Jesus with the Holy Spirit (Eph. 1:13). So believers can rest assured we are secured from God letting go of us or anything or anyone taking us from him. By being sealed, we are also identified as belonging to God, adopted children, and therefore Satan has not rights in regards to us.

1029. May God give the saints a spirit of wisdom and of revelation in the knowledge of him (Eph. 1:17).

1030. God's surpassing great power is toward those of us who believe in him (saints) (Eph. 1:19). God's power is available to each saint from the moment we are saved. This power is used to God's glory and cannot be used for personal gain.

1031. Jesus was raised from the dead and is seated at the right hand of God in heaven far above all rule, authority, power, dominion, and name, not only of this age but of the age to come (new heaven and new earth, which comes after the great white throne of judgment after the millennium). All things are in subjection under Jesus's feet (Eph. 1:20–22).

1032. Before each saint was saved, they were dead in their sins, living their life according to the way of the world, which is according to the prince of the power of the air (Satan), of the spirit that is working in sinners (Eph. 2:1–3). All people are sinners until they are saved and are easily influenced by Satan. Sinners are destined, as is Satan, to the second death, unless sinners repent.

1033. By the grace of God are people saved through faith, and not works, because of God's love for people. And this faith is not of ourselves lest we should boast (Eph. 2:4, 5, 8). Even our faith to believe in Jesus as Lord is given to us by God. Thank God for choosing me.

1034. Saints are raised up with Jesus and seated with him in heaven (Eph. 2:6). While saints are alive in the flesh, they are known in heaven and have access to all that is in heaven for the glory of God. When saints die, their soul goes to heaven to be with the Lord.

1035. Each saint is created in Christ Jesus by God for good works, which God prepared beforehand for each saint to do (Eph. 2:10). Our purpose is to do the good works God lays on our hearts to the glory of God.

1036. Before Jesus's crucifixion and resurrection, Gentiles as a whole had no hope of being with God. There were exceptions such as Rahab the harlot, Ruth, and any others who earnestly desired to be with God. God has now made peace and brotherhood between Jew and Gentile through Jesus, for those who choose to believe in Jesus as Lord. And we have access to God through the same Spirit (Eph. 2:11–18).

1037. The temple of God is the worldwide church, the body of believers, or all saints in the world. This temple is built on the foundation of the apostles and prophets, Jesus Christ being the chief cornerstone (Eph. 2:19–22).

1038. Mystery of Christ. The mystery of Christ is that through the gospel, the Gentiles are heirs together with Israel, members together of one body, and sharers together in the promise in Christ Jesus through faith in Jesus as Lord (Eph. 3:6).

1039. In Jesus, and through faith in Jesus, saints may approach God with freedom and confidence (Eph. 3:12).

1040. The Lord strengthens saints' inner beings, our souls, with his power through the Holy Spirit (Eph. 3:16, 20).

1041. Christians are to live a life worthy of the calling they have received from God (Eph. 4:1). Christians are worthy of going to heaven just by being a child of God, but how they live their lives is dependent on their actions, thoughts and speech. So a Christian's life varies with how faithful they are to God.

1042. Unity of the Saints. Saints are to be completely humble, gentle, and patient with one another, motivated by love for one another as God loves us. Saints keep their unity with one another, of the Holy Spirit, making every effort to be bonded together peacefully, without compromising on the word of God. There is one hope, one body, all believers of the world, so there should not be denominations or divisions. There is one Holy Spirit, one Lord, one faith, one baptism, and one Father God, who is over all, through all and in all (Eph. 4:2–6).

1043. Jesus descended to hell between His death on the cross and His ascension to heaven (Ac. 2:27–31, Eph. 4:9, 10). While there, he made proclamation to the fallen angels that did evil during Noah's time (1 Pet. 3:19–20). The eight souls delivered in 1 Peter is referring to Noah, his wife, Noah's three sons, and their wives, not to eight souls saved by Jesus's visit to hell. So then Jesus conquered both death and hell and has the keys to them (Rev. 1:18).

1044. Jesus and God, and therefore the Holy Spirit, fill the whole universe, not just the third heaven above earth (Eph. 4:10).

1045. Maturation of saints. Prophets, evangelists, pastors, and teachers, as was well as the apostles, have the job to equip saints for service to God, until saints become knowledgeable enough of the Bible and mature that they are unified in their beliefs and actions. We saints are to measure ourselves not against the standard other saints, let alone sinners, set but against the perfect standard Jesus set for us. So that we realize, since we are not perfect until we get to heaven, we need to be vigilant in our study and meditation on God's word, submitting our wills to

God, and as we do so our heart, and thus desires, change. Then we will hate evil, because to not hate evil is to not love God. Also, we will exhibit the perfect love of God in whatever we think, say, or do. In addition, we will not be deceived by the devil with false teachings. We then stop doing the sins we did before we were saved and stop lying to other people because God renews our conscience to what is right and wrong. We no longer steal, speak unwholesome words (curse words and criticisms of others without pure motives), slander others, and allow anger to stay more than an moment in, but only long enough for God to take it out of, us. We speak words of edification to one another, which may be words of praise for doing good or words of criticism (humbly, for we know we are not perfect) for sinning with the intent of helping one another to be godlier. Be kind to one another, Christians, tenderhearted, forgiving one another, just as God in Christ also has forgiven each believer (Eph. 4:11–16, 20–32).

1046. When people embrace sin their conscious becomes callous so that they lose their understanding of what is right and what is wrong and become involved in sensual sin, if not other sins (Eph. 4:17–19).

1047. We can be angry and not sin (Eph. 4:26). It is natural to feel anger when something does not go as we desire. That is the flesh in us, and God made us, so to have that initial response is not sin as long as we stop being angry as soon as we realize we are angry. Also, anger at evil is not sin. Instead, it motivates us to oppose evil. When we see injustice done to others, it should make us angry so that we do something about it right away. We should not let anger stay in our heart when we lay down to go to sleep but should resolve it by then. We should forgive all others by then, if not out of love, then out of fear of God, remembering God will not forgive us of our sins if we do not forgive others of their sins.

1048. Saints are to be imitators of God, living their lives motivated by love of God and other people, rather than continuing in sin as if sin did not matter anymore to someone who was saved. While it is true a saint cannot lose their salvation by committing so many sins, each of our sins has consequences. These consequences may be a change in our heart so that our thoughts are not pure, and so it becomes harder to not sin; it may mean we affect others in a bad way, and regardless, all people will give an accounting of their sins to the Lord (Eph. 5:1, 2).

1049. Saints are not to speak crudely; curse; say, or willingly listen to, dirty jokes; or speak silly talk so that it becomes difficult for people to know when we are saying the truth or not (Eph. 5:3, 4).

1050. No person whose life is habitually immoral, impure, or covetous, or who seeks anything more than God, will go to heaven, unless they repent and change their ways and are saved (Eph. 5:5).

1051. Do not believe those who say God will not send to hell people who do not repent, making Jesus their Lord, and as evidence of truly doing that, are obedient to God (Eph. 5:6).

1052. Saints are not to be partakers of those sinning (Eph. 5:7, 11). Saints are to be pious.

1053. Saints are to walk as children of Light, trying to learn God's word and exposing evil done by others where they see it, in attempt to stop Satan's control of themselves and others, not in attempt to hurt others (Eph. 5:10, 11, 17).

1054. Because the days are evil and Satan is constantly seeking whom he may take with him to the lake of fire, saints are not to waste time but make good use of their time in every effort to do the work of God, opposing Satan (Eph. 5:16).

1055. Saints are not to drink enough alcohol to become drunk (Eph. 5:18).

1056. Saints are to let the Holy Spirit control their lives and not the flesh or other people (Eph. 5:18). Saints are to conduct their lives in a manner worthy of the gospel of Jesus, standing firm in their faith, in unison of spirit with each other, and striving together for the faith of the gospel (Php. 1:27–28, 1 Thes. 2:12). So then we will not be hypocrites, which is repulsive to unbelievers.

1057. Saints are to sing psalms, hymns, and spiritual songs, making melody in our hearts (Eph. 5:19).

1058. Saints are to be thankful to God, in the name of Jesus, in all circumstances (Eph. 5:20). This tells us to pray in Jesus's name and to rest assured that God is in control, even when circumstances are currently bad for us.

1059. Saints are to be subject to one another in the fear of Christ (Eph. 5:21). This does not mean we are slaves to one another, but we are to help those who ask for our help or we become aware of them needing our help if we are able to help them. Saints are also to not be prideful but listen to the chastisement of other saints who seek to help them live more godly lives.

1060. Husband and wife relationship. Wives are to submit to their husbands because the husband is the head of the wife, as Christ is the head of the church. Husbands are to love their wives as Christ loves the church and gave his life for the church, despite the faults of those he chose. So wives are to obey their husbands once a husband has made a final decision. This does not preclude discussion by the wife and husband beforehand, in which the wife is free to speak her opinion. The wise husband listens to his wife's opinion before making a final decision. Eventually, a final decision has to be made by someone, even when the husband and wife do not agree, and God has said the husband is to be the final decision maker, with the wife submitting to his decision. The husband is then responsible for the consequences, or rewards, of the decision. None should be despondent or proud if they have prayed to God before making decisions and tried to be obedient to God, no matter the consequences, which are in the Lord's hands.

God has set principles though that we need to live by, and if we break those, there are predictable consequences, such as borrowing with no good plan on repaying the debt, spending more than one makes, and breaking laws. Husbands are to love their wives so much that they would die for them, despite their faults. Even as Christ nourishes and cherishes the church, so should husbands nourish and cherish their wives, meaning husbands are to speak kind words to their wives, speak and act in such a way as to let them know they can be confident in their never-ending love for them, take care of their wife's needs, help them grow to be the person God intended, help them grow in the knowledge and love of God, and love their wives more than anybody else. A husband is to not be bitter toward his wife for any reason because that gives place to the devil to work in the husband's heart. Of course, the Bible tells saints to not have bitterness, which is caused by unforgiveness, toward anyone, anyway.

A husband and wife are to leave their parents when they get married. When a man and woman marry, they become one flesh. There is no room in there for another person, so a person is not to be married to more than one person at a time. Paul further admonishes husbands to love their wives as a man normally loves himself, and wives are to respect their husbands. This points out the weakness of the man is to lose his love for his wife for lack of respect from his wife or whatever reason. He must maintain it no matter what. Also, a weakness of a woman is to lose her respect for her husband because of his failures or whatever reason (Eph. 5:22–33, Col. 3:18, 19).

1061.  Parents and children. Children are to obey their parents in the Lord, for this is right. This means children are to obey their parents in everything as long as it does not conflict with how God tells us to conduct our lives in the Bible. Children are to honor their father and mother, and God will, in return, bless them here on earth and give them a long life in the flesh. Honoring one's parents means loving, respecting, and obeying, out of this love and respect. The Bible does not say to only do this for good parents or when the parents are right. Parents are responsible for themselves and their children, and if they are doing something wrong like taking too many risks with finances or whatever, God will hold them responsible, not the children. Fathers are to not provoke their children to anger but bring them up in the discipline and instruction of the Lord. It is implicit here that God wants children to be raised by a father and a mother because that is the way He designed people; children need both a father and a mother. Also, disciplining, such as spanking, and instructing one's children is not provoking the children, unless it is abusive such as cutting off a hand of the child who steals, as is acceptable in non-Christian countries. How does one provoke a child? Abuse, as previously mentioned, which can take many forms. Spanking can be abusive and a clue as to whether that is the case is if the parent enjoys it. Unreasonable demand and restrictions provoke a child. Look at how life was for the first century, AD, Christian family for comparison to see if one is being unreasonable with one's children. To look at families of contemporary times is subjective because cultural norms and values change. Currently, in many industrialized countries, the standard is no discipline and anything goes-if it feels good do it. Also, the people of these countries do not even know what a family is anymore, sadly enough, so now in those countries a family is whatever you want it to be (Eph. 6:1–4, Col. 3:20, 21).

1062. Servants/employees and employers. Servants/employees are to obey what they are told by their employer, as long as it does not conflict with God's laws. Servants/employees are to work for their employer as if they were working for God, not just appearing to be good employee but actually being a good employee. God will reward servants/employees who are obedient to their employers when they get to heaven. Employers are to not even threaten physical harm to a servant or employee or they will have to give an accounting to God. Employers are to treat their employees justly and equally. While Jesus said in the parable of the workers in the field it is the right of the employer to do as he wishes with his money and if some people agree to work for less than others that is just, it is right in God's eyes to not take advantage of people and pay people equally for equal work (Eph. 6:5–9, Col. 3:22–4:1). Employee and employer alike are to fear God and to not do anything that is dishonest or in any other way would displease God.

1063. Armor of God and spiritual warfare. Our struggle is not against flesh and blood (people) but against the Satan and demons here on earth and in heaven. Our weapons are also spiritual: pray as directed by the Holy Spirit for all believers, and if there are needs that individual believers have, we are to pray for those. Pray for saints to be bold in their witness and that they speak what God would have them speak. Saints are able to stand firm in the battle with Satan and the demons and not fall because of the armor we have: gird our loins with truth; put on the breastplate of righteousness; shod our feet with the preparation of the gospel of peace; take up the shield of faith, wherewith we are able to extinguish the flaming arrows of the evil one; and take the helmet of salvation and the sword of the Spirit, which is the word of God. These verses are action verbs, not adjectives. The last two we just have to take, or accept, what is offered to us, meaning when we accept Jesus as Lord they become part of us.

That means the previous things are not part of a Christian automatically, but they become part of a Christian when a Christian makes those things a major part of who they are, in preparation for battle with Satan and his evil forces. Having our loins girded with truth, or truthfulness means we are to live uncompromising lives. We are not to compromise on the truth of the Bible either. We are not to compromise the way we live our lives, after we repent, so the enemy has nothing wherewith to accuse us. It is no coincidence that this girds the loins since sexual sin is the type of sin that entangles most people, at least in the mind.

As we live righteous lives, our heart is protected from the devil, less prone to sin because of our love for God. We are dependent on our feet to stand and there is no surer foundation of faith than the gospel of Jesus, able to withstand anything the devil would use against us. However, the verse says the preparation of the gospel, meaning we are to study and know the word of God, particularly the gospels so we have a sure foundation from which to attack the devil and defend against him. Taking up the shield of faith means we are to have faith in the Lord so we can defend against the attacks of Satan. Our faith is in the Lord God and not ourselves, and God is faithful. Satan knows our weaknesses, where we are prone to fail God, and that is where he will attack us. We must remember that, and when we are tempted to sin, we must recognize it for what it is: an attack by Satan. We can ward it off by faith in the Lord so that the attacks will fail. Faith comes by hearing the word of God (Rom. 10:17), so we must quote scriptures to ourselves and to Satan when these attacks come and our faith will be increased and we can push back the enemy. So the shield of faith can be used as both a defensive and offensive weapon.

Our salvation is assured if we truly believe in Jesus as Lord so all we have to do is accept, or take, this free gift from God. So then, our soul is secure. What reflects who owns our soul more than our thought life. The verse says to take the sword of the Spirit, which is the Spirit of God-this comes automatically into a person when a person becomes saved. The gates of hell will not be able to stand against the Lord's church (Mt. 16:18) because saints have the sword of the Spirit. This is the primary offensive weapon saints have, but it can also be used defensively. Remember we are in spiritual warfare and saints have the most powerful spirit, the Holy Spirit. This verse then says this Spirit is the word of God.

So then, the work of the Holy Spirit is done because of the word of God. Quoting scripture, as God intended it, in our prayer life is powerful! Just as God holds people accountable to their word, he honors his word. Whatever the scripture says God will do, he will do. We are to be on the alert for the schemes of the devil and pray, binding and rebuking the devil and his demons and asking God for help for those of us in battle, which should be all saints (Eph. 6:10–20). Those who are not with Jesus, as touching anything, are against him and those who are not bringing sinners to salvation are scattering (Mat. 12:30).

1064. Paul was imprisoned and in chains for publicly speaking the truth of God's word (Eph. 6:20).

# PHILIPPIANS

1065. God, who began a good work in each saint he chose, will perfect that work in each saint until the day of Jesus Christ's return (Php. 1:6, 2:13). God will improve these saints to become more like Jesus throughout their lives by the work of the Holy Spirit and the word of God in them. Godly love will abound more and more in saints as they gain real knowledge of God and discernment. This will cause saints to be more sincere about their faith live more blameless lives, which in turn increases the love of God inside them, to the glory of God (Php. 1:9–11).

1066. God can use the gospel for his good purposes even if it is taught out of wrong motives (Php. 1:15–18).

1067. To live is Christ and to die is gain. It is better to die and be with Jesus, but to live gives us more opportunities to help others while we are in the flesh (Php. 1:21–26).

1068. Saints are to conduct their lives in a manner worthy of the gospel of Jesus, standing firm in their faith, in unison of spirit with each other, and striving together for the faith of the gospel (Php. 1:27–28).

1069. Saints will suffer for their faith (Mt. 5:11, 12, Ac. 14:22, Php. 1:29, 30).

1070. The Holy Spirit provides love and fellowship between saints. This allows saints to be of the same mind, maintaining the same love, united together, intent on one purpose. That purpose is to reach lost souls with the gospel and make disciples (Php. 2:1, 2).

1071. Saints are to do nothing out of selfishness or pride but, with humility, regard one another as more important than oneself. We are to not just look out for our own interests, but the interests of others (Php. 2:3, 4). Just as Jesus humbled himself and took on the form of a man, even though he is God the Son, so should saints humble themselves and not think more of themselves than others (Php. 2:5–8).

1072. Jesus existed in the form of God but did not think to be equal with God (Php. 2:6). He and the Father are one, but they are not the same in that Father God is not the Son and the Son is not the Father.

1073. Because Jesus humbled himself and became a man and allowed himself to be crucified, God has highly exalted him and bestowed on him a name that is above all other names, and that every knee shall bow and every tongue confess that Jesus is Lord, to the glory of God the Father. This will occur at the judgment seat of God after the millennium (Rom. 14:10, 11, Php. 2:9-11, Rev. 20:12, 13).

1074. Saints are to work our their own salvation with fear and trembling (Php. 2:12). This does not mean we are saved by works we do. "Work out" is also used in reference to exercising, and that is how this phrase is used. So then, saints are to not be evil or lazy and live a life as an unbeliever after they are saved. Instead saints should fear and tremble knowing all people will stand before God and give an accounting of themselves to God. With this in mind, saints are to do the work of God. This is a good motivation if love for God and others is not enough for a saint to live holy lives and to do his work. Saints are not perfect, but we are to strive toward perfection, modeling after Jesus, our standard (Php. 3:12–16).

1075. Saints are to do all things without grumbling or disputing with one another so that they can be a shining example of a better way for sinners and not be hypocrites (Php. 2:14–16).

1076. Saints are to hold in high regard those who serve God faithfully (Php. 2:29).

1077. The flesh is not reliable to do what is right. Neither can anyone claim to inherit salvation through his or her fleshly bloodlines. Our righteousness comes from God through faith in Christ (Php. 3:3–9).

1078. The saints' citizenship is not of this world but of heaven (Php. 3:20). So saints' loyalties are to the kingdom of God and not to earthly kingdoms or nations because earthly nations and kingdoms serve themselves and not God, and they change as they allow themselves to be influenced by Satan.

1079. When Jesus returns saints will be given a body like Jesus's that will be imperishable and without sin (Php. 3:20, 21).

1080. Saints are to be anxious about nothing, but in everything by prayer and supplication with thanksgiving let your requests be made known to God. As a result, the peace of God, which surpasses all understanding, will guard our hearts and minds in Christ Jesus (Php. 4:6, 7). Being anxious, worrying, about anything never solved anything. We need to remember that God is in control and not ourselves, so we will not worry. We need to pray to God, as in the Lord's Prayer, humbling ourselves before God, making his will and the return of Jesus our primary desire, and, having already forgiven anybody who has sinned against us, asking God to meet our needs (though he promises to meet them regardless) with an expectation that he will and going ahead and thanking him for it. So then, we, being free of worry and thankful to God with the knowledge that he cares for us and will take care of us, will have the peace of God in our minds and hearts.

1081. Saints are to think on things that are true, honest, just, pure, lovely, of good report, virtuous, or worthy of praise

(Php. 4:8). If we think on such things there will not be room to think about things that are evil or immoral.

1082. Whatever state we saints find ourselves in, we need to be thankful to God. We may be in pleasant circumstances or horrible circumstances. No matter how hard times may be for us or how hard the task we have to do, Jesus Christ strengthens us to go through hardships and temptations and to do His will as winners (Php. 4:11–13).

1083. God will supply all the saints' needs according to his riches in glory in Christ Jesus (Php. 4:19). God has infinite riches, so there is no limit to what he may choose to do for us, but at least he will meet our needs.

# COLOSSIANS

1084. Saints do not know God's will automatically. We must always pray for one another to be full of the knowledge of God's will in all spiritual wisdom and understanding. This is a prayer I have rarely prayed for other saints. Usually I just pray to God with the requests other people have of God, such as healing, adding that God's will be done. But this scripture tells us saints that we need to pray for one another to become enlightened to God's will for each of us in each of our circumstances, and not only to be enlightened but to become full of the knowledge of God's will so there is no doubt as to what is God's will. And when we are full of the knowledge of God's will, we will walk in a manner well pleasing to the Lord in all respects, bearing fruit in every good work and increasing in the knowledge of God.

The knowledge of God comes from study of, and meditation on, God's word, the Bible. Also, as a result of being full of the knowledge of God's will, we are strengthened with all power, according to his glorious might, for the attaining of all steadfastness and patience, joyously giving thanks because we are partakers in the inheritance of the saints of Light. God's power in us will enable us to be steadfast in our faith for the work God has for each of us. It also gives us joy and a thankful heart. I hope more saints become aware of what these scriptures say and start praying for other saints to become full of the knowledge of God's will in all spiritual wisdom and understanding (Col. 1:9–12).

1085. When the Bible calls Jesus the firstborn of all creation, it immediately says all things were created by him, through him, and for him. Then it says he is before all things and in him all things hold together (Col. 1:15–18). Jesus was not created but has been with God from eternity. (Jn. 1:1–3). So the term firstborn here in Colossians means he is preeminent and ruler of a household as the firstborn male was in early world history. Jesus was also the first person (his fleshly body) to be raised from the dead, so again he is the firstborn, of the dead, making him to be first place in everything. All creation would fall apart if not for Jesus. He and Father God are the force yet unrecognized by many scientists that created and organized the universe and keeps it working properly. He made DNA. He makes gravity. He makes suns make heat and light.

1086. Jesus is the head of the church. Therefore all Christians are to submit to him and to his word, the Bible, regardless of our likes or dislikes (Col. 1:18).

1087. Because of the sacrifice of Jesus paying for the debt of sins by those who accept Jesus as Lord and Savior, believers will be presented before him as holy and blameless *if* those believers continue in the faith (Col. 1:22, 23). This implies some people might discontinue their faith in Jesus as Lord and Savior. In that case, they will not be holy and blameless. And it is necessary to be holy and blameless to be in heaven where everything is perfect and good. Jesus said those who deny him, he will deny before God, so they will be denied entry into heaven. This means people who were once saved and then no longer believe in Jesus as Lord and Savior will go to hell. There are some who would say these apostate Christians were never saved to begin with. If that were the case though, God would not classify them as believers in the first place.

1088. People should not be deceived by philosophy and deception, after the traditions of men, which are contrary to the teachings of Christ and the Bible (Col. 2:8). This tells us to expect that the people of this world will espouse teachings and philosophies that are contrary to the Bible and thus God. Anything that is contrary to the Bible, and thus God, is false and to be rejected. Even if the knowledge of mankind at the time seems to indicate it is right, it needs to be rejected. Mankind has been proven wrong on teachings contrary to the truths of the Bible for centuries. The majority of the world accepted these false teachings, each for a time. Such teachings included the world is flat, the earth is the center of the universe, cities and civilizations mentioned in the Bible never existed, no giants ever existed, and evolution (macroevolution) and denial of the Creator/God.

1089. In Jesus the fullness of the Deity dwelled in bodily form (Col. 2:9). While Jesus was here in human form he was God in the flesh.

1090. Saints are circumcised spiritually by Jesus. Jesus removes the filth of the flesh and makes us clean because saints are forgiven of their sins (Col. 2:11).

1091. New believers are to be baptized in water. This water baptism represents saints being buried after the old fleshly self has died (the old fleshly self dies when a person understands the truth and humbles him or her self to God and repents, giving up their own desires and will, and asks Jesus to be their Savior and Lord), as he was baptized, and rising from this burial into a new life with Jesus as Lord, as he was raised form the dead. The new believer is no longer dead because they are no longer slave to sin and destined for the lake of fire. The new believer is alive, in Christ, forgiven of all their sins and will live forever with Christ, released from the claim Satan had on them (Col. 2:12–15).

1092. Sabbath. We should honor God daily or on the Sabbath. We are not to judge people for working on the Sabbath (Mk. 2:23–28, Col. 2:16).

1093. Teachings that a person must do certain works to go to heaven or adding laws we must abide by that are not in the Bible are wrong (Col. 2:16–23).

1094. Worshiping of angels is sin (Col. 2:18).

1095. Saints are to set their affections on things above, not on things of this earth, and then seek those things which are above, where Christ sits on the right hand of God (Col. 3:1, 2).

1096. When Christ returns, the saints will be with him in glory (Col. 3:4).

1097. Saints are to mortify the sins we formerly committed. To mortify means to put to death, which is more than just sweeping under the carpet or avoiding so that they could come back in us. Putting to death our former sins means they are dead and are not able to come back to life in us. These sins include such things as fornication; enjoyment of sinful things, such as movies or television shows not portraying sin as bad; sexual affection for anything other than between one man and one woman who are married to one another; evil desires; and covetousness, which is idolatry; anger (for the wrong things and/or with selfish motives); wrath, which is hurting others out of anger; malice (intentionally hurting someone); blasphemy; filthy communication, such as cursing or telling dirty jokes; and lying. These are the types of sins that sinners (people who are not saved) commit and can even enjoy, once their conscience is seared from participating in the sin so long, and will receive the wrath of God, if they do not repent of their sins (ask for forgiveness and commit to no longer commit their sins) and become saved. When we are saved, we are a new person, renewed in knowledge so that we want to obey God rather than our fleshly desires and Satan (Col. 3:5–10, 1Thes. 1:10).

1098. Believers are all the same in God's eyes so that there is neither Jew nor Gentile, bond nor free, race, or nationality (Col. 3:11).

1099. Saints are to be merciful, kind, humble, meek, patient, forgiving, charitable, and thankful to God (Col. 3:12–15).

1100. Saints are to let the peace of God rule in their hearts (Col. 3:15). Thus there is no room for Satan or self to rule in a believer's heart so that sin has no place there.

1101. Saints are to let the word of God dwell in them richly in all wisdom (Col. 3:16). The only way the word of God can dwell in us richly is if we study the Bible on our own and apply it to ourselves. The beginning of wisdom is the fear of the Lord so that is the mindset to approach God as well as knowing he loved us so much he gave his Son to die on the cross for our sins while we were yet sinners. Starting with these attitudes in our study of scripture we will be made into the vessel the Potter, God, wants us to be.

1102. Saints are to teach and admonish one another in psalms and hymns and spiritual songs, being graceful to one another, knowing that we are not a horrible person by the grace of God (Col. 3:16).

1103. Whatever we do in word or deed, we are to do all in the name of the Lord Jesus, giving thanks to Father God in Jesus's name (Col. 3:17). Knowing this, we should not sin. We owe all that we are and have to God. We also represent God to others and so should be loving, holy, and sure in what we say and do, representing the Lord.

1104. Saints are to continually pray with an attitude of thanksgiving to God, knowing that he will answer our prayers in accordance to his will, which is always best

(Col. 4:2). God's will is not always our will, and so we need to submit our will to his, thanking him no matter what because he has our best interest in mind, as well as a perfect plan for the world.

1105. Saints are to pray for God to open doors for those who are evangelizing, and preaching and teaching God's word, and that God would make known to those doing this what they ought to speak and help them speak it (Col. 4:3, 4).

1106. Saints are to walk in wisdom toward sinners, bearing in mind that there is a limited time that we have to witness for God. Saints are to always speak with grace, seasoned with salt, and to know how to answer all people with their challenges and questions (Col. 4:5, 6). To be wise starts with the fear of God and develops with humbly studying God's word. There are also some people God gives the gift of wisdom so that they are particularly wise for God's purposes. Studying God's word and applying it to ourselves, as well as life experiences (both good and bad), helps us to answer sinners with their challenges and questions. We are to speak with grace, meaning with love for those we speak to and a heart desiring those we speak to to know the love of God, and the forgiveness and better life he offers.

Our speech needs to be seasoned with salt, meaning we do not compromise on what the Bible says to make it more acceptable to sinners. When salt is poured into wounds, it burns, but it also cleanses the wound, so the salt hurts the person with wounds, but it prevents the wounded person from dying from their wounds. The person with wounds has to first expose their wounds and accept the salt to be poured into their wounds. Likewise a sinner has to recognize they sin and need a savior and so repent of their sins (expose their wounds). Then the sinner has to accept the truth of the gospel of Jesus, including his virgin birth, his death on the cross for the sins of the world, and his resurrection from the dead in body and spirit, and accept him as Lord and Savior. This brings salvation from the second death that all people are destined for unless they are saved. This may cause contention with those who resist the truth, but we must not try to please people but God (1 Th. 2:2, 4–8).

# 1 THESSALONIANS

1107. Satan hinders those of us doing God's work (1 Th. 2:18). We are in a spiritual battle so we must submit ourselves to the Lord and pray that God's will be done and rebuke the devil and his demons, quoting scripture, so that God will not allow Satan to further hinder us from doing God's work. Saints can also make specific requests of God for the sake of his kingdom and other people. We should pray that God's word would be preached and have free course and that God would deliver us from those who oppose God (1 Th. 3:11–13, 2 Th. 3:1, 2).

1108. The hope and the joy to come, which causes joy now, of saints is the future of being with Jesus when he returns (1 Th. 2:19).

1109. Satan is called the tempter (1 Th. 3:5). Satan is the one who tempts people to sin.

1110. Saints can make specific requests of God for the sake of his kingdom and other people (1 Th. 3:11–13).

1111. Living our lives in obedience to God please God (1 Th. 4:1). Sinning displeases God whether it is done by a saint or a sinner. To obey is better than sacrifice (1 Sam. 15:22).

1112. The will of God is for the sanctification of saints, which is the process of becoming holy. Sanctification begins when a person is saved. It continues with abstaining from such things as fleshly lusts and desires, deceit, and hatred. It is completed when the Lord returns and we receive an incorruptible and imperishable body (1 Th. 4:3–8). Even the ability of a saint to not sin comes from God. God did not call and save saints to live as sinners but to be holy, even as he is holy (1 Pet. 1:15, 16).

1113. God teaches saints to love one another through the Holy Spirit (1 Th. 4:9). Saints love God and each other because God is love. Those so-called Christians who do not love other Christians are not saints but sinners, destined for hell unless they repent and become saved (1 Jn. 4:7, 8). Sinners will know who are truly Christians by their love for one another (Jn. 13:35).

1114. Saints interaction with the world. Saints are to try to not be disruptive and to mind their own business. We are not to meddle in other people's business nor are we to gossip. We are to work and not be lazy so that we do our best to not lack what we need. We are to be honest (1 Th. 4:11, 12).

1115. The return of the Lord Jesus. With the voice of the archangel and at the sound of the last trumpet of God, Jesus will return from heaven to earth. At this time, the dead in Christ will rise first, then we who are alive and remain will be caught up together with the dead who rose before us who are alive when Jesus returns, in the clouds, to meet the Lord in the air. Verse 14 implies there will be a slight delay, minutes or days perhaps, between the time that the dead in Christ rise and the time the alive in Christ rise. Saints are to comfort one another with these words. This implies saints will need comforting because of worldwide persecution of saints before the Lord returns. We need to know what the Bible says about the end times so we will not be deceived and troubled by others. Then saints are to speak to each other what the Bible says about the end times, particularly Jesus' return (1 Th. 4:13–18).

The return of the Lord will occur when the people of the world have forgotten the one true God and are no longer concerned about the wrath of God to come. It will come as a woman in labor, meaning it will be painful to the world and the pains will become more severe and more frequent the closer the day of the Lord approaches. These pains are the travails to come on the world, spoken of in Revelation, such as wars, famines, pestilence, and earthquakes. Once God starts the end times He will not stop them, as there is no escape the travail of a woman in labor (1 Th. 5:1–3).

The Holy Spirit will enlighten saints when God has started the end times (1 Th. 5:4). Until the Lord returns saint are to be sober, putting on the breastplate of righteousness, which comes through faith and love, and for a helmet the hope of salvation (1 Th. 5:8). As the day of the Lord approaches, persecution of saints will worsen but God has not appointed us to wrath but to reaching out to sinners to bring them to salvation (1 Th. 5:9). Saints are to comfort and edify one another with the truths from the Bible, especially with the knowledge we will one day be gathered together and forevermore be with the Lord, ever more as the day of the Lord approaches (1 Th. 5:10, 11).

1116. God has appointed some saints to be over the flock or majority of believers. These are prophets, evangelists, and preachers. Over smaller groups of believers, God has appointed teachers. The saints are to highly esteem these who are over the body of believers and to abide by their admonishments (1 Th. 5:12, 13).

1117. Saints are to encourage one another, and when a saint is continuing in a sin without repentance, the saints are to go to the one sinning without repentance and, with humbleness out of a desire to restore them to a right walk with God but boldness of the knowledge of scripture, admonish and exhort them. Saints are to pray for one another and help one another practically when the need arises. We are to be patient toward all people (1 Th. 5:14, Jas. 2:14–17).

1118. Saints are not to repay evil for evil done by anyone (1 Th. 5:15). We are not to get back or get even for wrongs done to us but turn the other cheek.

1119. Saints are to rejoice evermore (1 Th. 5:16). This is easy to do when things are going well for us, but Paul knew very well that the life of a Christian is often filled with trials. Therefore, for Paul to tell us this, he had this in mind. How can we rejoice evermore? By consideration of the blessed hope, we have of eternity with God and Jesus where all is well, free of the flesh, sin, and Satan.

1120. Saints are to pray without ceasing (1 Th. 5:17). Praying to God without ceasing is a way of life for some who have taken this scripture to heart. For saints who have not made this a way of life yet they can with practice, usually starting with praise and giving of thanks to God. Trials and tribulations improve the prayer life, which is communication with God, of saints. I would rather not neglect my communication with God so that he felt a need to motivate me to increase my communication with him. Truthfully, Christians in developed nations are blessed and, therefore, have cause to continually praise and thank God. But in everything give thanks to God, for this is the will of God in Christ Jesus concerning you (1 Th. 5:18). In good times an bad times, we are to give thanks to God. He will honor those sincere prayers of thanks. It is hard to think evil thoughts when one is praying.

1121. Saints are to not quench the Spirit (1 Th. 5:19). If we see the Holy Spirit at work, we should not interfere. If we feel the Holy Spirit at work in us, such as convicting us of sin, we should listen and obey. If we continually ignore the Holy Spirit convicting us of sin ,our conscience will become seared and callous so that we will not be able to feel or hear the Holy Spirit convicting us of sin. A person in such a state can truly be an evil influence on the world around them.

1122. Saints are not to despise prophesies (1 Th. 5:20). When someone claims to be giving a prophecy, we are to test it to see if it is consistent with scripture. If it is not, we are to reject it immediately and confront the one who is saying it is true, using the scriptures as our standard. If it does not conflict with scripture, each saint who hears it should pray to God to see what God would have us do in our own lives, if the Holy Spirit does not immediately convict us of what we need to do. We must act, without delay, on whatever God convicts us of, whether it is to repent and stop committing sins or to go and do work for God.

1123. Just as saints are to test prophesies, we must test all teachings with scripture and prove them true or false (1 Th. 5:21). Satan tries to influence all people by various means: temptation, trials, deceit, comfort, and wealth. One of his favorite ways, which is what he did with Jesus at the end of Jesus's forty-day fast, was to use quotes from the scriptures in ways God did not intend them to be used. Partial truths are a common way for the devil to get people to go down the path to hell, thinking they are on the path to heaven. Teachings that are true saints are to hold fast to and trust the word of God whether it seems they are not true at the time. In the end, God's word will prove true and faithful.

1124. Because saints represent Christ, we are to abstain from all appearance of evil (1 Th. 5:22). Saints are to avoid being evil of course, but Paul is telling us not to even appear to be evil. We need to be mindful of the influence we have on other people. If we act selfishly, using the excuse of trying to make things fair, for instance, we have the appearance of evil to many because they see our motives are not pure. Satan has trapped many people who pretended to be, or do, something evil and received power or pleasure from Satan as a result. Pretending then can lead to reality of evil.

1125.  God sanctifies saints. Saints do not sanctify themselves by their works (1 Th. 5:23).

1126.  God will make sure saints do what he has called them to do (1 Th. 5:24).

# 2 THESSALONIANS

1127. It is righteous of God to make saints suffer for the his kingdom (2 Th. 1:5). If we suffer for sins it is also righteous of God, but it is to our shame. If we suffer for the kingdom of God, it is for the glory of Jesus in us and us in him (2 Th. 1:12).

1128. When Jesus returns, he will come in flaming fire, executing vengeance on those who persecuted us (2 Th. 1:6–10).

1129. The day of the Lord's return and our gathering together to him is not imminent. First there must be a great many Christians fall away from their faith in the Lord and reject him. To some people it is easier to think of these people who fall away from their faith to have never been saved to begin with. Also, the Antichrist, or beast of the sea, must be revealed to the world before the Lord returns and the gathering together of saints to him. The Antichrist will be revealed for who he really is, at least to saints, when he exalts himself above all gods and even God, so that he sits in the temple of God as god. He will also oppose God and all that is God's. Some time after these things, the Lord will return and the saints will be gathered together to him. There will not be "rapture" of Christians any second now. That is not what "in the twinkling of an eye" refers to (Mt. 24:10, 2 Th. 2:1–4, 1 Tim. 4:1). That means the Lord's return will occur suddenly when it comes. The temple in which the Antichrist sits as a god has traditionally been thought of as a new Jewish temple yet to be rebuilt in Jerusalem because the verse says the temple of God. This may be the case; however, the wailing wall is part of the old temple so he could commit this abomination there. Or he could do it at the Dome of the Rock, which is generally considered to be over the sight of Solomon's temple. Another possibility is the temple of God refers to the Vatican because the Vatican is the headquarters of the largest Christian church in the world.

1130.   The Antichrist is called the man of sin, the son of perdition (2 Th. 2:3). This tells us he will sinful and perhaps not born of a woman married to a man. He will be under the influence of Satan, so he can be expected to oppose God and to steal, kill, and destroy. Lawlessness will increase under his rule. He will have power from Satan to do signs and lying wonders. Some of the signs and wonders will be truly amazing, and some will be tricks like a magician. Most of the people of the world, sinners, will be deceived and believe the lies he tells. The majority of people of the world prefer pleasures of unrighteousness to the truth and so they will be condemned to hell by God (2 Th. 2:9–12).

1131.   The Antichrist will be revealed to sinners for who he really is by the return of Christ. The mystery of lawlessness is already at work in this world (Satan is prince of this world). Satan restrains the time of the Antichrist and his revelation until the appointed time. When Satan is taken out of the way and bound a thousand years, the Lord will slay the Antichrist (lawless one) with the breath of His mouth (2 Th. 2:6–8). It is hard to imagine though that Satan restrains the time of the Antichrist's revelation to the world (abomination of desolation). Another explanation of these verses is that the Holy Spirit, or the worldwide body of saints, is the one doing the restraining. With this in mind, the time of the Antichrist is restrained until the appointed time.

When the Holy Spirit, or worldwide body of believers, is taken out of the way, the Antichrist will be revealed for who he is by the abomination of desolation. This would either mean a rapture of the church before the abomination of desolation, which is contrary to what Jesus said in Matthew 24:29–31, or that the Holy Spirit is removed from the earth from just before the abomination of desolation until the return of the Lord. If the Holy Spirit is removed from the earth during this three-and-a-half-year period, known as the great tribulation, then no one could be saved during this period [the Holy Spirit is the one who convicts people to repentance and salvation (Jn. 16:8)]. This contradicts Revelation 10:6 and 7, which say that the mystery of God/Christ will not end until the last (seventh) trumpet sounds that heralds the Lord's return. Yet another explanation is that an angel, like Michael, is the one who restrains for the Antichrist to be revealed (by the abomination of desolation). When the angel is taken out of the way, then the abomination of desolation will occur and the Antichrist be revealed to the world. This last explanation seems the most plausible.

1132. Saints need to ask God for his love to increase in their hearts, so much the more as we see the day of the Lord's return approaching (2 Th. 3:5).

1133. Saints are to patiently wait for the Lord's return (2 Th. 3:5). Patiently means we do not get mad when it doesn't happen in our lifetime. It also means we do not do things that are foolish such as build up huge bills, thinking we won't have to pay them because we think the Lord is returning soon. Waiting means we anticipate it will happen. We look forward to it. We know it will happen. Waiting means we do not have an active part in determining when it will be; only God does that.

1134. Saints are not to associate with saints who live as sinners, willfully sinning (2 Th. 3:6, 14, 15). We are to pray for them and try to speak to them in a way that would bring them to repentance and a right walk with God.

1135. We are not to be lazy. We are to provide for ourselves so that if a person chooses not to work, they should not eat. This is not cruel but prevents laziness and idleness, which gives place to the devil to do more work in a person's life (2 Th. 3:8–12).

1136. Though it can be hard to do God's work because of opposition from others and the devil, we are to not be weary in doing God's work but confident God will accomplish good through us if we continue to be obedient to him (2 Th. 3:13).

# 1 TIMOTHY

1137. We should not believe fables, legends, and attempts to trace our origins, which cause questions that can lead away from the truth (1 Tim. 1:4). There is almost no end to the imaginations of people and spending time on those that are contrary to the Bible can be harmful. It is better to spend our time together edifying one another in faith.

1138. One of the things God asks of saints to do while here on earth is charity out of a pure heart, with good conscience, and full of faith (1 Tim. 1:5).

1139. The Mosaic law is beneficial for sinners to better know right from wrong (1 Tim. 1:8–10).

1140. Christ Jesus came into the world to save sinners (1 Tim. 1:15).

1141. God is the eternal king, immortal, invisible, and the only wise God (1 Tim. 1:17).

1142. Prophecies did not end with the first incarnation of Christ but will end with the second incarnation of Christ Jesus (1 Tim. 1:18).

1143. There comes a time that we are to no longer pray for the salvation of someone (1 Tim. 1:19, 20). Those who once professed a belief in Jesus as Lord and then turn away from their faith in him as Lord are the most likely ones God will have us cease from our efforts, including prayer, to bring them to salvation (if they really never were saved to begin with, because it is impossible to be saved more than once per Heb. 6:4–6).

1144. Saints are to pray with thanksgiving for all people, including kings and other leaders, so that we may lead a tranquil and quiet life in all godliness and dignity (1 Tim.

2:1, 2). If God influences those around us and our leaders as a result of these prayers then the country we live in will be more godly, allowing us to live a tranquil and quiet life with godliness and dignity.

1145. God desires all people to be saved and to come to the knowledge of the truth (1 Tim. 2:4). Even though omnipotent God desires this, it will not happen (Mt. 7:13, 14) because prophesies have to be fulfilled. For these prophesies to be fulfilled most people must reject Christ Jesus as Lord and Savior. Also, God gives people free will to decide whether or not to be a believer and follower of God (Jn. 3:36, Ac. 17:30). However, God gives people the faith to believe (Eph. 2:8), and he predestined who would go to heaven before the foundation of the world (Jn. 6:44, Ac. 13:48, Rom. 8:29, 30, Eph. 1:4–6). Those he predestined to go to heaven must hear the word of God first somehow though to be saved (Rom. 10:17, 2 Th. 2:13, 2 Tim. 2:10). So then the main reason not all people will be saved, even though God wants them to be saved, is fulfillment of prophecy. God does not want people to sin, but he gives us free will to sin or not to sin. Also, God has no pleasure in the death (neither the first or second death) of those who do choose not to follow and obey him (Ez. 18:23).

1146. One God and one Mediator. There is one God and one Mediator, the man Christ Jesus (1 Tim. 2:5). There is one God, comprised of God the Father, God the Son, and God the Holy Spirit. There is only one mediator between God and man, and that is Jesus, so we pray in Jesus's name (Mt. 18:20, Jn. 14:13).

1147. Jesus willingly gave his life on the cross as a ransom for all (1 Tim. 2:6).

1148. Men should pray in every place lifting up holy hands, without wrath and dissension (1 Tim. 2:8). Holy means pure, with pure motives and contrite heart. We must forgive others before we go to God in prayer. This verse does not mean men should always pray with their hands lifted up, but it does say in every place, such as home or church, a man should at various times pray with uplifted holy hands.

1149. Women in church. Women are to be dressed modestly in church, not in a way that gathers attention to themselves away from God (1 Tim. 2:9, 10). Paul gives the example of not wearing costly jewelry. A woman needs to be honest with herself when she dresses for church, and if she can say to herself and to God she dressed modestly without desiring to look attractive (since worshipping God, seeing people made right with God, and studying of his word is supposed to be the desire of the heart for church) or distracting, then she can attend church with a good conscience. If a woman reads this and determines to intentionally look her worse, that is also distracting. Stop thinking about oneself, and think about God.

Her attitude needs to be of obedience and service to God. I should say that the same goes for men. Also, a man should not dress in a way that is distracting either such as flamboyant clothes. Christians are not to be so strict on this and judge others for what they wear so that they miss the point of worship of God, bringing people to a right relationship with God, and study of God's word at church. People can get carried away in judging others as well as in rebellion. Each person needs to consider what is in his or her heart. Are they more focused on God than themselves and more concerned about other people, with Godly love, than themselves? Women are not to be preachers (1 Tim. 2:11, 12). Women are not to teach or exercise authority over men in church, including in Sunday school (1 Tim. 2:12). Before the time of the early Christian church, women were treated as chattel. The Christian church was liberating to women in that it allowed them to be in houses of worship with men and said women were equal with men in God's eyes. God does instruct us though that men have authority over women and women are not to have authority over men in the home or church. It is necessary to have hierarchy to limit confusion and anarchy. The Bible does not comment on differences between the sexes at the workplace separate from church.

1150. There is a difference in the identity and roles of men and women because God created Adam first, and Eve was the initial one to sin. Women have the opportunity to make the world a better place though by raising godly children (1 Tim. 2:13–15). A woman is not saved through childbearing but can be the initiator, because of her unique role on motherhood, of godly influence on her children just as Eve was the initiator of sin. Women were esteemed less than men during Biblical times, partly because Eve was the one who was the first to sin. This scripture does not mean women are saved from going to hell for their sins by bearing and rearing children, but their stigma in society can go away by bearing and rearing godly children, and they continue in the faith of the Lord.

1151. Requirements for a pastor/bishop/overseer and deacons. A pastor must be above reproach; the husband of one wife; temperate; prudent; respectable; hospitable; able to teach; not addicted to wine; not pugnacious but gentle, peaceable; free from the love of money; one who manages his own household well, keeping his children under control with dignity, and if his children are old enough, they should be saints; and not a new convert. He must also have a good reputation with those outside the church, hospitable, loving what is good, sensible, just, devout, self-controlled. He must always hold fast the faithful word of God so that he will be able both to exhort in sound doctrine and to refute those who contradict the truth of scripture (1 Tim. 3:1–7, Tit. 1:5–9).

First of all, it is a given that pastors are to be men as implied in these verses and overtly stated in 1 Tim. 2:11, 12. The good reputation goes along with above reproach and the other qualifications, but it also implies he has good relations with those outside of the church. Scripture says marriage is to be only between one man and one woman (Gen 2:24, Mt. 19:5, 6, Mk. 10:6–9, Eph. 5:31, 33). God allowed polygamy and divorce (Mt. 19:8, 9) in times past but neither one is his will (Mal. 2:16, Mk. 10:6–9, Eph. 5:31, 33) for anyone. Polygamists could not even be church members of the early Christian church. It is a sad commentary on the church today that polygamy is allowed among church members in cultures where polygamy is allowed. Some missionaries give the excuse of not condemning polygamy to the new believers in these countries because they are afraid people there would not then accept Christianity.

It is understandable that those new believers who are already married to multiple wives not be required to divorce any of their new wives, for that would add harm to some. Monogamy was the norm in Greek and Roman culture at the time of the early church also (though sinners frequented prostitutes), so an injunction against polygamy was unnecessary. The question then becomes was a pastor to be simply as God required of other people of not remarrying except allowing it after death of a spouse or divorce from a spouse because of infidelity? This may very well be the case. If it means a pastor is to have only one wife during his life, regardless of divorce from, or death of, a spouse it would put the focus on the marital status of the person rather than the obedience of the pastor to God.

In today's time, some pastors are divorced despite their wishes by wives who leave them for another man or other sinful reasons. This should not disqualify the pastor from pastoralship because it is beyond his control. Also, if we use the strictest interpretation of the husband of one wife requirement a single man is disqualified from being a pastor. This would have disqualified Paul, who wrote the scripture, so a strict interpretation of the scripture is obviously not God's intent. The pastor is not to be quarrelsome, violent, or bad tempered. He must not be an alcoholic or crave alcohol. He must not love money. He must manage his household well, including keeping his children under control.

This is probably the hardest requirement since our children are responsible for their own sins and become more and more independent, out of sight of their fathers, in their teenage years. It is not to say one crazy bad act by a child of a pastor disqualifies him from being a pastor or there would be no men qualified. Otherwise, it would require perfection in the children of pastors, which Jesus did not even ask of his disciples. The overall behavior of a pastor's children though should be good. Deacons have similar qualifications as pastors except the do not have to keep their children under control and do not have to be able to teach. They are to be tested by the local church before becoming deacons to ensure they qualify (1 Tim. 3:8–13).

1152. Women are not to gossip but be dignified, temperate, and faithful in all things (1 Tim. 3:11). Women are to control their tongue and speak in a temperate fashion, and act dignified. Faithful in all things means full of faith in God, trustworthy, and pure in mind and body.

1153. The Holy Spirit explicitly says that in the later times, some will fall away from the faith, paying attention to deceiving spirits and doctrines of demons, by means of hypocrisy of liars with seared conscience (1 Tim. 4:1, 2). The later days, also called the last days or end times, is the period of time when Israel is invaded by the Antichrist and his armies, Christians will be persecuted for their faith, the two witnesses' ministry occurs on earth, and the seven seals, seven trumpets and seven bowls of judgment occur. The later days did not start with Jesus' first incarnation or Paul would not have used the term later days. He would have used words more like "these days."

Also, in 2 Tim. 3:1 Paul says these days shall come. He did not say they are here. Indeed there was a rapid increase in the number of new believers during the time Paul wrote to Timothy and not a falling away from the faith. The Spirit has made it known to those who are his that the last days have not occurred yet and, perhaps, the only way we will know for sure is when we see the ministry of the two witnesses. There has been speculation about who is the Antichrist for centuries, but there will be no doubt who the two witnesses are when they doing God's work here on earth. The Antichrist will be the one who kills them. Some say these professed Christians who leave the faith in the later days never truly believed in the first place. Others say that if that were the case they would not be falling away from the faith, but merely revealing their true hypocrisy, and so verse 1 would have been worded that way. Those who deceive those who fall away from the faith are described as liars and hypocrites teaching false doctrines. Examples of their teachings are given in verse three: forbidding marriage (encouraging people to live together in a sexual relationship out of wedlock) and created rules or laws of God (falsely so-called) such as abstaining from certain foods or drinks (1 Tim. 4:3).

1154. Grace or blessing over food. We are to pray blessings, including quoting scripture, over food before we eat it if we want it sanctified, thus making it safe to eat (1 Tim. 4:5).

1155. Spiritual discipline is more profitable than bodily exercise because while both have benefits while in this present life, spiritual discipline holds promise for the life to come. Spiritual discipline brings godliness, which benefits others as well as oneself (1 Tim. 4:7, 8).

1156. Youthfulness does not prevent usefulness for God (1 Tim. 4:12). No matter our age God can still use us, even when we are old also.

1157. Saints are to be good examples in speech, conduct, love, faith and purity (1 Tim. 4:12).

1158. Saints are to read scripture in public, which usually means in church out loud (1 Tim. 4:13). Saints should not be ashamed to read scripture in public outside of church also if God tells them to do so.

1159. Saints are to exhort and teach one another from our reading of scripture (1 Tim. 4:13).

1160. Saints are to not neglect the gifts God gives us to use them for our own benefit as well as the benefit of others. This helps us stay faithful to God (1 Tim. 4:14–16).

1161. Those who are our elders we are to treat with the respect God would have us give our parents. We can exhort them but it needs to be with respect (1 Tim. 5:1, 2).

1162. Progeny, such as children and grandchildren, are to care for their parents and grandparents as needed and not leave it up to others (1 Tim. 5:4).

1163. People are responsible for their own families and are not to depend on others for help except widows at least sixty years old without family to care for them (1 Tim. 5:3–16). Those men who neglect to care for their families are worse than unbelievers.

1164. Young widows (at least less than sixty years old) are encouraged to marry again, bear children and keep house. This will prevent Satan from occasion for causing sin such as sexual sin temptation (1 Tim. 5:14).

1165. Christian leaders, especially those who preach and teach, are worthy of more honor than those who listen and learn. The leaders whose job it is to preach or teach are to be paid well enough for their work that they do no have to be concerned about the welfare of themselves and their families (1 Tim. 5:17, 18).

1166. Do not listen to an accusation against an elder, or leader, in the church except it be in the presence of two or three witnesses (1 Tim. 5:19). This should prevent people accusing leaders or elders of wrongdoing without facts to support their accusations.

1167. Those saints who continue in sin after another saint has gone to him or her to show him or her their sin, and then doing the same with one or two witnesses if they do not repent and change their ways, are to be rebuked in the presence of the congregation of the local church. This will make the congregation fearful of sinning (Mt. 18:15–17, 1 Tim. 5:20). If they still refuse to repent and change their ways, they are to be removed from church membership and treated as a sinner. This means they are still loved and witnessed to, but if they continue to refuse, there is a point believers are to no longer spend time witnessing to them and are to be left alone (Mt. 10:14, 15).

1168. Saints are not to be biased, or prejudiced, against people because of the race, creed, nationality, wealth, or sex or age (except where specifically mentioned elsewhere in the Bible such as women are not to be pastors) (1 Tim. 5:21).

1169. We are not to commission people for God's service too hastily. We must make sure they are fit for the work they are attempting to do (1 Tim. 5:22).

1170. Alcohol and healing. Paul instructed Timothy to drink wine for medicinal purposes (1 Tim. 5:23). This tells us drinking alcohol is not a sin and can have medicinal purposes. It also tells us that God can keep us healthy by healthy living and we are to attempt to stay healthy by healthy eating and drinking habits. It also tells us God can heal through medicine. God does not just heal by miracles. We also know sometimes God does not heal a person of their sickness, though some like to say death is the ultimate healing because they are going to heaven. Sickness and mortality of people entered the world with the original sins of Adam and Eve and so a person does not become ill because of a specific sin they did routinely (there are some illnesses that come specifically because of sin such as sexually transmitted illness from sex outside of God's laws). Lack of faith is not why people are not healed by God, except in rare circumstances possibly.

1171. Masters and slaves who are saints are to treat each other as brothers in Christ (1 Tim. 6:1, 2). Some people entered into slavery by asking a person to pay their debts that were too much for them to pay, and in return, they would be their slaves. Their owners gave these slaves food and shelter. In Israel, slaves were to be freed every seven years. People do not do this in modern times, and so slavery is never right.

1172. Anyone who does not agree with sound doctrine from the Bible and advocates conflicting doctrine is conceited and understands nothing. He or she has a morbid interest in controversial questions and disputes about words, out of which arise envy, strife, abusive language, evil suspicions, and constant friction between men and women of depraved mind and lack the truth, who suppose the appearance of godliness is a means of gain (1 Tim. 6:3–5). These people do not want to know the truth so it is best to not get involved in disputations with them. Some of these people think they appear more intelligent if they can stump a Christian with a question. Because the verse says controversial questions, it tells us we cannot answer all questions with an indisputable answer.

1173. Contentment and pursuits. Contentment with godliness is great gain. We have brought nothing into this world, and we can take nothing to the hereafter either. We should be content with food and covering. Those who want to be rich fall into temptation and a snare and many foolish and harmful desires, which plunge people in to ruin and destruction. For the love of money is a root of all sorts of evil, and some longing for it have wandered away from the faith and have hurt themselves with many griefs. We are to flee from the pursuit of wealth and instead pursue righteousness, godliness, faith, love, perseverance and gentleness (1 Tim. 6:6–11). This does not mean we should not earn money to provide for our family and ourselves, otherwise we would be in disobedience to what the Lord would have us do as written in the last chapter of 1 Timothy.

1174. Saints are to fight the good fight of faith, being faithful in all things. Behaving, thinking, and speaking in a holy manner and not as the world, which is devoted to it's own lusts. We are to be obedient to God, without stain or reproach, until the Lord returns (1 Tim. 6:12–14).

1175. God will bring about the return of his Son at the proper time. God is the blessed and only Sovereign, King of kings and Lord of lords, who alone possesses immortality and dwells in unapproachable light, whom no man has seen or can see. No one has seen God completely (1 Tim. 6:15, 16, Ex. 33:20, Ps. 104:2, Is. 6:1–5).

1176. Instructions for the wealthy. Those who are rich in this present world are not to be conceited or put their hope on riches, which are uncertain. Instead they are to put their hope on God, who richly supplies people with all things to enjoy. The rich are to be rich in good works, generous, and ready to share with others, storing up for themselves the treasure of a good foundation based on Christ and Christ alone (1 Tim. 6:17–19).

1177. Science, or knowledge, falsely so-called. Sciences, or knowledge, that professes things contrary to the word of God are not true. With time they are discovered to be wrong, such as macroevolution. These sciences, or knowledge, have caused some believers to gone astray from the truth. We are to avoid arguments with them (1 Tim. 6:20, 21).

# 2 TIMOTHY

1178. Under times of discouragement and trials, such as faced by the church during the first century AD, we are tempted to not be bold in our witness. This was the case for Timothy and Paul, so Paul encouraged Timothy to rekindle the gift of preaching and teaching God gave him. This occurred at a time when Paul laid his hands on him, probably at his conversion to Christianity (2 Tim. 1:6).

1179. God has not given Christians a spirit of fear but of power and love and of sound judgment (2 Tim. 1:7). When saints face tribulation, we are not to fear because God has given us the Holy Spirit of him, which gives us power to do God's work, love for those who persecute us, and sound judgment so that we the elect are not confused, or deceived by false teaching, but know the truth.

1180. Saints are not to be ashamed of the gospel and fellow believers who are faithful to God but join with them in suffering for the gospel in gratitude for God saving us. For we were saved not by our own doing, but God chose us, giving us the faith to believe the gospel. God did not save us saints just to save us but called us to a holy calling. Each of us is called to do tasks, each a different member of one body, for God to further his kingdom (2 Tim. 1:8, 9). But all saints are called to witness to sinners about the gospel and then to baptize them and teach them the Bible (Mt. 28:19, 20).

1181. Jesus conquered death and brought life and immortality to light through the gospel (2 Tim. 1:10). The gospel has the power to save sinners from the punishment we all deserve for our sins and the second death and to give them eternal life with God.

1182. Paul was appointed by God as a preacher, apostle, and teacher (2 Tim. 1:11).

1183. Saints can be confidant God will keep his word and his word is true. So we are not to be ashamed of God or the Bible. Saints are to remember the Bible, which means we need to study it to begin with. We may not be able to quote scripture and verse but we should know if anything we hear is consistent with the Bible or not. The Bible is inerrant. There are 5,300 documents from the first century that are consistent with the New Testament as written in English, because great care has been given in interpretations from the first century documents till now. Some have purposely changed some of the truth for evil purposes and made apostate bibles like the homosexual bible. Some have left out parts or changed parts of the Bible that can be significant so they are not as good interpretations.

The New King James version has adjusted the King James Bible to better reflect early writings that have been discovered since the King James version was written and it is written in modern English, which is easier to understand. Other versions that accurately reflect the original documents are New American Standard and perhaps the English Standard versions. There may be more I am not aware of. The Catholic Bible has more books, and more chapters in the book of Daniel, than the protestant Bible but they were left out of the Protestant Bible because they did not add to our understanding of the Bible or God. We are to guard the truths we have learned from the Bible in our heart and not waver from them (2 Tim. 1:12–14).

1184. Saints are to teach the Bible to others, who are trustworthy, so that they will then teach even more people what the Bible says (2 Tim. 2:2).

1185. Saints are to be as soldiers, separated from civilian life. We are called to duty to serve God and not ourselves or the world. We are not to become entangled in the affairs of everyday life so that we may please God (2 Tim. 2:3, 4). We are in the world, so it is impossible to separate completely from the world, but we are to not let the affairs of this world distract us from doing God's work he has for us such as witnessing and studying the Bible. God has us in this world so we can influence it for his sake, leading others to him, showing mercy and love to others, and dealing justly with others.

1186. Saints are as athletes in that not only do we train for our service to God by studying God's word, but we compete according to the rules or we do not win the prize (2 Tim. 2:5). Competing by the rules means we cannot cheat or compromise. We cannot compromise on the word of God. If the Bible says something we personally do not like we must submit to it and obey. Otherwise we may lead others astray from living lives the way God desires and not just live part of our lives in disobedience. Also, a little leaven leavens the whole loaf. So a little compromise can lead to many more compromises in others and ourselves, which multiplies over time. Over time then, these compromises lead to people living lives and preaching doctrine that is mostly unbiblical.

1187. Just as the hardworking farmer ought to be the first to receive his share of the crops, the saint who works the hardest, most obedient to God, will receive the greatest reward in heaven (2 Tim. 2:6). This reward will most likely be leading more people to Christ, but it may be some reward from God yet unknown. We do not want to be lazy and neglect the work God has for each of us. This is at least the great commission, which Christ commissioned all Christians to do: making disciples of others, baptizing new believers, and teaching them the Bible (Mt. 28:19, 20).

1188. Predestination and free will. Those people who will be saved were chosen by God for salvation before the world began (Jn. 6:44, Ac. 13:48, Rom. 8:29, 30, Eph. 1:4–6) but are not saved until they hear the word of God (Rom. 10:17, 2 Th. 2:13, 2 Tim. 2:10). So then saints must witness the gospel of Jesus to bring the called to salvation. This is the motivation that helps us endure trials and tribulations for our faith.

1189. If a saint dies a martyr's death, he or she will go to heaven. A martyr is one who dies for their faith (2 Tim. 2:11). This is obvious to most people.

1190. If we endure trials and tribulations for our faith, we will reign with Christ during the millennium (2 Tim. 2:12).

1191. If we deny Jesus as Lord and Savior, he will also deny us (2 Tim. 2:12). Peter denied Jesus during his trial and yet we know Jesus used him afterwards and he went to heaven so how do we reconcile these facts? The answer is in the mind and soul. If a person denies Jesus, for fear of life or harm, and yet believes Jesus is Lord and Savior Jesus will not deny her or him to God. If, however, that person actually does not believe Jesus is Lord and Savior, Jesus will deny her or him to God, and they will go to hell. If this person though was never saved to begin with, they could later be saved by the grace of God, sparing them from going to hell.

1192. During trial and tribulations, saints can struggle with their faith but not lose our salvation because Jesus is faithful (2 Tim. 2:13).

1193. Debates are to be avoided (2 Tim. 2:14). If a person does not respond to one or two admonitions from scripture we are to stop talking to them and pray for them to ask God to open their eyes and minds to the truth. It is useless to continue and leads to the ruin of the hearers. The hearers can become calloused to the word of God if we continue (2 Tim. 2:14, Tit. 3:9, 10).

1194. Saints are to be diligent in their work for God, accurately handling the word of truth, the Bible (2 Tim. 2:15). Saints are to interpret the Bible accurately and preach or teach it accurately. We are to do this diligently and not neglect it so that we will not be ashamed.

1195. Saints are to avoid much talk about worldly matters because it can lead to ungodliness. 2 Tim. 2:16. Strife over worldly matters is unprofitable and can lead others and us to sin.

1196. Premillennialism. It is false teaching to say the resurrection has already come or we are in the millennium now (2 Tim. 2:18, Rev. 20:4–6).

1197. Saints are to flee wickedness and lusts of the flesh and pursue righteousness, faith, love, and peace so that we will be useful to the Master, prepared for every good work he has for us and so we can call on God from a pure heart (2 Tim. 2:20–22).

1198. How to oppose false teaching and foolish speculations. Saints are to know scripture and teach the truth of scripture, correcting those who teach false teachings or have foolish speculations. We are not to be quarrelsome, but patient, gentle, and kind when we correct them in hopes, with prayer, that God would grant them repentance, leading those who oppose the truth to the knowledge of truth and escape from the snare of the devil, having been held captive by him to do his will (2 Tim. 2:23–26).

1199. In the last days difficult times will occur. The reason they will be difficult is because people will be lovers of self (selfish), lovers of money, boastful, arrogant, revilers, disobedient to parents, ungrateful (feel they have rights, or are entitled, to things they do not), unholy, without natural sexual affection (homosexual, bisexual, transgender, transsexual, pedophilia, necrophilia, bestiality, etc.), unfaithful to their word, false accusers, without self-control, brutal, despisers of those that are good, traitors, proud, conceited, lovers of pleasure more than lovers of God, having a form of godliness but denying the power thereof from such turn away (2 Tim. 3:1–5).

During the last days, we are not to try to reason with these people but to turn away from them and avoid them. These people will have a form of godliness, perhaps even saying they are being loving Christians by accepting all manner of sin and saying God loves all people just the way they are so these people do not need to repent or change. There are people today who do charity work in the name of God or Jesus but at the same time deny that unless a person accepts only Jesus as Lord and Savior they are going to hell, thus de facto denying the Lord. These sorts of people lead astray women who are laden with sin, led on by various impulses, ever learning and yet never able to come to the knowledge of the truth (2 Tim. 3:6, 7). These people resist the truth and are reprobate concerning the faith (2 Tim. 3:8). So then we are not to attempt to reason with them but avoid them. Evil men and women will become worse and worse over time, deceiving and being deceived (2 Tim. 3:13).

1200. All who will live godly in Christ Jesus shall suffer persecution (2 Tim. 3:12).

1201. Evil men and women will become worse and worse over time, deceiving and being deceived (2 Tim. 3:13). From this verse and Genesis 15:16, we know that the more sins a society accepts, the more immoral it will become. From the Bible and history, it is evident that sexual sin is the common denominator sin among societies that reject God. Sexual sin is sex, or thinking of having sex, outside of that between a man and woman married to each other. Other sins that enable a society to participate in sexual sins then become acceptable (eg. Making it illegal to publicly declare sin a sin and stealing from others who oppose sin and call it a tax or penalty).

1202. Saints are to continue in the things we have learned from the holy scriptures, which are able to give wisdom that leads to salvation through faith in Christ Jesus. All scripture is profitable for teaching, reproof, correction, and for instruction in righteousness; so that the believer may be adequately equipped for every good work (2 Tim. 3:15–17). We are to not lose faith in the Bible but continue to trust what it says. It is useful for leading others to salvation (faith comes by hearing the word of God), teaching, correction and instruction so we will be equipped for every good work God has us do.

1203. Jesus will judge the live and the dead when he returns in that the saints who are dead will rise first and then the saints who are alive will meet him in the air. The sinners who are alive will be judged then in that he will destroy many who are against Him and with the Antichrist. He will spare some of the people who are alive on earth and they will worship him (2 Tim. 4:1). See notes on Mt. 25:31–46. The great white throne of judgment, where all people will be judged and give an accounting of their lives will occur after the millennium.

1204. Saints are to reprove, rebuke, and exhort one another as needed with great patience and instruction from God's word (2 Tim. 4:2). Everyone sins, but saints are not to overlook a saint who is living a sinful lifestyle. Instead we are to reprove, rebuke and exhort. If possible, we are to do this before a saint falls into a sinful lifestyle if we can.

1205. Approaching, and in, the last days people will not endure sound doctrine, but wanting to have their ears tickled, they will accumulate for themselves teachers in accordance to their own desires, and they will turn away their ears from the truth and will turn aside to myths (2 Tim. 4:3, 4).

1206. Even though not all saints are called to be a full-time evangelist, we are all called to evangelize, regularly witnessing to people and discipling new believers. We are to be sober minded, recognizing we have a limited time to do this. This stirs us to endure hardships to evangelize rather than hide from those who oppose Jesus (2 Tim. 4:5).

1207. God allows sinners to oppose us in the work he has us do. The opponents may have victories against us because God allows it. We are to be on guard against them (2 Tim. 4:14, 15).

1208. All saints who are faithful to Jesus and look forward to his return will be rewarded when he returns with a crown of righteousness (2 Tim. 4:8).

1209. When saints die, they are rescued from all evil, and their soul goes to heaven (2 Tim. 4:18).

# TITUS

1210. The pure in heart desire things that are pure. To the defiled and unbelieving nothing is pure, but both their mind and conscience are defiled. These may even profess to know God, but their actions are disobedient to God, showing that they are not God's children (Tit. 1:15, 16). The defiled and unbelieving reach a point where they no longer feel they have done wrong when they sin. Then they live detestable lives.

1211. Older men are to be temperate, dignified, sensible, and sound in faith, in love and in perseverance (Tit. 2:2).

1212. Older women are to be reverent in their behavior, not malicious gossips nor enslaved to much alcohol, teaching what is good, so that they may encourage young women to love their husbands and children, to be sensible, pure, workers at home, kind, submissive to their own husbands, so that the word of God will not be dishonored (Tit. 2:3–5). The part of this that is hard for industrialized nations' people to accept is the encouraging of women to be workers at home on par with being kind and loving their husband and children. But it is encouraged in 1 Tim. 5:14 as well. So the priority of married women is to keep their home a safe, loving environment and caring for their husband and children.

Men were made by God to be the provider of funds for their family (1 Tim. 5:8), and this scripture from Titus tells us God intends women to be the homemaker. Being submissive does not mean the wife does not voice her opinions. The husband and wife need to be in agreement on decisions. If that is impossible sometimes, then the husband is the final decision maker, but he bears the responsibility for his decision. He does not have the support of scripture to make a decision that is contrary to God's word though. It should be noted these instructions are for couples where both spouses are Christian. There are exceptions because of health issues or other reasons that may lead to a reversal of roles but it is better to abide by God's direction for the roles of women and men to make a better family environment.

The scripture does not say married women cannot do work at home to earn money. But if she is working for money so much at home that she is not raising her children then one of the main reasons for her to be home is lost. Also, single women and men are obviously free to work as they please but the Bible says they would do well to do work for God (1 Cor. 7:7–40). Fathers are not to work so much that they are not helping in the rearing of his children either. Both parents must impart Biblical values and teachings to their children.

1213. Young men (males age twelve to perhaps forty or fifty) are to be sensible, full of good deeds, pure in doctrine from scripture, dignified, and sound in speech which is beyond reproach, so opponents will have no occasion or reason to say anything bad about them (Tit. 2:6–8, 1 Pet. 2:12). From this, it is obvious that young men should not participate in deeds displeasing to God, telling of dirty jokes, and other wrong doings. Rather they are to be examples of good rather than trying to be as bad as they can be without being *too* bad.

1214. Slaves who are saints are to be submissive to their own masters, well pleasing and not argumentative. Slaves are not to steal from their masters but honest so that their masters will not have excuse to think or speak evil of the Lord or the Bible (Tit. 2:9, 10). When this was written, slavery was legal and common in society. Scripture does not condone slavery. There are some Mosaic laws on slavery such as banning it for his people among themselves, freeing the slaves every seven years, and loss of right to keep a slave one harmed. People sold themselves into slavery to pay off debts. God did not create sin, even though he created good and evil. Sin is the result of man choosing self, or evil, rather than God. Just as God did not create sin, the bad decisions of people made slavery come into being and not God. Scripture tells us our spiritual life is more important than this temporal fleshly life on earth. Scripture helps us live through deplorable conditions that mankind makes, such as slavery, and how to influence the world around us for good, leading others to a saving knowledge of Jesus and of how God would have them conduct their lives. The Bible is God's word, and the Bible did not say to get rid of slavery per se (Phm. 1:16). If God had told the disciples to condemn slavery, then Christianity would have been banned from all societies and the gospel would not have spread. It was only after the gospel spread through the world that it was possible for enough men that the Holy Spirit could convict that slavery was wrong. These men then rid the world of slavery wherever they could. Slavery is legal now only in a small minority of the world where evil has triumphed.

1215. The grace of God has appeared, bringing salvation to all people (Tit. 2:11). Bringing salvation to all people means it is offered to all people. It does not mean all people are saved. Scripture says more people will reject it, and thus go to hell, than will accept it (Mt. 7:13, 14).

1216. Saints are saved to be a peculiar people. After we are saved, the Holy Spirit instructs us to deny ungodliness and worldly desires, and to live soberly, righteously, and godly, looking for the glorious appearing of our God and Savior Jesus. Jesus thus is God. Jesus gave himself for us to redeem us from all sin and to purify to himself a peculiar people, zealous of good works. Saints are to continue this message to others (Tit. 2:12–15). We are not sinless after we are saved, but God desires us to not sin. We are to be zealous to not sin and to do good works for the Lord's sake. This makes us peculiar to the world. We are not to be like the rest of the world. We are not to conform to this world but be transformed by the renewing of our minds so that we will think, speak, and do what is acceptable to God (Rom. 12:2).

1217. Saints are to be submissive to our worldly rulers and authorities and to be ready for every good deed God presents opportunity for us to do (Tit. 3:1, Rom. 13:1–7, 1 Pet. 2:12–17). Saints are to obey God rather than rulers or authorities when there is conflict between the two (Ac. 5:29).

1218. Saints are to not speak evil of other people and not be brawlers, but be gentle, showing meekness to all (Tit. 3:2).

1219. When we were sinners we were disobedient to God, deceived by Satan, enslaved to various lusts and pleasures, spending our lives in malice and envy, hateful and hating others (Tit. 3:3).

1220. People are saved not by righteous deeds but, because of the love of God and according to His mercy, by the washing away of our old self and sins and renewing of us completely, including our minds, by the Holy Spirit. The Holy Spirit is poured out richly on those who make Jesus Christ their Savior because of his sacrifice so that we are justified by the grace of God and not works (Tit. 3:4–6). Saints are then fellow heirs with Jesus (Rom. 8:17, Tit. 3:7, 1 Pet. 1:3, 4).

1221. Saints are to be engaged in good works, which are good and profitable for men (Tit. 3:8, 14). Only works that come from love for God are good.

1222. Saints are to avoid foolish controversies, genealogies, strife, and disputes about the Jewish Law for they are unprofitable and worthless (Tit. 3:9). Such things come about because of pride generally. Saints are to reject a factious person after a first and second admonition, knowing that such a person is perverted and is sinning, being self-condemned (Tit. 3:10, 11). If a person does not respond to two admonitions, showing them the scriptures that correct them, they are not submissive to God but rebellious to the truth and will not change with further admonition. One should pray for them that God would be merciful and open their eyes to the truth and be saved and pray that they not interfere with the gospel of Jesus.

# PHILEMON

1223. Paul showed us we are to express thanks to those who have helped us (Phm. 1:7). This encourages the one who helped the other.

# HEBREWS

1224. The last days. The last days can be the time from Christ's ascension to heaven to his return (Heb. 1:2). This is also called the church age or age of the Gentiles (Lk. 21:24, Rom. 11:25).

1225. God has spoken to us through his Son Jesus (Heb. 1:2, 2:8; Jn. 12:49, 15:15).

1226. Jesus is heir of all things, as God made all things through him (Heb. 1:2, Rom. 8:17).

1227. Jesus is the radiance of God's glory, and the exact representation of God's nature. The universe exists and is sustained in working order by Jesus's word. When Jesus had made purification of sins, he sat down at the right hand of the Majesty on high. When Jesus was crucified he paid the price for all people's sins, if they will accept he is Lord and Savior. When he ascended he sat at the right hand of God (Heb. 1:3). Jesus is much better than the angels, as he has by inheritance obtained a more excellent name than they (Heb. 1:4). For God never said to any angel, "You are my Son, today I have begotten You?" and again, "I will be a Father to Him and He will be a Son to Me."

And when Jesus was born, God said, "And let all the angels of God worship Him." Of the Son God says, "Your throne, oh God, is forever and forever, and the righteous scepter is the scepter of His kingdom," "You have loved righteousness and hated lawlessness; therefore God, Your God, has anointed You with the oil of gladness above your companions," and "You Lord (Jesus), in the beginning laid the foundations of the earth, and the heavens are the works of Thy hands; the earth and heavens will perish, but You will remain; and they all will become old like a garment, and like a mantle you will roll them up; like a garment they will also be changed. But You are the same, and Your years will not come to an end." God never said to an angel, but he did to Jesus, "Sit at My right hand until I make your enemies a footstool for your feet" (Heb. 1:5–13). The Son, Jesus, was God before all creation, but Jesus is called begotten because he was born in the flesh with his first incarnation. He was not created by God in any way before that. The Son has always existed as has the Father and the Holy Spirit (Gen. 1:2, 26, Mt. 28:19, Rev. 1:8). He was God and man at the same time while he was here on earth.

1228.  Angels are ministering spirits sent out to render service for the sake of those who will inherit salvation (Heb. 1:14, Mt. 18:10). Angels protect us as God directs and are messengers of God to us when God tells them to speak to us. The latter is rare but, by reports, is happening in Muslim countries where the gospel is forbidden, to leads people to Christ.

1229.  Just as people, including his children the Jews, who were disobedient for sinning against God before Jesus came were punished for their disobedience if they continued in them, so to will God's children, Christians, receive penalty if they continue in disobedience to God. God testified the truth of the gospel of Jesus with miracles and wonders and gifts of the Holy Spirit (Heb. 2:1–4).

1230.  God created man (people) a little lower than the angels, but he put man in charge of the world and not angels (Gen. 1:26–31, Heb. 2:5–8).

1231.  While Jesus was in human form on earth he was a little lower than angels also because his flesh was not immortal, and he could feel temptation, hunger, and thirst. This was necessary for Him to empathize with, and help, those that are tempted and to die on the cross, the sacrifice for the sins of the people of the world. Because Jesus was in the flesh for a time, he called saints his brethren (Heb. 2:9–11, 16–18).

1232. Singing praise to God was part of the early church service (Heb. 2:12).

1233. We are to put our trust in God. This is why this is on American money, showing all that America at one point was as God intended and put its trust in God and nothing else, including money. Saints are to teach their children that they are to put their trust in nothing else but God also (Heb. 2:13).

1234. Satan has the power of death over all mankind since the original sin. But those who accept Jesus as Lord and Savior are freed from Satan's claim to them (Heb. 2:14, 15).

1235. We are to confess our sins to God and Jesus (Mt. 6:12, Heb. 3:1).

1236. Evidence of a true saint is faithfulness till their death. Those who claim to be saved (Christian) and lose their faith were either never true believers to begin with or they once believed and later stopped believing. Christians are to encourage one another daily to not return to sin and then become hardened to unbelief (Heb. 3:6–19).

1237. Those who hear God's word, including the gospel of Jesus, and yet never believe in Jesus as Lord and Savior will not go to heaven but will go to hell (Heb. 4:1–11).

1238. The word of God is quick (living and active) and powerful and sharper than any two-edged sword, piercing even to dividing soul and spirit, and of the joints and marrow and is able to judge the thoughts and intentions of the heart. No creature is hidden from God, but all things are open and laid bare before him (Heb. 4:12, 13). This is not to say all people have a spirit in them. People are made of flesh and blood and each person has a soul in them that is the part of them that lasts beyond their fleshly death (first death). All people who are saved have the Holy Spirit in them so they cannot have an evil spirit (demon) in them. People who are not saved can be possessed, inhabited, and controlled by an evil spirit (demon). The wording "dividing soul and spirit" is for emphasis like "heart and mind." Our heart is not the part of us that thinks and has intentions, but the term "heart" is often used for the most meaningful desires of the mind. The point is the word of God is powerful and effective in all aspects of humans and the spirit world, and nothing in the natural world or spiritual world can hide from God.

1239. Because Jesus was tempted and yet sinless, saints can pray to him with confidence that he will give us the mercy and grace to help us in our time of need (Heb. 4:15, 16).

1240. Jesus was called by God to be the high priest forever after the order of Melchizedek (Heb. 5:1–10, 6:20). Melchizedek was king of Salem (later called Jerusalem) and priest of God during the time of Abraham (Gen. 14:18–20). Melchizedek was not without father or mother, but his genealogy was not known. His birth and death were not recorded. He was not a preincarnate Christ. He was a universal priest of God that all people that knew him recognized him as such and was not appointed by another. The tithe of 10 percent of our income is what God expects us to give to him, which is used to support those who do his work full time and pay the bills of the church. Jesus holds his priesthood forever because he continues forever. He is the perfect priest because he is holy, perfect, and without sin and sits at the right hand of God. He did the ultimate sacrifice of himself so no more sacrifice will be needed for those who are saved through faith, and faith alone, in him as Lord and Savior (Hebrews chapter 7; 8:1, 2).

1241. The Son, Jesus, was God before all creation, but Jesus is called begotten because he was born in the flesh with his first incarnation. He was not created by God in any way before that. The Son has always existed as has the Father and the Holy Spirit (Gen. 1:2, 26, Mt. 28:19, Rev. 1:8). He was God and man at the same time while he was here on earth (Ps. 2:7; Ac. 13:33; Heb. 1:5, 5:5).

1242. Saints who do not study God's word and continue to work for God are as infants, not able to handle harder things of the Bible to understand, not having trained their senses to discern good from evil. These babes in Christ are only able to handle and understand the simple truths of scripture so they become dull of understanding God's word. They should mature in their faith through obedience to God, resulting in regular study of God's word and doing God's work, which at least entails witnessing for Jesus to lead others to Christ. As they mature, they will be able to be used by God for more works for Christ's sake (Heb. 5:11–14).

1243. People who are saved (saints) are filled with the Holy Spirit when they become saved. If they later fall away (reject the faith in Jesus as Lord and Savior and not simply have doubts and questions or are backslidden), they can never be saved again, seeing they crucify to themselves the Son of God afresh and put him to an open shame (Heb. 6:4–8). This is probably the most definitive set of verses about falling away from the faith because only a person who is saved can be partakers of the Holy Spirit. A person does not lose their salvation by sinning too much. God does not reject his saints (Jn. 6:37), and nothing can take saints away from God (Rom. 8:38, 39), but we have the free will to reject him, which these verses say can occur after salvation resulting in a person no longer being saved and not capable of being saved again.

Since God is omniscient, he knows who will and will not be faithful to him. Those who are faithful are the chosen by God (Mt. 22:14). These Christians who later reject Jesus as Lord would not later have a desire to repent of their sins and want Jesus as their Savior and Lord. A person who wonders if they have sinned or doubted in the Lord too much and desire a relationship with the Lord are not those who really rejected the Lord. If a person had those feelings, it would mean they were never saved to begin with and are now ready to become saved or they were a backslidden Christian who never rejected Jesus as their Lord and Savior in their heart.

1244. New Covenant. God promised a new covenant to the house of Israel where He will put His laws into their minds and write them on their hearts and they will be His people; He will be merciful to their iniquities and will remember their sins no more (Jer. 31:31-34, Heb. 8:7-13). God has done, and will continue to do until Jesus returns, this to those who have believed the Son, Jesus, is Lord and Savior (Gentiles are grafted into the vine of Abraham) and will do to the third of Jews he spares from the Antichrist and will be tried by fire (Zec. 13:8, 9). Jesus was both the high priest and the sacrifice for this new covenant (Heb. 9:11–14). A blood sacrifice is necessary for a covenant, and Jesus was that, and thus the mediator, for the second covenant (Heb. 9:15–22). The holy of holies of the Old Testament tabernacle was replaced by heaven itself with Jesus. Jesus presented himself before Father God directly for us. It was only necessary for Jesus to do this once, and when he returns, he will be without sin for salvation of those who eagerly await him (Heb. 9:23–26, 28).

1245. Only two things are guaranteed in life for people: death (of the fleshly body) and judgment by God (Heb. 9:27).

1246. It is impossible for the sacrifice of animals to take away the sins of the world. Jesus, by sacrificing himself, was able to do this for those who believe he is Lord and Savior (Heb. 10:1–10).

1247. Sanctification of believers. Sanctified means set apart or holy. Believers are sanctified by the sacrifice of Jesus (Heb. 10:10, 14–18). So then saints can go to God in prayer with a clean conscience, knowing the blood of Jesus has washed us pure. This gives us confidence God hears our prayers (if we forgive others who sin against us), so we are not to waiver in our faith (Heb. 10:19–23).

1248. Saints are to provoke one another to love and good works (Heb. 10:24). Provoke means more than encourage. Saints are to let other saints know that it is expected of them to love one another and to do good works.

1249. Church/Assembly. Saints are not to forsake the assembling of ourselves together, but exhort one another the more as we see the day of the Lord's return approaching (Heb. 10:25).

1250. Those who once were saved (Heb. 10:29; someone who never truly believes is never sanctified) but then reject God shrink back to destruction and sin willfully (Heb. 10:26–39).

1251. The first century Christians endured many tribulations, including seizure of their property. They did it with joy, knowing that this world is not our home, but we have an inheritance coming from God, prepared for those who love him (Heb. 10:34, 11:13–16).

1252. God will judge all people, including saints. It is a fearful thing to fall into the hands of the living God. (Heb. 10:30, 31).

1253. Faith. Faith is the substance of things hoped for, the evidence of things not seen (Heb. 11:1). If we saw all things, we would not need faith to believe that they exist. By faith, we please God. By faith, we believe God created all things. Without faith, it is impossible to please God. Those who pray to God must believe that he is and that he is a rewarder of those who seek him (Heb. 11:1–6).

1254. Noah, by faith, believed God when God told him he was going to destroy the world by flood. Noah built the ark despite ridicule by other people because he believed God and was obedient to God. By this, he condemned the world because the world would not head the warnings he gave to the world of the coming destruction. His faithfulness was accounted to him as righteousness (Heb. 11:7).

1255. By faith, Abraham moved to a foreign land and believed God would give it to him as God had told him. Abraham believed God could give him the ability to father a child with Sarah in their old age. Abraham was willing to offer up his only begotten son to God as a sacrifice, in obedience to God's test of his faith, believing God could raise up the dead and fulfill his promise. This was accounted to him as righteousness (Rom. 4:21, 22, Heb. 11:8–10, 17–19).

1256. By faith Sarah believed God would give her the ability to conceive in her old age, and so she did conceive the father of the great nation Israel in her old age (Heb. 11:11, 12).

1257. By faith, Isaac blessed Jacob and Esau even though he did not have the power on his own to make the blessings come true (Heb. 11:20).

1258. By faith, Jacob blessed the sons of Joseph even though he did not have the power on his own to make the blessings come true (Heb. 11:21).

1259. By faith, Joseph believed God would bring the nation of Israel back to Canaan, so he gave instructions about his bones (Heb. 11:22).

1260. By faith, Moses's parents hid Moses, not afraid of Pharos's command. They trusted God would protect the child Moses (Heb. 11:23).

1261. By faith, Moses chose the life of the slaves of Egypt rather than the life of a prince of Egypt. By faith, he kept the Passover. By faith, he and Israel passed through the red sea on dry land (Heb. 11:24–29).

1262. By faith, the walls of Jericho fell down (Heb. 11:30).

1263. By faith, Rahab the harlot did not perish (Heb. 11:31).

1264. By faith, others, like the prophets of old, shut the mouths of lions; quenched the power of fire; escaped the edge of the sword; from weakness made strong; became mighty in war; put foreign armies to flight; received their dead by resurrection; were tortured, net accepting release by denying their faith, so that they might obtain a better resurrection; experienced mockings, scourgings, and imprisonment; were stoned, sawn in two, tempted, put to death with the sword; and they went about in sheepskins or goatskins, being destitute, afflicted, ill-treated, wandering about in deserts, mountains, caves, and holes in the ground (Heb. 11:32–38).

1265. All who have faith in God have, and will, not receive their full reward until Jesus returns (Heb. 11:39, 40, Rev. 6:11).

1266. Since we are surrounded by the world that observes us, we are to lay aside every encumbrance and sin that so easily entangles us. Each of us knows the weaknesses that cause us to sin or not fully serve God. We are to actively forsake these and strengthen our weaknesses. We are to be faithful until we die (Heb. 12:1, 12, 13).

1267. Jesus is the author and perfecter of faith. He showed the perfect example of faith and humbleness for us while he was here on earth, endured the cross and is set down at the right hand of God. The Lord gives us our small faith of a mustard seed to believe in him to begin with and perfects it through our lives. This faith is how we endure tribulations and trials and do great things in Jesus's name (Heb. 12:2, 3).

1268. When our conscience bothers us before we repent of sin, it is chastisement from God. Some of the trial and tribulations we endure are from God to discipline us. As an earthly father disciplines his children to correct their behavior so too does God discipline his children when he needs to. If anyone does not suffer any while here on earth, he or she is not a child of God. Even though suffering can cause sorrow for a while, it trains us and results in our behaving more righteously here on earth, doing what is right in the sight of God (Heb. 12:4–11).

1269. Saints are to pursue peace with all people, and the salvation, which results in sanctification, of all people. Bitterness, which is caused by not forgiving those who do wrong, leads to trouble and defilement. So we must forgive all people and encourage others to forgive so they will not be defiled and come to salvation (Heb. 12:14–17).

1270. God is now approachable by all his children with the new covenant, unlike the time of the old covenant, when God could only be approached by Moses and then the high priests (Heb. 12:18–24).

1271. After the millennium, the present heaven and earth will be replaced by a new heaven and a new earth (Heb. 12:26–29, Rev. 21:2).

1272. Saints are to love each other (Heb. 13:1).

1273. Saints are to be hospitable and helpful to strangers, for by this, some have entertained angels without knowing it (Heb. 13:2). We must be sensitive to the direction of the Holy Spirit with strangers because there are times when strangers are evil people meaning to do us harm.

1274. We are to minister to inmates in jails and prisons as though we are in prison with them. Likewise, we are to minister to people who are treated poorly by society (Heb. 13:3).

1275. Saints are to honor their marriage to their spouse and to not commit adultery [or fornication (sex outside of marriage with one's spouse) if they are not married], for God will judge adulterers and fornicators (Heb. 13:4).

1276. Saints are to not love money and be content with what they have, being confident in God who said, "I will never leave you, nor forsake you." The Lord is my helper, and I will not fear what man shall do unto me (Heb. 13:5, 6).

1277. We are to imitate the faith of those who are good examples of the faith for us (Heb. 13:7).

1278. The Lord is the same yesterday, today, and forever. Any teachings then contrary to the Bible are false, and any teachings from the Old Testament are valid today, unless the New Testament says otherwise (e.g. circumcision necessary to go to heaven) (Heb. 13:8, 9).

1279. Sacrifices under the new covenant. Sacrifices that saints should offer to God now are: continual praise of him, giving him thanks, doing good to people, and sharing the gospel of Jesus with others (Heb. 13:15, 16).

1280. Saints are to submit to their spiritual leaders, which are pastors, teachers, prophets, and evangelists. This eases their burdens. This does not mean those who are listening and learning should blindly follow these who might be called spiritual leaders; otherwise, it would be a cult. If a spiritual leader says something contrary to what we have thought, we need to investigate the matter in scripture and conform our ideas of truth to what the Bible says. If what the spiritual leader said seems to contradict scripture, we need to go to that leader with that issue and lovingly try to conform his/her, or our, beliefs to what the Bible says. All Christians are to hold each other accountable to scripture. If it is evident the leader does not conform to what the Bible says, with this one on one encounter, we need to go to him/her again with two or three witnesses and discuss the matter. If the leader still does not conform to what scripture says, the church needs to be informed, and the church needs to confront the leader as a whole with the matter. If the leader still does not conform to what the Bible says, they need to be voted out of the church membership and leadership. Other Christian churches need to be informed of this rebellious leader so they will not be lead astray (Heb. 13:17).

# JAMES

1281. Trials, temptations, and sin. Saints are to count it joy when we encounter trials. These trials are allowed by God and test our faith. If we do well with these trials and not sin, we increase our ability to not sin when tested in the future, thus increasing our ability to endure trials. If we consider sinning, then the trial becomes a temptation to sin to us. If we do not give into the temptation, then we do not sin but also increase our endurance. Then we will be able to resist sin more in the future and thus be more Christlike (Jas. 1:2–4). Scripture helps saints endure and do well with trials and tribulations (Rom. 15:4). When a saint perseveres under trials, they will receive a crown of life, which is promised to those who love the Lord (Jas. 1:12). God is neither tempted by evil and he does not tempt anyone to do evil. When a person is tempted, they are carried away, when God allows their faithfulness to be tried, and enticed by their own lust. If then he or she gives into the temptation, he or she does sin. Sin then brings death. Our flesh is not immortal because of sins worthy of death (Jas. 1:13–15, 1 Cor. 11:30, 1 Jn. 5:16, 17).

1282. Prayer. When a saint prays, they must pray for things that are godly, and they must not doubt. Someone who doubts is like the surf of the sea, driven and tossed by the wind. In other words, affected by the world around them, which is Satan's now and he wants to make saints ineffective by decreasing their faith in God. A saint who doubts when they ask of God for something they know is godly should not expect to receive anything from God (Jas. 1:6–8). When we ask God for something godly, it must be in the light of God's word. So asking God to save the whole population of the world may sound godly but it is counter to scripture since he told us most people will not be saved. Asking God to save a particular person is good, but ultimately, it is in God's hands once we tell that person the gospel of Jesus. If we demand anything of God in prayer or think anything we ask of him without doubting, it will be answered the way in which we prayed we are playing God. Even Jesus said, "Your will be done" when he prayed to Father God. So when we pray, we ask for godly things without doubting and trust God will do what is best because he is God. If we do not doubt that God will answer our prayer for the best, however that is, then we can be at peace. We can be at peace even when others around us reject God because we know that God is good and in control.

1283. Wisdom. If we lack wisdom, we need to ask God to give us wisdom. God, who gives generously, will give it to us, if we do not doubt (Jas. 1:5–8). Wisdom from God is first pure, then peaceable, gentle, reasonable, full of mercy and good fruits, unwavering, without hypocrisy. Imagine having these traits generously, given by God. By exhibiting these godly traits, we will bear fruit of righteousness; God will use us to bring others to salvation and help other saints exhibit these traits (Jas. 3:17, 18).

1284. Poor saints are to glory in their honorable state in heaven as a brother or sister of Christ. Wealthy saints are to glory when they are humiliated by trials because it reminds them that their wealth is fleeting. Their wealth can be taken away by God just as it was given by God (Jas. 1:9–11).

1285. Every good gift and perfect gift is from the Father of lights (God) who changes not (Jas. 1:17). Whatever is sinless and good is from God.

1286. Christians became into being because of God's word of truth. Christians are a kind of first fruits among his creatures (Jas. 1:18). Christians are God's first children who will live forever with him under the new covenant by repenting and accepting Jesus as Lord and Savior. God is creative and will create a new heaven and a new earth after the millennium. We do not know all there is to know about it, but Christians will be there when it is created.

1287. Anger. We are to be quick to hear, slow to speak, and slow to anger, because the anger of a man of woman does not achieve the righteousness of God (Jas. 1:19, 20). When we feel we are about to become angry we need to listen to the person we are angry toward because what they have to say may explain things to us that would take our anger away. Also we need to listen quickly to the Holy Spirit when we are about to become angry so we can feel the Holy Spirit convict us so that we do not sin. We must also be slow to speak because we can do more harm than good when we speak out of anger. Only after we feel the Holy Spirit telling us we would not sin in saying certain things are we to speak those things. This would then be the case of God being angry about something motivating us to speak. If our anger is self-motivated, it does not achieve good. A general test for whether anger is of ourselves is the motivation for the anger. If greed or pride, or any other part of our flesh, motivates the anger, then it is of ourselves and will not achieve the righteousness of God.

1288. We are to do away with sin in our life, particularly the sins that were our most common ones before we were saved. If we listen to God's word and call ourselves Christian but do not do as the word of God tells us, we will no longer be convicted of our sins, having our conscience seared. We must do as the word of God tells us and not hearers only; then we will be blessed (Jas. 1:21–25).

1289. Someone who calls himself or herself Christian but routinely speaks the same as sinners is not saved (Jas. 1:26).

1290. Pure religion and undefiled is this: to visit the orphans and widows in their distress and to keep oneself unstained by the world (Jas. 1:27). Helping the helpless is a sign of loving our neighbor as ourselves. Keeping oneself unstained by the world means not influenced by the world or our own lusts and thus sinless. This is only possible by loving God more than anything or anyone. No one is perfect. But sin occurs the moment we love someone or something more than God, so then we give in to temptation at that moment.

1291. Exhibiting personal favoritism is wrong. God chose the poor people of the world to be rich in faith and heirs of the kingdom, which he has promised to those who love him. So then we need to not show more favoritism to those who are more wealthy or less to those who are poor. We do well to do in accordance to the royal law of scripture: "You are to love your neighbor as yourself" (Jas. 2:1–9).

1292. Sin. When we transgress against one law of God, we are guilty of transgressing all laws. So even though we do not commit a sin against a Mosaic law that was punishable by death, we are guilty of it regardless. So then we are worthy of death, and our fleshly body will die. This then seems to equalize sinners, if not the sins (Jas. 2:10, 11).

1293. Judgment by God will be without mercy to the one who has shown no mercy. Mercy triumphs over judgment (Jas. 2:13). A genuine believer will show mercy to others, so saints will be shown mercy by God come judgment day.

1294. Faith without works is dead. A man or woman is justified by works and not by faith alone. Our works, out of love for God and others, shows our faith. This does not mean a person needs to do good works as well as have faith in God to get to heaven but if we do not do good works for God's sake to other people we do not have faith in God. It also does not mean works replace faith to be saved. Works without faith is dead also. The demons even believe in the one true God, but they do not do God's work, so they are not justified; therefore belief in the truth of who God is is not enough to go to heaven. One must love, and be obedient to, him and good works is evidence of that. However, doing works to help others physically without faith will not justify a person before God. One must have a faith in the triune God. Abraham and Rahab exhibited both a faith in God as he was known at the time and good works. They were justified to God as a result (Jas. 2:14–26).

1295. Not many Christians should be teachers because teachers of God's word will have a stricter judgment by God, and we all stumble (sin). If anyone does not stumble (sin) in what they teach from the Bible they do well, able to bridle their body, thus not able to be accused of being a hypocrite (Jas. 3:1, 2).

1296. The tongue can do great and terrible things. It is as a small flame that starts a forest fire. It is set on fire from hell, and it can change the course of a person's life. With the tongue, saints both bless God and curse men, who are made in the image of God. This should not be. We must master it (Jas. 3:3–12).

1297. Jealousy and selfish ambition are earthly, natural, and demonic. When we have jealousy or selfish ambition, it is because we are allowing Satan to influence us. This then leads to disorder and every evil thing. Wisdom from God is pure, peaceable, gentle, reasonable, full of mercy and good fruits, unwavering, and without hypocrisy. The work of an obedient saint is done with peace in that saint's heart, knowing they are doing their best to do God's will, and results in righteousness (Jas. 3:18).

1298. Quarrels and conflicts between people because of lust for pleasures or power, that sometimes conflict, and envy (Jas. 4:1, 2).

1299. Unanswered prayer. Sometimes the reason we have unanswered prayer is because we ask things of God with wrong motives so that we may use it to please our own lusts (Jas. 4:3). We are not to live or pray seeking pleasure but seeking God. Other reasons for unanswered prayer are: not being reconciled with a fellow believer we have wronged (Mt. 5:23, 24), if we regard sin or wickedness in our heart (sin willfully and not repentant, Ps. 66:18), and not forgiving other people since that is sin in itself (Is. 59:1, 2; Mt. 6:15).

1300. Friendship with the world is hostility toward God; therefore whoever wishes to be a friend of the world makes himself or herself and enemy of God. To desire things of this world causes a separation between God and us. By doing as the world does, such as watch movies or shows, we know we would be ashamed of God seeing us watch, we are choosing the world over God. Such desires and acts demonstrate that we love the world more than God, at least in those moments, so they cause God to be jealous for our heart. Despite this, God is graceful enough to forgive us if we humble ourselves (Jas. 4:4–6).

1301. God resists the proud but gives grace to the humble (Ps. 138:6, Prov. 3:34, Jas. 4:6, 1 Pet. 5:5). Submit therefore to God (Jas. 4:7a). A person cannot be saved or helped by God if they are too proud to submit to God. Only when a person humbles himself or herself to God will God save them, if they are not saved, or help them. Draw near to God, and he will draw near to you. We must be willing to stop sinning, change our desires, and repent. Then he will save that humble person who does this (Jas. 4:8–10). Also, God cannot use a proud person because they want to do things their way. Only when a person is humble can God use them, to his glory.

1302. Resist the devil, and he will flee from you (Jas. 4:7). This is a great verse to quote when rebuking the devil, such as when a saint feels tempted to sin.

1303. Saints are not to speak against a fellow believer with intent to hurt them, such as gossip. This is wrongful judgment because the one doing this seeks to be the punisher and not leave it to God (Jas. 4:11, 12). This does not preclude going to a fellow believer who is unrepentant of sin with intent of restoring them to a right relationship with God, as Jesus said (Mt. 18:15–17).

1304. We need to be humble in our successes in the worldly realm, recognizing God has allowed us to do so, knowing that we did not do it ourselves. We need to plan our lives with the realization that God can give and take away (Jas. 4:13–16).

1305. To know to do good and to not do it is sin (Jas. 4:17). This verse tells us that God has a higher standard that goes beyond doing bad things is sin. To not do something good that one feels convicted to do is disobedience to the leading of the Holy Spirit/God.

1306. The evil rich man or woman who does not consider God and does not honor his or her agreements with those who are powerless and poor will receive judgment from God, even though life is pleasurable for them in the flesh (Jas. 5:1-6).

1307. Saints are not to be envious of, or complain against, one another but be merciful and compassionate, just as Christ has been with us, all the while anticipating the return of the Lord (Jas. 5:7-11). Saints are not to grumble against the Lord (Phil. 2:14) as the children of Israel did in the wilderness, lest they lose some of their reward from God after the Lord returns (2 Jn. 8).

1308. We are not to swear by anything, or anyone, but let our yes be yes and our no be no. We are to be honest. God holds us to our oaths or what we swear to. We do not have control of the world, as God does, so things may change beyond our control making it impossible for us to fulfill our oath (Jas. 5:12).

1309. If anyone is suffering, such as persecution, they must pray. And on the contrary, if anyone is cheerful, they should sing praises to God (Jas. 5:13). Each saint has a different life God makes for them, influenced by our own decisions, and we are to realize God cares for us whether we are suffering or doing well. He wants to hear from us regardless, and he deserves our praise.

1310. If a saint is sick then he or she should call for the elders to pray over, and anoint with oil in the name of the Lord, him or her. Then, if the God wills, God will heal him or her. The one who is sick will have their sins forgiven them, since during their time with the elders they would confess and repent of their sins (Jas. 5:14, 15). Saints are to confess their sins to one another and pray for one another so that they may be healed (Jas. 5:16).

1311. Confess sins to fellow Saints. Saints are to confess their sins to one another (Mt. 5:23, 24, Jas. 5:16).

1312. The effective, fervent prayer of a righteous man accomplishes much. Jas. 5:16. Saints today and Elijah are alike in that both are of the same nature. Elijah prayed earnestly that it would not rain on the earth for three and a half years, and God made it so. Then Elijah prayed for rain, and the rains came abundantly, then the earth produced fruit (Jas. 5:17, 18). This tells us that a saint can do the same as Elijah today, if God so leads them.

1313. If a so-called Christian, who in reality is a sinner, strays from the truth and a saint turns them back, let him who turned the so-called Christian to God know that he saved a soul (actually God saved the soul, using the saint) and prevented a multitude of sins (Jas. 5:19, 20). This so-called Christian could not have been saved before this (Heb. 6:4–6).

# 1 PETER

1314. Peter's letter is to Christians of Jewish blood since he uses the term aliens (but could also be to Gentiles since we are of the kingdom of God and not of this world), in various parts of modern day Turkey. Saints, having been chosen by God, are born again, reborn by the Spirit after being born of the flesh, when they believe in Jesus, whom they have not seen. Our faith will be tested by fire (various trials). May we be found faithful to God in these trials, proving that we love the Lord, to his praise, glory, and honor. The outcome of our faith is salvation of our souls, the Holy Spirit indwelling and sanctifying saints, and an imperishable inheritance for the saints. The prophets prophesied of such things (1 Pet. 1:1–12).

1315. Saints are to prepare for action for God and act as he directs. Saints are to be holy even as the Lord is holy in all our behavior, because it is written, "Be you holy, for I am holy." Therefore, we are not to conform to our sinful nature but be sober and vigilant for God. We are to conduct ourselves in fear of God while we are here on earth, recognizing he will judge all according to their work here on earth. Jesus was the sacrificial lamb unblemished and unstained from the world (sinless), God having predetermined this before the foundation of the world (1 Pet. 1:13–21).

1316. Saints are to fervently love one another (1 Pet. 1:22).

1317. Saints are born again of the Word of God, which endures forever (1 Pet. 1:23–25).

1318. After a saint is born again, they are to do away with malice, deceit, hypocrisy, slander, envy, sensuality, lusts, drunkenness, carousing, drinking parties, and idolatry but instead desire and love God and the Bible. This will make the saint grow spiritually (1 Pet. 2:1–3, 4:2, 3).

1319. The worldwide body of believers is a spiritual sanctuary, or spiritual house, made of the chief cornerstone Jesus and the saints being the other stones. These stones, or saints, are living built up for a holy priesthood to offer up spiritual sacrifices acceptable to God through Jesus Christ. To those who do not believe in Jesus as Lord and Savior, Jesus is a stumbling block and a rock of offense. Sinners are offended by the word of God, including the gospel of Jesus (1 Pet. 2:4–8).

1320. Saints are a chosen race, a royal priesthood, a holy nation, a people for God's own possession, so that we may proclaim the excellencies of him who has called us out of darkness into his marvelous light; for we once were not a people, but now we are the people of God. We had not received mercy, but now we have received mercy (Dt. 26:19, 1 Pet. 2:9, 10). Saints across all potential boundaries, including nationalities, the world, and time are united as one holy people of God, because of the mercy of God.

1321. Saints no longer belong to this world, so we are to abstain from fleshly lusts, which war against our soul. We are to keep our behavior excellent among sinners, so that in the evil thing they desire to accuse us of doing, they cannot accuse us because of our good behavior obvious to all. This then may lead these sinners to salvation when the Holy Spirit visits them, and then they will glorify God when he returns (1 Pet. 2:11, 12).

1322. Saints are to honor governments, rulers, and other people by abiding by their rules and laws as long as these do not conflict with the way God wants us to be (1 Pet. 2:13–17). God establishes and brings down rulers and nations so by doing this we obey God.

1323. We are to be submissive to our employers, even the ones who are unreasonable. If we patiently endure suffering such as this, we find favor with God. We are called for purposes such as this because Jesus suffered without doing anything wrong, and he himself bore our sins in his body on the cross so that we might die to sin and live to righteousness (1 Pet. 2:18–24).

1324. By his wounds, we are healed. This speaks of spiritual healing until he returns; then, we will receive an imperishable body. He is the Shepherd and Guardian of our souls (1 Pet. 2:24, 25).

1325. Wives are to be submissive to their husbands, and by doing so, they may lead their unsaved husband to salvation by their chaste and respectful behavior. For a woman to exhibit a gentle and quiet spirit is precious in the sight of God (1 Pet. 3:1–6).

1326. Husbands are to live with their wives in an understanding way, as someone weaker, which means in a merciful manner. Husbands are to show their wives honor as a fellow heir of the grace of God so that their prayers are not hindered. 1 Pet. 3:7. Remember unforgiveness of others leads to unforgiveness by God of that unforgiveness and him not listening to our prayers (Ps. 66:18, Mt. 6:14, 15), and unresolved conflicts that the Holy Spirit reminds us of leads to God not listening to our prayers (Is. 59:1, 2, Mt. 5:23, 24). To honor one's wife means to hold them in high position, and a husband respects everything his wife says and does, unless it is evil. This then should make the wife careful of what she says and does.

1327. Saints are to be harmonious, sympathetic, brotherly, kindhearted, and humble in spirit, not returning evil for evil or insult for insult, but giving a blessing instead, for we were called for this purpose so that we might inherit a blessing (1 Pet. 3:8, 9).

1328. The one who desires a good life on this earth must keep his tongue from evil and speaking deceit. He or she must turn away from evil and do good, seeking peace. For the eyes of the Lord are over the righteous, and he hears their prayers, but the face of the Lord is against those who do evil (1 Pet. 3:10–12).

1329. Suffering for our faith. There is little chance of suffering if a person does what is good, but if a saint does suffer for the sake of righteousness, then they are blessed. Do not fear sinners' intimidation, and let not your heart be troubled (1 Pet. 3:13, 14). Saints need to trust God that he will make things right so that whatever the outcome it is his will. God is in control (1 Pet. 4:19).

1330. Saints are to always be ready to give a defense of our faith and give an account of our hope, yet with gentleness and reverence, and do our best to not sin so that we will have a good conscience. Then those who would slander us will only be able to revile our good behavior and speech, putting them to shame. It is better to suffer for doing right, if God wills, than for doing wrong (1 Pet. 3:15–17, 4:2).

1331. Jesus went and made proclamation, between his crucifixion and ascension, to the fallen angels (demons) that did evil during the days of Noah. There were only eight people saved during the flood on board Noah's ark (1 Pet. 3:19, 20, Gen. 7:13, 2 Pet. 5).

1332. Baptism does not save people. It is the first act of obedience after a person is saved. One can only have a good conscience before God if they have repented and made Jesus their Lord and Savior. To say baptism saves is contrary to the gospel message (1 Pet. 3:21).

1333. Jesus. Jesus sits at the right hand of God in heaven. All angels, all authorities, and all powers are subjected to him (1 Pet. 3:22).

1334. Death brings perfection. When saints suffer as Jesus suffered (die in the flesh), they will be free of sin (1 Pet. 4:1). The worst Satan has against saints is death of the flesh, but he is powerless over the soul of the saint. God makes death of the flesh into perfection of the saint.

1335. Sinners are surprised that saints do not do as they do such as attend drinking parties, view pornography, and have sex outside of marriage so they malign us (1 Pet. 4:4).

1336. Saints are to be sober and to watch for the end of this age in prayer (1 Pet. 4:7). There have been generations of saints since this was written and the end has not yet come. How are we to continue to do this, with this realization? We do not know when the Lord will return. If we did, many saints through the ages would have been tempted to live their lives centered on the pleasures of this world rather than working for God, knowing their life would have been more pleasant here on earth. Then there would have been less people saved over the ages perhaps.

1337. Saints are to fervently love one another because love covers a multitude of sins. We are to be hospitable with other saints (1 Pet. 4:8, 9).

1338. Saints are to use their spiritual gifts for the benefit of one another as good stewards of the grace of God. He who speaks is to speak as one speaking the utterances of God, whoever serves is to do so as one who is serving by the strength of God, so that in all things God may be glorified through the Son Jesus, to whom belongs the glory and dominion forever (1 Pet. 4:10, 11).

1339. Saints and crimes. If a saint suffers for Christ's sake, they are to rejoice but we need to make sure we do not suffer for wrongdoing. This means saints need to not commit crimes against God and man such as murder and theft. If they are accused of such crimes and are innocent, they are to defend themselves to preserve their reputation and ability to witness without being accused of hypocrisy (1 Pet. 4:12–16).

1340. The Lord will judge saints and sinners. The Lord will first judge saints and then sinners at the great white throne of judgment (1 Pet. 4:17, 18, Rev. 20:11–15).

1341. Pastors in churches are to shepherd the church not out of compulsion or desire for wealth but a desire to do it out of love for God and their fellow believers. They are to lead by good example and not lead by domination or intimidation. Pastors who do this will receive an unfading crown of glory (1 Pet. 5:1–4).

1342. Younger men who are saints are to be submissive to the elder men saints. All saint are to be humble (1 Pet. 5:5).

1343. God resists the proud but gives grace to the humble (Ps. 138:6, Prov. 3:34, Jas. 4:6, 1 Pet. 5:5). Submit therefore to God (Jas. 4:7a). A person cannot be saved or helped by God if they are too proud to submit to God. Only when a person humbles himself or herself to God will God save them, if they are not saved, or help them. Draw near to God, and he will draw near to you. We must be willing to stop sinning, change our desires, and repent. Then he will save that humble person who does this (Jas. 4:8–10). Also, God cannot use a proud person because they want to do things their way. Only when a person is humble can God use them, to his glory. God will exalt, at the proper time, those who humble themselves to him (1 Pet. 5:6).

1344. We are to cast all our cares on God for he cares for us (1 Pet. 5:7). God truly cares about us, so we are to pray to him about our needs, fears, etcetera. He will then help us with these. He may not take away the thing we fear but give us more love or faith so we may endure it.

1345. The devil prowls like a roaring lion, seeking whom he may devour, so we need to be sober and on the alert for him. This tells us the devil is not passive but active in his efforts. We must be on the lookout for him and his actions and pray always, even before we see his efforts (1 Pet. 5:8). Satan seeks to steal, kill, and destroy (Jn. 10:10). The devil wants to steal faith, love, and peace from saints. He also wants to steal people from God and steal people of an eternal life full of grace, love, peace, joy, and mercy from God. The devil seeks to get as many people to die and go to hell and then suffer the second death in the lake of fire as he can. The devil seeks to destroy God's creations (people's lives, marriage, families, the church) causing such things as discord, divorce, mental illness caused by unforgiveness of others, and murder.

1346. Sufferings can be brought by Satan, as allowed by God to test our faith. We must resist the devil, knowing that other saints face similar sufferings and trials. These sufferings and trials will last a little while, and when we resist them, we will be made stronger, closer to perfection by God. This perfection of us will occur when Jesus returns and we receive our incorruptible and imperishable bodies (1 Pet. 5:9, 10).

1347. Peter sends greetings from the church in Babylon (1 Pet. 5:13). Some have conjectured this Babylon is Rome. But nowhere else in letters from apostles do they refer to Rome as Babylon so this is unlikely. It is unlikely that in a friendly salutation from a church that Peter would use the name Babylon for the location of the church in Rome. Babylon was the center from which the Asiatic dispersion whom Peter addresses was derived. Philo (*The Embassy to Gaius*, 36) and Josephus (*Antiquities*, book 18, chapter 9) inform us that Babylon contained a great many Jews in the apostolic age [whereas those at Rome were comparatively few, about eight thousand (Josephus, *Antiquities*, book 17, chapter 11)]; so it would naturally be visited by the apostle of the circumcision.

It was the headquarters of those whom he had so successfully addressed on Pentecost (Acts 2:9), Jewish "Parthians…dwellers in Mesopotamia" (the Parthians were then masters of Mesopotamian Babylon); these he ministered to in person. Those he wrote this letter to were most likely Jewish believers in Cappadocia, Pontus, Asia, Phrygia, Pamphylia. So it would make sense he wrote a salutation from a large group of Christians of Jewish heritage who were in Babylon of Mesopotamia. This does not mean Peter was never in Rome. Christian church tradition is that Peter was crucified upside down in Rome. Tertullian, *in The Demurrer Against the Heretics* (AD 200), noted of Rome, "How happy is that church…where Peter endured a passion like that of the Lord, where Paul was crowned in a death like John's [referring to John the Baptist, both he and Paul being beheaded]."

Church tradition is that both Peter and Paul were martyred at Rome, most likely during Nero's persecution of Christians in the sixties. In the same book, Tertullian wrote that "This is the way in which the apostolic churches transmit their lists: like the church of the Smyrnaeans, which records that Polycarp was placed there by John; like the church of the Romans, where Clement was ordained by Peter." This Clement, known as Clement of Rome, later would be the fourth pope. (Note that Tertullian didn't say Peter consecrated Clement as pope).

# 2 PETER

1348. Saints, as much as possible, are to add to their faith virtuous thought and behavior, and to virtue add knowledge of God through prayerful study of the Bible, and to this knowledge, self-control, patience, godliness, brotherly kindness, and love. As we increase in these, we become more useful to God. One who neglects these is blind and forgets what manner of person they were before they were saved. This person then may not be truly saved (2 Pet. 1:5–11).

1349. All scripture in the Bible is either eye-witnessed accounts of what happened and the teachings of Jesus or divinely inspired by the Spirit of God (2 Pet. 1:16–21).

1350. There are so-called Christians who teach false teachings contrary to the Bible, even denying that Jesus is the only way to heaven and everyone who does not believe in him as Lord and Savior is going to hell. These same so-called Christians follow their sensuality, or lusts of the flesh, the ways of the world, and Satan. They will suffer at the hands of God just as the false prophets before Jesus's first incarnation did. This justice at the hands of God may not occur until after these false prophets and false so-called Christians die (2 Pet. 2:1–3).

1351. God cast the rebellious angels who sided with Satan into hell, reserved for the day of judgment to come (2 Pet. 2:4). The fallen angels that followed Satan when he rebelled against God have been bound in hell since the days of Noah, awaiting the day of judgment after the millennium. These fallen angels had sex with women somehow (perhaps directly or by possessing men's bodies), and that is how the race of giants, the Nephilim, came into being (Gen. 6:1–6, Nu. 13:33, 2 Pet. 2:4, Jude 1:6).

1352. Rescue for the righteous and punishment for the unrighteous by God. God destroyed Sodom and Gomorrah for the sensual sins, which tormented Lot's righteous soul day after day. God knows how to deliver the godly from temptation, just as he did with Lot, when sin became too great in his society. The Holy Spirit can help us overcome temptation; sometimes God uses other means. Sometimes this rescuing is by death at a relatively young age (e.g. Samson, from temptation of pride, idolatry, and fornication), imprisonment (Joseph, from temptation of adultery), and physical removal (Lot, from various sins such as homosexuality). Although God always provides a way to escape temptation, we do not always do what is right, as we know from many Bible accounts and our own experiences.

The godly are rescued finally from temptation when we die in the flesh though. The unrighteous people (those that are not saints), especially those who indulge their fleshly desires and despise the authority of God, are kept under punishment in hell, just as the fallen angels (demons) are, until the day of judgment. All people are born sinners and have natural desires of the flesh they were born with to sin. This does not make these natural desires acceptable. Instead, God calls on all humanity to forsake these natural desires that he gave us for him. In this way, we prove we love him more than ourselves. Sinners are self-willed, rather than submitting to God, daring even to revile angels and God, which are greater than they. Sinners, driven by their instincts like animals, will suffer for their sins in hell. Sinners are stains and blemishes on society, even deceiving saints by associating with them and pretending to be saints. They never cease from sinning, having desire for all kinds of sexual sin, enticing those who are indecisive as to whether or not to follow God.

These so-called Christians, who are sinners, having forsaken the gospel of Jesus they have heard are accursed, greedy, and deceptive. They appear to have the truth in them but do not, like springs without water. These false teachers, by arrogant words, entice people who are indecisive about the truth, promising freedom when they themselves are slaves of sin. The people they entice are typically people tired of consequences of bad decisions and looking for a new way of life, a new explanation of life, or a new religion. So false teaching that is contrary to the Bible is a way to recognize so-called Christians that are not saved (2 Pet. 2:6–19).

1353. So-called Christians who once escaped defilement by the knowledge of the Lord and Savior Jesus Christ but then are again entangled and overcome by sin so that they reject Jesus are in a worse state than before they were free from these defilement. It is worse for them than had they never come to the knowledge of the truth. This happens though to fulfill the proverb, "A dog returns to its own vomit" and "A sow, after washing, returns to wallowing in the mire." The latter proverb is not in the Bible but perhaps a proverb of Peter's time (Prov. 26:11, 2 Pet. 2:20–22). These scriptures may mean that a person who professes a faith in the Lord but never really does is in worse shape than a sinner who never professes a faith in the Lord because the former will never repent and come to salvation, whereas the latter may. However, it is remarkably similar to Hebrews 6:4–6, which says for a person once saved who then turns away from God (not taken from God's hand by anyone or anything nor released by God by God's initiative) it is impossible to be saved again. This would explain how their state is worse after rejecting Christ, after having once having possessed a saving knowledge of him, than had they never been saved, or possessed a saving knowledge of Jesus, to begin with. One cannot escape defilement without being saved.

1354. In the last days, mockers will come who will mock and say, "Where is the promise of his coming? For since the fathers fell asleep, all continues just as it was from the beginning of creation." In this, they neglect the proofs of the flood of Noah's day. Since these people say creation, these people are probably unsaved people belonging to religions that teach creationism in one form or another (2 Pet. 3:3–6). This would be one way the devil would use to bring about a great falling away from the faith (Mt. 24:10, 2 Th. 2:3, 1 Tim. 4:1).

1355. The world will end with fire, kept for the day of judgment and destruction of ungodly men (Mal. 4:1; 2 Pet. 3:7, 10–13; Rev. 20:9, 21:1, 5).

1356. One day is as a thousand years, and a thousand years as one day to the Lord (2 Pet. 3:8). God does not look at time the same as humans. This may be taken literally in some cases and figuratively in others. There have been prophecies where God gave length of times that were understandable to us.

1357. The Lord is not slow in his return but is patient toward those that are his, not wishing that any would perish but for all to come to repentance (2 Pet. 3:9). The "any" and "all" in this verse appears to refer to those people God has chosen to go to heaven from the foundation of the world. God desires all people to be saved and to come to the knowledge of the truth (1 Tim. 2:4). Even though omnipotent God desires this, it will not happen (Mt. 7:13, 14) because prophesies have to be fulfilled. For these prophesies to be fulfilled, most people must reject Christ

Jesus as Lord and Savior. Also, God gives people free will to decide whether or not to be a believer and follower of God (Jn. 3:36, Ac. 17:30). However, God gives people the faith to believe (Eph. 2:8), and he predestined who would go to heaven before the foundation of the world (Jn. 6:44, Ac. 13:48, Rom. 8:29, 30, Eph. 1:4–6). Those he predestined to go to heaven must hear the word of God first somehow though to be saved (Rom. 10:17, 2 Th. 2:13, 2 Tim. 2:10). So then the main reason not all people will be saved, even though God wants them to be saved, is fulfillment of prophecy. God does not want people to sin, but he gives us free will to sin or not to sin. Also, God has no pleasure in the death (neither the first or second death) of those who do choose not to follow and obey him (Ez. 18:23).

1358. The day of the Lord will come as a thief in the night, in which the heavens will pass away, the elements will be destroyed with intense heat and the earth with its works will be burned up. What manner of people then we should be in holy conduct and godliness. There will be new heavens and a new earth (2 Pet. 3:10–13). This day of the Lord is the end of the millennium since it describes this present earth and heavens being destroyed by fire, being replaced by new heavens and a new earth (Rev. 20:9, 21:1, 5).

1359. Since God will judge the earth with fire, what manner of people then we should be in holy conduct and godliness. Saints are to be diligent to be found blameless by God, unstained from the world, steadfast in our faith. We are not to be moved by others who would dissuade us from our faith (2 Pet. 3:11, 14–18). We will not be perfect until we die and go to heaven, or until the Lord returns, and we receive our new imperishable bodies, but we are to do our best to not sin. It is a dreadful thing to fall into the hands of the living God (Heb. 10:31).

# 1 JOHN

1360. God is Light, just as Jesus is Light (Jn. 1:4, 4, 3:19), and in him, there is no darkness at all (1 Jn. 1:5). This helps us see that Jesus and God are one.

1361. Sins in saints and sinners. Saints are to acknowledge they sin, but saints tend to not sin but choose to do right. A sinner tends to sin and not do right. If a person walks in the Light, the blood of Jesus cleanses him or her of their sins (1 Jn. 1:6–8, 10).

1362. Forgiving and confessing sins. If we confess our sins to God, he is faithful and just to forgive us of our sins and to cleanse us from all unrighteousness (1 Jn. 1:9). See notes on Mt. 6:12, 14, 15 and Mk. 11:25, 26.

1363. Jesus is the Advocate for saints with the Father for their sins (1 Jn. 2:1). Jesus defends saints from Satan's accusations about saints to God.

1364. Jesus was the payment for the sins of all people (1 Jn. 2:2). This does not mean all people's sins are forgiven because people who do not repent of their sins will not be forgiven of their sins and will perish in hell (Lk. 13:3, 24:47).

1365. Obeying God's commands and loving God are what Christians do. If a person does not do these, then they are not saved, even if they think they are saved (1 Jn. 2:3–8). This does not mean a person has to be perfect to show they are saved but that their desire should be to obey God, out of love for him.

1366. Saints love one another. Sinners do not love saints. If a person who claims to be a Christian and yet hates other believers, he or she is not a Christian. This kind of person is blinded by Satan so that he or she does not know they are not saved, and they walk in darkness, even though they have the appearance on the outside of being a Christian. These people have hatred in their heart for others (1 Jn. 2:9–11, 3:10). Hatred is as murder (1 Jn. 3:15).

1367. Cannot love God and the world. Saints are not to love the world nor the things of the world, such as riches and pleasures of the world. If anyone loves the world, he or she does not love God. The lusts of the flesh, the lusts of the eyes, and the pride of life are of the world and not God. The world is passing away, but the one who does the will of the Father will live forever (1 Jn. 2:15–17). Sometimes saints get caught up in these things of the world and lose our focus on God. This is sin. We are to repent and turn from our wicked ways as soon as we realize this.

1368. Those who deny that Jesus is God's Son and the only way to heaven are of the spirit of the Antichrist. Some of them at one point will have said they were Christian (1 Jn. 2:18–27).

1369. We should abide in, and thus obey, Jesus so that we will not be ashamed at his coming. He is the Light and reveals all things that are hidden and done in secret (1 Jn. 2: 28).

1370. People who practice righteousness are of God. Doing good things that appear righteous are not righteous without a heart made clean by salvation of Jesus (1 Jn. 2:29, 3:7).

1371. Saints are children of God and the world does not know, or understand, us because it did not know Jesus (1 Jn. 3:1).

1372. What saints will be after Jesus returns has not all been made known to us. When he returns, saints will be like him because we will see him as he is (1 Jn. 3:2). We are not perfect yet, but when Jesus returns, we will become perfect.

1373. Saints have their hope on Jesus's return and want to purify themselves, just as he is pure. Saints are made pure when they become saved so that they can go to heaven but we continue to sin because we are in a fleshly body, with lusts and pride. Saints want to be more and more like Jesus though, free of sin as much as possible until Jesus returns, because we love him and want to not hurt him by sinning. This desire is one way of knowing if one is saved (1 Jn. 3:3–9).

1374. The Lord Jesus came to earth in the flesh to destroy the works of Satan (1 Jn. 3:8). The works of Satan include: turning the hearts of people away from God, accusing saints before God to attempt to convince God to test the faith saints, ruling this world and the power of death. The gospel of Jesus brings hope from the power of Satan to those who listen and obey. Jesus is our Advocate to God against the devil on our behalf (1 Jn. 2:1). While all people die in the flesh because of sin, those who belong to Jesus will be rescued from the second death. God will make a new heaven and earth after Satan is cast into the lake of fire, so the devil will not rule the new earth.

1375. Saints are to love one another so much that we would be willing to lay down our lives for each other just as Jesus did for us (1 Jn. 3:13–16).

1376. A saint who has the capability to help another saint in need and yet closes his or her heart and does not help the needful saint is in rebellion against God, and it is questionable if he or she is saved. Helping others shows love is in the heart. Just saying one loves another does not mean anything if there is not truth to it and deeds to show the love (1 Jn. 3:17, 18).

1377. Saints who are obedient to God are not condemned by their heart because they have not committed sins to be ashamed of. When saints keep God's commandments and do those things that are pleasing in his sight, their prayers are directed by God, and so their prayers are answered.

They do not pray for their own lusts or desires (1 Jn. 3:20–22).

1378. God's commandment. This is God's commandment, that we believe in the name of God's Son Jesus Christ and love one another, just as Jesus said. Those that keep God's commandment abide in him, and he in them by the Holy Spirit whom he has given to us who believe. The Holy Spirit testifies to believers' souls that they are saved and, therefore, children of God (1 Jn. 3:23, 24).

1379. Saints are to test spirits and teachings to see if they are from God. We do this because demons and the devil can appear to be good, or truthful, to deceive people. The devil and demons also influence people to deceive others. People being used by Satan are either deceived by Satan or work for him willingly. Either way, their end is death. Every spirit that does not testify that Jesus is the Son of God, come in the flesh from God, is the spirit of the Antichrist. Every spirit that testifies that Jesus is the Son of God, come in the flesh from God, is from God. People are to test spirits and teachings by comparing them to the Bible, the word of God (1 Jn. 4:1–3). Even teachings in churches can be false. If saints determine teachings or spirits are not of God, they are to let others know and not have membership of churches that, or partnership with people who, accept false teachings (2 Cor. 6:14).

Unsaved people speak and understand the same language of the world. The devil is prince of this world so it is not surprising. Seeking wealth and power over other people are the main goals of the world. Ways of doing this are controlled by Satan, because God has allowed it. People learn the devil's ways and become successful, as the world defines success. That success is defined as wealth and power. The more of those a person has, the more successful they are in this world. The way of a Christian is not to seek power over other people and wealth but to seek God and his will; to love God with all one's mind, soul, and might; to love other people as one loves oneself, and to treat other people as one wants to be treated. This does not mean a Christian does not work and provide for themselves and their family. That is just common sense that that has to be done to survive, and it is biblical (1 Tim. 5:8). The unsaved do not listen to saints because they choose darkness over the Light (Jn. 3:19, 1 Jn. 4:5, 6).

1380. Greater is he who is in saints than he who is in the world (1 Jn. 4:4). God is the one in saints and the devil is the one in the world. This means saints have the power of God in them to oppose, and overcome, Satan wherever they are (Mt. 16:18, 19, Heb. 2:14, 15).

1381. God is love. God is the essence of love. Love would not exist without God. Without God, there is no love (1 Jn. 4:7, 8, 16).

1382. Saints love one another because the love of God is in them. This is evidence of who is a saint and who is not a saint. Those that are not saints will not love saints or God. The Holy Spirit in saints gives saints this love for each other and for God. This testifies to saints' souls that they are part of the family of God. We do not need to earn love from other saints just as we did not earn God's love. While we were yet sinners, God loved each of us so much that he sent his Son Jesus to die on the cross for our sins so that we might inherit eternal life (1 Jn. 4:7–14). Saints love because God first loved us (1 Jn. 4:19). If a person claims to be a Christian but hates a Christian, they are not a Christian (1 Jn. 4:20).

1383. No one has seen God at any time but Jesus. Moses saw his back but not his face, or he would have died (Ex. 33:20, Jn. 1:18, 1 Jn. 4:12).

1384. Saints confess that Jesus is the Son of God. Those who do not confess that Jesus is the Son of God do not have God in them and they are not saved (1 Jn. 4:15).

1385. God is love, and perfect love casts out fear. Saints do not fear the judgment of God because of the love of God in us. Love casts out fear because fear involves punishment and there is no punishment for saints at the judgment seat of Christ (1 Jn. 4:16–18).

1386. Christians are as Jesus was in this world (1 Jn. 4:17). Saints are not perfect until their body dies and their soul goes to heaven, but they have the Holy Spirit in them to guide and direct them to act and speak as Jesus would.

1387. God commands saints to love one another (1 Jn. 4:21).

1388. Whoever believes that Jesus is the Christ is born of God, and whoever loves the Father loves the Son born of him. "Born of God" is being born again, as Jesus described it. So saints are born of God (Jn. 3:3–7, 1 Jn. 5:1).

1389. Saints love other people not just by doing acts of kindness but by loving God and keeping his commandments. These commandments are not burdensome, and the Holy Spirit helps us obey them. By loving God and keeping these commandments, we are a better person and are motivated to minister to others. By this, saints demonstrate God's love for mankind, allowing God to love through us (1 Jn. 5:2, 3).

1390. Whatever, or whoever, is born of God overcomes the world. The faith of saints that Jesus is the Son of God overcomes the world. The world in this verse is sin and the powers of darkness, which are the devil and the evil forces that serve him (1 Jn. 5:4, 5).

1391. Three things testify of Jesus as the Son of God, the Savior: the water, the blood, and the Holy Spirit. It is an indisputable, historical fact that Jesus was born in the flesh (born of water, as John 3:5 says) and that he claimed to be the Son of God who takes away the sin of the world (Matthew 16:16, 17, John 1:29). It is also an indisputable, historical fact that Jesus was crucified (the blood) without denying his claims in order to save his life (Matthew 27:11–14, John 18:33–38). The Holy Spirit testifies to the souls of those who are saved that Jesus is the Son of God. Those who do not believe in Jesus as God the Son cannot hear the Holy Spirit, so they are deceived (1 Jn. 5:5–10).

1392. Eternal life is given to those who believe in Jesus as God the Son (1 Jn. 5:11, 12).

1393. Saints are to be confident that whatever they ask of God, he hears us and will receive what we ask for (1 Jn. 5:14, 15). This verse has been misunderstood by many to mean God is like a genie that will give saints whatever they ask for, but that is contrary to scripture. Scripture plainly shows us that this means whatever that God wills that we ask for, he will provide it. This is demonstrated by Jesus in the garden of Gethsemane where he says, "Father, if You are willing, remove this cup from Me, yet not My will, but Yours be done." (Luke 22:42). Asking God for things with wrong motives, such as for our own pleasure, will not be answered by God as we might hope (James 4:3). All things are in God's hands, and we are to submit our will to him, even if it means pain for us. He knows what is best for us and is doing just that. We just need to trust God.

1394. Saints are to pray for one another when we see each other sin. There is a limit to God's patience and so, at some point, God decides to take the life of those who deliberately sin. Saints are not to pray for God to keep these persons alive when we see this. God is preventing these rebellious people from being further bad influences on other people (1 Jn. 5:16, 17).

1395. No one who is born of God sins, but he who is born of God keeps himself and the evil one (devil) does not touch him. This does not mean saints never sin. It means saints do not willingly continue to sin. Saints love God too much to continue to willingly sin. We may willingly sin, but the Holy Spirit in us convicts us, and we love God too much to continue to willingly sin. The devil has no part in saints and not authority over us (1 Jn. 5:18).

1396. Satan has the power over the world given to him by God (he rules the world) but he does not rule saints (1 Jn. 5:19).

1397. Jesus has given saints knowledge of him. This leads to repentance and salvation, and further understanding of Him, as we mature in our faith (1 Jn. 5:20).

# 2 JOHN

1398. There is no guarantee that all the children of a faithful Christian parent will be saved, as seen in 2 John where only some of the lady's children were waling in the truth (2 Jn. 1:4).

1399. Love is obeying God's commandments (2 Jn. 1:6).

1400. Many deceivers have come into the world, teaching that Jesus is not the Christ, the only way to heaven (2 Jn. 1:7).

1401. Christians who are disobedient run the risk of not receiving all of the reward in heaven they could if they were obedient to scripture (2 Jn. 1:8). These disobedient saints will not be punished in heaven (1 Jn. 4:16–18), but they will receive less reward than they otherwise could have had. An example of disobedience is not forgiving other people who have wronged them (Mt. 6:15).

1402. Saints are not to greet or invite into their home those people who teach, or openly speak their beliefs, contrary to the teachings of Jesus (2 Jn. 1:10, 11). This does not mean saints are not to greet or invite into their home people that are not saved who are searching for the truth. It also does not mean saints are to not greet or invite into their home those who teach on minor points differently than they, such as Calvinism versus Arminianism. If saints avoided greeting all sinners, then they would not be able to fulfill the great commission, so it is sinful to avoid contact with all sinners.

# 3 JOHN

1403. Saints are to defend themselves against unjust accusations and defend the word of God (3 Jn. 1:10).

1404. Saints are to house full-time servants of God who are visiting from out of town (3 Jn. 1:10).

1405. Saints are to imitate what is good and behave and speak in a goodly manner and not imitate what is evil because what is evil is not of God (3 Jn. 1:11). Then, we should not imitate evil even if it is for humor.

# JUDE

1406. Deceivers who claim to be Christian have infiltrated the church since the first century AD, grumbling, lusting, causing dissension, and teaching false doctrine. In their heart, they deny that hell is the destination of those who are not saved and that Jesus is the only Lord, the only way to heaven, and they will deny it openly when it they feel they can. They flatter with words to gain advantage. Their message leads to destruction, and they will go the lake of fire after the day of judgment. Just as God did not spare, but destroyed, those who were of the children of God (Israel) who did not truly believe in him, so too he will do to those who are claim to be Christian but are not (Jude 1:4–16).

1407. The fallen angels that followed Satan when he rebelled against God have been bound in hell since the days of Noah, awaiting the day of judgment after the millennium. These fallen angels had sex with women somehow (perhaps directly or by possessing men's bodies), and that is how the race of giants, the Nephilim, came into being (Gen. 6:1–6, Nu. 13:33, 2 Pet. 2:4, Jude 1:6). Typically, it is believed that the fallen angels who rebelled with Satan against God are the demons that do the devil's work. However, since the fallen angels are bound, as it says here in Jude, they are not free to do anything. We know from many Bible accounts that demons are active since the days of Noah. With that in mind, demons would have to be some other creation of God than these fallen angels. Another explanation would be that not all of the fallen angels had sex with women and thus bound in hell by God. Then, the other fallen angels would be what we call demons.

1408. Sodom and Gomorrah indulged in gross immorality and went after strange flesh (homosexuality) and were punished by fire. This is an example to all people that God will punish all who are not his by eternal fire, in the lake of fire. In that God calls homosexuality gross immorality, and not just immorality, tells us that it is more repugnant to him than some other sins. Homosexuality and transgenderism is rebellion against God's design for mankind (Jude 1:7). However, when a person transgresses one of God's laws, they are guilty of transgressing all of them (Jas. 2:10). Just one sin is enough to condemn a person to hell. Only by repentance and loving God so much to make Jesus your Lord and Savior can a person receive forgiveness from God and not be condemned to hell and then the lake of fire. There is a difference between committing sin and espousing sin, though, because God looks at the heart of a person. When a person commits a sin and is sorrowful about it, their heart is in the right place when they are sorrowful about it. But when a person promotes sin, and may even be angered when a person calls it sin, their heart is in the wrong place.

1409. Michael the archangel is the chief angel of God who leads the angels (Rev. 12:7). He fought against Satan over the body of Moses. In this fight, Michael did not bring a railing accusation against Satan but said, "The Lord rebuke you!" This is an example to saints to not converse with the devil but say, "The Lord rebuke you!" (Jude 1:9). Moses's body was buried in a secret place (Dt. 34:5, 6). This may have been to keep Satan from making Moses's body an object of worship.

1410. Many thousands of angels will come with the Lord, when he returns, to execute judgment on the ungodly (unsaved) people on earth at that time (Jude 1:14, 15).

1411. Sinners mock saints and their beliefs. Sinners follow their own lusts rather than God and God's laws. Sinners cause divisions. Sinners are worldly minded, devoid of the Holy Spirit (Jude 1:18, 19).

1412. Saints are to pray in the Holy Spirit. This means letting the Holy Spirit guide our prayers. This may take the form of praying in other tongues, or it may not. When a person prays in other tongues it does not necessarily mean it is of God. Some people do it copying others. Some people also do it under the influence of Satan. We are to discern good from evil. If we witness praying in other tongues that is not consistent with scripture, we know it is not of God (Jude 1:20).

1413. Saints are to be merciful to those who doubt the validity of the Bible (Jude 1:22).

1414. Saints are to hate sin but love the sinner enough to witness to them to save them from eternal fire (Jude 1:23).

1415. Jesus is able to keep saints from stumbling, or sinning, if saints will only let him control them (Jude 1:24).

1416. Saints will stand before Jesus blameless, with great joy, after their fleshly bodies die, because they are forgiven of their sins (Jude 1:24).

# REVELATION

1417. The Revelation of Jesus Christ, which God gave to him to show his bondservants (saints) of things to come was shown to the apostle John by Jesus' angel (Rev. 1:1). So Revelation(s) is about things to come, and not things that had happened by the late first century AD (when it is felt John wrote Revelation), regarding Jesus. Irenaeus of Lyons, who learned from the student of the apostle John, Polycarp, wrote that the vision John wrote, called the book of Revelation(s) occurred toward the end of Domitian's reign. This is recorded in Irenaeus's book *Adversus Haereses* in book 5, chapter 30, and paragraph 3: "The apocalyptic vision. For that (the vision) was seen on no very long time since, but almost in our day, towards the end of Domitian's reign." It is well known the Domitian was emperor of Rome AD 81–96. So the vision given to John that he recorded as the book of Revelation(s) occurred in the midnineties AD, well after the destruction of the temple in Jerusalem by the Romans in AD 70. This will help in interpreting Revelation(s), in that it is clear the destruction of the Jewish temple in AD 70 was not the abomination of desolation written about in Revelation 13:6, and throughout the Bible, yet to be done by the ant-Christ.

1418. Blessed is he who reads and those who hear the words of the prophecy of Revelation(s), and heed the things written in it, for the time is near (Rev. 1:3). Revelation is a hard book to understand, partly because it mixes allegory with nonallegorical writings. So it is tempting to many people to dismiss it and just live with the philosophy of "what will be will be" and not ask God to help them understand

Revelation. After all, God wins in the end. Eschatology, the study of end-times, is rarely preached on. However, it says blessed are those who read it, hear it and heed to the writings. God said that to encourage saints to study it, probably because He knew it was tempting to Christians to dismiss it because of the difficulty in understanding it. Knowing what the Bible says also helps us not to be deceived by Satan.

1419. The apostle John addressed the book of Revelation to seven of the churches in Asia Minor because Jesus told him to write Revelation and send it to the seven churches: Ephesus, Smyrna, Pergamum, Thyatira, Sardis, Philadelphia, and Laodicea. The letters to these churches are as relevant to churches today as they were then. The word church here means a local body of professed believers, obviously, and not the worldwide body of believers. Churches (local bodies of professed believers) include people who are truly believers in Jesus and people who say they are but are not. So what Jesus has to say to the churches is for saints and sinners who appear to be saints (wolves in sheep's clothing). Some have said today's true believers are represented by the Philadelphia church, in order to fit their philosophy of pretribulation rapture of the church, but that is simply not true. To say that Christian churches today are not represented by each of these seven churches ignores fact. Also, to say that Christians being persecuted throughout the world (represented by the church at Smyrna) are not true Christians is wrong (Rev. 1:4, 10, 11).

1420. John blesses the seven churches with grace and peace from God (him who is and was and is to come), the Holy Spirit and Jesus (Rev. 1:4, 5).

1421. There are seven Spirits before God in heaven, which are the seven lamps of fire burning. This is a description of the Holy Spirit in heaven. These seven lamps are the eyes of the Lord, which range to and fro throughout the earth (the Holy Spirit searches the earth) (Zec. 4:2, 6, 10; Rev. 1:4, 4:5).

1422. Jesus is the Christ, the faithful witness, the firstborn of the dead (he is the first of all who have had a fleshly body which is raised from the dead), ruler of the kings of the earth (all authority was given to Him by God-Mt. 28:18), the one who loves all people and released those of us who accept him as Lord and Savior from our sins by his blood, the one who has made saints to be a part of the kingdom of God, priests to Father God (Rev. 1:5, 6).

1423. Jesus refers to Father God as not only his Father but also his God. God the Father, Son, and Holy Spirit are God, but Jesus has received power and authority from God the Father and holds reverence to God the Father (Jn. 4:34, 5:19–26; Rev. 1:6, 3:2).

1424. Jesus is returning to earth in the clouds and every eye will see him return, even those who are dead (including those who pierced him), and all the people of the earth who do not repent of their sins will mourn and fear at his return (Rev. 1:7).

1425. Jesus is the Alpha and Omega, the beginning and the end: "Who is and who was and who is to come, the Almighty" (Rev. 1:8, 17). Jesus has always been, just as God the Father and God the Holy Spirit have always been. They will always be also. God is the same yesterday, today and forever (Heb. 13:8).

1426. John was exiled on the island of Patmos for speaking God's word and witnessing about Jesus Christ (Rev. 1:9).

1427. John was not asleep but awake and praying in the Spirit on the Lord's day (the day of his resurrection, Sunday), when the Revelation was given to him by the Lord. Praying in the Spirit may (1 Cor. 14:14) or may not mean praying in other tongues. It means void of cares of this world, worshiping God. The Lord's day has been Sunday since early church history. Sunday is called that because it is the day the Lord was resurrected from the dead (Rev. 1:10).

1428. Vision of Jesus by the apostle John. John saw Jesus standing in the middle of seven golden lampstands, which represented the seven churches to which Jesus told John to write. Jesus looked like a man, clothed in a white robe reaching to his feet, girded across his chest with a golden sash. His head and hair were white like white wool, like snow, and his eyes were like a flame of fire. His feet were like glowing, hot bronze, and his voice was like the sound of many waters. In his right hand he held seven stars, which are the angels of the seven churches in Revelation 2 and 3. Out of his mouth came a sharp two-edged sword, and his face was like the shining sun. With this sword that comes out of his mouth, he will judge those who oppose him and rule (Rev. 1:12–20, 2:16, 19:15).

1429. Jesus told John he has the keys of death and Hades (hell). Death and hell are in his power, in other words. No one dies or goes to hell without the Lord being in control of it (Rev. 1:18).

1430. Jesus told John to write what he had seen up to this point (chapter 1), the things which are (chapters 2 and 3), and the things which will take place after these things (chapters 4–22) (Rev. 1:19, 4:1). So the prophecies in Revelation were for the future from when John wrote them. The events in chapters 6–22 are yet to occur from now because there have never been such worldwide events as described in those chapters. For instance, it is obvious we are not in the millennium because the world is not going to Jerusalem worshiping Jesus there, as He rules the world. The letters to the churches can apply to the majority of churches in a country, local churches and individuals today.

1431.   To the church in Ephesus (love grown cold church). Good deeds: perseverance, cannot tolerate evil people and false teachers, putting to the test those who claim to proclaim God's word or prophecies. They hated the way of the Nicolaitans, who claimed to be Christian but were not, as evidenced by their deeds: they perverted grace, gave in to sensual pleasures. Area of the Lord's displeasure: the church at Ephesus left their first love (their love for Jesus had grown cold). They were doctrinally correct but their love for Jesus, and thus their love for sinners, had grown cold. Jesus told them to remember from where they had fallen before they were saved, repent of their losing their first love, and return to leading people to Jesus and helping them know God's word. If they did not do this Jesus said he would remove the lampstand out of its place. This means he would bring an end to the church in Ephesus because of its spiritual death, physical death would follow (Rev. 2:1–7).

1432.   To the church in Smyrna (persecuted church). Jesus encouraged the church by letting them know he knew of the persecutions and poverty and of the blasphemy from those who said they were Jews but, while they may have been genetically Jews, were actually of the household of Satan. Jesus foretold this church that God was going to test them by allowing the devil to cast some of them into prison soon, and that they would have tribulation for ten days. He told them to be faithful unto death, and he would give them the crown of life. Those who overcome (never lose their faith and love for Jesus despite trials and temptations) will not be hurt by the second death. Saints do not suffer the second death, which is eternity in the lake of fire. This is the only church that Jesus does not criticize (Rev. 2:8–11).

1433. Pergamum (Pergamos) is described as the location of Satan's throne. This may be in reference to a large throne like altar to Zeus that was in the acropolis there. There were also other gods worshipped there. However, there were other cities where false gods were worshiped, so one has to wonder if present-day Turkey is the center of evil in the world. Could Turkey, then, be where the Antichrist comes from (Rev. 2:13)?

1434. To the church in Pergamum (compromising church). Good deeds: faithful despite persecution. Areas of the Lord's displeasure: allowing teaching, and membership, by those who are in rebellion to God. These people teach perversion of grace and turn freedom from sin into freedom to sin. Those who repent and overcome He will give hidden manna and write new names that He will give them on white stones. Only these overcomers will know the new names the Lord gives them (Rev. 2:12–17).

1435. To the church in Thyatira (corrupt church). Good deeds: love, faith, service, and perseverance. Areas of the Lord's displeasure: Tolerance of woman Jezebel, who calls herself a prophetess, but leads Christians astray so that they commit acts of immorality, exploring the occult, and eat things sacrificed to idols. Jesus searches the minds and hearts of people, and he gives to each one according to their deeds. This means sometimes Jesus lets saints and sinners alike suffer here on earth because of our deeds but suffering does not necessarily mean one is being punished for doing wrong, as in the case of the blind man Jesus healed (Jn. 9:1–3). Christians who are faithful to the Lord until the end (overcomers) will be rewarded by the Lord with giving them authority over the nations. Those saints will rule the nations with a rod of iron, as Jesus will, during the millennium. Saints who overcome will have Jesus to the full because we will be in his presence (Rev. 2:18–29).

1436. To the church in Sardis (hypocritical church) (Rev. 3:1-6). They appeared alive but were dead spiritually. Jesus admonished them to remember the word of God they had heard and then repent and obey. Yet there were a few who were faithful to the Lord. This is the only good remark Jesus made about the church here. Those who would be faithful Jesus would not erase from the book of life. The book of life contains the names of those people who will live forever with God because they love and obey God and Jesus. This does not mean that those who sin too much would be erased from the book of life. Those who reject Jesus as Lord and Savior since he came to earth will not be in the book of life. Only those who initially believe in Jesus as Lord and later reject him (not a mere backsliding because of doubt or self indulgence) would possibly be erased from the book of life (Heb. 6:4–6).

1437. To the church in Philadelphia (faithful church). Though this church was not influential in the world, they kept their faith in Jesus and kept his word, and they did not deny his name. So Jesus has kept the door to heaven open for them. Only Jesus has the key of David, which opens and closes the door to salvation/heaven. Jesus will cause those who are of the synagogue of Satan, but say they are Jews but are not, to bow down at the feet of the people from this church. This will most likely occur during the Great White throne of judgment at the end of the millennium. Jesus also said he would keep this church from the hour of testing, which is to come on the whole world to test them, because they have been faithful to his word despite testing now. Testing from God is usually hardship, as it was with Job.

Jesus said this would come onto the whole world. That has not happened yet and the only prophecies that teach on that are the ones about the tribulation period of the last days, which is yet to come. The tribulation period of the last days is felt to last seven years because that is the time period that the Antichrist is felt to rule (Dan. 9:26, 27). The great tribulation is during the last three and half years the Antichrist rules before he is destroyed by the return of the Lord. The great tribulation is the tribulation caused by the bowls of judgment God pours out on the earth because of its evil. If Jesus means all Christians here, then he means all Christians will be raptured from the earth prior to the last three and half years of the Antichrist's reign and the great tribulation. If he means only those Christians that have been tested and proven faithful to the Lord up until the great tribulation will be spared going through the great tribulation, then there will not be a rapture of all Christians prior to his return at the end of the great tribulation. These faithful Christians will have the name of God and the name of the new Jerusalem written on them. They will be pillars in the temple of God and will not go out from it (Rev. 3:7–13). Jesus told how the end times will be in Mark 13:14–27. There, he told us that Christians will go through the great tribulation just as sinners would and that he would return at the end of the great tribulation and gather all the saints then.

1438. Jesus was not created, but he is preeminent of all creation. He created all of creation with Father God and the Holy Spirit. He was the first of creation to be resurrected from the dead (Col. 1:15–20, Rev. 3:14).

1439. To the church in Laodicea (lukewarm church). Jesus said he wished them to be either cold (unrepentant sinner) or hot (Christian who is on fire for the Lord). Because they were lukewarm (half hearted effort at serving and loving

Jesus) and neither hot nor cold, he would spit them out
of his mouth (reject them). These are people who thought
they were, or at least claimed to be, Christian but had
not really repented in their heart and made Jesus their
Lord. They knew Jesus was Lord in their mind but had
not repented of their sins and loved Jesus enough to make
Him their Lord and Savior. Because they were wealthy,
they thought they had no need of anything. But Jesus said
they did not know they were actually wretched, miserable,
poor, blind, and naked. Jesus said true repentance and
loving him enough to make him their Lord and Savior
would take care of these needs. Jesus said those whom he
loves he reproves and disciplines. He loves everyone, (Jn.
3:16) so everyone feels this at sometime in their lives. He
then urged them to be zealous and repent. He knocks on
our door trying to get us to open the door of our heart to
him. When we open the door of our hearts to him, he will
come into our heart and dine with us and be with us. He
who overcomes Jesus will grant to sit on his throne with
him (Rev. 3:14–22).

1440. Throne of the God the Father. The throne of God the
Father is in heaven, and the God is in appearance like a
crystal clear jasper stone, or diamond, and sardius, which
is a fiery ruby red stone. Around the throne of God is a
rainbow like an emerald in appearance. This would mean
a several-colored rainbow with an overall emerald hue to
it (Ez. 1:26, 28; Rev. 4:3, 21:11). Out from the throne
come flashes of lightning, sounds, and peals of thunder.
Before the throne of God are the seven burning lamps,
which are the seven spirits of God, the Holy Spirit. Before
the throne is something like a sea of glass or crystal (Rev.
4:6). We know this is Father God from Rev. 5:1 and 7.

1441. Around the throne of God are twenty-four elders, who
sit on their own thrones and have on white garments and

golden crowns. These elders fall down before God, on his throne, whenever the four living creatures glorify and thank the Lord and worship him and cast their crowns before the throne, saying, "Worthy are you, our Lord and our God, to receive glory and honor and power, for you created all things and because of your will they existed and were created." These elders may be the twelve apostles (with Matthias or Paul replacing Judas Iscariot) and twelve men called by God from before Jesus's first incarnation: Adam, Noah, Abraham, Isaac, Jacob (Israel), Moses, Joshua, David, Isaiah, Jeremiah, Ezekiel, and Daniel, but it is unknown who they really are (Rev. 4:4,10, 11).

1442. Glory thunders and Holy Spirit. Around the throne of God are lightnings and sounds and peals of thunder. These are probably seven peals of thunder. Also around the throne of God are the seven spirits of God (Holy Spirit) (Ps. 29:3; Rev. 4:5, 10:3, 4).

1443. Four living creatures. Around the throne of the Lord are the four living creatures, which are the four beings Ezekiel saw in his vision. They do not cease to say, "Holy, holy, holy is the Lord God, the Almighty, who was and who is and who is to come" (Ez. 1:5–21, 10:15, 17, 20; Rev. 4:6–9).

1444. Jesus is the Lamb who is worthy to take the book sealed with seven seals from the right hand of God and to break the seals and read it. The book reveals the future tribulation period yet to come. The Lamb is described as having seven horns and seven eyes, which are the seven Spirits of God, the Holy Spirit, sent into all the earth. The Holy Spirit was sent out into all believers in Jesus as Lord after he ascended to heaven (Rev. 5:1–7).

1445. Prayers of saints are incense to God (Rev. 5:8).

1446. Jesus died that men from all tribes and tongues and people and nations would be saved and become part of the kingdom of God and priests of God. These saints will reign upon the earth during the millennium (Rev. 1:6, 5:9, 10).

1447. There are thousands of thousands of angels in heaven (Rev. 5:11, 12).

1448. All creation praises and worships God the Son. This is probably done by animals daily such as birds singing (Rev. 5:13). Sinners will also do this come judgment day at the end of the millennium (Rom. 14:11).

1449. First seal: white horse the conqueror. White horse and he who sat on it had a bow and a crown was given unto him, and he went forth conquering and to conquer. This may or may not be the Antichrist. A bow is for shooting arrows at prey or enemies. This would be used in conquests of other lands. A crown indicates a ruler, which may be the Antichrist. He goes forth conquering and to conquer, indicating he will set forth to conquer more than he does. There have been many who have attempted to rule the earth since the Roman Empire: Napoleon and Hitler for instance (Rev. 6:1, 2).

1450. Second seal: red horse of conflict. Red horse goes out and to him who sat on it was granted to take peace from the earth and that men would slay one another, and a great sword was given to him. This corresponds to the white horse of conquest. Taking peace from the earth means world war. There have been two wars called world wars. The first one was caused by an individual trying to conquer the world. The second was Hitler and the Nazis. There will be at least one more world war, given this prophecy. It may or may not be the last. If it is the last, it will be associated with other prophesies of the last days/

end of this age. This is one of God's ways to tray to restore a rebellious people to him, such as he did with rebellious Israel (Rev. 6:3, 4).

1451. Third seal: black horse of famine. Black horse of famine causing the price of wheat and barley (and perhaps all foods) to rise dramatically so that a day's work would only provide enough food for one person to eat on. A voice from the center of the four living creatures said, "Do not damage the oil and the wine." This probably means oil for preparation of food and wine will be spared. Grapevines are hardier than some grains. Oil can be made from a variety of sources. This is also one of God's ways to bring his people to repentance that are in rebellion (Rev. 6:5, 6).

1452. Fourth seal: ashen horse of death. This is the same as the dapple horse in chapter 6 of Ezekiel. Death, with hell following, is to go forth throughout the earth and authority is given death to kill a fourth of the world population by sword (red horse—conflict and war), famine (black horse—famine), with pestilence (another way God tried to get Israel to repentance), and by wild beasts of the earth (the Lord used this with Israel to bring them to repentance also but this has never happened on a worldwide scale). World war could cause large-scale death, famine, and pestilence because of resources wasted on warfare and destruction of crops by war. If a large amount of people die as a result, then people would be vulnerable to wild beasts (Rev. 6:7, 8).

1453. Zechariah 6 also prophecies about these four horses of the Apocalypse and that they start from between two bronze mountains. Bronze is associated with God dealing with sin, as was the case with the bronze serpent (Num. 21:9) and the bronze altar (Ex.27:2). God said judgment would begin with the Jews (Rom. 2:9), so it would make sense that these four horses of Apocalypse start their effect in and around Israel.

1454. Fifth seal: cry of the Christian martyrs. When Jesus broke the fifth seal, the saints who will have been martyred cried out to the Lord judge and avenge their blood on those who dwell on the earth who killed them for their faith. The Lord told them to wait awhile longer, until the number of their fellow servants and brethren who were to be killed as they had been (martyred for their faith) would be completed (Rev. 6:9–11). Various people, including the Romans, Hitler (martyred the obedient Christians like Dietrich Bonhoeffer), communist China and Russia, and Pol Pot, have martyred Christians through the ages. It is not clear if martyrs through the ages like these are the ones who cry out here or if they are Christians martyred by the world during the early years of the tribulation period. What is clear is that the martyrs Jesus tells them to wait for until they are martyred before He will judge and avenge their blood on the earth are the Christians killed by the Antichrist during his last three and a half years of reign, during which God allows him to overpower the saints (Rev. 13:5–7). God has already determined who is going to be martyred and when and by whom. Gods final wrath on the earth can not occur until after these saints are martyred.

1455. Sixth seal: the Lord Jesus Christ's second coming. When Jesus broke the sixth seal, there was a great earthquake (causing every mountain and island to move out of their places), the sun will become black as sackcloth and the whole moon became red like blood, the stars will fall from the sky to the earth, and the powers of the heavens will be shaken. The people of the world will know it is the day of the Lord, the day the Lord returns, and try to hide from him to escape his wrath (Mt. 24:29–31; Rev. 6:12–17, 16:17–20).

1456. To protect from the trumpets and bowls of God's wrath on the earth to take place during the great tribulation before the Lord returns, God seals 144,000 of the tribe of Israel, twelve thousand each from the tribes: Judah, Reuben, Gad, Asher, Naphtali, Manasseh, Simeon, Levi, Issachar, Zebulun, Joseph, and Benjamin. These 144,000 will be the remnant of Israel God protects not only from the effects of His wrath but also from the Antichrist. This may be done by miraculously bringing them up to heaven since they are with Jesus on Mount Zion in Rev. 14:1. These 144,000 Jews will be virgins, innocent of lies, purchased by Jesus from the world. They will follow Jesus, the Lamb, wherever he goes and learn a new song that only they can know (Zec. 14:2; Rev. 7:1–8, 13:16, 14:1–5). The twelve tribes of Israel were initially Reuben, Simeon, Levi, Judah, Dan, Naphtali, Gad, Asher, Issachar, Zebulun, Joseph, and Benjamin (Gen 29:32–30:24; 38:15). The twelve tribes of Israel during the days of Moses were: Reuben, Simeon, Judah, Issachar, Zebulun, Ephraim (son of Joseph), Manasseh (son of Joseph), Benjamin, Dan, Asher, Gad, and Naphtali (Num. 1:5–15). The reason Levi is not mentioned in Numbers is because they were not given land in the promised land. Joseph was blessed with a double portion by his father Jacob so each of his two sons received a tribes portion (Gen 48:5, 22). It is not certain why Dan is not mentioned among the twelve tribes in Revelation. They did commit idolatry before the captivity (Judges 18) but so did other tribes. Regardless, they will receive an inheritance during the millennium (Ez. 48:1).

1457. There will be a multitude in white robes who will be the saints who are on earth during the great tribulation before the Lord returns. These saints are persecuted by the Antichrist and his followers for three and a half years, during the great tribulation. They will be rewarded by God spreading his tabernacle over them (Rev. 7:9–17, 13:5–7).

1458. Seventh seal: silence in heaven for about half and hour and each of the seven angels who stand before God will be given a trumpet to sound. The prayers of all the saints mixed with incense will go up to God, then an angel will take fire, with a censer, from the alter that is before God's throne and cast the censer that is filled with the fire from the altar to the earth. Then there will be peals of thunder, lightning, and an earthquake (Rev. 8:1–6).

1459. First trumpet sounded: hail and fire, mixed with blood, thrown to the earth, and a third of the earth will be burned up, a third of the trees will be burned up, and all the green grass will be burned up. This could be in reference to volcanoes erupting, in association with the earthquake in verse 5, where the rocks, ash, and lava might appear this way (Rev. 8:7).

1460. Second trumpet sounded: something like a great mountain with fire (probably a meteor or asteroid) will be throne into the sea, and a third of the sea will become blood, and a third of the creatures in the sea die, and a third of the ships destroyed. The sea could turn red from red tide (algal bloom), or it could turn to literal blood, depending on if the scripture is allegorical or literal about blood. It is understandable how the sea creatures would die, but as to how a third of the ships would be destroyed is not clear (Rev. 8:8, 9).

1461. Third trumpet sounded: star named Wormwood. A star, named Wormwood, falls from heaven, like a torch, over a third of the rivers and springs of waters, and these waters will become wormwood. Many men die from the waters because the waters become poisonous. These are the fresh water sources of earth; the water that is heavily relied on for drinking water. Wormwood is a bitter, poisonous in larger amounts, substance derived from the root of a plant by the same name. This falling star could be a meteor or comet since it has a torch. A meteor burns up as it travels through our atmosphere, leaving a trail like a torch. This could leave poisonous substances that fall on a third of fresh water, making it poisonous (Rev. 8:10, 11).

1462. Fourth trumpet sounded: heavens struck. A third of the sun and a third of the moon and a third of the stars will be struck, so that a third of them would be darkened, and the day would not shine for a third of it and the night in the same way. This does not say that the intensity of the light from these is reduced a third but that for a third of the duration of the day the sun would not shine and for a third of the duration of the night the moon and stars would not shine. This would be a supernatural event that would make disbelief in God a willful act because there would be no doubt that this was done by God. This is the first of the events of the tribulation period that God causes that would not be able to be explained away as a natural occurrence. Undoubtedly, there will be many people attempt to explain it in other ways than a fulfillment of this prophecy. An eagle declared, as it flew in midheaven, "Woe, woe, woe to those who dwell on the earth, because of the remaining blasts of the trumpet of the three angels who are about to sound." This indicated more severe events to come (Rev. 8:12, 13).

1463. Fifth trumpet sounded: locusts from the bottomless pit. A star falls from heaven, which has the keys to the bottomless pit given to him. This falling star is an angelic being, perhaps Satan. He will unlock the bottomless pit, where all the other fallen angels are bound (2 Pet. 2:4), and releases smoke from the pit that darkens the air and the sun (the sky). Then out of the smoke will come locusts upon the earth that have the power of scorpions (painful stings). These will not have the power to hurt grass, trees, or any green thing but only people who are do not have the seal of God on their forehead. These sealed people of God will include the 144,000 Jews from chapter 7, if there is not rapture before the Lord's return. If there is a rapture, then these sealed ones of God will be the 144,000 Jews. These locusts will do their harm for five months. In those days, people will seek death because of the pain from the locusts stings, but death will escape them. These locusts will have a king over them, the fallen angel Abaddon, Apollyon in Greek. Since these locusts do not have the power to hurt grass, trees, or anything green, nor saints, these verses are not allegorically speaking of helicopters or other military equipment, when speaking of locusts (Rev. 9:1–12).

1464. Sixth trumpet sounded: angels from the Euphrates. Four angels bound at the river Euphrates are released will be released and kill a third of mankind. The numbers of the armies of the horsemen will be two hundred million. The riders will have breastplates of fire, hyacinth, and brimstone. The heads of the horses are like the heads of lions and their tails are like serpents. Out of their mouths proceed three plagues: fire, smoke, and brimstone. These four angels are not holy angels, since they are bound before God releases them. These riders and their horses could be demons. They could also be human armies with weaponry that John did his best to describe. The rest of mankind who were not killed by the plagues of these horses will not repent of the works of their hands, so as not to worship demons, idols, nor repent of their murders, sorceries, immorality or of their thefts. Because this verse says the rest of mankind, some believe there are no children of God on earth at this time. However, there is no mention of a rapture or return of Jesus between then fifth and sixth seals. The verse most likely means the rest of mankind that are not children of God (Rev. 9:13–21).

1465. Then a strong angel swore by God that there will be delay no longer of the Lord's return and in the days of the voice of the seventh angel, when he is about to sound his trumpet, then the mystery of God is finished. This seventh angel's trumpet sound is the last trumpet sound. This is sounded when the Lord returns and the dead in Christ are resurrected from the dead, then those saints who are alive on the earth will meet the Lord in the air (Mt. 30, 31, 1 Cor. 15:52, 1 Th. 4:16, 17). The mystery of God/Christ (they are one God) is this: that all people who believe (through faith and not sight) in Jesus as Lord and Savior become children of God (Jn. 20:29, Eph. 3:1–6, Col. 1:27). The mystery of God/Christ is finished when the Lord returns because it will then be evident to all that he is Lord God, so that faith is no longer required to know that He is Lord. The last (seventh) trumpet is sounded on the day the Lord returns (Rev. 10:6, 7).

1466. The two witnesses. During the last three and half years of the Antichrist's reign, when he and his gentile army will be in Jerusalem, two witnesses of God will prophecy for 1,260 days (three and a half years). The abomination of desolation begins the last three and half years of the Antichrist's reign. They will be clothed in sackcloth because of mourning about the sinful state of the people of the world and the abomination of desecration of the temple in Jerusalem (Rev. 11:2, 3). The remnant of Jews will escape from him, so he will pursue and persecute Christians for his last three and half years on earth until the Lord returns and destroys him and his armies at Armageddon (Dan. 7:21–27, 9:27, 21:11; Mt. 24:15–28; 2 Th. 2:1–4). These witnesses prepare the way for the Lord's return (Mal. 3:1, 2). The spirit of Elijah will be in one of them, as he was in John the Baptist (Mal. 4:5, 6, Lk. 1:17). Enoch was the only other person to not die, but simply go to heaven, so his spirit could be in the other one. Some have also conjectured Moses as being one of them. It is fitting that there will be two prophets to prepare the way for Jesus's second coming, as there was one, John the Baptist, for his first incarnation.

These two witnesses are the two olive trees and the two lampstands that stand before the Lord of the earth in heaven (Zec. 4:3, 11, 14, Rev. 11:4). They are two anointed ones for the Lord. If anyone wants to harm them, fire flows out of their mouth and devours their enemies, so if anyone wants to harm them, he must be killed in this way (Rev. 11:5). This is necessary so they can boldly speak God's word to the world, because otherwise the world would kill them, or at least imprison them, quickly. The Antichrist and his followers will have largely silenced Christians during the great tribulation (last three and half years of the Antichrist's time on this earth) so that the only effective way that the gospel will be preached is by means of the two witnesses. They will be the world's last chance of hearing the gospel to bring as many as possible to repentance and salvation. The two witnesses will receive power from God to stop rain on the earth for three and a half years, while they prophecy, and they will have powers over the waters to turn them into blood, and to strike the earth with every plague, as often as they desire. They will be so obedient to God that what they will desire will be what God desires. The beast that comes out of the abyss (bottomless pit), the Antichrist, will make war with them and kill them. Their dead bodies will lie in the street of Jerusalem. This would indicate two things: first, that the Antichrist will not be able to harm them until their ministry is finished, and second, that their ministry will be in Jerusalem, at least during their last days.

People from all over the world will look at their dead bodies for three and a half days, and will not permit their bodies to be buried. This viewing by people from all over the world is now possible with television. The people on earth will rejoice over their death and celebrate and will send gifts to one another because these two prophets will have tormented those who dwell on the earth (Rev. 11:6–10). This indicates that so many of the world's population will be disobedient to God that the two prophets will cause at least some of the plagues previously described. The first six bowls of judgment in Revelation 16 are most likely done at the word of these two witnesses. For instance the second and third bowls involve turning water into blood. It is most likely literal blood. The sixth bowl of judgment may be the result of a three and a half year drought, preparing the way for the battle of Armageddon. The drought prophesied to occur in Egypt may also be a result of this drought (Is. 19:5).

The words "those who dwell on the earth will rejoice" indicates that there will be few Christians left alive on earth. If it meant there would be no Christians left on earth, as would be with the case of a pretribulation rapture, then that would conflict with Matthew 24:15–28 and many other scriptures. After three and a half days of being dead, God will bring them back to life and, in a loud voice, speak to them, "Come up here." They will go up into heaven in a cloud and all their enemies (the majority of the world) will watch that. This has not been possible to occur until twenty-four-hour news channels came into being. In that hour, there will be a great earthquake and a tenth of Jerusalem will fall, seven thousand people will be killed by the earthquake, and the rest will be terrified and give glory to God (Rev. 11:11–13).

1467. After the two witnesses ascend into heaven, the seventh angel sounds his trumpet (the last trumpet), and loud voices in heaven will say, "The kingdom of the world has become the kingdom of our Lord and of His Christ; and He will reign forever and ever." The four and twenty elders will give thanks to God saying, "You have taken Your great power and have begun to reign. And the nations were enraged, and Your wrath came, and the time came for the dead to be judged, and the time to reward Your bond-servants the prophets and all the saints and those who fear Your name, the small and the great, and to destroy those who destroy the earth" (Rev. 11:15–18). This would indicate that the Lord returns and destroys his enemies soon after the two witnesses ascend to heaven, which is confirmed by Rev. 11:14.

1468. The Ark of the Covenant that the Israelites carried through the wilderness, that contained Aaron's rod that bloomed and the two tablets with the Ten Commandments written on them, is in heaven (Rev. 11:19). When the seventh trumpet is sounded, there are flashes of lightning, sounds and peals of thunder, and an earthquake (the earthquake when the Lord returns) and a great hailstorm (Rev. 11:19). This coincides with the seventh bowl of judgment (Rev. 16:17–21).

1469. The red dragon (Satan) tried to kill the boy child (Jesus) of a woman (Israel) clothed with the sun and a moon under her feet and a crown of twelve stars (twelve tribes of Israel) but failed. Herod was inspired by Satan to kill the male children two years old and younger in Bethlehem, but failed to kill Jesus. The dragon has seven heads and ten horns, which are seven kingdoms and ten kings. This means Satan has dominion over these kings and kingdoms. The sixth kingdom was Rome, the seventh was a future kingdom from the apostle John's time. The eighth, and final, kingdom will be one of the previous seven but not Roman (Rev. 17:8). The scarlet beast is the eighth kingdom, which is the same as the fourth kingdom shown to Daniel. The ten kings give their power and authority to the eighth kingdom for one hour (symbolic of a short period). The Antichrist will arise after the ten kings and subdue three of the ten kings. He will claim to be a god. The son of the woman (Jesus the Christ) will rule all the nations with a rod of iron during the millennium. He was caught up to Father God and to his throne after his crucifixion (Dan. 7:7, 20–25; Rev. 12:1–5, 17:8–14).

1470. Satan took a third of the angels (stars) in heaven with him when he rebelled against God. Or, in other words, a third of the angels in heaven rebelled, with Satan, against God (Rev. 12:4).

1471. Besides being named the red dragon, Satan is also called the great dragon and the serpent of old (Rev. 12:9).

1472. Satan and his angels will be cast out of heaven to earth, as a result of a future war between him and his angels against Michael and the angels of God. Then there will no longer be a place for Satan and his angels in heaven. Satan has been going before God to get God's approval to hurt people since creation, as recorded in Job, so this is a future event. The devil has also been accusing saints of their faults to God since creation. Saints overcome the devil's accusations by the blood of the lamb and continued faith in the Lord. Satan only has a short time left after this before he is bound for a thousand years. Satan will then persecute the woman (Israel) who gave birth to a son (Jesus), who was caught up to heaven, as written in verse

5. Satan will do this through people on earth—the eighth kingdom from Revelation 17 (fourth kingdom from Daniel 7). This eighth kingdom will invade Israel, during a time of peace after the Jews have been gathered together into Israel, and kill many and plunder, but God will allow half of the Jews in Jerusalem to escape into exile.

The Jews returned to Canaan in the 1940s and became the nation Israel again in 1948, for the first time since the time of Christ's first incarnation. Some have conjectured that the eagle wings that take the remnant of Jews to safety is America because America uses an eagle as it's symbol, but this is not likely. Because scripture says the remnant will go to the wilderness where God will care for them for three and a half years, it is more likely that the remnant will escape to the wilderness in the Middle East. This may be in Sheba (part of modern day Saudi Arabia), Dedan (part of modern day Saudi Arabia), and modern-day Jordan since it is not listed among the allies of the Antichrist. Tarshish (Spain or western countries) may also be a place of refuge from the Antichrist for the Jews, but it is not known. The Bible does not say these remnant of Jews that God rescues from the eighth kingdom is the 144, 000 Jews sealed by God in Revelation 7 and currently Jerusalem has more than 288,000 Jews.

The army that Satan sends into Israel will be like a river because it will be so overwhelming in size and force. God will open up the earth and drink up this river (army). Because the Antichrist will set up his tent in Jerusalem following this invasion (Dan. 11:45), this destruction of the army of the eighth army is either a partial destruction of the army of the eighth kingdom or is referring to a yet future battle of Armageddon, in which the eighth kingdom and the Antichrist's rule is finally terminated with Christ's return. The devil will be enraged that God has rescued some Jews from him, so he will make war with Christians (God's children who hold to the testimony of Jesus) (Ez. 38:7–14, Zec. 14:1, 2, 5, Rev. 12:6–17).

1473. Beast of the sea. The dragon (Satan) will make a beast (kingdom) arise out of the sea with ten horns and seven heads, and on his heads will be ten diadems (crowns), and on his heads will be blasphemous names. This is how Satan will make war with the saints. Coming out of the sea means the beast will be derived from many peoples (Gentile). Some have thought this means it would be from the west (European or American) since the main sea is the Mediterranean Sea, and it is on the west side of Israel. However, the Antichrist is described as coming from the north in Ezekiel 38. The ten horns are ten kings or leaders of nations (Dan. 7:24). Kings wear diadems or crowns. The seven heads are seven kingdoms, five had fallen by the time the apostle John was given the vision of Revelation, one existed at the time of John's vision (Rome), and one was yet to come. The seventh beast (kingdom) will be replaced with the eighth kingdom after the seventh head (kingdom) was and is not and will come [perhaps the seemingly deadly wound that it survives (thus becoming the eighth kingdom)].

The ten kings (national leaders) will give their power and authority to the beast for one hour (limited time). The beast is described as being like a leopard, and his feet like those of a bear, and his mouth like the mouth of a lion. We know from Daniel that the lion represents Babylon (a winged lion was the national symbol), the bear represents Medo-Persia (a bear was used as a common symbol for Medo-Persia), and the leopard represents Greece (the Grecian army used leopard skins as part of the uniform for some of their military). So modern-day Iran, Iraq, and Greece will be part of the kingdom that the Antichrist rules. The Antichrist comes after the initial ten kings of the last kingdom and subdues three of them (Dan. 7:24). These three kings may be from Babylon (today's Iraq), Medo-Persia (today's Iran), and Greece, given these three characteristics of the fourth beast in Daniel. However, the scripture does not say certainly. Satan gives this beast his power and his throne and great authority.

Since Satan is prince of this world and has power to influence people for evil, the beast (final kingdom) will have power over the world and influence it for evil. One of the heads will suffer a fatal wound as if it was dead. From Daniel 7:6, we know that heads can also be used to symbolize leaders because there it represents the four generals to whom the Greek empire was divided after Alexander the Great died. So the fatal wound to one of the beast's heads may mean a fatal wound to the man whom we refer to as the Antichrist. The wound will be healed, and the whole earth will be amazed and follow after the beast; they will worship Satan because he will have given his authority to the beast, and they will worship the beast, saying, "Who is like the beast, and who is able to make war with him?"

Since the scripture here says people will worship the beast it has transitioned to meaning an individual when speaking of the beast. The beast will speak arrogant things and blasphemies against God, God's tabernacle, and those who dwell in heaven, and authority will be given to him for forty-two months (three and a half years). During this three-and-half-year period God will allow him to make war with the saints and to overcome them. Authority will be given to the beast over every tribe, nation, tongue, and people. Everyone on the earth whose name is not written from the foundation of the world in the book of life will worship him. If any saints kill, they will be killed, and those destined for captivity will be taken into captivity (Jer.15:2; Dan. 7:7,8; Lk. 21:24; Rev. 13:1–10, 17:1–18).

1474. Beast of the earth (Rev. 13:11–18). A second beast will arise, and he will come up out of the earth. Coming up out of the earth may only mean that his origin and inspiration will come from hell. He will exercise all the authority (granted by Satan) of the first beast (Antichrist) in the presence of the Antichrist. Since the scripture says in his presence then it is clear these scriptures are referring to individuals instead of kingdoms when using the term beast. The second beast (beast of the earth, also commonly called the false prophet) will make the earth and those who dwell on it (those not written in the book of life since other scripture is clear that not all people on earth will worship the Antichrist or he would not kill or imprison them) to worship the Antichrist, whose fatal wound was healed. The Antichrist does not claim to be God until the abomination of desolation, when he has three and a half years left before the Lord returns and destroys him. Therefore, the work of the false prophet described here is subsequent to the abomination of desolation. He will perform great signs so that he will make fire come down out of the sky to the earth in the presence of people.

This is similar to the magicians of Pharaoh mimicking miraculous things done by God at the hand of Moses, so that people will continue to be deceived by Satan in following the Antichrist and rejecting the Lord. The false prophet will tell the people of earth (those not written in the book of life) to make an image of the Antichrist, and he will have the power given to him to make the image come to life or appear to come to life, such that the image will speak. The false prophet will cause as many as do not worship the image of the Antichrist to be killed. The false prophet will cause all people to be given a mark on their right hand or on their forehead and that no one will be able to buy or sell unless they have the mark of the Antichrist.

It would be very difficult to survive without the mark: one could not buy food at a grocery store, pay rent or buy a home, etcetera. There will be two choices for the mark of the Antichrist: his name or the number of his name-six hundred sixty-six. The similarity between the Muslim teachings of end-times and the Bible may be meaningful. In their teachings, the twelfth Imam, or Mahdi, is very similar to the Antichrist. They also say that Jesus will come back and tell people to the world to worship the Mahdi, like the false prophet. There is also similarity between the Arabic writing of crossed swords and the word "Allah" and the Greek writing of 666. However, it is not known if the Antichrist will be Muslim.

1475. The Lamb (Jesus) will stand on Mount Zion, with the 144,000 undefiled Jews who are to be sealed in Revelation 7. Mount Zion is a hill in Jerusalem just outside of the old city wall. The Lord will reign over the earth, during the millennium, from Mount Zion (Jerusalem). The 144,000 Jews will sing a new song that only they can learn. The placement of chapter 14 in Revelation after chapter 13 does not mean that the Lord will return immediately after the mark of the beast is placed on those who follow him. In verse 6, it says the gospel is to be proclaimed to all people throughout the earth. This will be done most effectively by the two witnesses because they will be able to speak the gospel for three and a half years without being killed or imprisoned. Also the mystery of the gospel does not end until the Lord returns (Rev. 10:7), so the scripture would not say the gospel is to be proclaimed to the people of the earth if the Lord returns immediately after the mark of the beast is placed on his followers (Rev. 14:1–7).

1476. Immoral Babylon will fall some time during the great tribulation. The scripture is not clear if Babylon is a revived city Babylon in modern-day Iraq or an immoral religion, country, or financial system (Rev. 14:8).

1477. People who receive the mark of the beast and worship the Antichrist and his image will go to the lake of fire and receive the wrath of God from the coming bowl judgments on the earth. God assures saints that they will have the perseverance to not receive the mark of the beast (Rev. 14:9–12).

1478. A voice from heaven and the Holy Spirit said blessed are the saints who die during the great tribulation before the Lord returns. This argues against a "rapture" before the tribulation (Rev. 14:13).

1479. Reaping the harvest of the earth. One on a cloud like a son of man, with a crown and sharp sickle, will put in his sickle to the earth and reap for the harvest of the earth will be ripe. This one on the cloud is an angel because Jesus said angels would do the harvesting. Another angel will put in his sickle, and the clusters of the vine of the earth will be throne into the wine press of the wrath of God and blood will come out up to the horses' bridles for a distance of two hundred miles. This is the battle of Armageddon, where Jesus destroys the Antichrist and his followers when he returns. This is consistent with the doctrine of the resurrection of the dead in Christ, then those saints who are alive meeting the Lord in the air when he returns, at which time he destroys the Antichrist and his followers. It is possible that there could be some days between the resurrection of the dead and the Lord's return, but scripture is clear that the battle of Armageddon occurs when the Lord returns. Scripture is also clear that it is when the Lord returns that saints who are alive on earth will meet the Lord in the air, and not before he returns (Is. 63:2–4; Mt. 13:39–42; Rev. 14:14–20, 19:11–21).

1480. The seven bowls containing the seven last plagues, in which the wrath of God is finished, occur during the great tribulation. The great tribulation occurs after the abomination of desolation by the Antichrist. Saints will go through the great tribulation. There is not a "rapture" of Christians before the tribulation. Saints will be victorious over the Antichrist, his image, and the number of his name as seen by John. For saints to be victorious, they would have to not worship the Antichrist or his image and receive his number or his name. This is a good promise that God will give to saints the ability to not do these things but be victorious over tribulation from the Antichrist and his followers (Mt. 24:15–31, Rev. 15:1–8).

1481. First bowl: loathsome sores on people who receive the mark of the beast and worship his image. The Septuagint uses the same Greek word to describe the boils that plagued the Egyptians at the hand of Moses and that covered the beggar Lazarus (Lk. 16:21). This is remarkably similar to Methicillin resistant *Staphylococcus aureus* sores that are plaguing the world now, and this may be the cause of these prophesied boils, but the Antichrist has not come yet so the current problem with these is not what is described here. This does not typically cause death but a painful existence. This will give the people of the world who do not love God a foretaste of the eternal suffering they will endure forever (Rev. 16:2).

1482. Second and third bowls: water turned into blood. The sea will become blood like that of a dead man and every living thing in the sea will die. The sea may mean one sea or all seas. Since this is representative of God's wrath, then I would have to assume this means all seas. With the third bowl, all the rivers and springs of water will become blood.

This is also like the plague of God on Egypt at the hand of Moses, where the Nile and all the fresh water were turned into blood. Just as the fish in the Nile died and it was difficult for the Egyptians to drink water, so it will be for the entire world during the great tribulation. The rebellious people will then have to drink blood, which is fitting because they will have spilled the blood of saints and prophets (Rev. 16:3–7).

1483. Fourth bowl: scorching heat from the sun. God will cause the sun's heat to be so fierce that people will be scorched. Instead of repenting, the people of the earth will blaspheme the name of God. This will also cause melting of the polar ice caps, which will cause flooding of coastal cities and lands (Rev. 16:8).

1484. Fifth bowl: darkness and pain. Darkness and pain will come upon the Antichrist and his followers, starting at the Antichrist's throne. They will blaspheme God instead of repenting (Rev. 16:10, 11). Darkness was also one of the plagues on Egypt before the Exodus of Israel. Just as Pharaoh did not relent with this plague, so will the Antichrist and his followers be stubbornly rebellious against God.

1485. Sixth bowl: Euphrates River dried up. The king of Assyria and his armies are referred to as the Euphrates River (Is. 8:7). Isaiah 8:7, 8 tell of the king of Assyria sweeping over the promised land or Holy Land. This prophesied of the Assyrian invasion before the Babylonian empire. It may also prophecy about a future invasion. In Rev. 16:12 it is prophesied God will dry up the Euphrates River so the way for the kings from the east would be prepared for invasion of the Holy Land for Armageddon. This means either the river Euphrates will literally be dried up for the kings of the east to invade the Holy Land or the Assyrians will be destroyed before the armies, including these from the east, gather to Armageddon. These kings from the east are not the same as the country from the east that disturbs the Antichrist, along with news from the north, because these kings from the east help the Antichrist at the battle of Armageddon.

1486. Seventh bowl: entire earth shaken by the greatest of all earthquakes and hailstones, of a talent's weight (about one hundred pounds), fall to the earth. This is started by a loud voice from the throne saying, "It is done." This is much like Jesus's words on the cross: "It is finished." Then there will be flashes and lightning, and sounds and peals of thunder, and then the earthquake and hailstone plague will occur. So great will the earthquake be that cities of nations will fall, and mountains and every island will disappear. Still people will not repent but blaspheme God. The hail that fell on Egypt prior to the Exodus was mixed with fire. The great city, Jerusalem, will be split into three parts with this earthquake. This earthquake is the one that occurs when the Lord returns. Babylon the Great will be remembered by God to receive his fierce wrath (Zec. 14:4, Rev. 16:17–21).

1487. Babylon the Great. The identity of Babylon the Great has been a mystery for ages. Is it a city, such as a rebuilt city Babylon in modern day Iraq, or an immoral religion, country, or financial system? The references to Babylon in Revelation are all to the same Babylon. It is also called the harlot, the mother of harlots and abominations of the earth, and woman clothed in purple and scarlet sitting on a scarlet beast. The central theme of Babylon is its immorality (Rev. 17:2). It sits, or is based, on many peoples, nations and tongues (Rev. 17:1, 15). Babylon will sit on seven mountains (kingdoms), five of which had occurred before the vision of Revelation was given to John, one existed during John's life (Rome) and one was yet to come.

Some Protestants have tried to say that Babylon is the Catholic Church because the church is located in Rome, which is situated between seven hills. However, the scripture is clear that these seven mountains are seven kingdoms, or kings. The scarlet beast, Antichrist, will carry her and yet hate her (Rev. 17:3, 16). The ten kings (national leaders) will hate her also and, with the Antichrist, will make her desolate, naked (make her obvious for what she is and no longer able to hide behind appearances), and burn her up with fire (v. 16). So God will use the ten kings who will be allied with the Antichrist and the Antichrist to punish Babylon. Babylon is the great city, which reigns over the kings of the earth (Rev. 17:17). Since the Antichrist will reign over the kings of the earth during this time, then Babylon will most likely be his city headquarters. It is likely to be where ancient Babylon was located.

Since it is where the Antichrist's headquarters will be and he reigns over the world, then that would explain how Babylon sits on many peoples, nations and tongues. It should also be mentioned that the Antichrist will pitch his tent (live for a while) in Jerusalem (Dan. 11:45). Looking at this through the current world situation, it is understandable how one might consider New York, where the United Nations is located, to be Babylon. But Zechariah prophesied that wickedness will be exalted in the last days. People will build a temple in the land of Shinar, Babylon (today's Iraq), in the last days. An image, most likely a statue, of wickedness will be made and put on a pedestal in the temple. So Babylon in Revelation is most likely a rebuilt city Babylon in today's Iraq (Zec. 5:8–11, Rev. 17:1–17). Babylon will be full of demons and every kind of evil. Kings of the earth will commit acts of immorality with her and merchants will become rich by all her sensuality. Sensual sins are sins like pornography and other sexual sins. These will financially benefit those who are in those businesses there and the kings of the earth and all the nations will participate in her immorality.

It will be so bad that God will tell saints to leave there so that they will not participate in her sins and receive her plagues. This is similar to God getting Lot away from Sodom and Gomorrah. Because Babylon will be proud and confident of not being harmed God will punish it in one day. God will punish it because of its pride, immorality, and cruelty (including murder) to saints. Its punishments will include pestilence, mourning, famine, and fire. Merchants will also become rich by trading in luxuries and slavery in Babylon. When Babylon is destroyed, those who participated in her immorality and made rich by her will lament. Heaven will rejoice at the fall of Babylon (Rev. 18:1–19:9).

1488. The worldwide kingdom that is the Antichrist's will not be Roman but will be one of the other six kingdoms that rule over the Jews because in Rev. 17:8 it says it *is not* during the apostle John's time. But in verse 10 it is evident that the king(dom) that *is* is Rome. The seven kingdoms that have reigned over the Jews, in order, are: Egypt (during the time between Joseph and Moses), Assyria, Babylon, Medo-Persia, Greece, Rome, and Islam (starting with Caliph Umar in 637 AD. After the split of the Roman Empire, the remnant of the Roman Empire (Byzantium) ruled over the Jews, with a few years of freedom, until the Muslims conquered the Middle East, Near East, Africa, and parts of Europe. The Islamic kingdom, or even religion, had not existed yet during the apostle John's time. The Antichrist's kingdom will be one of the seven, but not Roman, putting verses eight and ten together. The greatest threat to the Jews currently is from Islam and Babylon (Iraq) is controlled by Islam, so it is reasonable to expect the eighth kingdom (the Antichrist's kingdom) to be a one world Islamic kingdom. Things could change, but that is the current world situation.

Islam is both a religious and governing system. Since the Antichrist will eventually declare himself to be God (2 Th. 2:4), it is understandable how the Antichrist will hate and destroy the city Babylon if the city Babylon is the future headquarters for a worldwide Islamic kingdom whose god is Allah, an unapproachable god in heaven. The Antichrist will make the world worship him rather than any other god. Islam would give the Antichrist the avenue through which to reach world domination until then though. Except for Greece and Rome, Islam currently dominates the other regions that have ruled the Jews: Egypt, Assyria (modern-day Turkey, northern Iraq, and northern Syria), Babylon (Iraq), and Medo-Persia (modern-day Iran). Egypt is conquered by the Antichrist (Is. 19:4) and Iran (Persia) assists the Antichrist (Ez. 38:5). So an Islamic Antichrist kingdom would fulfill scripture with the Antichrist coming from Turkey, Iraq, or Syria.

The ten kings will support the Antichrist in waging war on Jews and Christians. Based on rhetoric from Islamic leaders, the common enemies of Muslims are Jews and Christians. They even label Israel the little Satan and the United States of America the great Satan. That is interesting, considering that Israel and the USA are the only two countries based on the teachings of the same God. The commonality between the prophesies of the Antichrist waging war on Jews and Christians and the current situation with Islam waging war on Jews and Christians is undeniable. However, prophecy could also be fulfilled with a secular Antichrist kingdom (Rev. 17:3, 8–14).

1489. Jesus, the Word of God and who has a name that only he knows, will come in the clouds, with the armies of heaven and destroy the Antichrist, the false prophet and the armies of the Antichrist at Armageddon. The armies of heaven may just be angels, but some have thought it may also include saints who died before the day of the Lord's return. On Jesus's robe and on his thigh he has a name written: "King of kings and Lord of Lords." The Antichrist's armies will have time to assemble to wage war with the Lord and his army. The false prophet and the Antichrist will be seized and thrown into the lake of fire, which burns with brimstone. His army will be killed with the sword that proceeds out of the Lord's mouth. Birds will feast to their fill on the flesh of the dead armies of the Antichrist (Dan. 12: 1, 2, Rev. 19:11–21).

1490. Millennium. At the conclusion of the battle of Armageddon, Satan will be bound and thrown into the bottomless pit in hell by an angel. There the devil remain and will not be able to deceive people until one thousand years has passed. Then he will be released for a short time to deceive the nations to make war with the Lord. During the millennium, Old and New Testament saints will be priests and reign over, or judge, the earth with the Lord (1 Cor. 6:2, 2 Tim. 2:12). This implies there will be people on earth who will not be saints or part of the Antichrist's armies. This is the first resurrection: all saints are given an imperishable body when the Lord returns. The rest of the dead will not come to life until after the millennium, and they will face the second death, which is an eternity in the lake of fire. These people are all people who will have not loved and followed God. Rev. 20:1–6.

1491. When the one thousand years of the millennium are completed, Satan will be released to deceive many people from throughout the world. They will become a vary large army. These people and their army will be called Gog and Magog. This is not the Gog of Magog in Ezekiel 38 and 39. The Gog of Magog from Ezekiel is defeated and then the millennial reign of the Lord begins with a temple in Jerusalem. This battle with Gog and Magog is not followed with the millennium and a temple in Jerusalem but with a new heaven and a new earth. Gog and Magog will surround Jerusalem, where the Lord and the saints are located. Then fire will come down from heaven and devour Gog and Magog. And the devil who deceived them will be cast into the lake of fire and brimstone, where the beast (Antichrist) and false prophet will have already been cast, and they will all be tormented constantly forever and ever.

1492. Great white throne of judgment. After Satan is cast into the lake of fire and brimstone, those people who will have not love and follow God will come to life for judgment by Jesus (Jn. 5:22) at the great white throne of judgment. Then death and hell will be cast into the lake of fire. Books containing the deeds of all people (saints and sinners) will be opened, and all the deeds that all people did will be exposed and judged (Rom. 14:10). There is no other place in scripture where saints give an accounting for their words an deeds. Jesus plainly said all people will have to give an accounting. All people will be accountable for what they say. Our words could justify us or condemn us before God (Mt. 12:36, 37). This does not mean a Christian will go to the lake of fire if they say too many bad things.

Jesus said people will have to give an accounting for every careless word they say. Christians will be justified by their repentance and acceptance of Jesus as Lord, but they should minimize their careless words to minimize how much they have to give an accounting. All people will kneel and bow to Jesus and confess that he is Lord, and all people will give praise to God (Rom. 10:11, Php.

2:10, 11). Those people whose names are not written in the book of life (sinners, those who will not have loved and followed God), which will be the majority of people (Mt. 7:13, 14), will be cast into the lake of fire. The eternal punishment in the lake of fire is the second death—the death that all sinners will suffer (Rom. 2:5, 6, 3:19, 20; Rev. 20:5, 11–15).

1493. God will destroy this heaven and earth with fire and heat and make a new heaven and a new earth (without any sea) (Dt. 32:22, 2 Pet. 3:10, 12, 13). This will occur after the millennium and judgment day at the great white throne of judgment. The New Jerusalem will come down to the new earth from heaven. God himself will be with his people, whom he will call his children, and there will be no more tears, mourning, pain, nor death. The New Jerusalem will have a great and high wall with twelve gates, three gates on each side (three on the east, three on the west, etc.). The gates will each be made of a single large pearl and will have written on them the names of the twelve tribes of the sons of Israel. There will be an angel at each gate. The wall of the city will have twelve foundation stones, and on them will be the twelve names of the twelve apostles of the Lamb, Jesus.

New Jerusalem will be shaped in a square and will measure, with the wall, 1,500 miles on each side and in height. The wall will be 72 yards in width by human measurement, which is the same as angelic measurement. The wall will be made of jasper, and the city will be made of pure gold, even thee street, like clear glass. The foundation stones of the city will be adorned with every kind of precious stones. There will be no temple in the New Jerusalem because the Lord God Almighty and the Lamb will be its temple. There will be no need for the sun or lights on the new earth for the glory of God will illumine it. Therefore, there will be no night there. The saints of God will be there from all nations. Kings of countries will visit there. There will not be anything unclean in the New Jerusalem. The gates will always be open because there will be no danger. A river of the water of life, clear as crystal, will be in the middle of the street of gold, coming from the throne of God and the Lamb.

On either side of the river will be the tree of life, bearing twelve different kinds of fruit, a different fruit for each month, and the leaves of the tree will be for the healing of nations. It is not clear why there will be leaves from the tree of life for the healing of nations if there will only be saints in their imperishable bodies, angels, and other heavenly beings with the triune God in the new heaven and the new earth. The answer is in the latter part of Isaiah 65. God will create a new heaven and new earth, in which people will not remember the former things and people other than those with new imperishable bodies (the saints) should live to be one hundred years old (Is. 65:17–20). These people will also build houses and plant vineyards (Is. 65:21). Former enemies will live at peace with one another such as the wolf and lamb (Is. 65:25). So God will create more people in the new earth. This explains why in Revelation 22:24 is written that the nations will walk by the light of God, and the kings of the earth will bring their glory into Jerusalem.

Revelation 22:14 and 15 is written that saints have the right to the tree of life and enter the gates freely into New Jerusalem and outside of the New Jerusalem are immoral sinners. The immoral sinners in verse 15 refers to those in the lake of fire, and not people outside of the New Jerusalem, because there will be no more curse, meaning no more sin since sin brings the curse, in the new earth (Rev. 22:3). Also, if sin were to be in the new earth then people would remember the former things, which contradicts Isaiah 65:17. Since Isaiah 65 gives a life expectancy for people who are not saints on the new earth, then that would explain the leaves from the tree of life for healing; healing of hurts and illnesses. The Lord's bond-servants, saints, will serve God; they will see his face, and his name will be on their foreheads (Rev. 21:1–22:15).

1494. The book of Revelation is not likely to lead sinners to repentance (Rev. 22:10). But saints are to read and learn from it (Rev. 1:3).

1495. Jesus is the Alpha and the Omega, the first and the last, the beginning and the end (Rev. 22:13). He has always been and always will be. He was not created. He is God the Son, the Lamb.

1496. Jesus told the apostle John he is coming quickly. Quickly to God is different than to us because he has an eternal perspective (Rev. 22:12, 20).

1497. The Holy Spirit and saints say, "Come" (Rev. 22:17).

1498. If anyone adds to the book of Revelation, God will add to him/her the plagues which are written in this book, and if anyone takes away from the words of Revelation, God will take away their part from the tree of life and the New Jerusalem. By extension, one could say this is a warning to all about any of the holy scriptures of the Bible (Rev. 22:18, 19).

1499. Even so, come Lord Jesus (Rev. 22:20).

# APPENDIX

## TOPICS

Topics is a quick reference to scripture on various topics. The numbers following each topic correspond to the number preceding each commentary in *Truth*.

God bless those who use this reverently.

Abortion: 54 (Ex. 20:13), 190, 307

Angels: 18, 153, 240, 244, 305, 330, 341, 395, 405, 480, 484, 514, 531, 534, 535, 550, 564, 641, 920, 994, 1043, 1094, 1227, 1228, 1230, 1231, 1273, 1333, 1352, 1409, 1410, 1428, 1447, 1458, 1462, 1464, 1470, 1472, 1479, 1489, 1493

Anger: 871, 946, 1017, 1047, 1287

Baptism: 402, 403, 446, 551, 594, 611, 648, 732, 740, 789, 795, 904, 1091, 1332

Comfort: 257, 411, 737, 766, 966, 976, 988, 1058, 1080, 1115

Conflict/Confronting Evil: 331, 417, 425, 426, 499, 518, 527, 750, 881, 946, 1047, 1061, 1062, 1122, 1172, 1217, 1269, 1298, 1300, 1322, 1326, 1345

Creation: 2, 3, 5, 6, 7, 50, 154, 244, 257, 351, 470, 635, 636, 647, 683, 713, 839, 961, 1035, 1085, 1088, 1177, 1214, 1227, 1241, 1286, 1438, 1441, 1493, 1495

Decision Making/Seeking God's Will: 189, 287, 290, 425, 434, 507, 655, 666, 682, 706, 777, 807, 868, 884, 941, 112, 1024, 1084, 1104, 1107, 1120, 1126, 1297, 1309

Demons/Fallen Angels: 18, 74, 110, 111, 244, 330, 409, 441, 442, 443, 473, 476, 506, 589, 595, 706, 738, 754, 788, 871, 937, 992,

Relationships: 881

Salvation: 14, 79, 166, 186, 188, 237, 278, 295, 299, 305, 339, 340, 342, 390, 395, 413, 425, 426, 435, 444, 446, 450, 451, 472, 473, 499, 503, 533, 552, 555, 589, 602, 611, 612, 614, 621, 625, 636, 647, 654, 657, 662, 663, 664, 670, 681, 703, 706, 707, 708, 711, 737, 740, 741, 747, 749, 760, 798, 812, 820, 830, 838, 854, 857, 902, 905, 907, 910, 927, 962, 970, 971, 973, 1001, 1048, 1063, 1074, 1077, 1106, 1115, 1143, 1188, 1192, 1202, 1215, 1243, 1321, 1353, 1378, 1384, 1397, 1398, 1408, 1414, 1436, 1439, 1446, 1466

Satan: 5, 12, 16, 76, 111, 139, 167, 191, 244, 254, 257, 275, 313, 331, 333, 346, 405, 425, 426, 431, 439, 440, 466, 479, 480, 499, 534, 549, 602, 635, 664, 674, 675, 680, 682, 683, 695, 706, 788, 821, 871, 900, 923, 939, 945, 964, 974, 992, 994, 995, 997, 1028, 1032, 1053, 1054, 1063, 1078, 1097, 1100, 1107, 1109, 1123, 1124, 1130, 1131, 1135, 1219, 1234, 1297, 1302, 1334, 1345, 1346, 1363, 1374, 1379, 1380, 1395, 1396, 1407, 1409, 1418, 1433, 1463, 1469, 1470, 1471, 1472, 1473, 1474, 1490, 1491, 1492

Souls: 8, 76, 240, 252, 278, 456, 503, 509, 534, 536, 537, 550, 576, 581, 655, 677, 934, 961, 977, 979, 1012, 1016, 1034, 1040, 1209, 1238, 1321, 1324, 1391

Stress: 706, 852, 966, 1179

Tithe: 28, 62, 67, 205, 366, 387, 542, 865, 991, 1240

Tribulation Period/End Times/The Resurrection and Return of the Lord and Thereafter: 76, 129, 145, 161, 166, 231, 237, 238, 239, 240, 243, 246, 247, 248, 252, 256, 259, 280, 286, 291, 292, 301, 305, 306, 307, 308, 309, 311, 317, 318, 319, 320, 321, 323, 327, 329, 330, 331, 334, 335, 337, 338, 339, 340, 341, 342, 343, 344, 345, 346, 348, 352, 353, 355, 356, 357, 358, 359, 363, 364, 365, 369, 370, 371, 372, 373, 380, 381, 382, 384, 385, 388, 389, 440, 460, 503, 536, 544, 545, 546, 547, 548, 549, 550, 551, 554,

565, 610, 629, 657, 659, 663, 680, 702, 714, 716, 720, 723, 737, 821, 822, 839, 855, 862, 902, 956, 957, 958, 1115, 1128, 1129, 1130, 1131, 1132, 1133, 1153, 1190, 1196, 1199, 1201, 1203, 1205, 1224, 1244, 1245, 1249, 1264, 1336, 1354, 1358, 1359, 1401, 1410, 1417, 1418, 1419, 1424, 1425, 1428, 1429, 1430, 1433, 1437, 1444, 1446, 1448, 1449, 1450, 1451, 1452, 1453, 1454, 1455, 1456, 1457, 1458, 1459, 1460, 1461, 1462, 1463, 1464, 1465, 1466, 1467, 1468, 1469, 1472, 1473, 1474, 1475, 1476, 1477, 1478, 1479, 1480, 1481, 1482, 1483, 1484, 1485, 1486, 1487, 1488, 1489, 1490, 1491, 1492, 1493, 1494, 1496, 1497, 1498, 1499